2—

FRANCE

Publisher: Aileen Lau
Editors: Emma Tan
                  Aileen Lau
                  Irene Khng
Design/DTP: Sares Kanapathy
DTP Assistant: Manvinder K. Sran
Illustrations: Mabel Chung
Cover Artwork: Susan Harmer
Maps: Elizabeth Ng

Published in the United States by
PRENTICE HALL GENERAL REFERENCE
15 Columbus Circle
New York, New York, 10023

ISBN 0-671-87904-9

Titles in the series:
Alaska - American Southwest - Australia - Bali - California - Canada - Caribbean - China - England - Florida - France - Germany - Greece - Hawaii - India - Indonesia - Italy - Ireland - Japan - Kenya - Malaysia - Mexico - Nepal - New England - New York - Pacific Northwest USA - Singapore - Spain - Thailand - Turkey - Vietnam

USA MAINLAND SPECIAL SALES
Bulk purchases (10+copies) of the Travel Bugs series are available at special discounts for corporate use. The publishers can produce custom publications for corporate clients to be used as premiums or for sales promotion. Copies can be produced with custom cover imprints. For more information write to Special Sales, Prentice Hall Travel, Paramount Communications Building, 15th floor, 15 Columbus Circle, New York, NY 10023.

Printed in Singapore

FRANCE

Text by Christine Pemberton

Editors
Emma Tan
Aileen Lau
Irene Khng

Prentice Hall Travel

New York   London   Toronto   Sydney   Tokyo   Singapore

C O N T E N T S

INTRODUCTION

Bienvenue en France 1
*Welcome to one of Europe's most varied &
beautiful countries*

HISTORY, GOVERNMENT &
ECONOMY

From Fossils to Fortuitous Fighting –
History 9
*Roman Gaul - Charlemagne - Hundred
Years War - Wars of Religion - Cardinal
Richelieu & the Defeat of the Huguenots -
Thirty Years War - Louis XIV, the Sun King
- Seeds of Revolution - 1789 Revolution -
Rise of Napoleon - First Consul - Napole-
on's Military Prowess - Louis XVIII Return
from Exile - Charles X - Louis-Philippe & the
Second Republic - Second Empire - The
Paris Commune - Third Republic & the
Dreyfus Affair - Into the 20th Century -
Surging Economy*
    La Belle Epoque 14
    Napoleon Bonaparte 22
    Joan of Arc.................................... 24

Political Self-Analysis – Government
.... 33
*World War - The Great Depression and the
Advent of Socialism - World War II - Vichy
France - The Resistance - Iron Arm of Colo-
nialism - De Gaulle & the Fifth Republic -
France Post-de-Gaulle - Socialism under
Threat - 1986 Parliamentary Elections -
Foreign Policy in the 1990's*
    German Occupation 38
    Charles de Gaulle....................... 42

Technological Triumphs – Economy
.... 47
*Nationalization - Car Industry - Energy
Resources - Channel Tunnel Technology -
Aerospace*
    The Silk Industry of Lyon 56

PHYSICAL PROFILE

Nourished by Water – Geography &
Climate... 59
*Massif Central - Massif Armoricain - North-
Eastern Plateau - Alps, Jura Pyrenees -
Valleys & Plains & Basins - Rivers of France*
    The Windiest Place in France 66

Native Plants & Animals – Flora &
Fauna 71
*Holarctic Floral Zone - Mediterranean Flora
- Forests, Fires & Fun - Perils of Endangered
Species - Encouraging Environmentalists*

C O N T E N T S

French Agriculture 74
Transhumance in Cevennes 78

MEET THE PEOPLE

Gallic Tradition – People 83
*The French Character - Family Ties - Mores
& Manners - Divisions of Class - Life in the
City - Regional Differences - Independence
Movements - Brittany Americanization -
Colonial Immigrants*
    The French Language & the
    Academie Française 90
    The Mystique of French Women ....
    92
    French Fashion Visionaries 94

Religious Beliefs & Practices – Religion
.... 101
*Religion & the Revolution - Napoleon
Bonaparte - 1801 Concordat - Anti-
Gallicanism - Dreyfus Affair - Separation of
Church & State - Modern Day Religion*
    Miracle at Lourdes 110
    Muslim Minority 112

Joie De Vivre – Festivals 115
*Religious Holidays - Civic Holidays - Festivals
- Hot Summer Fun - Maudlin Memories -
Single's Day - Begging Pardon - Balancing
Acts*
    Festivals of the Cote d'Azur 118
    Les Saintes – Maries-de-la-Mer . 124

Flourishing Arts – Art 129
*Architecture: Awesome & Avant Garde -
Canvas Creations - Literary Lights - The
Twentieth Century - Crescendo - Figurines
& Flirtatious Dance - Classic Cinema -
Unexpected Art*
    French Impressionism 136

FOLLOW THAT BUG

City of Lights – Paris 143
*Overview of the City - From La Place de la
Concorde to the Louvre - Notre Dame & the
Ile de la Cité - Marinas & Squares - The
Marais Museums & Multi-Culture - Modern
Art - Architectural Incongruity & Revival -
Promenades along les Grands Boulevards -
Arc de Triomphe - Eiffel Tower - Lesser
Known Sites*
    Treasures of the Louvre 150
    Catacombs 156
    Pigalle 160

Palaces & Abbeys – Ile de France 167
Holy Places - Chateaux - Cathedrals
    Euro Disney 173

C O N T E N T S

Versailles "A Garden for a Great Child".............................252

Of Castles & Kings – Loire Valley..183
Chambord - Blois - Cheverny, Chaumont & Chenonceau - Amboise - Of Horses & Wine - Historic Retreats - From Poitiers to Cognac
Chenonceau 190
Atlantic Islands 198

Bracing Beauty – Brittany & Normandy 175
Mont Saint Michel - Chic Resorts - Fishing Towns & Villages - Normandy - Battle Beaches - After the War - Lisieux & Bayeux - Norman Cuisine - Northwestern France
Brittany's Parish Closes 210

Connoisseur's Country – The Eastern Wine Region 223
Champagne - Lorraine - Verdun - Nancy - Industries - Strasbourg - Alsace Region- Wine Routers - Dijon - Burgundian Countryside & Wines - Wine Sales - Lyon - Rhône Valley Wines - La Loire - Roman & Romanesque
How to Appreciate Fine Wine .. 230

Mountain Peaks & Historic Towns – Heartland 251
The Challenge of the Puy-de-Dômes - Dore & Cantal Mountains - Famous Mineral Spas - Michelin's Home - Berry & Limousin - Bordeaux, A History of Trade & Occupation - Bordeaux Wines - Dordogne Valley - A Drive Along the Dordogne Valley - Chateaux Galore - Black Périgord, the Land of Truffles - La Maison de la Boétie - Green & White Périgord-Valley Lakes & Plateaux
Jacques Coeur - A Role Model for the Bourgeoisie? 258

Forts & Mountains of the Borderland – Southwest 273
Barque Resorts - The Pyrénées Mountain Area - Languedoc-Roussillon - Toulouse - Birthplace of Toulouse-Lautrec - North of Toulouse: Fortresses & Castles - Border Territory
Foie Gras – Cuisine or Cruelty . 280

Alpine Activities – French Alps ...287
Ski Resorts - Summertime Beauty - Grenoble & Environs - Post-Olympic Worries
The Liqueurs of La Grande Chartreuse 295

Azure Sea & Ancient Relics – South east 301
Prestigious Resorts - "Villages" of the Rivi-

C O N T E N T S

era - The "Little Rome" of Provence - Marseille - Corsica: Beauty Bespoiled - Corsican Cultural Museum

Monaco 312

WHAT TO DO

Partisan Pursuits – Sports & Recreation 321
Team & Spectator Sports - Formula One - Individual Sports & Hobbies - Museums - Theatre French - Theme Parks - Summer Holidays - Truly French Sport

Tour De France 327
Guignol Puppet Theatre 329

The Art of Contentment – Cuisine 335
Culinary Brotherhoods - Haute Cuisine & Recent Trends - Famous Regional Cuisine - Bread & Cheese: Vignettes of French Life - Wine: Contentment for Connoisseurs - French Eating Habits

Black Diamonds – Truffles 338
La Bouillabaisse 346

The Temptations of Luxury – Shopping 351
Beyond Shopping - Food & Wine - Books &

Films - Department Stores - Antique Appeal - Museum Shopping - Customs

The Economics of Luxury 354

EASY REFERENCE

Travel Tips 363
Supplement essential for travel planning
Directory 366
Useful listings
Photo Credits 394
Index 395

MAPS

France 140
Paris 146
Ile De France 171
Loire Valley 186
Brittany 202
Normandy 212
Burgundy 236
Lyon 245
Bordeaux & Périgord 256
Bordeaux 262
Southwest 276
French Alps 290
Cote D'azur 304

Women have been the subject of many of

the most exquisite

artists.

and sensitive paintings by French masters and many other

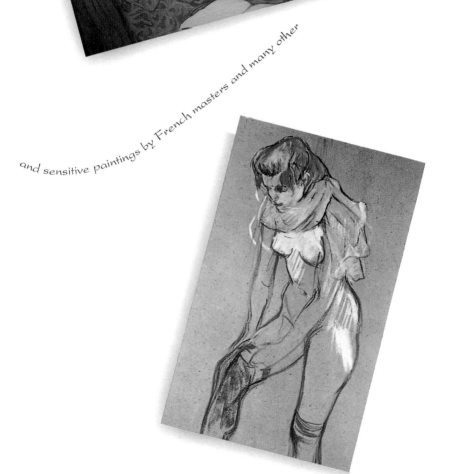

The people of France reflect

various European

temperament.

influences in their lifestyle, culture and

elegant,

Sometimes quaint, sometimes grand, sometimes

or simply

rustic, the French take great pride in their homes.

France like many other countries

has its

domestic institutions, so recognisably French.

Bienvenue en France. Welcome to France, one of Europe's most varied and beautiful countries. Whether you feel like admiring some of the world's major art collections or going skiing, shopping for the latest in high-fashion clothes or joining in the grape harvest, eating in top-class restaurants or visiting pre-historic sites, *la belle* France has all this, and more. France has something for everyone, whether you are a city person or a country lover, a fan of the mountains or the beach, a historian or an epicure, a frantic shopper or the lingering-over-a-coffee type.

French people often refer to their country as the *héxagon*, because of its hexagonal shape. Within its boundaries, France is the European land of plenty, for it has an extremely rich and varied geography, a significant factor for both agriculture and tourism. Mountains, beaches, or-

Towers, steeples and old lampposts mark the Parisian skyline.

Introduction

1

Annecy is a typical example of a historic provincial town.

chards, vineyards, and forests are complemented by big cities, an excellent road and rail network, enormous hypermarkets and major industrial infrastructure.

France is lucky enough not to be economically dependant on any one commodity or industry, manufacturing and exporting aircraft and cars, perfumes and clothes, as well as top quality wines and foods.

A visitor to France will inevitably arrive with certain preconceived ideas about the country and the people. Fashionably dressed women, exquisite food served in elegant restaurants; the **Mona Lisa** and the **Eiffel Tower**; crowded Mediterranean beaches and Olympic-class ski slopes; each and everyone of these images of one of Europe's largest countries is valid.

Elegance and a certain formality are integral parts of the French make-up, and you only have to look around you, as you travel through the country to realise this. The French like symmetry not untidiness, simple neatness rather than fussiness. It is hardly surprising, therefore, that the French are leaders in the world of fashion and design. *Haute couture*, literally high fashion, is a major industry in France, for even though very few people can actually afford the high prices that *haute couture* today commands, the off-shoots are a major and highly lucrative business – *"prêt à porter"* (ready to wear) lines, perfumes, cosmetics, and accessories are especially popular.

The French sense of style is perhaps not as individualistic as the Italian approach to fashion, but their intuitive eye for design makes them natural leaders in setting new trends.

Just think for a moment : who gave the world the little black dress and trouser suits, trench coats and the coveted Hermès® silk scarf? The French, of course. Other nations may well adapt, copy or re-interpret Paris vogue but the original inspiration for any new fashion statement is usually French.

A natural complement to the Gallic love of good clothes and elegant appearance is their passion for food and wine, which are treated with a respect and appreciation missing. France gave the world *haute cuisine* and no-one can challenge them. The varied climate and geography of the country certainly helps, for France produces probably the world's best wines, most of the world's best cheeses, as well as meat, fish, dairy products, all kinds of fruit – from Normandy apples to kiwis – wonderful bread and excellent mineral water springs – the list is endless. The French love for food means that you can eat well just about anywhere, be it in top-class, top-price restaurants or in private homes, in local *cafés* or old-fashioned, noisy *bistros*.

Having swept away her monarchy in a bloody revolution, just over 200 years ago, France today is a Republic, with a democratically elected President. But that does not mean that it is a classless society – far from it.

There are very distinct upper, middle and working classes, and in the countryside you can meet robust villagers, in overalls and a beret, who will proudly describe themselves as *paysans* (peasants). They may well live in centrally-heated homes with a television, video cassette recorder and telephone, but working as they do on the land, they see themselves as belonging to a certain class.

Many of the French upper-classes have retained their titles, and a quick glance at the society columns of the

Fast Facts

Area: France covers an area of 210,026 square miles, and shares common borders with eight other European countries – Belgium, Luxembourg, Germany, Switzerland, Italy, Spain, and the two principalities of Andorra and Monaco. Its northern coast is bordered by the English Channel, under which the long-awaited Channel Tunnel is being constructed, which will soon link England and France. The country's two major mountain ranges also act as boundaries: the Pyrenees to the southwest border and Spain, and the Alps to the east border and Switzerland.

Highest Point: The highest point in France is Mont Blanc in the Alps, at 15,771 feet.

Population: 56,411,000 (1990 figures).

Capital: Paris is the capital city, and is the seat of government, the country's principal financial and business centre, as well as the country's prime cultural attraction for visitors.

Government: France's multi-party democracy operates under the constitutional guidelines of the 1958 Fifth Republic. The head of state is the President, who is elected in a popular vote for a seven year term. There are two Houses of Parliament, the National Assembly and the Senate.

The National Assembly has 577 members, all elected to five year terms by popular vote, whereas the Senate's 321 members are elected by a special electoral college. Senators have a nine-year term of office, but limited legislative powers.

People: The French people regard themselves essentially as a single race and a single nation, although centuries of migration have historically led to different ethnic backgrounds. Today, those few dissenters form the commonly accepted view of an ethnically and linguistically united French race and tend to live on the country's perimeters. There are strongly nationalistic political parties in the southern Basque country, in Brittany, and in Corsica, a French island off the Mediterranean coast. The Corsicans are currently the most vociferous and potentially the most disturbing of these nationalistic groups, but for the average French man in the street, there is no doubt in his mind, *"Je suis Français, et j'en suis fier"* (I am proud to be French).

Religion: Officially, three-quarters of the French population are Roman Catholic, with the other

newspaper *Le Figaro*, will prove just how many counts and barons still remain in Republican France.

France has her high society, just like any other country and *le grand monde* (high society) includes an eclectic mix of aristocrats, high-profile sports personalities, fashion designers, artists and rock stars.

If the role-models for French teenagers are more than likely to be successful footballers and tennis stars, their parents will follow with equal interest the highly publicised and gossiped about lifestyles of the leading French filmstars, and the nearest thing to an indig-

enous Royal Family – the princely family of Monaco.

The French are quick to appreciate art, and attend exhibitions and visit museums with an impressive frequency, and are keen movie-goers, especially the urban French. There is a tolerance of anything that is *nouveau* (new), even if it is iconoclastic, indeed, perhaps, even more so.

Controversial architecture is discussed, loudly criticised and accepted as another facet of life. Many of the major Parisian architectural projects of the last twenty years may have initially aroused controversy, such as the **Pompidou Cen-**

main religious groups being Christian of other denominations, Jews, and Muslims the majority of the latter being settlers from France's former colonies in Africa.

National Language: French is the national language, and it is the only language that is understood in most of the country. In big cities, people may well understand English, and may reluctantly speak it with visitors, but in *"la France profonde"*, (the rural areas), it is rare to find French people who speak a foreign language. In areas close to the German, Italian and Spanish borders, people will usually understand their neighbours' language.

Currency: The currency of France is the French Franc, which is sub-divided into 100 centimes.

Economy: The country's economy is one of the most powerful in the world, and is a mixture of manufacturing industries, agriculture and the service industry.

National Flag: The French flag, *"le tricolore"* consists of three plain vertical bands of blue, white and red.

National Anthem: The national anthem is the stirring revolutionary song, *"La Marseillaise"*.

tre or **Les Halles**, but since the French like a good argument as much as they like being known to be *avant garde*, sooner or later, everything gets assimilated into the mainstream.

A probable reason for this acceptance of anything that is new and unusual is the pronounced streak of individualism that seems to run through every French person you meet.

An orderly queue or a passive wait in a traffic jam are not for the French : it is part of the national characteristics to push and shout, and these are some of the world's most aggressive and horn-happy drivers.

To the visitor, all of this can seem puzzling, for they are also a polite people : the French language is full of courteous expressions, there is a formal as well as a familiar form of address, and when people pop into their local bakery to pick up their morning *baguette* (long loaf of bread), they will often say a general *"Bonjour Messieurs, Bonjour Mesdames"* (Good morning ladies and gentlemen) to everyone in the shop – though it will more often than not sound like *"Bonjour M'sieurs dames"*.

Yet these same people will ruthlessly drive across pedestrian crossings, shamelessly block entrances with their cars, and will blaze away on their car horns should someone ahead not start off from the traffic light with the speed of a Formula One racing driver!

Critics may call it rudeness, but the French, even if they live in the extreme north of the country, will describe themselves as "Latins", to explain away their noisiness, their volubility, their excitable gesticulating and their erratic driving.

France is a country which is rich in history, and her people are fully aware of their past, both the triumphant moments of history, as well as their brushes with war and defeat.

The present status of France in the world is one befitting a major economic and industrial power, a committed leader in the increasingly important European Community, a military power coming to terms with its often troubled colonial past.

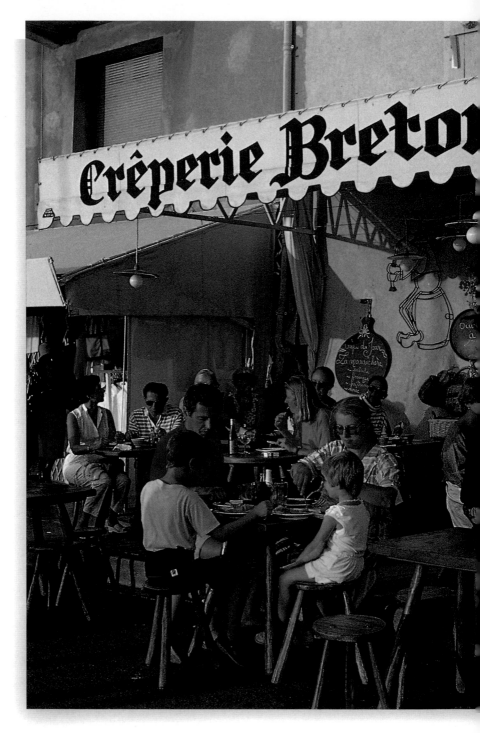

Al fresco dining in the summer.

Curious children at a market.

And what does the future hold for the country? In common with many of her European neighbours, the short-term outlook is of a somewhat leaner economic climate.

There will be the necessary adjustments needed to balance the traditionally warm French welcome for refugees of any kind, with the harsh realities of increasingly limited housing and infrastructure. The strengthening economies of the Far East will challenge the highly unionised French labour unions, but the highly perfected French technology will always be in demand.

In short, a challenge, and one to which the country of reason and pragmatism *par excellence* will rise with her customary aplomb.

Deciding the precise date when a country's history begins is an impossible task, and archaeologists usually have only fragments and fossils to help them. In France, paleolithic remains have been found across the country: in the northern Somme Valley, around Paris, and in the caves of the Dordogne. Thousands of megaliths and monuments thought to have been constructed between 5,000-2,000 BC have been found in Brittany, especially around Carnac.

The Celtic culture is thought to have originated around 1200 BC, on the upper Danube. As society shifted from a bronze-based culture to an iron-based one, the Celts gradually moved both westwards and southwards.

■ ■ ■ ■ ■ ■

Louis XIV, the flamboyant "Sun King".

Roman Gaul

The Romans gave the name Gaul to France, calling it Trans-alpine Gaul, to distin-

ANGLETERRE

Isles Sorlingues

LA MANCHE

Pas de Calais
Boulogne
Montreuil
Somme
S. Valery
Abbeville
Dieppe
Neuchatel
Yvetot
Forges
Rouen

C. Cornwall
Lands End
Falmouth
Cap Lezard
Dartmouth
S'art P.te

Hartland
Newport
Plymouth
Dorchester
Exmouth
I. et Chan. de Portland
L. de Wight
Southampton
Chichester
Rie
Douvres

I. d'Ouessant
Brest
S.t Pol
Tregnier
Morlaix
S.t Brieux

I. Aurigny
I. Grenesey
I. Jersey
I. Hermes
de Cetenil
S. Heliers
I. Chausey
S. Malo

de la Hague
C. de Barfleur
Cherbourg
I. S.t Marcoul
Barfleur
Ileomes
le Havre
Lillebonne
Lisieux
Honfleur
Pont l'Eveque
Evreux

Bayeux
I. Bo
Caen
Carentan
Coutances
Avranches
S. Michel
Granville
Falaise
Mortain
Mayenne
Domfront
Seez
Argentan
Verneuil
Mortagne
Alençon
Nogent

NORMANDIE
MAINE
ORLEANS

L'Aigle
Mantes
Chartres

BRETAGNE
Quimper
Brieux
Carhaix
Rohan
Malestroit
Redon
RENNES
Vitré
LE MANS
Vendôme
la Fleche
Blois
Amboise

Quimperlé
Lorient
Hennebont
Port Louis
Vannes
Coislin
I. de Glenan
I. de Groais
Presqu.t de Quiberon
Belle Isle
Redon
la Roche Bernard

ANJOU
ANGERS
P.t de Cé
Saumur
TOURS
TOURAINE
Loches
Amboise

Montreuil Belay
Doué
Richelieu
Ch. au Blanc

OCÉAN

I. de Noirmoutier
I. Dieu
les Sables
d'Olonne
I. de Re
LA ROCHELLE
I. d'Oleron

Fontenay
le Comte
Luçon
Pouille
Niort
POITOU
POITIERS
Vivonne
Lusignan
Chizé
Melle
Civray
le Dorat
MARCHE
Bourganeuf

Maulion
Villeneuve

AUNIS
Brouage
Rochefort
Marennes
T. de Cordouan
Tailebourg
S. Jean d'Angely
Jarnac
SAINTONGE
Cognac
Pons
ANGOUMOIS
ANGOULEME
LIMOGES
LIMOUSIN

ECHELLE
Milles Romains de 75 au Degré.
20 40 60 80 100 120 140 160
Milles Géographiques de 60 au Degré.
30   60   90   120
Lieues communes de France de 25 au Degré.
10   20   30   40   50
Lieues Marines de 20 au Degré.
10   20   30   40
L.s de Gascogne et du Languedoc de 18 ¾ au D.s
10   20   30   37¼

PERIGUEUX
PERIGORD
Bergerac
Sarlat
Dordogne R.
Bassin d'Arcachon
BORDEAUX
GUIENNE
Tête de Buche
AGENOIS
Gabarre
Garonne
Bazas
Nerac
Agen
CAHORS
QUERCY

GOLFE DE GASCOGNE
LANDES
MEDOC
BORDELOIS

C. Pinas
Castrapol
Villaviciosa
S. Andreo
Vermello
Bilbao
C. Machicaco
S. Jean de Luz
Fontarabie
Bayonne
S. Jean
Pied de Port
LABOUR
Orthes
ARMAGNAC
CONDOMOIS
Condom
GASCOGNE
Marsan
Aire
Tarbes
Isle Jourdain

ESPAGNE

Monts Pyrénées

LA FRANCE
PAR GOUVERNEMENTS,
dreſſée par Mr BONNE,
Ingénieur-Hydrographe
de la Marine,
Juillet 1779.
Avec Privilège du Roi.

Charlemagne – King of the Franks and Emperor of the Occident.

guish it from their other large province of Cisalpine Gaul, which comprised northern Italy. As a political entity, Gaul existed from 50BC to the end of AD400. Julius Caesar conquered large parts of Gaul between 58 to 50BC, despite one major attempt at Gallic resistance, from Vercingetorix in 52BC. From 50BC to AD250, the rule and influence of the Romans was speedily assimilated into Gallic life. This was especially so for the south of the country, which acquired a series of city-states which were peopled with retired Roman soldiers. The degree of sophistication of these cities can be judged from the Roman remains still in existence today, notably in the Provençal towns of Nîmes, Arles, Orange and Vaison-la-Romaine, as well as the im-

pressive 2,000 year old aqueduct, the Pont du Gard.

Roman rule also spread northwards, and existing cities such as Paris – known as Lutetia Parisiorum – became Roman administrative centres. The Romans built the Lutèce arena in Paris, which still stands. During the second half of the Roman Empire (AD250 to AD400), the rule from Rome was weakened by foreign invasions and military priority was given to defending the eastern borders of the Roman Empire. Gaul, to the west, was neglected, a neglect which caused increasing political stress over the decades. Gaul was invaded by Germanic armies, and civil war followed.

By AD418, the Franks and the Burgundians had settled west of the Rhine, and the Visigoths settled in Aquitaine. As the power of the Roman Empire declined, the invaders asserted their authority. The Visigoths encroached steadily eastwards on Roman territory during AD460 and AD470. In AD476 , the last Roman possessions in Provence were ceded to the Visigoths. The Burgundians likewise expanded westwards from their base in Savoy.

The period from AD476 to 887 is known as the Early Middle Ages, and was characterised by Frankish rule in Gaul, and by Merovingian and later Carolingian rule in an area roughly located between the Loire and the Rhine, and extending further into Germany. The most dynamic figure of this period was Clovis, who ruled from AD481 to 511, and who unified all of Gaul except the southeast. Clovis chose Paris as the capital of his new kingdom, and in AD496, converted to Christianity.

Charlemagne

Charlemagne (AD742-814) was King of the Franks, King of the Lombards and Emperor. On the death of his father in AD768, Charlemagne inherited half the kingdom, his brother inheriting the other. On the death of the latter three years later, Charlemagne gained sole control. He defeated the Lombards, and the Saxons, whom he converted to Christianity, and from AD794 his court at Aix-la-Chapelle became a political and administrative centre. Charlemagne was a loyal ally of the pope, who needed a strong presence in the west to counter the strength of the eastern Byzantines. In Rome, on Christmas Day AD800, the Pope crowned Charlemagne as Emperor. Thus it is that history books refer to Charlemagne as both the Holy Roman Emperor as well as Charles I of France.

After the death of Charlemagne, and over the ensuing generations, political power was gradually fragmented, as the power of the west Frankish kings disintegrated. New smaller kingdoms emerged as centres of rule with all the contingent rivalries and conflicts. One power base centred on the Paris-Orléans area, which was later known as the Ile de France, and which in time would become the heart of the new kingdom of France. In the north, powerful princes ruled over the largely independent principalities of Normandy, Flanders, Brittany, Anjou, Blois-Champagne and Burgundy.

By the 12th century, the king struggled to impose his sovereignty over these northern principalities, some of which had links to the English crown. This situation culminated in the Franco-English Hundred Years War, two centuries later. In the southern half of the country, south of the River Loire, were the kingdoms of Provence, Auvergne, Toulouse, Aquitaine and Barcelona, the latter controlling the eastern Pyrenean area.

Philip II Augustus, who ruled from 1180-1223, was instrumental in strengthening the power of the French monarchy, and in wresting much of northern France back from English control. Philip's grandson, Louis IX, who ruled from 1226-1270, is another major figure in French history. A self-professed Christian ruler (he was canonized in 1297) he enjoyed a reputation for fairness and was deeply respected by his subjects. During his long reign, more territories came under the control of the king, a process which continued under his grandson Philip IV the Fair, who ruled from 1285 to 1314.

Hundred Years War

In 1328, when King Charles IV died without a male heir, the collateral House of Valois succeeded to the throne of

La Belle Époque

If the words "Belle Époque", literally meaning the beautiful era, conjure up an image of the Moulin Rouge cabaret and can-can dancers, Maxim's restaurant and champagne, it is not entirely false, for the turn of the 20th century was a progressive time for France, and partying had almost become a way of life.

After the political upheavals of the 1871 Commune uprising, the French settled down in the 1880s and 1890s to enjoy the best of their talents, and like most Europeans, they were blithely ignorant of the build-up to the horrors of WWI – just over a decade away. But, in the closing years of the 19th century, the country lived the exciting years of "La Belle Époque", trying to erase the memory of one war, and heedless of the next one. In the three decades preceding the First World War, Paris was the cultural capital of the world, and the undisputed arbiter of fashion and gastronomy. Everything seemed to be happening in Paris, and everyone who was anyone in the world of letters and fashion seemed to be there. There was a palpable vitality about the city, fuelled by new artistic movements, new buildings, technological discoveries, scandals, and the arrival of American tourists with their refreshingly different views.

In 1898, César Ritz opened his soon-to-be-legendary hotel in Place Vendôme, bringing with him Escoffier, a cook from London's Savoy Hotel. Émile Zola wrote prodigiously – rumour had it that he penned either 100 lines of poetry or 20 pages of prose every day. Toulouse-Lautrec glorified the decidedly louche world of cabarets and music halls, immortalising Jane Avril, a singer at the Moulin Rouge. The actress Sarah Bernhardt was at the height of her popularity, with her 1899 performance of *Hamlet* regarded as one of her major triumphs. Colette wrote hugely successful novels, cut her hair unfashionably short, and scandalized even blasé Paris society with her behaviour. Garnier opened his Opera house, which was generally agreed to

The Paris Opera House, designed by Garnier.

be suitably lavish, but far too expensive to patronize. Music-halls and dance-halls flourished, as did the new form of entertainment, "le cinéma" (cinema). In 1907, Serge Diaghilev brought the Russian Ballet to Paris, where a young dancer by the name of Nijinsky would soon triumph, dancing to music by contemporary composer, Stravinsky. The much derided Impressionist painters of the late 19th century were slowly beginning to gain respectability, whilst bourgeois taste was shocked yet again, in 1905 when the works of a new school of painters were exhibited at the Autumn Salon. Following this exhibition, Matisse and his fellow painters were immediately dubbed *les fauves* (the wild beasts). As the 20th century began, Paris was host to the International Exhibition of 1900, where the new icon of Technology was displayed in all its glory. The huge crowds thronging the 80,000 exhibits in the Champ de Mars were equally impressed by one of Paris's recent landmarks, the Eiffel Tower, opened only eleven years earlier in 1889, and at that time, the world's tallest construction. The underground Métro train system opened in 1900, to ferry people to the exhibition, some of the station entrances being designed by one of the pioneers of *Art Nouveau*, Hector Guimard.

The Parisians' love affair with their cars, and their scathing disregard for any form of control over them, was already taking root : the first *Salon de l'Automobile* (motor-show) opened in 1898, the driving licence was introduced in 1899, to be quickly followed by a 30 kilometres speed limit in 1901, yet the figures of dead and wounded on the roads alarmingly increased. Technical progress was rapid, and by 1906, an aircraft factory in Paris was manufacturing biplanes and car exports in that same year mounted to 140 million francs.

WWI

However, WWI shattered "La Belle Époque" for ever, as a whole generation perished in the trenches, the days of endless partying disappeared, and in the words of Paul Valéry, "civilisation found out that it was mortal".

what was then the most powerful European kingdom. On the accession of Philip VI of Valois, only four areas remained outside direct royal domination – Flanders, Brittany, Burgundy and Aquitaine, where the English Plantagenets held sway.

This situation would lead to the Hundred Years War, a struggle between the French and the English which raged intermittently for much of the 14th and 15th centuries, involving, amongst other disputes, the issue of the succession to the French throne. Although historians date the war as lasting for just over 100 years, from 1337 to 1453, the groundwork had been laid back in the 12th century, when the English held sway over many French principalities.

Edward III of England, a grandson of the French King Philip the Fair, was also Duke of Guyenne in Aquitaine, and on the death of Charles IV in 1328, Edward claimed the throne of France. The House of Valois prevailed, but when, the King of France tried to confiscate Guyenne in 1337, Edward III landed in Flanders with his army.

Much of the Hundred Years War consisted of long, wearing and expensive sieges of major, fortified cities, interspersed with decisive battles. The English won a major victory at the Battle of Crécy on 26th August, 1346, and captured Calais, after a long seige. Under the Treaty of Calais in 1360, Edward III re-gained the former sovereignty he had over his French possessions, but the French king later repudiated these trea-

The Battle of Agincourt 1415, saw France's defeat at the hands of the English.

ties. By 1380, after over 40 years of war, both England and France faced their own internal power struggles, and the war subsided into an uneasy peace.

Civil war between the Armagnacs and the Burgundians broke out in France in the early 15th century, and seeing an opportunity to revive the English claim on the French throne, Henry V of England invaded France in 1415. On 25th October, 1415, the English defeated the French in the Battle of Agincourt, where the French suffered major losses and the English minimal losses.

By 1418, the Burgundians were in control of Paris, and the *dauphin* (King's eldest son and heir) Charles was in exile, an exile from which a young peasant girl named Joan of Arc would lead him to the throne, after decisively defeating the English with the seige of Orléans in 1429 (see box story p.24). The tide turned against the English, with the French regaining control over Normandy and Aquitaine: only Calais remained in English hands, to be handed over to the French in 1558.

With the expulsion of the English from France, the French began to look towards other European power blocs. In 1494, they invaded Italy, in the first of a series of wars that would last for the next 60 years. The French economy was strained with having to recover from the devastating effects of the Hundred Years War and financing this new military activity. One way of doing this, in addition to taxation, was by the selling of offices, with both judicial and financial positions up for sale as well as titles, which, for an extra payment, could be made hereditary.

Wars of Religion

One of the major areas of internal conflict during the 16th century was religion as Protestantism, under its French form of Huguenotism, began to take an increasing hold on the country, especially amongst the poor people in areas such as Brittany, Normandy and Languedoc. The policy of the Huguenots' French throne vascillated between the harsh repression of Henri II and the more moderate approach of Catherine de Médicis, the queen mother, who ruled as regent for Charles IX. In 1562, when Catherine issued the *Edict of January*, allowing a degree of toleration of the Huguenots, this served to create an uproar amongst France's Roman Catholics.

Headed by the Duc de Guise, the Catholic party massacred the Huguenots, sparking off the Wars of Religion. These wars continued for the next decade. Amidst all the fighting and assassinations, the Massacre of Saint Bartholomew's Day in August 1572 stands out as one of the most horrific events – over 3,000 Huguenots who had gathered in Paris for the wedding of the Huguenot leader, Henri III of Navarre with Marguerite de Valois (the daughter of Catherine de Médicis) were killed,

leading to renewed civil war. The vicious intrigues and fighting of the Wars of Religion were only brought to a close with the 1598 *Edict of Nantes*, which granted substantial religious freedom to the Huguenots, and gave them a number of fortresses, including La Rochelle and Montpellier.

The *Edict of Nantes* remained in force for nearly a century, until its revocation in 1685, and with it, Henri IV was granted a breathing space, during which he could tackle the problem of restoring the power and position of the monarchy. France had come close to disintegration after so many years of civil war, and the throne was under direct threat.

Cardinal Richelieu & The Defeat of the Huguenots

In 1610, King Henri IV was assassinated, and his widow, Marie de Médicis ruled as regent on behalf of their infant son, Louis XIII. Cardinal Richelieu (1585-1642) then Bishop of Luçon, came to the notice of the queen mother, who appointed him as her secretary. Richelieu, known as *L'Éminence Rouge* (Red Eminence), probably the greatest minister of the Bourbon Dynasty, determined to secure absolute obedience to the crown, to enhance its international reputation and to put an end to the potential border threats from the Spanish and the Hapsburgs.

Richelieu became a Secretary of State in 1616, a Cardinal in 1622, and in

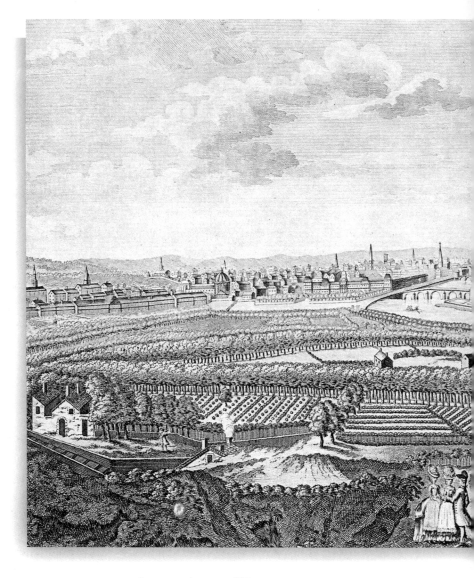

A general view of Paris, circa 1783.

1624, was appointed Chief Minister to King Louis XIII, a post he held until his death in 1642. He was ruthless in stamping out palace revolts and conspiracies, and since it was in Louis's interests that all such intrigues be controlled, Richelieu retained the king's support throughout.

Richelieu believed that the rights of the Huguenots to maintain armed fortresses were a threat to the king's supremacy, and Protestant rebellions in 1625 and 1627 goaded him into an attack on the Huguenot town of La Rochelle in 1627, which fell only after a year's siege.

The Thirty Years War

The Thirty Years War (1618-1648) was a war of savagery and destruction, waged across most of Europe, involving many nations fighting for various reasons. The theatre of war was largely outside France, in Germany. In 1635, Richelieu committed Catholic France to support the Protestants and aligned her against her hated enemy, Catholic Spain. This action, which intensified an already horrific war, has led history to judge Richelieu harshly. In 1648, when the *Treaty of Westphalia* brought the war to an end, the map of Europe had been drastically changed.

Louis XIV, the Sun King

Louis XIV, the Sun King, had as his motto *Nec pluribus impar,* ("None his equal"), and throughout his long reign, from 1643-1715, he aimed to live up to this statement. Louis ruled from his spectacular palace at Versailles, during one of the most dazzling and brilliant periods of French history. He also became the symbol of absolute monarchy. Louis became King of France in 1643, as a minor of four years old. His childhood was largely unhappy and neglected, especially during the Fronde civil war, 1648-1653, when the nobility and the Paris *Parlement* (parliament) revolted against the crown. The humiliations and poverty suffered by the young Louis

A peace treaty allowed the Huguenots religious liberty, but they lost their military power, thus removing a threat to the monarchy. In foreign policy, Richelieu's aim was to secure France's frontiers, and his antipathy to both the Spanish and the Hapsburgs, drew France into the Thirty Years War, one of Europe's most brutal.

Liberty. Egality. Fraternity. –
Symbols of the Revolution.

during this uprising shaped the character of the future king, who would never forgive either the nobility or the common people. The Prime Minister, Cardinal Mazarin, who was almost universally hated had been a principal cause of the Fronde war. When he died on 9th March, 1661, Louis announced that he was going to take over ruling France.

Louis XIV believed in his own divine right to rule, a task to which he diligently applied himself for the next 54 years. He genuinely believed that he was God's representative on earth, and that any manifestation of disobedience to his rule was sinful. To contain the power of the aristocracy Louis XIV made two important changes. First, he built his hugely expensive architectural legacy, Versailles, so large that it would require the continued presence of the aristocracy. Secondly he wove a spider's web of ever-more elaborate forms of etiquette around the increasingly dissipated nobles. The result was that the nobles ceased to be a factor in French government, being reduced to mere courtiers.

After the popular adulation following his successes in the wars against the Dutch, and the extension of France's borders, Louis's personal standing began its slow decline. Under the influence of his mistress Madame de Maintenon, whom he later secretly married, Louis imposed sobriety and piety on his court, a move which could not succeed, leading only to an atmosphere of total hypocrisy! In 1685, Louis revoked the *Edict of Nantes*, which had granted liberties to the Huguenots. This action earned him the enmity of the Protestant French and drove many talented artisans out of France. The last decade of Louis's reign was dominated by the War of Spanish Succession (1701-1714), from which the country emerged with its territories intact, but its hegemony damaged.

The Seeds of Revolution

Three-quarters of a century separated the death of the Sun King from the storming of the Bastille in 1789, and it was during those years of brewing discontent that the revolutionary seeds were sown. There were many factors which

La Carmagnole, dance of the Revolution.

made 18th century France ripe for revolution. The monarchy could not control the enormous deficit, much of which stemmed from the prohibitive cost of wars and colonial expeditions and the French involvement in the American War of Independence was another huge drain on finances. Attempts at reforming certain acknowledged ills of society especially those proposed by Turgot, the comptroller general of Louis XVI – alienated the conservative factions in society, and the subsequent failure to implement these reforms also alienated radical opinion. The Queen Marie-Antoinette was personally detested, and with the highly publicised affair of the diamond necklace, in which the queen was actually innocent, but perceived to be amenable to bribes, the royal family's popularity reached a nadir which further plummetted when a bad harvest, followed by an unusually harsh winter led to food shortages and high prices.

1789 Revolution

The Paris Parliament which was exiled in 1787, was recalled a year later, and in May 1789, the king finally decided to convene the Estates General, a representative body of three "estates"– the clergy, the nobility and the Third Estate, representing the majority of the people. Faced with the growing financial and constitutional crisis in the country, the reform-minded deputies of the Third Estate hoped that at long last the king would recognise their cause. The meeting at Versailles rapidly deteriorated into a predictable deadlock of entrenched interests. On 17th June, the Third Estate took the initiative, declaring that they were no longer the Third Estate, but a National Assembly.

Within a month, the citizens of Paris, stirred up by inflammatory leaders, took to the streets, and on 14th July, 1789 believing that gunpowder was stored in an old fortress used as a prison, the mob stormed the Bastille, in what was to become the symbolic start of the French Revolution. The importance of the fall of the Bastille was certainly more symbolic than actual, since the prison only contained seven bemused prisoners–

four forgers, two lunatics and a dissolute young nobleman. As armed mobs of peasants roamed the French countryside, in Paris, the National Assembly published the *Declaration of the Rights of Man and the Citizen*. By the time of the guillotining of "Citizen Capet", as Louis XVI had been named, on 21st January, 1793, the Republic was in trouble. The economy was out of control, French armies were fighting on five different battlefronts and civil war had broken out in France. By the autumn of the same year, the Reign of Terror had started, thousands of citizens were imprisoned and guillotined. Although no precise figure of people killed under the Terror exists, estimates put the number of those arrested at 300,000.

The Rise of Napoléon

Coups and counter-coups took place over the next few years, as radicals and conservatives within the new Republic struggled for power, one faction decided that a military figure was needed, and General Napoléon Bonaparte was given a central role in The *Brumaire Coup*, of November 1799. Napoléon called for the scrapping of the constitution, and he quickly assumed power in the newly created executive of three consuls.

First Consul

He designated himself as the First Con-

Napoléon Bonaparte

Whether you call him by his French name, Napoléon Bonaparte, or by his original Italian name, Napoleone Buonaparte, or even by one of his nicknames, "The Corsican" or "The Little Corporal" or "Little Crop-head", the fact still remains that a poor Corsican became the Emperor of France, ruled over a huge domain, and profoundly influenced the French military and judicial systems.

Napoléon was born on 15th August, 1769 in Ajaccio, on the island of Corsica. He was educated in France, was an army officer by the age of 16 when he was caught up in the turmoil of the French Revolution, and was influenced by current political ideas. By 1795, he had risen to the rank of Brigadier-General, and assumed command of the army of the interior within two years.

Italian & Austrian Campaigns

Successful Italian and Austrian campaigns were followed by defeats in 1798 and 1799 in his Egyptian and Syrian campaigns. But events were in his favour, for there was a coup in 1799, and Napoleon assumed power as the First of the three Consuls and set up a military dictatorship. The first decade of the 1800s saw Napoleon's military successes continuing: in 1800 he defeated the Austrians, he signed a peace treaty with the British in 1802, and he literally crowned himself Emperor, in Notre Dame Cathedral in 1804 – dramatically taking the crown from the Pope at the last minute, and putting it on his own head.

King Of Italy

In 1805 he was crowned King of Italy, and the military successes continued with the defeat of Russia and Austria at the Battle of Austerlitz in 1805. Despite set-backs in Spain and Portugal, he continued to consolidate his European empire, and by 1810, Napoleon was at the pinnacle of his career: his second wife, the daughter of the Emperor of Austria had given him a son and heir, and his large empire was surrounded by states and kingdoms, all ruled by chosen members of his family. One brother ruled over the Kingdom of Westphalia, another over the Kingdom of Spain, and his brother-in-law over the Kingdom of Naples.

The Downfall Begins

His downfall began in 1812, with his disastrous Russian campaign. Napoléon set out with his *Grande Armée* (Great Army) of 453,000 men, but faced with Russian might, he razed towns and villages and withdrew and at the unexpectedly early on-set of winter, less than 10,000 able-bodied men made the retreat from Moscow many dying of cold and starvation. Defeat on such a massive scale encouraged the other European nations to defy Napoléon, and both the Prussian and Austrian contingents of the decimated *Grande Armée* deserted.

Back in Paris, Napoléon somehow managed to raise more money and troops, yet when war broke out with the Austrians in the summer of 1813, contingent after contingent of Germans deserted to the other side, and the Battle of Leipzig in October saw the remnants of the *Grande Armée* reduced to shreds. The allies took the offensive against Napoleon: the Spaniards defeated the French, the British attacked them north of the Pyrénées, and the Austrians went on the offensive. Even Murat, Napoléon's brother-in-law, negotiated with the Austrians against the man who had made him the King of Naples.

A Coalition of Four Allies

In March 1814, a coalition of four allies, Russia, Prussia, Austria and Great Britain was formed, with the avowed intention of overthrowing Napoleon, and when their allied army marched to Paris, the French authorities were open to negotiation. Napoléon had only escaped as far as Fontainebleau when he heard that Paris had sided with the allies against him, and on 6 April,

Napoléon Bonaparte.

1814 he abdicated and was exiled to the island of Elba.

Less than a year later, with France disenchanted with the restoration of the Bourbon Monarchy, Napoléon escaped from Elba, returned to France (landing at Cannes on the southeast coast) and marched to Paris, gathering support as he advanced. His return to power lasted for only 100 days, and the decisive defeat of the French at the Battle of Waterloo on 18th June, 1815 marked the end for Napoléon.

Forced Abdication

He was forced to abdicate for a second time, and was exiled to the island of Saint Helena, where he died on 5 May 1821. Twenty years later, the body of the "Corsican ogre" was brought back to France, and buried with all due pomp in Les Invalides in Paris.

Joan of Arc

On Tuesday 10th May 1429, Clément de Fauquembergue, a clerk to the Parliament of Paris, wrote down the latest political and judicial news in his registers, as he did every day : among his notes that day was news from the battle campaign in Orléans, which was pitting the French *Dauphin* (Crown Prince) against the English occupiers. De Fauquembergue noted that the *Dauphin's* troops "had in their company a maid (sic) alone bearing a banner in the midst of the said enemies" and added, somewhat laconically, "if it be as they say". It was indeed as they said, and Jeanne d'Arc (Joan of Arc), the "maid (sic) alone bearing a banner", became not only a leader of the fight to drive the English invaders out of France, but she found a place in the hearts and minds of all Frenchmen. Joan of Arc, made a Saint by the Catholic Church in 1920 is still, today, one of the most revered saints, figurehead, and rallying point for the French.

From 1337-1453, war raged almost continuously between the French and the English, and over the course of this Hundred Years War, the English invaded France and inflicted on the French demoralising defeats such as at Agincourt in 1415, when the French Army was wiped out. In 1418, the English took Paris, and by the *Treaty of Troyes* in 1420, the French *Dauphin* (Crown Prince) Charles was disinherited in favour of Henry V of England. Two years later, on the deaths of both Henry V of England, and Charles VI of France, a struggle for succession erupted between Henry's ten-month old son, and the *Dauphin*, a weak, insecure man, plagued by doubts of his own legitimacy.

The exact date of birth of Saint Joan of Arc is not known, but is generally taken to be 1412. She was born into a poor, simple peasant family and was a shepherdess noted for her religious devotion. From the age of 13, and over a period of four or five years, she began to hear "voices", and claimed that various saints and angels visited her, telling her that her destiny was to leave her family and, in her own words "that I should raise the siege laid to the city of Orléans".

In early 1429 Joan set off for Chinon, where the *Dauphin* held court, to persuade him of her divine mission. The sceptical courtiers tried to discredit her – a courtier was dressed as the *Dauphin* and seated on the throne, but Joan went straight to the hidden Dauphin, and told him that the King of Heaven had sent her "to lead thee to Reims, that thou mayst receive thy coronation". Joan was sent to Poitiers, where most of the academics still loyal to the *Dauphin* were based, and there she underwent three weeks of cross-examination and also a physical examination by a panel of noblewomen, to ascertain that she was indeed a virgin, since she called herself "la pucelle", (the Maid).

The conclusion of the examinations was "that there was in her nothing evil nor anything contrary to the Catholic faith", and thus vindicated, she returned to Chinon, where she was given arms and men, and on 20th April, 1429, she set off on the first stage of her historic and ultimately tragic destiny. Nine days later, she arrived in the besieged garrison town of Orléans, winning the loyalty of most of the soldiers and commanders, and on 6th May, she led a triumphant first sortie, to recapture part of the city defences.

The next day, 7th May, she fell in battle, badly wounded by an arrow, to the jubilant English cries of, "The witch is dead", but Joan herself pulled out the arrow and resumed battle to the panic of the English, who retreated, lifted the siege on the town, and later that day, surrendered. On 8th May, a triumphant Joan entered Orléans.

The successes continued throughout the month of June, and by the end of the month, Joan persuaded the *Dauphin* to go to Reims, to be crowned King, a ceremony which took place on 17th July, with Joan kneeling before her King, "embracing him round the legs, She (sic) said to him whilst shedding copious tears Gentle King, now is done God's pleasure".

Over the next year, Joan fought various campaigns, always totally loyal to her king, yet when she was captured by the Burgundians in May 1430, Charles, who had never shown the same ardour and courage as Joan, was more interested in reaching a truce with the Duke of Burgundy and made no attempt to save her.

She was imprisoned, failed in an attempt to escape and was handed over to the church

sul, and, as his position was strengthened by a string of military victories over the next couple of years, in 1802, he was named First Consul for life.

Proclaimed Emperor

Two years later, he was proclaimed Emperor. Napoléon brooked no opposition to his rule and his ideas: political clubs were banned, politicians were deported and censorship was re-imposed.

He sought to instil confidence in his rule via his religious policy, and under the 1802 *Concordat*, the Roman Catholic church was reintegrated into French life, a decade after it had been banned.

Napoléon's Military Prowess

Much of Napoléon's power over his countrymen was derived from his military prowess and over the next 10 years, major defeats were to progressively lead to his downfall. The *Battle of Trafalgar* (1805) saw the French fleet shattered by the British.

The disastrous Russian campaign of 1812 and the ignominious retreat of the French from Moscow, led to the inevitable defeat of the Grand Army. In 1814, Napoléon was exiled to Elba, and despite his escape and the Hundred Days in 1815, when he once again ruled France, he was a spent force. The decisive British victory at the Battle of Waterloo (1815) led to his abdication, and

French heroine, Joan of Arc.

authorities, who put her on trial in January 1431, accusing her of heresy, because of her claims to communicate with God through her voices and visions.

Over the ensuing months, Joan resolutely refused to admit that her behaviour had been blasphemous, claiming that she held herself answerable to God and his saints. She was handed over to the secular authorities, namely the English and their French collaborators, and on 30th May 1431 surrounded by two monks and over 800 soldiers, Joan was burned at the stake in the Place du Vieux Marché in Rouen, dying with such dignity that "even several Englishmen were provoked to tears".

Less than 20 years later, the King who had done nothing to save her life, ordered an enquiry into the trial, and five years later the Pope revoked her sentence and Joan of Arc was officially recognised.

final exile (see box story on Napoléon).

Louis XVIII Return From Exile

Louis XVI's brother, Louis XVIII, returned from exile in 1814, to be proclaimed king, promising to rule under a constitution. The new king fled during Napoléon's Hundred Days, and returned a second time in 1815.

Charles X

On his death in 1824, his younger brother Charles X succeeded to the throne. Charles X was a bitter reactionary who sought to compensate the *émigré* nobles and to re-affirm the authority of the church. Confrontations with his political opponents led to inexorable protests, which culminated in the Revolution of July 1830, the king's abdication, and the appointment of Louis-Philippe, Duc d'Orléans as king.

Louis Philippe & the Second Republic

The rule of Louis-Philippe, the "Citizen King" was marked by a greater degree of stability and peace than the country had known in decades, but there was still a bed-rock of discontent, and when the 1846 harvest failed, and an economic crisis ensued, opposition to the constitutional monarchy grew. Follow-

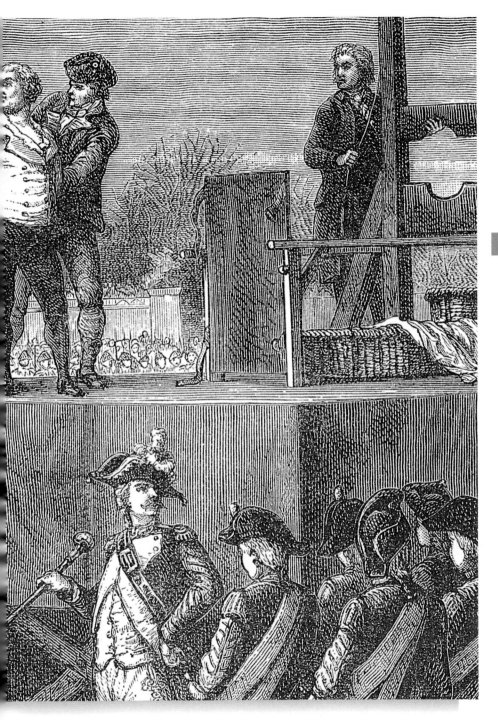

Execution of Louis XVI in Paris.

ing the Revolution of February 1848, the king abdicated and the Second Republic came into being.

Barricades Up Again

By June of the same year, Parisians were once again rioting, the barricades went up, and during the December elections, Louis-Napoléon Bonaparte, the Emperor's nephew was elected President of France. The mood of his government was increasingly conservative; a-third of the electorate were disenfranchised, while a rift developed between the government and the slightly left wing Louis–Napoleon. In December 1851, he staged a *coup d'état* against his own government, held a plebiscite on a new constitution, and a year later was proclaimed Emperor Napoléon III.

The Second Empire

The Second Empire (1852-1870) poses an interesting paradox for historians, for given the Emperor's own enigmatic character, and the contradictions of his regime, he can either be judged as an opportunist or as a man of vision. The first years of his rule were marked by authoritarianism – civil liberties were reduced and opponents of the regime were exiled: yet, the possible negative effects of these measures were offset by an unprecedented economic growth, and a peaceful foreign policy.

The second half of his rule was marked by a more liberal policy, but the electorate surprisingly voted more and more for his political opponents. Napoleon III's handling of foreign policy in these later years was less than successful and in 1870 war broke out with Germany. The French were defeated by the Prussians at Sedan, and the Emperor was taken prisoner on 4th September, 1870, the same day that a mob in Paris demanded that a republic be declared. Thus, the Second Empire collapsed in a bloodless revolution.

The Paris Commune

The Prussians advanced on Paris, which was surrounded and besieged and an armistice was eventually signed with the Germans in January 1871. One of the terms of the peace treaty was the handing over of Alsace and half of Lorraine to the German Empire. Discontent in France, especially Paris, was rife, and in March 1872, the capital broke out again in rioting which escalated into civil war.

The Paris Commune, an elected council supported by the national Guard, aimed at municipal self-government, but it was hindered by internal factions and the brief rule of the Commune was brought to a violent conclusion during the last "Bloody Week" of May.

Street fighting drove the cornered Communards into Père Lachaise cem-

Strasbourg in olden days.

etery, where the surviving members of the Commune were shot by the French army against the Mur des Fédérés, which has become an obligatory place of pilgrimage for all French left-wing politicians. The government was ruthless, and killed over 20,000 Communards and deported thousands more.

The Third Republic & the Dreyfus Affair

In 1875, the constitution of the Third Republic was adopted with a President elected for seven years (which is still the case today), a cabinet and a bicameral legislature.

Although there was constant political in-fighting, the early years of the new republic saw important educational reforms, and colonial expansion. Paris became a magnet for artists, designers and socialites. The next three intellectual decades would be known as *La Belle Époque* (the Edwardian era). (See box story on p.14.)

Crisis of the Third Republic

The greatest crisis of the Third Republic took place in the closing years of the 19th century. In 1894, a secret court-martial of a young Jewish army captain named Alfred Dreyfus took place. Dreyfus was accused of passing military secrets to the Germans, but although the evidence was non-existent, prevalent anti-semitic feelings made Dreyfus a convenient scapegoat. He was convicted, cashiered and deported for life; re-tried, convicted a second time of high treason, and sentenced; pardoned, cleared of all charges in 1906, given the *Légion d'Honneur* (Legion of Honour), a distinguished award and reinstated in the army. He died in 1935.

L'affaire Dreyfus (Dreyfus Affair) was a controversy that would have repercussions over many generations, dividing the nation into "dreyfusards" and "anti-dreyfusards". Émile Zola who wrote his famous open letter, *J'accuse* written to the President of the Republic, in defence of Dreyfus, was tried as a result, found guilty and fled to England. The blatant anti-semitism of large segments of the French establishment was the precursor of an ugly spectre that would raise its head 50 years later during WWII.

Into the 20th Century

France entered the 20th century in comfort and prosperity. A stable government engineered the separation of the church and state, and signed an *Entente Cordiale* (Friendly Agreement) in 1904 with their traditional enemy – Britain.

Surging Economy

Meanwhile the economy was growing, and the extent of France's colonies were second only to Britain.

The Paris wine market was already an organised industry, 1860.

Tthe relative peace of France was shattered, along with that of all of Europe, on 28th June, 1914, when the Austrian Archduke was assassinated in Sarajevo. On 3 August, Germany declared war on France, who had voiced her support for the Russians and Serbs. The French, under the Commander-in-Chief, General Joffre, confidently expected the war to last a matter of weeks. In the circumstances, it took four years of debilitating trench warfare, huge losses of life, and economic devastation before an armistice was signed in Compiègne on 11 November 1918.

■ ■ ■ ■ ■ ■

Marianne – the symbol of the Republic of France.

Government

33

World War

The statistics of French suffering in WWI are overwhelming: in the first four months alone, France lost 850,000 men – dead, wounded or prisoners – this horrifying rate of human attrition continued, so that by 1918, over 1.3 million men had been killed,

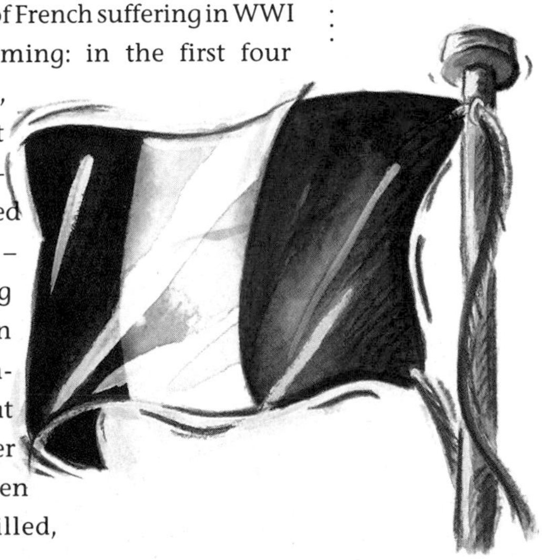

Monument to the casualties of WWI.

The Great Depression & the Advent of Socialism

The initial German inability to pay its war damages and the 1923 hyper-inflation of the Deutschmark, were mirrored in the weakness of the French Franc during the same period. By the late 1920s the Great Depression was beginning to spread throughout Europe, and although the effects did not hit France until 1931, when they finally did, the country suffered just as much as its neighbours.

The growing strength of the trade unions and internal political struggles pre-occupied the government, and after a series of coalitions and elections, the left-wing parties, communists and trade unions came together in 1935, to form the *Front Populaire* (Popular Front), in a concerted effort to counter increased right-wing militancy.

The Bastille Day procession of 1935 saw a combined force of socialists, communists and radicals, numbering anywhere between 300,000 to 400,000 marching together through the streets of Paris. The *Front Populaire*, with its slogan "Bread, Peace and Liberty", won the 1936 general elections, and the Socialist leader Léon Blum became Prime Minister – the first French Jewish premier. However, strains soon emerged, as the communists refused to join Blum's government and an immediate series of workers' strikes led the government to introduce a series of social reforms, in-

and another one million crippled. One of the most disastrous scenes of battles, for both French and Germans, was Verdun where almost half a million men lost their lives fighting here in 1916. Today, Verdun is a poignant place to visit, with its peaceful war memorials and well-tended cemeteries.

After the blood-letting, came the peace negotiations, and on 28th June, 1919, the *Treaty of Versailles* was signed, detailing the war reparations to be paid by Germany, as well as defining territorial limits.

France, along with the rest of Europe, entered the 1920s trying to rebuild its shattered economy and recover, both physically and psychologically, from the traumas of the war.

Upper flagged balcony of the Council of State, Paris.

cluding the 40-hour week, and *congés payés* (paid holidays).

Whilst France was mired by costly social reforms, without a counter-balancing programme of economic reform, Germany and Italy were becoming even more powerful.

Hitler was elected Chancellor in 1933, Mussolini invaded Ethiopia in 1935, and Germany re-occupied the Rhineland in 1936.

Hitler's supremacy continued unabated: Germany invaded Austria in March 1938, and Czechoslovakia in March 1939, with mere remonstrances from France and Britain, but the invasion of Poland finally prompted a declaration of war and on 3 September, 1939 WWII began.

World War II

As a permanent defence against any future German attacks, Maginot, the French Minister of War from 1929-1931, had ordered the construction of a fortified barrier along the Franco-German border, known as the Maginot Line. Completed in 1938, the elaborate defence system boasted recreation and living areas, storehouses, and even underground railway lines, all of which gave the French a sense of confidence bordering on complacency.

However, the Maginot Line covered only the German border, so when the Germans invaded France in May 1940 through Belgium, the fortifications of

Liberty. Egality. Fraternity. The philosophy of the Republic, inscribed on virtually every Town Hall Building.

the Maginot Line were of no use. The Germans rapidly advanced on Paris and despite the frantic efforts of the British under Winston Churchill, the French government, under Pétain, surrendered to the Germans in June 1940. Ironically the armistice agreement was signed in the very same railway car at Compiègne, where the 1918 armistice had been signed. France was divided into two zones, the north and the west which became the occupied zones, and the south which remained unoccupied.

Vichy France

The government of occupied France was centred in Vichy, with Pétain and Pierre Laval in charge, whilst the former Under-Secretary of war, General Charles de Gaulle, escaped to London, from where he called on his fellow countrymen to resist the Germans, a call that went largely unheeded in the early days of occupation. Laval was persuaded that Germany was the new European power, and that France accordingly should come to terms with her occupiers. He engineered the voting out of the Third Republic and publicly called for Franco-German collaboration, which was to leave a bitter legacy of hatred and resentment between fellow Frenchmen in the years ahead. Collaboration was a misconception, for Laval it meant that France's compliance would be favoured by Germany, whilst for Germany, col-

Chamber of Deputies, Paris, illuminated.

laboration was but an empty theory, made merely to pacify French politicians. The Germans continued in their ruthless programme of the Germanization of Alsace-Lorraine and of the conscription of French workers for German factories. A compliant Vichy Government supplied the conscripts and tried to stamp out the Resistance, whose activities were aimed at sabotaging supplies and conscripts to Germany.

The Resistance

The resistance movement grew steadily, gaining the support of the Communists, after Hitler invaded Russia in 1941. As the pace of conscription speeded up, escaped draftees also went underground, calling themselves the *maquis* thereby increasing the potential of resistance power. The *maquis*, meaning dense thickets of drought-resistant shrubs are named after plants in the plateaux of Roussillon which provided perfect hideouts for the Resistance. As the tide of war swung in favour of the Allies, and despite the Allied tensions caused by de Gaulle's often high-handed behaviour, the goal of an invasion of occupied France became more feasible. The Allied landing in Normandy on 6th June, 1944, and the by now considerable strength of the underground resistance forced the gradual retreat of the Germans. Paris was liberated on 25th August, 1944, with de Gaulle becoming the

German Occupation

When the Germans invaded Belgium on 10 May 1940, they continued to advance straight into France marching on Paris, virtually unhindered by the Maginot Line, in which so much French confidence had mistakenly been placed. On 10 June, the French government fled to Tours, declaring Paris an open city, four days later the Germans entered Paris, sweeping on southwards. By the end of the month, the French government had signed an armistice with the Germans. Under the terms of the Armistice, France was divided into two zones, Occupied (Vichy France) and Unoccupied France, the former under German military occupation, and the latter under French rule. The French Navy and Air Force were neutralized and the French army was disarmed.

Both the passive French and the victorious Germans considered the end of the war to be imminent, both sides firmly believing that Britain, alone among the European powers, would be incapable of resisting German might.

Thus it was, that two further clauses of the Armistice agreement, instead of being short-term measures, turned into a long-term noose around France's neck. The Germans insisted on retaining all French POWS, and they decreed that France would have to pay the expenses of the army of occupation.

Whilst the politicians manoeuvred for position both vis-à-vis the invaders and within the French government, now based in Vichy, the French economy was soon crippled by the occupation. The Germans requisitioned machinery and raw materials, for which the French had to pay. Nearly two million POWS were still in German hands. An artificially imposed exchange rate, fixed in favour of the Germans, gave them immense spending power, at the expense of the French, whose situation worsened with the bad harvest of 1940 and the continued lack of manpower. The winter of 1940-41 saw the country on the verge of starvation and rationing and strict price and wage controls were introduced. The latent anti-semitism of the French quickly rose to the surface, and by October 1940, there were laws prohibiting Jews from holding any position in government, the teaching profession, and any state-subsidized industry and

quotas were fixed for entry into other professions.

Invasion Of Russia

When the Germans invaded Russia in June 1941, the Communists joined forces with the fledgling French underground Resistance movement, which started attacking individual Germans: German reprisals were harsh, shooting batches of 50 hostages at a time, usually Jews.

As more and more workers were needed for the German armament factories, they started to conscript French workers: those who escaped often fled to join the Resistance, or the "*maquis*" (the name given to tough drought resistant shrubs, amongst which members of the Resistance often hid) guerrilla bands.

Allies Landing

The Allied landing in Normandy on 6th June, 1944 was the beginning of the end for the German forces in France. The Germans slowly retreated, under the pressure of the advancing Allies and the effective sabotage tactics of the Resistance. Paris was liberated on 25th August, 1944 by free French forces, but not before desperate hand-to-hand street fighting had killed many "*résistants*" (members of the resistance). Memorial plaques to these Resistance fighters, many of them barely out of their teens, can still be seen all over Paris – a row of them are on the corner of the Tuileries and the Place de la Concorde, a couple are opposite Notre Dame, amidst the second-hand book stalls, and there are many more isolated ones, suddenly discovered on a quiet street. In the last few days before the Allied liberation of France, an increasingly desperate Hitler ordered the German military commander of Paris, General Dietrich von Choltitz, to blow up much of the city, rather than hand it over to the Allies. Bridges across the River Seine were mined, as were many of the capital's palaces and monuments, along with most of the strategic installations. Luckily for France, and the world, the Prussian general chose to disobey orders, and Paris survived.

recognized head of state (see box story on de Gaulle p.42). The retribution and blood-letting of an impoverished and demoralised country began. There was a massive purge against Vichy officials, during which the Resistance is estimated to have executed more than 10,000 people, and there were trials and yet more executions of collaborators. In October 1945, elections were held, which granted female suffrage, and in November 1946 the Fourth Republic was voted in.

The Iron Arm of Colonialism

Amidst all the domestic political and economic upheavals of the post-war years, France also had her colonial headaches, especially in Indochina. Where her involvement had effectively begun after the Second Empire. A small skirmish in 1847 was the start of France's military presence in Vietnam, to be followed over the years by a succession of battles, which culminated in a French stranglehold over both the territory and the economy. In 1887, the French proclaimed the setting up of the Indochinese Union, consisting of Cochinchina, Tonkin, Annam, Cambodia, Laos and the Chinese port city of Kwangchowan.

The French, despite their frequently proclaimed *mission civilisatrice* (mission to civilize), were principally motivated by profit, and in order to generate the high returns on capital demanded by Paris, invested in rubber plantations,

coal, tin and zinc mines in the colonies, all of which became notorious for the exploitation of local workers. Taxes were cripplingly high, leading to a landless, impoverished peasantry. In Vietnam although the majority of Vietnamese peasants had owned their own land prior to the arrival of the French, by the 1930s, 70 percent of them were landless.

Discontent was rife, and over the years, there were many failed attempts at over-throwing the colonial rule, but it was not until the early years of the 20th century that an organised, nationalistic movement grew up. The most committed, and the most successful, anti-colonialists were the communists, and in 1941 Ho Chi Minh founded the Viet Minh. When France capitulated to the Nazis in 1940, the Vichy Government accepted the presence of Japanese troops in Indochina, and it was Ho's Viet Minh which resisted the Japanese invasion, thereby earning the (temporary) gratitude and funding of the Americans.

In 1945, the turmoil of post-Hiroshima Japan was reflected in the growing unrest in Vietnam: the Emperor abdicated, and on 2nd September, 1945 Ho Chi Minh proclaimed the independence of the Democratic Republic of Vietnam. The reaction came just three weeks later, when French settlers and troops rampaged through the streets of Saigon, vowing to reclaim their inheritance. To counter an invasion in the north of the country by Chinese Kuomintang troops, Ho was reluctantly obliged to accept the temporary return of the French, for an

The Arc de Triomphe, a monument to Napoleon's victories.

agreed period of five years. The French shelling of Haiphong in 1946 precipitated the last stage of the Franco-Vietnamese crisis. War broke out, Ho and his forces fled to the hills to wage an eight year guerilla war against the French, who were given huge amounts of American aid. The *coup de grace* came on 7th May, 1954, with the surrender of 10,000 starving French forces at Dien Bien Phu, after a 57-day siege. Any remaining French support for a colonial effort that had cost 35,000 French lives in eight years was shattered by Dien Bien Phu and the French Assembly voted for the withdrawal from Indochina – a considerable recession in French Colonial power.

The year 1954 also saw the North African colony of Algeria rebelling against French rule, and, determined to hold onto a territory it claimed as an integral part of France, the government proceeded to send out more than half a million French soldiers over the next three years. The Algerian War was a brutal, expensive and domestically unpopular war and when extremists plotted the downfall of the Fourth Republic, and the installation of a tougher regime, possibly backed by the military, the country was once again plunged into a constitutional crisis. By September 1958, de Gaulle's Fifth Republic had been accepted, which constitutionally granted greater power to the President. In December of the same year de Gaulle himself was elected President for seven years. The Algerian problem was to take four years to solve, before independence was finally granted on 1st July, 1962.

De Gaulle & the Fifth Republic

De Gaulle's first seven-year term brought peace and prosperity to the country, and he embarked on a campaign to retrieve some of France's lost stature in foreign affairs, blocking the entry of Britain into the Common Market, and forcing NATO forces to leave France. But his second term was not so peaceful, and in May 1968, what had been sporadic student protests erupted into national strikes and rioting. The students were affected by general feelings of unease against the Vietnam war, the government's control of the media and the archaic values of the older generation. One minor incident, the police break-up of a demonstration staged by radical students at the Sorbonne in Paris, became the spark that ignited a huge civic conflagration. The barricades went up, students all over the country joined in the protests, and millions of workers went on strike. The riots, strikes, and protests lasted a month, but as middle-class Frenchmen gradually lost their enthusiasm for the fight, de Gaulle took the issue to the country, winning a landslide victory. France had been profoundly shaken by the depth and passion of the riots, and a series of concessions were made to both workers and students.

France Post de Gaulle

After de Gaulle's death in 1970, there was some doubt as to whether his party could continue to exist without him personally at the helm. But, it did under the markedly less autocratic leadership of Georges Pompidou, whilst the fragmented left-wing parties gradually coalesced under the leadership of François Mitterrand. After the death of President Pompidou in early 1974, the presidential elections saw the Gaullists splitting into two groups, with Valéry Giscard d'Estaing barely defeating the socialist candidate, Mitterrand. Giscard's Prime Minister, the ambitious young Jacques Chirac harboured leadership ambitions, and was soon replaced, in turn forming his own party. The 1973 oil crisis undermined any hope of economic reforms, and the government's austerity programme was unpopular. The 1978 parliamentary elections were an ideal time for the left wing factions but internal squabbling between Socialists and Communists allowed the right to retain power, with Chirac's party becoming the largest party in the Assembly. Rivalry between Giscard and Chirac intensified and they both stood as candidates in the 1981 presidential elections, whilst the left-wing vote was divided between Mitterand and the communist leader, Georges Marchais.

The second round of voting saw Giscard and Mitterrand opposing each other, with victory going to the Socialist

Charles de Gaulle

Charles-André-Marie-Joseph de Gaulle was born on 22nd November, 1890, and during his long life and career, played a major role in the wartime history of France, and in her post-war political development.

After distinguished service in WWI, de Gaulle earned a certain degree of notoriety from his writings on military affairs. On the outbreak of WWII, he entered Paul Reynauds' government, as Under-Secretary for defence and war, but when Reynaud was replaced by Marshal Pétain who declared his intention of seeking an armistice with Germany, de Gaulle left both the government and the country and fled to England.

In London, de Gaulle began broadcasting appeals to his countrymen to resist the Germans, under the banner of his "Free French" movement. On 18th June, 1940, he made his first broadcast, and by 2nd August, 1940, a military court in France had tried him in absentia: the verdict – death. Although the British government gave de Gaulle both moral support and material facilities, relations were not always easy, for the General's touchiness and his single-minded commitment to the cause of France (sometimes interpreted as obstinacy by the British) often caused strains. In 1943, de Gaulle moved his headquarters from London to Algiers, and was named joint head of the French Committee of National Liberation. To his military prowess, he now added political prowess, for he successfully edged out his co-president to become the acknowledged leader of the Free French outside the country, and the resistance movement inside France. On 9th September, 1944, de Gaulle and his government in exile returned to Paris, whilst the war passed into its final stage. In a referendum in 1945, the French voted against the continuation of the Third Republic which had been part of Vichy France, but de Gaulle was unhappy with the new constitution of the Fourth Republic which was voted in November 1946 and he continued to oppose the Fourth Republic until 1958. In 1947, he founded a new party, the RPF – Rally for French People – which

won 120 seats in the 1951 elections. Through the RPF, de Gaulle expressed his continued hostility towards the constitution, and towards his former Resistance allies, the Communists. By 1953, disillusioned with his new party, he resigned, and the RPF was disbanded in 1955. The General retired to the country, and started writing his memoirs, only to be called back to power on 1st June, 1958, with France facing the threat of civil unrest because of troubles in Algeria. Yet another constitution, the Fifth Republic, was voted in, and in December 1958 de Gaulle became President of France. The Fifth Republic changed the balance of French politics, since it transferred effective power from the Assembly to the President as he had wished. During the Algerian War, de Gaulle was seen as the only hope of containing the threat of civil war in France, but once Algeria gained her independence in 1962, he was no longer politically indispensable and he had to consolidate his position. The general elections of November 1962 gave him a fresh mandate, and de Gaulle now turned his attention increasingly towards the fledgling EEC, – European Economic Community; he withdrew France from NATO and advocated the withdrawal of American troops from Vietnam.

May 1968 saw France (especially Paris) plunged into a ferment of student and labour unrest and once again he turned to the electorate, who, voting more for peace than for the President himself, gave him a landslide victory. But when de Gaulle presented yet another referendum on electoral reform to the country, with a mandate, as before, to accept the issue or his resignation, the voters this time chose the latter, and on 28th April, 1969, General de Gaulle resigned, retiring permanently to his country home and to the continuation of his memoirs. He died on 7 November, 1970.

The French flag flies regal over Marseille.

candidate. The country was euphoric, parliamentary elections were rapidly called which also returned a socialist majority. So for the first time in French history, the Socialists were totally in control.

Socialism Under Threat

Banks and major industrial units were nationalised and a packet of social reforms were introduced, upper income groups were taxed more heavily, but as France embarked on a left-ward journey, most of their European neighbours were turning to the right.

Economically, France soon found itself out on a limb, the economy suf-

fered, with a marked flight of capital out of the country. The communists, who had been rewarded for their electoral support with four cabinet jobs, resigned from the government, and on the far right, the xenophobia of the National Front party, under Jean-Marie Le Pen was increasing its share of the vote in local elections.

1986 Parliamentary Elections

The 1986 parliamentary elections resulted in a conservative victory, and France entered into an uneasy two years of what was termed "cohabitation": co-existence of a Socialist President and a right wing Prime Minister, namely

Mitterrand and Jacques Chirac respectively in the leadership of the government.

Mitterrand, ever the astute politician, kept increasingly aloof from the more problematic parts of government, including more violent student riots, and a campaign of terrorism in Paris, and when the 1988 Presidential run-off pitted President against Prime Minister. Mitterrand won.

Foreign Policy in the 1990's

The political situation at the beginning of the 1990s sees France resolutely turning towards the strengthened, larger political entity of a Europe without barriers, whilst also embarking on an attempt at gaining a sphere of influence in her former colonies. Mitterrand's 1992 visit to Vietnam and Cambodia, especially his pilgrimage to Dien Bien Phu in the company of the Vietnamese General who had defeated the French, nearly 40 years earlier, was significant.

France wants to be an economic power, in a part of the world with which she has had past colonial links. France's few remaining overseas possessions, are usually referred to as "les Dom-Toms", a nickname for the much more impressive sounding title of "Overseas Dominions and Territories". Some of these tropical islands, including French Polynesia and New Caledonia have problems, and New Caledonia, in particular, has a recent history of violence.

La Défense, Paris, against a modern skyline.

Economy

France is one of the world's major economic powers, an impressive statistic for a country that, 50 years ago, at the end of WWII, had been stripped of food and raw materials, and faced a severe manpower shortage.

In the 30 years from the end of the war to the oil crisis of 1973, France enjoyed a period of unprecedented growth. A marked rise in unemployment followed the oil crisis, whilst the end of the 1980s saw the economy picking up with renewed vigour. Now, however, the worldwide recession of the opening years of the 1990s is beginning to affect France, something she has in common with most of her European neighbours.

The economy of France has a great deal to do with its agriculture.

47

Nationalization

The tradition of a mixed economy is well established in France, with the private and the public sectors co-existing. This was particularly so since the end of the war, when successive governments

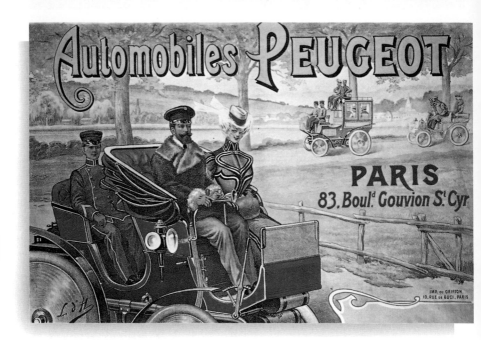

Peugeot transport has been à la mode for a long time.

have regularly intervened to protect or promote different sectors of the French economy and this state directed industrial policy called *dirigisme* can be clearly seen in the domain of nationalized industries.

Immediately after the end of WWII, the French government initiated a series of nationalizations, including the public utilities, such as gas and electricity; large industrial corporations, such as Renault®; and some of the country's largest banks, for example, Crédit Lyonnais and the Banque National de Paris, known to everyone as the "BNP".

The Socialist government of the early 1980s re-introduced an extensive nationalization programme, which was temporarily halted, and slightly re-versed, by the short-lived right-wing Jacques Chirac government of 1986-88.

As a general rule, France is one of the European countries at the forefront of technology. Take the Minitel® for example, a computerised information system, accessible via telephone. The Minitel® terminals are provided free to homes and offices and by dialling a short code, you can access a wide range of services easily, from reserving a train ticket (the Minitel® will ask you, whether you require smoking or non-smoking, facing the engine or not, window or aisle), to finding a phone number when you do not even know the address, to locating a special item of clothing: suppose you want to buy a particular outfit, you can enter the type of garment, the

The Bourse, the hub of the Paris stock-market.

colour required, the material and the price you are prepared to pay and the Minitel® will reply with a list of shops, country-wide, stocking your ideal garment!

The concept of accessing computerised information banks has so caught on, that you can now book train tickets via a machine in the station, without having to queue up at a *guichet* (ticket booth) and in Paris, you can interrogate route-finder machines that are placed on the street, to find out the quickest way from A to B – the machine will even tell you which bus to take, or at which underground Métro station you should change from one line to another.

Banks have long had highly sophisticated computer information systems, and ATMs, (Automatic Teller Machines), from which you can withdraw money, find out the balance of your account and check which transactions have gone through, are increasingly commonplace.

Major banks, such as Crédit Lyonnais, which have heavily invested in information systems, have a series of *"Agences libres"*, which are special unstaffed branches, open 24 hours a day: they consist of rows of machines, ATMs, as well as cheque deposit and coin machines.

A recent development that has been fuelled, sadly, more by the need to combat crime rather than anything else, is that all credit card transactions are now validated on the spot via a personal

Sheep shearing is part of the life of many a French farmer.

code, that the card-holder himself enters. By the time you walk out of the restaurant after dinner, the bill has already been debited to your credit card account.

The Car Industry

The French love driving, they love their cars, and feel attached to them in both

and tyres were being developed and the sport of car racing was in its infancy, the French car industry is now entering a period of heavy retrenchment.

Peugeot®, a major automobile manufacturer, was founded in 1890 by Armand Peugeot. It merged with Citroën®, in 1976 and the new company was called – naturally enough, Peugeot-Citroën®, though three years later the name was shortened to Peugeot SA®. The Citroën company, started by André-Gustave Citroën, was initially a manufacturer of munitions during WWI and it was only after the war that the arms factory was converted into a plant manufacturing small, inexpensive cars, the first of which rolled off the assembly line in 1919. The Great Depression badly affected the company, and by 1934 Citroën had gone bankrupt and was sold to Michelin®, after which further mergers took place during the 1960s. In the mid-1970s, to avert another potential bankruptcy, the government funded the sale of Citroën to the Peugeot group.

The other great name of the French automobile industry is Renault®, or, to give it its full name, the *Régie Nationale des Usines Renault*®, the largest manufacturer and exporter of motor vehicles in France. It is owned by the government. Like the other French car companies, Renault was originally a family concern, founded in 1898 by the three Renault brothers. Like the Citroën company, Renault also produced arms during WWI, as well as aeroplane engines and light tanks. WWII was disastrous

a personal and a vaguely patriotic way, but the hard facts of overseas competition, especially from the Japanese, and the present global recession, means that the automobile industry has recently suffered. From its heyday at the beginning of the century, when the first cars

Michelin's first car with pneumatic wheels, one in
a long line of French motor inventions.

for the company. In the early stages of
the war, the Germans took over the
factories, and retaliatory Allied bomb-

ing damaged a large number of plants.
By the end of the war, more than 80
percent of the Renault installations had

a suburb of Paris, became a powerful symbol in the country, representative of the trade union movement, of the power of the working class, and, in its own way, a laboratory for social reform. Amidst a climate of economic downturn and the recession, Billancourt was permanently closed down in the spring of 1992. A division of Renault, Renault Véhicules Industriels® has also felt the effects of the recession on the world truck industry, with profits of FF23 million in 1991 plunging to losses of close to a billion francs in 1992, amidst more cuts in the labour force.

New factors are also influencing the car industry, such as ever stricter rules on pollution control, which means that much-loved older models such as the Renault 4 – known universally as the 4L – have been phased out, to make way for a new generation of small cars, such as the 1993 Twingo®.

The central French town of Clermont-Ferrand is the headquarters of the Michelin® company, the leading manufacturer of tyres and other rubber products.

Energy Resources

The French are firm believers in nuclear power, and while many countries are quietly dropping their plans for new nuclear reactors, France is doing exactly the opposite.

Currently, three-quarters of French electricity is generated by nuclear power,

been destroyed. In 1945, the remaining property was confiscated by the French Government, which nationalized it, setting up the *Régie Nationale des Usines Renault*. Its headquarters at Billancourt,

more than anywhere else in the world and the government is continuing to invest in its future use. The state-owned *Electricité de France*, (EDF), has asked for the go-ahead to order their 62nd nuclear reactor, at the same time advising that similar requests will be made roughly every 18 months. France has coal reserves, but output is limited, since the stocks are not of a good quality and are difficult to extract, making them expensive. Supplies of natural gas and oil are very limited, so nuclear power appears as an economic alternative.

Using economies of scale, one broad design of reactor was developed, perfected, and repeated all over the country, cutting both design costs and time. Admirable as such an efficient, single-minded attitude may be, there is an opposite point of view. A recent report made by a branch of the OECD (Organisation for Economic Cooperation and Development), called the International Energy Agency, made a pertinent observation: should a design flaw ever appear, all of France's nuclear reactors would be at risk.

Channel Tunnel Technology

The Anglo-French joint project to build the Channel Tunnel has been an example of the effective harnessing of French technology, where earlier investments in technology have paid off, whereas the British half of the project has not been so impressive. For example, the French have had their *Train à Grande Vitesse*, (TGV, or high-speed train), for years, it is in daily use throughout much of the country, and the state-owned railway company, SNCF, is constantly extending its network within France, and into neighbouring countries. The proposed implementation of a luxury, cross-Channel rail service linked to the Channel Tunnel does not, therefore, pose any major technological problem for France. However, on the British side, there is no high-speed train, so when the future Eurostar Train crosses from France at 300 kph it will have to reduce its speed to 160 kph once it reaches Kent in England.

The TGV, France's high speed train.

Aerospace

France, long a believer in the value of a united Europe, has been quick to enter into European industrial projects, a prime example being the aerospace industry. In 1970, a European aircraft manufacturing consortium, called *Airbus Industrie®*, was formed between France and West Germany, with the aim of competing with the American manufacturers of large capacity, short and medium-range planes. Airbus® has manufactured the A300, the A310 and now the A320, and although the consortium headquarters are in Toulouse, the component parts are actually separately manufactured in the European member countries and assembled in France.

France was at the forefront of supersonic space technology, symbolized by the most beautiful looking aeroplane in the world – the Concorde®, which, was the first commercial, passenger-carrying airplane to fly at speeds of Mach 2. Concorde was a joint Anglo-French government project (the name must surely have been slightly ironic, after so many historical battles!). Concorde was tested in the early 1970s and went into regular service on 21st January, 1976, with a double inauguration, the French jet flying from Paris to Rio de Janeiro and the British plane flying from London to Bahrain. Sadly, despite its aesthetics and *avant garde* technology, Concorde has

The Silk Industry of Lyon

Silk has been an integral part of the fabric of Lyon, literally and metaphorically, since the 16th century, bringing the city first wealth and then political activism. In the 16th century, most European silk came from Italy, so when in 1536, Étienne Turquet suggested setting up a silk and velvet weaving factory in Lyon, using imported Genoese labourers, his plan was well received by the king, François I. Earlier moves had already been made to regularize the silk business: King Louis XI had tried to encourage local producers by abolishing taxes on silk manufacture and François I was delighted at the idea of halting the export of currency from France, used to purchase Italian silk, by encouraging local industry.

Silk Manufacturing Capital

By the 17th century, Lyon was the silk-manufacturing capital of Europe, but the French Revolution brought about a slump in the silk industry, leading to the collapse of both the domestic and the foreign market.

Joseph-Marie Jacquard, who was born in Lyon in 1752, was one of the figures who once again galvanised the Lyon textile industry. He developed a revolutionary idea for a loom, a system of punched cards with holes to guide the threads, enabling the loom to be set for a variety of patterns, which could then be automatically obtained. Such an innovative technique was bound to provoke controversy. However, Jacquard's experimental work was interrupted by the French Revolution, where not surprisingly, he defended Lyon, fighting on the side of the Revolutionaries. Then, when his machine was finally put into service in 1805, it aroused total opposition from the hostile weavers, who feared for their jobs since his invention allowed one man to do the work formerly done by six. They burned the machines, and even attacked their inventor. Opposition was relatively short-lived, however, for by 1812, 11,000 looms were in use in France – with Jacquard earning royalties on each machine!

Special *ateliers* (workshops), were built to house the big looms, centred on a hill called La Croix Rousse. A system of *traboules* (covered passageways) were also built, linking the different workshops, so that a worker carrying a bolt of silk could walk from one *atelier* to another and on to the buyer's office, without getting his work spoiled by the rain.

The silk weavers of Lyon were called "*canuts*" and in the first half of the 19th century, there were 30,000 *canuts* working on La Croix Rousse. Bloody riots broke out twice – in 1831 and 1834, when the *canuts* fought waving black flags with the words "Live by work, or die by fighting". In 1854, there was a devastating silkworm plague, whose cause, and means of control, were discovered by Louis Pasteur, only in 1865. Although the Italian industry managed to recover, the French one never really did. The American Civil War put an end to the booming trade it had established with the southern states: sales fell from 138 million francs in 1859, to one million francs in 1865. Three-quarters of the city's looms were idle.

Mechanical Looms

In 1875, the ailing industry was further buffeted by the introduction of mechanical looms, which coincided with a downturn in the use of silk for clothing. In Lyon, only a few looms survived to handle orders for extremely expensive silks. Today, the Lyon textile industry is dominated by the manufacture of rayon and silk, and specialises in highly technical work, involving the use of silk for the aeronautic and electronic industries. However, visitors to Lyon can still see traditional silk-weaving at the silk workers' co-operative, *La Maison des Canuts*, where serviceable handlooms, including a Jacquard loom can be viewed.

Maison des Canuts

The *Maison des Canuts* is partly an *atelier* (workshop), partly a museum, with a display of old fabrics and partly a shop. The excellent *Musée Historique de Tissus* (Museum of Textiles) in Lyon contains gorgeous samples of silks.

France's dynamic space industry on the move.

not been a commercial success, and by 1982, all the routes were cut, except the Paris to New York route.

Today, Air France®, the state-owned airline, has seven Concordes in its fleet, all capable of cruising at a speed of Mach 2.02, or 2,200 kph. France manufactures fighter aircraft, notably the Mirage combat aircraft, which are produced by the Dassault-Breguet Aeronautics Factory. The first Mirage was developed in the 1950s, but has undergone significant modifications and improvements over the intervening 40 years.

The recent Mirage 2000, a multipurpose fighter with a delta-wing design, was introduced into the French Air Force in 1984. The Mirage has recently been at the centre of a Far Eastern political storm: in November 1992, the French signed a deal to provide Taiwan with 60 Mirage 2000 planes, a much needed boost for the French industry, worth some 21 billion francs.

However, this sale angered the Chinese, who initially retaliated by closing the French consulate in the southern port city of Guangzhou, and in early 1993, froze French telecommunications projects in China worth an estimated 2 billion francs. The telecommunications industry needs the contracts, as does the aircraft industry, and the government must now tread carefully, balancing domestic and foreign politics, and weighing diplomacy against the need to keep French jobs.

59

The hexagonal shape of the French land mass covers a total area of 543,965 square kilometres, and encompasses a considerable diversity of landforms. France has two of Europe's major mountain chains, some of Europe's major rivers and beaches, as well as forests, vineyards, industry-filled plains and a long and varied coastline.

Mountains, forming France's major natural boundaries correspond, fairly logically, with many of her political borders: the Pyrénées form the southwestern frontier with Spain and the tiny principality of Andorra and the eastern mountainous chains of the Vosges, Jura and the Alps form her boundaries with Germany, Switzerland and Italy respectively. Only the extreme northeastern plains, bordering on the Duchy of Luxembourg and Belgium, are an exception. The British Isles are to the north, across the English Channel, and the two countries, historically

The rugged splendour of the Pyrénées.

such long-standing rivals, will soon be physically linked, once the Channel Tunnel – an ambitious rail link under the sea is completed.

The western coast of France opens straight onto the Atlantic Ocean. The tiny, independent Principality of Monaco is tucked into the Alpes Maritimes and the island of Corsica is off the southern Mediterranean coast.

Climatically, most of France lies in the southern part of the temperate zone, but within this, are variations. The climate in France can vary considerably, and on any given day in the winter, it can be snowing in the Alps, raining and chilly in Brittany and sunny on the Côte d'Azur. The northwest of the country, which essentially means Brittany, has an oceanic climate – low seasonal variations, moderate rainfall, cloudy skies and, for Europe, high humidity.

The northeast has a continental climate – cold winters, with frost and snow and early storms preceding warm summers. In the southeast, the thin strip of Mediterranean coastline is the only part of France with a sub-tropical climate, enjoying mild winters and hot, dry summers.

Generally speaking, the French

landscape comprises lowlying plains, plateaux, older mountain blocks, known as "massifs" and the younger, higher ranges of the Alps and the Pyrenees.

The physical structure of France is dominated by a group of ancient mountains, whose folding and formation took place between 345 and 225 million years ago. These Hercynian massifs formed the Ardennes massif, the Vosges, the Massif Central and the much lower Massif Armoricain in Brittany. The composition of these mountains is essentially a mixture of resistant metamorphic rocks and Paleozoic sedimentary rocks, which are sometimes found to contain coal deposits.

Massif Central

Despite the inevitable exceptions and the danger of generalizations, the geography of France can conveniently be broken down into nine main land areas. The huge plateau of the Massif Central covers about 86,000 square kilometres, which is almost one-sixth of the total area of France.

To the east, the Massif Central is

Icing on the Alps.

bordered by the Rhône-Saône valley, to the north is the flat Paris Basin, to the south are the lowlands of Languedoc, with the Aquitaine Basin to the southwest. The eastern and southeastern slopes of the Massif Central, those nearest to the Alps, are steep, whilst the western and northern slopes are much gentler. In the north-eastern corner of the massif is the forested region of Morvan.

Earlier volcanic activity caused faulting and led to the formation of the mountains of Cantal and Monts Dore, where the highest summit of the Massif Central, the Puy de Sancy (1,886 metres) stands. Further to the west, is the extraordinary Châine des Puys, or Monts Dôme, a 30 kilometre stretch of 112 extinct volcanoes, which are, geologically speaking, relatively young, being a mere 10,000 years old. The many well-known mineral springs, such as those in Vichy in the central Auvergne, are also relics of earlier volcanic activity.

To the southwest, the rocks of the Massif Central are covered by a thick layer of *causses* (limestone), a sparsely populated area, with dramatic gorges cut into the massif by the rivers. Some of the most spectacular gorges called the Gorges du Tarn are found here. The whole area has an extensive cave system, some of which contain prehistoric art, notably Pêche-Merle in the Lot valley and Lascaux. Just south of the area known as the Cévennes, is a cave called the Grotte des Demoiselles, where mid-

Ocean blue, a vision of serenity off the coast of Marseille.

night mass is celebrated underground every Christmas Eve.

There is an organ, choir and a large congregation, perched on rocks and standing on any available piece of ground, amongst the stalagmites and stalactites, to participate in one of France's most picturesque masses.

Massif Armoricain

The Brittany-Normandy hills, better known as the Massif Armoricain, are

tral, for its highest point, the Mont des Avaloirs, only stands at 417 metres above sea level. The coastline of Brittany is highly indented and rugged.

Northeastern Plateau

The Northeastern Plateau is another of the old mountainous formations of France, although neither the Ardennes massif nor the Vosges achieve the same altitudes as the Massif Central. The Ardennes Massif is a continuation into France from Belgium of the Rhine Uplands, and the erosion of the Paleozoic sedimentary rocks has formed a landscape of long ridges and valleys crossed by the Sambre and Meuse Rivers.

The Vosges form almost an internal barrier, between Alsace to the east, and Lorraine to the west. The steep eastern slopes of the Vosges sweep down to a rift valley and the plains of Alsace and of Baden (in Germany), whilst on the west, the slopes descend rather more gently into Lorraine. The maximum altitudes of the Vosges are found in the south, near the Alps, where the more resistant, crystalline rocks are exposed. The higher summits are called "*ballons*" and the highest is the Ballon de Guebwiller at an altitude of 1,423 metres.

The Alps, Jura Pyrénées

The Pyrénées are considerably younger than the Massif Central. Their forma-

formed from essentially the same rock structures as the Massif Central – Hercynian rocks, which have been folded into their current shapes.

The Massif Armoricain is principally situated in the western peninsula of Brittany and continues eastwards beyond Brittany and south across the Loire. It is much lower than the Massif Cention probably took place about 1.6 million years ago, making them the oldest of the more recently formed French mountains. The Pyrénées stretch for more than 450 kilometres across the southwestern corner of the country, forming a natural barrier between France and Spain.

The French Alps and the Jura Mountains are also, geologically speaking, "young" mountains. The Jura Mountains are composed of folded limestone, and the northeastern part of the Jura, which has the most pronounced folding, extends across into Switzerland. The French Alps are part of the major mountain chain that also extends across the frontier and into the rest of Europe, but it is in France that the highest peak of the Alps, Mont Blanc (4,807 metres) is situated. The Alps include the two greatest regions of permanent snow and glaciers in Europe.

The Northern Alps are relatively easy to cross, due to the numerous valleys, created by the movement of glaciers, whereas the valleys of the Southern Alps, which were not formed by glaciation, are narrow, winding gorges. The Alps form a natural barrier with Switzerland and Italy along France's southeastern flank.

Valleys & Plains & Basins

The mountains are in some respects, the bone structure of France. Between the main mountainous zones are plains, whose usage includes habitation, agriculture and industry. One of the largest of these lowland areas spreads across much of the northern half of the country, and can be generally classified as the Northern French plain. This area of lowlying land can be further sub-divided, as it is broken up by mountainous outcrops.

The gorgeous lushness of Provence.

Surrounded by the Ardennes, the Vosges, the Massif Central, and the Massif Armoricain is the huge Paris Basin, which is mainly composed of tertiary rocks, such as limestone. The plateaux of the Ile de France, Soisson and Valois are occasionally punctuated by the eroded remnants of higher rock formations, which have been left behind as isolated *buttes* (hills). Probably the most famous *butte* is in Paris – the Butte de Montmartre. The sandy parts of the Paris Basin are covered with forest, such as the Forest of Fontainebleau located

The Windiest Place In France

A meteorological station that is only 60 kilometres away from the Mediterranean should be a nice, sunny place. Right? wrong, that is if the meteorological station in question is on Mont Aigoual in the Cévennes, which in winter is the windiest and wettest place in France. Far from basking in the hot Mediterranean sun, in winter the meteorologists live in quasi-Siberian conditions.

The weather at the top of the mountain is unique, and lends itself to all kinds of statistics. In February 1964, 519.7 millimetres of rain fell there – as much as the annual rainfall of Paris – whilst only 60 kilometres away, the Camargue, is the driest spot in France. Rainfall records (or, more precisely, precipitation records) have been maintained since 1896, and show that the summit of the mountain receives more than 2,000 millimetres annually. In 1914, nearly 10 metres of snow fell, whereas in the winter of 1989-1990 just a few snowflakes fell. In winter, the wind is so strong that it sometimes exceeds the maximum speed of the wind-gauge – 250 kilometres per hour. Average annual wind speed in a "normal" region is calculated to be between 7 and 9 kph. On Mont Aigoual it is 60 kph.

Construction of the meteorological observatory began on 17 June 1887, but it was not completed until 1893. At that time, the weather was just as inclement, but in addition, there were also wolves to contend with. Inaugurated on 18th August, 1894, today nearly a century later the observatory has taken on an enlarged role. It is still one of the most important weather stations in France, but it is also a popular tourist attraction.

Every year 500,000 people climb up the mountain, hoping for one of the stunning views found on picture postcards and in the books they buy from the meteorologists, who are trying to make their profession slightly more accessible to the public, and to capitalize on the tourist trade.

Climbing all the way up for the view is something of a gamble, since Mont Aigoual averages 240 misty, hazy days a year, so opportunities of seeing the stunning view from the 1,567 metre summit are fairly rare. However, when the mist does lift, the view is really exceptional, for you can see nearly a quarter of France in one 360° view: the mountains of the Auvergne, the distant peaks of the Alps, the Camargue, the Mediterranean and all the surrounding peaks of the Cévennes. In summer, it is advisable not to climb up during the hottest part of the day – you will be exhausted and almost certainly the view will be very hazy. Really hardy souls climb during the night, in order to witness sunrise from the summit – September is the best time whilst in January you are most likely to be able to see Mont Blanc and the Spanish Costa Brava simultaneously. In July, an open-air Mass is celebrated on the mountain in honour of the Jour de la Montagne (day of the mountain).

southwest of Paris.

Going east, the Paris Basin spreads towards the chalky countryside of Champagne, further eastwards to Lorraine, and southeastwards to Burgundy and the limestone Plateau de Langres, which forms a watershed between the major river systems of the Seine and Rhône-Saône river systems.

The western part of the Paris Basin, is marked by the spectacular meandering and picturesque cliffs of the River Seine. Further north, are the wide chalky, fertile plateaus of Picardy and Artois, which are rich agricultural areas and much of the coast along the English Channel is lined with white chalk cliffs.

The Flanders Plain, to the extreme north, marks the French-Belgian border. To the extreme east of the Paris Basin is the thin strip of the Alsace Plain, bordered by the Vosges to the west, the

Jura Mountains to the south, Germany to the north, the River Rhine to the east, and beyond that, Germany and the Black Forest.

To the southwest, the plains of the Paris Basin follow the course of the Loire River Valley: the Loire and its tributaries cut through the Touraine Hills and the *plateaux* of Anjou and Vendée. The Loire Valley is justly famous for its procession of beautiful *châteaux*.

The Aquitaine Basin, which is much smaller than the Paris Basin, is situated between the Pyrenees to the south, and the low foothills of the Massif Central to the northeast. It is traversed by the River Garonne and the River Gironde which boasts a wide, deep estuary. The Landes, an area lying between the Garonne and Adour Rivers to the west, was once marshy, but has been reclaimed and is now planted with pine. South of the Landes and before the terrain starts rising to form the foothills of the Pyrenees, are lagoons which are sheltered from the sea winds by enormous sand dunes.

Between the ancient mountainous block of the Massif Central and the younger block of the Alps, is a series of plains and river valleys, the Rhône-Saône Valley being of particular interest. The valley stretches down to the triangular-shaped delta of the River Rhône as it flows into the Mediterranean Coast. The western, seaward face of the delta is home to the marshy Camargue region, which is one of Europe's most important wetland nature reserves. West of the Camargue is the broad Languedoc coastal plain, which has been developed into a series of holiday resorts, and further southwest the rocky Roussillon Coast meets with the foothills of the Pyrenees. To the east of the Rhône Delta is only an extremely narrow strip of lowlying land, known the world over as the Côte d'Azur. The combination of beaches, bays and the foothills of the Alpes Maritimes, all make the Riviera the country's most famous holiday area.

The Rivers of France

France has several major river systems, as well as smaller rivers and lakes, some volcanic in origin (mainly in the Massif Central) and some coastal lagoons, such as in the Landes. The main river of the Paris Basin is the Seine, 485 miles (780 kilometres) long, it has three main tributaries – the Yonne, the Marne and the Oise. Although the Seine generally has a regular flow throughout the year, there may be flooding in the spring and, occasionally in autumn and winter. Efforts have been made to reduce flooding of the Seine and its tributaries by the construction of reservoirs, and the spectacle of the Paris quais (embankment) under water is becoming increasingly rare. There are several small islands in the Seine, the most famous of which, the Ile de la Cité, forms the historical nucleus of Paris. The Seine enters the English Channel at Le Havre.

The Loire, is the the longest French

Shades of autumn.

river, flowing for 632 miles and draining the widest area (444 square miles). It rises in the Massif Central, flows northward through the Paris Basin giving every appearance of intending to join the River Seine before instead, turning west, and entering the Atlantic. The Loire is artificially joined to the Seine by a series of canals. The Garonne, in the southwest, rises in the central Pyrenees, and is the shortest of the main French rivers, with a length of only 35 miles, it drains only 22,000 square miles. The Garonne flows through the centre of the

The desolate winter landscape
provides poetry for the soul.

Aquitaine Basin to Bordeaux where it merges with the Dordogne River forming the Gironde estuary which empties into the Atlantic Ocean.

The Rhône is the main river of southeast France, rising in the Alps, and flowing through Lake Geneva before it enters France. The total length of the river is 505 miles, of which 324 miles run through France. At Lyon the Rhône meets its major tributary, the Saône. The course of the river has been modified by a series of dams, built both to generate power and also to permit navigation up to Lyon. The Rhône Delta starts about 25 miles from the Mediterranean Sea.

The Rhine is the river which links France, both physically and symbolically, to her neighbours. For 118 miles, the river forms the eastern boundary of France with Germany. Two tributaries of the Rhine – the Moselle and the Meuse drain the eastern Paris Basin. The Moselle then flows through Luxembourg before joining the Rhine in Germany, and the Meuse flows first through Belgium and Holland before joining the Rhine Delta.

Since vegetation is so naturally related to climate, in any discussion of the French landscape, it makes sense to divide the country according to her two major climatic systems: the Holarctic, northern zone and the Mediterranean zone.

Holarctic Floral Zone

Sunflower brilliance to rival the skies.

This division between climatic zones is however unequal, since most of France falls within the northern zone, which can be further subdivided into three parts. A large area of western France forms one part, including most of the Paris basin. Trees found in this area commonly include oak, chestnut, pine and beech, though much woodland has also been cleared for agricultural cultivation. Heathland, gorse, heather and bracken are also common. The Aquitaine Basin has a mixture of heath and gorse on the plateaux and oak, cypress, poplar and willow in the valleys. Broom, heath,

Flora & Fauna

Purple paradise, lavender in Provence, grown for the scent industry.

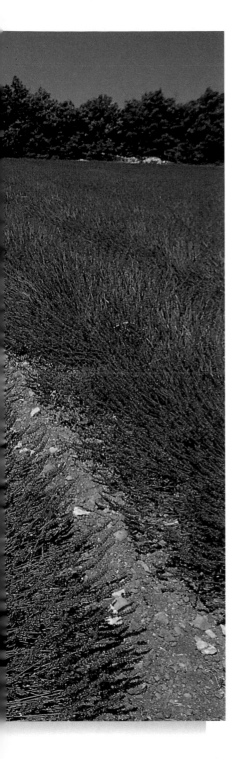

lavender and juniper are found among the otherwise bare rocks on the Massif Central and on limestone plateaux.

Eastern France forms a second part of the Holarctic division, but it is of a more central European type with trees such as the Norway maple, beech, oak, and larch. The third part comprises the high mountain zones of France whose cloudy and wet conditions provide ideal breeding ground for beech woods at lower elevations and fir, mountain pine and larch at higher altitudes. Above the tree-line are high mountain pastures which are now increasingly abandoned and have only stunted trees and lots of wild flowers which bloom in spring and early summer.

Mediterranean Flora

The second major type of landscape is found in the south of the country, where the dry and sunny Mediterranean climate makes for a type of vegetation very different from the rest of France. The Mediterranean areas often suffer from summer droughts, so naturally plant life has adapted itself to these conditions. There is a preponderance of plants that retard water loss by means of spiny, woolly, or glossy leaves, these include the evergreen oak, the cork oak, heather and lavender.

Umbrella pines and plantations of cypress are a typical part of any Mediterranean landscape. The predominant life of the plateaux of Roussillon is the

French Agriculture

Despite its large industrial areas, and its increasingly urban lifestyle, France is still a country that is profoundly attached to the countryside and, particularly, to its agricultural heritage. The days of Queen Marie-Antoinette and her ladies in waiting dressing up as shepherdesses may be long gone, but the average French person still has an illogical soft spot for *les paysans* (the peasants) and their often outrageous political clout.

But first the facts. Approximately 57 percent of the French land mass is arable or pastoral land, which translates into 77,582,000 acres (31,397,000 hectares). Of this more than half is devoted to arable farming, 40 percent for permanent grassland and four percent for permanent crops (such as vines and orchards). Although agriculture in France actually employs only seven percent of the workforce, and contributes less than four percent to the GDP, the country is still the leading agricultural nation in the EEC. France accounts for about a quarter of the total value of the output, and is responsible for more than one-third of the EEC production

of wine, oilseeds and cereals. Arable farming predominates in the northern and western regions of the country. Permanent grasslands are common in mountainous regions, where the soil is often not fertile enough to sustain crop notably in the Massif central, the Alps and the Vosges. Permanent cultivation is prevalent in the Mediterranean region.

Produce of the land

Half of France's arable land is used for cereals, principally wheat and corn, and the majority of arable farming is located in the Paris Basin and the southwest of the country, though there are in fact very few areas of the country where cereals are not grown. Vines, fruit, and vegetables represent more than a-quarter of the total value of the country's agricultural output. France is world famous for its wines, which can range in quality from *vin ordinaire* (ordinary wine) which is, as its name suggests, bottom of the range through to excellent champagnes and superla-

Life on the farm.

tive burgundies. The country's major concentrations of vineyards are in the Rhône valley, the Loire valley, Bordeaux, Alsace, Champagne and the southern regions of Languedoc-Roussillon and Provence. Apples, pears, and peaches are mainly produced in the Rhône Valley, the Garonne Valley and in the Mediterranean region. The lower Rhône Valley and the Mediterranean are also vegetable growing areas. Cattle are a feature of the French countryside, with the one notable exception of the Mediterranean. Milk and beef production constitutes approximately a-third of the total value of France's agricultural production.

Protectionism & the EEC

The problem with French agriculture, as seen by nearly everyone in Europe except the French themselves, is that it is overly protectionist, and out-of-step with the requirements of the Common Market. French agriculture receives vast subsidies, both from the government and from the European Community. But, almost from the inception of the Common Market, when the *Treaty of Rome* was signed, one of her overriding priorities was the protection of her own agriculture – it still is. The French regularly refuse to accept imports from other community countries, no doubt fearing for their own heavily subsidised agriculture. Thus, many disagreements result over agriculture in the EEC and French farmers have become known for their obstinacy which in-turn has promoted hostility between the international community of farmers. The simple unsophisticated *paysan* (peasant) of nostalgic fiction has become a smart political operator. Farmers in France seem to protest regularly and vehemently against EEC rulings, and always in ways designed to gain a maximum amount of attention – a favourite method is to tip lorryloads of fruit or vegetables in front of the local town hall, or in the town square, or across the main roads. These stocks, which are then deliberately destroyed by the very men who have produced them, are usually some of the infamous EEC food "mountains" (excess stocks) accumulated from over-production.

maquis (dense thickets of drought resistant shrubs) and during WWII this vegetation gave its name to the Resistance fighters – a reference to the difficulty of access to these remote, rural areas, which provided perfect cover for the Resistance.

A large part of Provence's hottest and driest terrain is covered by *garigue* (a kind of rock heath), and there are extensive vineyards, and lemon and orange trees. Provence also grows a lot of the flowering plants that are used in the perfume industry, which is centred around the town of Grasse. In the early spring, lavender and mimosa grow in the hills. In the Mediterranean coastal town of Eze, high on a hill overlooking the entire Riviera coastline, there is a garden devoted entirely to growing cacti: the temperature is high enough for this plant which is usualy associated with desert landscapes to survive in the open, unprotected by green-houses.

Forests, Fires & Fun

More than a quarter of the French land mass is covered with forest, an impressive 56,400 square miles (146,200 hectares). Most forests are found in the mountainous regions – the **Ardennes**, the **Vosges**, the **Jura**, the **Alps**, and the **Pyrénées**, but there are also extensive lowland forests. Three thousand six hundred and eighty square miles in the Landes have been planted with maritime pines, making it one of the most

Elegance of autumn gold on a wooded estate.

extensive forests in western Europe.

Forest fires are an annual problem, and every summer, France loses a considerable portion of its forest cover to fire, with an increasing loss of human life, for more and more people are holidaying in the forests, or building week end homes – a macabre aspect of the current vogue for back-to-nature living. The south of France bears a major part of this burden, with its increasingly fatal combination of hot temperatures and high numbers of visitors. As the strain on urban space increases, the role

of the forests is changing. Today, they are no longer perceived as sources of wood and food, but rather as places for recreation.

For people living in the big cities, such as Paris, forests such as Bois de Boulogne, Vincennes, Rambouillet and Fontainebleau are highly prized as early morning jogging tracks or weekend picnic areas.

Fauna

The animal and bird life of France are typical of the neighbouring western European countries. Red deer, roe deer, and wild boar, which are still hunted

Transhumance in Cevennes

Transhumance is the centuries-old transfer of flocks from their summer pasture to their winter home, and vice versa. In the 20th century world of instant communications and high-speed trains, one could be forgiven for imagining that the practice of transhumance has died out from the French countryside. Not so, in the remote Cévennes of southern France, every spring and every summer, flocks of sheep are transferred from one pasture to another using centuries old *drailles* (tracks) across the hills.

The trip up to the summer pasture never takes place before St Médard's feast day on 8 June since according to tradition, on that particular day you can predict the following days weather. But preparations for the trip will already have been made well in advance. For one thing, all the sheep are decorated with coloured woollen pompons, which the shepherds and their families make themselves. On the actual day of departure, the sheep will be decorated with the bright woollen pompons and *dralhons* (big bells) not only to protect the animals from storms and cold during the migration, but also from witches and evil spells. According to tradition, the deep sound of the *dralhons* has the power to ward off evil and to attract good. Today very few shepherds and farmers will admit to believing this, but tradition is, after all, tradition, and the colourful decorations and the deep sound of the bells, add to the festive atmosphere which surrounds the journey.

It can take anything up to six days to cover a hundred kilometres on foot, following the well worn drailles (trails) and as the procession winds its way across the countryside, custom dictates that each village must offer a glass of red wine. It would doubtless be much faster to load all the sheep into lorries and transport them by road – but that would mean the end of the cultural tradition of transhumance, pompons and bells, and who knows, the return of evil spirits.

are among the larger mammals. In the high Alps live the rare chamoix and the re-introduced ibex. Common rodents, hares and rabbits are found extensively, foxes are much rarer and the wild cat even rarer still. As far as bird life is concerned, the south of France is at the extreme northern limit of the range of exotic species, and such species as the flamingo, the Egyptian vulture, and the bee-eater have habitats in southern France.

The Perils of Endangered Species

Sadly the country has several endangered species, including the badger, the otter, the beaver, the Alpine marmot, the brown bear and the lynx, which are normally confined to the Pyrenees.

The French gov

Roosting pigeons on a bough.

ernment is endeavouring to tackle the wildlife issue and is currently undertaking several projects to reintroduce animals which have disappeared from a given region, or to protect the habitat of potentially threatened species. But, although the country's ecologists applaud this programme, there are other considerations, with opposition coming from the local people, especially the farmers. One such case in point is that of the Pyrénéan brown bear.

For over two years, the bear has been at the centre of a tussle between local villagers and locals on the one hand, and by environmental lobbyists and ecologists on the other. The latter are often perceived to be out-of-town technocrats.

The Pyrénéan brown bear may appear cuddly but it can kill; in 1991, 188 animals (mainly sheep) were killed by bears in the Pyrénées. Amidst protests from fearful farmers, the Ministry of the Environment suggested capturing the bears, and fitting them with a tracking collar allowing officials to follow the animals movements and thus warn local shepherds if their flocks are at risk.

The locals scorn at such a suggestion, (voiced by one local mayor who even sarcastically wondered why the authorities did not also give the bear a pair of earrings), appeared vindicated when an operation in July 1992 to capture and stun a killer bear failed; the animal escaped whilst the officials were

A farm horse and its owner.

still looking for a syringe with which to administer the anaesthetic! But although local shepherds might mock at officialdom, they are beginning to fee frightened not only for their sheep bu for their own lives.

Encouraging
Environmentalists

The re-introduction of the vulture one of the largest birds in Europe, has been

more successful, and far less controversial. Extinct in France for nearly 90 years, a combined operation by the French Ministry of the Environment, Frankurt Zoo, the authorities of the Cévennes National Park, and various French and European zoos saw the release of five young vultures, who had been born in captivity, into a controlled environment in the Lozére region.

Initially, game warders built nests for the birds, and during three months monitored them non-stop, to protect them against both natural predators, and more sadly, the disturbances of human curiosity.

In the Camargue region of south western France, amongst the flat marshes and the fingers of the Rhône delta, there are herds of wild bulls and wild horses.

The number of wild bulls is estimated to be 6,000. Originally, the bulls were raised for Provençal bull-fights, the horses being used to round-up the herds and *le gardien* (the Camargue equivalent of a cowboy) to supervise the animals.

Large free-roaming herds of bulls and horses still exist, though now they are principally found around the Etang de Vaccares, which is at the nucleus of the huge Camargue regional park. Yet, the fact that so many animals can exist in freedom is an encouraging sign. The future of the Pyrenean brown bear may not be assured, but the wild horses and bulls of the Camargue are in no danger of extinction.

I n 1990, the population of France was reckoned to be 56,411,000 – and to their less charitable neighbours, each and every one of these 56 million souls is a highly voluble, quick-tempered, often arrogant, vociferous individual. It is difficult to draw an accurate thumb-nail sketch of such a noisily diverse people: self-professed Republicans, who hanker after expensive status symbols; ruthlessly logical except where anything French is concerned; unashamedly bad at foreign languages, yet who are intrepid travellers with an insatiable thirst for adventure.

People

83

Farmer with a traditional scarf.

If a 1992 survey conducted by Eurostat (the statistical office of the European Community) is to be believed, the French eat more meat and drink far more wine than any of their European partners, they work an average of 39.9 hours per week, the country has the highest percentage of females in college and university, French women live longer than their European

Miss Prim.

sisters, the country has the second high-est number of road deaths, and one of the highest expenditures on medical and health care. Armed with all these conflicting figures, let us promptly ig-nore them, and set out to meet the real, rather than the statistical, French.

The French Character

It is always difficult to define a nation character without resorting to stereo type, but some aspects of the Frenc character are fairly prevalent. Th

Family ties in modern society.

French talk with their hands, waving them about in-tune to their beautiful language. They are extremely interested in food and drink and relish talking about great meals they have eaten, the latest restaurants they have visited and particularly good vintages they have drunk. Food is considered to be one of life's pleasures, to be shared and indulged. Interestingly and perhaps naturally, given their love of good food and wine, the French can often seem to verge on hypochondria. The highly subsidised national healthcare system, with its huge deficits, is fully utilised by the French, who can discuss medicine with almost as much accuracy and enthusiasm as their food. The French are great drinkers of after-dinner herbal teas, and in such a restaurant-oriented city as Paris, there is one with a *carte* (menu) entirely devoted to herbal teas. The beautiful French language has a subtlety which is particularly well expressed when it comes to food and drink; for example, the rather delicate matter of a morning-after head-ache deserves nothing as prosaic as the Anglo-Saxon "hangover" and is instead expressed, as a delicate *crise de foie* (crisis of the liver)!

Sometimes it seems as though the word contradictions was designed specifically with the French in mind. The French patronise health spas and drink gallons of mineral water, yet they also drink strong coffee and smoke far too much.

Although three-quarters of the

population would describe themselves as belonging to the Roman Catholic Church, France is one of the few countries to have legalized the institution of unmarried cohabitation. Although the French are as conscious as anyone else of the global problems of pollution in all its manifestations, almost everyone owns a car which they drive at great speed, with one hand placed semi-permanently on the car-horn. And, although France has always traditionally been a haven for refugees, now there is a growing xenophobic nationalist movement.

Most French people display a large dose of scepticism in their make-up, and show a particularly healthy disrespect for their politicians: they take a keen pleasure in the discomfort brought about when political scandals erupt which given the open nature of government, and an unfettered press happens not infrequently although France is by no means an especially corrupt or immoral country.

Whenever political or financial scandals arise, there is, also a little sense of let-down or disillusionment amongst the French electorate, who generally shrug their shoulders (a very Gallic trait) with a "what else can you expect from politicians ?" However, personal scandals are a different matter for unlike the Americans, whose obsessive concern with family values and moral rectitude puzzles the French, a person's private life is deemed to be just that – private. A person is judged without any reference

to his marital status and perhaps it is a legacy of the Mediterranean and Middle Eastern macho ethos, that French politicians will rarely fall out of favour because of a marital peccadillo. After all, in a country where the women strive to look elegant and well-groomed, and the men are reared to be charming and well-dressed, what is more natural than

The less glamorous aspect of Parisian life.

a degree of attraction – French pragmatism to the fore, again.

Family Ties

A respect for one's personal life and privacy is in line with the French attitude towards family ties. Although nuclear families are getting smaller and more self-sustaining, the French are by and large a family-minded people. The ritual of Sunday lunch *en famille* (for the whole family) is still adhered to, as are

Street mime artists entertain.

Beauty in diversity at a carnival in Marseille.

big family meals for major festivals and events. The French education system does not encourage youngsters to flee the parental nest: the concept of boarding schools is anathema to the French, and, most French students attend their local university, living at home rather than in a hall of residence. So family ties remain strong, and given the natural demonstrativeness of the French, and their lack of reserve, affection is freely shown – grown men hug and kiss each other freely, with none of the inhibitions of their northern neighbours.

Mores & Manners

Essentially a polite people, growing less restrained and more exuberant the further south one journeys, French customs and manners are very much based on social interaction.

There is a long list of ritual French greetings, from the simple *bonjour* (good day), through *bonne continuation* (keep on with whatever you are doing, and I hope it goes well), to the *bon appetit* (enjoy your meal) you wish each other before meals, (including waiters in smart restaurants!) The French are an affectionate people, strong believers in welcoming kisses on the cheek – and it is definitely kisses in the plural, ranging from a minimum of two, to perhaps three or four.

French office workers will do the rounds of their co-workers each morn-

The French Language & The Academie Francaise

"What's the water in French, sir?" "L'eau," replied Nicholas. "Ah!", said Mr Lillywick, shaking his head mournfully. "I thought as much. Lo, eh? I don't think anything of that language – nothing at all". (**Nicholas Nickeleby**. Charles Dickens).

Happily for the French language, very few people share Mr Lillywick's xenophobia, least of all the French themselves, who are robustly proud of their linguistic heritage, and who increasingly voice resentment at the predominance of the English language in international affairs. The French like their language to be well spoken, although they are not particularly linguistically talented themselves. Brusque Parisians will impatiently detect a foreign accent, but outside the capital, foreigners speaking French will always be well-received and politely praised. For a native English speaker, learning French has a few initial pitfalls, such as the gender of nouns, *le* for a masculine object, *la* for a feminine one, and you just have to memorize the genders of inanimate objects such as tables, doors and cars (feminine) and bread, wine and cheese (masculine).

French also has two forms of the word "you" – *tu* which you use to children, people you know well, God and animals, and *vous* which is used to strangers, to superiors, in formal circumstances and when you are addressing more than one person. There is always a moment in any relationship when one party suggests passing from the *vous* to the friendlier *tu* form, but as a rule of thumb, let the French person make the first move!

Despite French pride in their language, there is a growing encroachment of the English language, especially in technical and scientific domains. The French tend to have a love-hate relationship with the Anglo-Saxons and their language, so at the same time as they decry the proliferation of American fast food outlets, they will make it a point to see the latest American film in *version originale* (VO or original version) – with French subtitles – just in case.

The French have borrowed many words from *l'anglais* (English) and adapted them to *le Français* (French) from where you get the peculiar language known as *Franglais*. Examples of *Franglais* include: *Le weekend* (the weekend) *le sandwich* (the sandwich), *le rugby* (rugby), *le tennis* (tennis), *le foot* (football), as opposed to *le footing* which is jogging and even *le cricket* (cricket), which the French claim is an incomprehensible game, anyway!

Trying to protect the language of love and diplomacy from such linguistic horrors is the *Académie Française*, an association of 40 academics, known as "the Immortals". The *Académie Française* was founded by Cardinal Richelieu in 1634, with the aim of maintaining standards of literary taste and language. Some of France's major literary figures were once "Immortals" – Corneille, Racine, Voltaire, Victor Hugo, but there are some surprising omissions – Descartes, Molière, Balzac, Proust and Zola, all of whom

ing, dutifully shaking hands with acquaintances, and kissing particular friends, French politicians kiss not only babies but their adult constituents, and when the French President pins medals on worthy chests, he, too, usually concludes with a kiss.

French children are taught to be polite to adults, in a very mature, dutifully composed way: they appear quietly to be kissed by their parents' guests, they are allowed to eat with the adults from a very early age and are regularly taken out to restaurants.

Divisions of Class

Despite its Republicanism, France is notable for its social classes, with even a few extra categories such as "peasants" and "intellectuals", both of which are happily achieved literary immortality, despite not being "Immortals".

Women have at long last broken into this former masculine enclave where a new member is only admitted upon the death of another, and suitably attired in a dark-green, hand-embroidered uniform and armed with a sword, makes a formal speech praising his or her predecessor, in reply to which the Director makes an equally formal speech praising the successor. There is a permanent committee of "Immortals" at work on updates and revisions to the French language. The *Academie* decides whether or not a new word is acceptable, and they give rulings on things like the use of the circumflex accent – important issues in a country where people describe themselves, without a hint of self-mockery, as intellectuals.

The perceived threat to the French language from the English language often has political overtones, almost inevitable in a country that has a Ministry of "Francophonie"! With the approach of a truly politically-unified Europe, some French people are beginning to worry about the wide-spread use of English in international affairs, for in a recent letter to the President of France, signed by 250 intellectuals and politicians, the following remark was made: "If Europe has to have only one language, we fail to see why it should be the language of the United States, especially since there are more Francophones than Anglophones in Europe. *Compris* (understand)?

Joie de vivre!

descriptions taken completely seriously. When a Frenchman describes himself as being an intellectual, he is not being tongue-in-cheek.

Although the French Revolution swept away the monarchy and the aristocracy, France abounds with counts and barons and people with "de" in front of their surname denoting social stature.

Since education is highly regarded in France – it is, after all the land of intellectuals – upward mobility can often be obtained through a good education, especially from the *Grandes Écoles* (big schools), which are the country's prime universities and colleges.

These *grandes écoles* in addition to a top-class education also provide access to the most powerful networks in the country, and an almost guaranteed placement in the best jobs on offer. A school such as the *École Nationale d'Administration* (School of National Administration known universally as ÉNA) is a virtual passport to top slots in government, all-party ranks. In fact, the higher echelons of the civil service are all filled with ÉNA graduates, known as *Énarques*.

PEOPLE

91

The Mystique of French Women

Have you ever heard anyone describe a French woman as being sensibly dressed? Or casually turned out? Or comfortably dressed? What are the adjectives that immediately spring to mind when describing *les françaises* (French women)? Inevitably, words like chic, smart, elegant, impeccably dressed, svelte. When you look in magazines, do you ever see pictures of French mothers wearing comfortable clothes for walking the dog or doing the gardening, or wearing an old jacket, whilst driving the children to school?

What exactly is it about French women that makes them appear to be elegantly turned out, no matter what the circumstances are, or the time of day? Is there really some mystique about French women, or is it a myth? A cliché or a statement of fact? To decide, take a walk down one of the main streets of Paris and discreetly, watch the women.

You can immediately discount anyone holding a camera or a guide-book, as she will be a visitor, whereas any woman clutching a miniature, be-ribboned dog and wearing a designer label handbag *en bandoulière* (slung over the shoulder) will be French, probably Parisian. Interestingly, the fashion for wearing handbags diagonally across the body, rather than hanging from the shoulder, came about as a reaction to pick-pocketing and handbag snatching, but has now become a definite fashion statement. More than likely, our smart French woman will have a silk scarf draped around her shoulders, usually arranged so that the designer's name is discreetly visible. This expensive piece of drapery will never, ever actually be seen on her head: that fashion is left exclusively for the British Royal Family!

Even in winter, she will wear a heavy silk scarf, or a cashmere stole around her shoulders or over her coat, and there will be no question of anything as un-chic as wrapping it snugly round her neck to keep warm. Why wear something beautiful and then hide it, or crease it? As a rule, French women dress in simple, uncluttered, strong colours – lots of black and navy, with white or a bold, flamboyant contrast, and they resolutely steer away from flowery fussiness. Not only do classic colours like black and white look elegant, they also never really go out of fashion. In such an appearance-conscious country as France, staying in fashion is very important.

Other than being super-rich, the French solution is to have a wardrobe of timeless, classic clothes, which can be re-worked with different accessories and jewellery, and to invest in one really up-to-date outfit each season. The French are an eminently practical race, and not by nature sentimental, so there is no question of hanging on to clothes for years once they are hopelessly out of style or shape. Why save out-of-fashion clothes for walking the dog, or going to collect the children from school, when you can wear something smart?

There are certain things French women do and do not. Do nots include never wearing something ugly, just because it is decreed to be in fashion: if baggy clothes and clashing colours are deemed to be the season's fashion statement, well, that is *tant pis* (too bad). French women just will not wear them. Their innate sense of pragmatism precludes them ever looking unglamourous, just for the sake of a

Life in the City

Parisians have an expression to describe city life, saying it consists only of "*métro-boulot-dodo*", rhyming slang which can be roughly translated as "train, work, and sleep". Although not as frenetic as New York or Hong Kong, Paris is a city constantly on the move, and just as beset with problems of housing, transport and pollution as other capitals in the world. Although the city has specific districts, such as the financial district,

fashion whim. French women do not go out in track-suits, unless they are running, nor do they wear shorts and sandals, unless they are on the beach. Nor, to be honest, do they carry moral scruples into the domain of fashion – fur coats are not considered socially unacceptable, the way they are in many other countries.

Their list of do(s) includes having a good, sleek-looking hair-cut, usually a short, tidy trim. Older women, especially, avoid the floppy long-haired look. Most French women wear a lot of jewellery, especially gold chains and bracelets, which they usually wear all the time: that way, even at the weekend, in jeans (smart, well-cut ones, of course) they always look dressed. A French woman always has smart accessories: no bulging hand-bags, or comfortably worn-down shoes, but expensive designer makes, classic styles which last and wear well.

Training towards achieving this elegance starts young. If you look at little French girls, they will not be wearing shapeless school uniforms, but instead neat, cotton blouses, with large, pretty collars – hardly sensible, admittedly, but definitely feminine.

There will be no regulation navy-blue hair ribbons, but cute little head-bands, holding their neat little bobbed hair in place. Somehow, little French girls always manage to look like miniatures of their mothers: no self-respecting mother would dress her child in the eminently sensible and practical clothes favoured by Anglo-Saxons. Her little girl should always look *mignonne* (cute), and they do, and they all seem to grow effortlessly into elegantly turned out women.

Romance in the parks.

the garment district and the shopping district, all of these areas are also residential, so Paris never completely closes down. Although areas around the Stock Exchange and the Grands Boulevards will be quieter than normal at weekends and in the sleepy heat of an August afternoon, they are never totally deserted. No part of Paris is without its residents, and as a result there is little inner-city decay, usually experienced when the working population leaves the city *en masse*. French city dwellers rely heavily on public transport, and on shops and supermarkets that stay open late: sensibly, many shops close for a couple of hours in the afternoon, but then stay open until eight or nine o'clock at night – timings geared towards working families.

A French city dweller will often have his breakfast in a local *café*, standing at the counter to have a quick cup of coffee and a croissant, and he will more than likely buy his newspaper from a stall, since home-delivery is very much the

French Fashion Visionaries

If imitation is indeed the sincerest form of flattery, Coco Chanel must be deeply flattered. What woman does not possess, or dream of possessing, a "little black dress"? Her signature suit, with its distinctive collarless and braid-trimmed jacket, has been copied, imitated, and fiddled with, by countless designers and manufacturers the world over, ever since its debut in 1954. Wherever you buy it – Chanel's headquarters on Rue Cambon in Paris, or perhaps a fake from a street market in Hong Kong – possessing a "Chanel" product means something. Something chic, sex and with class, be it a suit, a little black hand-bag with the trademark chain strap and the inter-twined C logo, or the ultimate perfume, Chanel No.5. Chanel sets style the world over and now at 70 years old it is still going strong.

Coco Chanel, born in 1883, was orphaned at six years old, remained unmarried had numerous affairs, and was always an unconventional woman living in conventional times. She urged women to abandon uncomfortable, complicated clothing and aim, instead, for simplicity and comfort. She advocated cutting hair short into a "bob", wearing costume jewellery, and, of course, she launched the "little black dress". So many of today's classics owe their origin to Madame Chanel – the trench coat, the turtle-neck sweater, the jersey dress.

Every generation in France seems to throw up another iconoclastic fashion designer, who shocks, provokes and is ultimately wildly successful.

Christian Dior, pioneer of the post-war "New Look", which was a controversial departure from current fashion norms, was a major influence on world fashion during the 1950s. Dior's protégé, Yves Saint Laurent, who took over as head of Dior, after the latter's death, lengthened hems, then shortened them and introduced the concept of "chic beatnik". Yves Saint Laurent later founded his own fashion house, where he popularised trousers for women. In the mid-1970s, he revolutionized fashion shows, changing them from a silent viewing of motionless models to today's high-tech, multimedia shows, where music is *de rigeur*, sometimes classical, sometimes rock, sometimes both, and wave after wave of very tall and very thin models strut unsmilingly down the cat-walk.

In the mid-1980s, Christian Lacroix burst on the scene, dazzling Paris with his highly original and very brightly coloured clothes, whose colours and styles were inspired by the designer's native Provence.

Like most things in France, the world of high fashion is a highly regulated one. *Couture* (sewing), is under the authority of the *Chambre Syndicale de la Haute Couture*, which has its own definition of a *couturier* (dressmaker): the *couturier* must have his own studio, must employ at least 20 people, and must present a minimum of 75 designs, with a minimum of three models, in each collection. But discontent is brewing, as more and more foreign *couturiers* want to show in Paris, and independent designers and smaller fashion houses feel excluded by the cliquey nature of the *Chambre Syndicale*, which has only 21 members.

Because fashion is such big business in France, this simmering discontent has led to governmental concern, and a commission was set up, under the Industry Minister, to revise the *couture* (sewing) regulations, the general idea being to cut down the high costs of each *couture* collection, thus encouraging new entrants.

The world of *couture*, of the now indispensa-

exception. Combining a good dinner with a busy work schedule is not always easy, but in France there is a wonderful category of shops called *traiteurs* (elaborate delicatessens), which stock everything for a meal, from cooked food, to bread, wine, cheese and desserts.

Regional Differences

Outside the big cities, which, like cities

ble complementary fashion accessories and designer fragrances has always been dominated by a few visionaries, but working alongside these acknowledged stars are many equally famous names, whose quietly consistent quality has earned them the loyalty of generations of women. Names such as Hermès, Céline, Patou and Givenchy all epitomise the elegance and longevity of classic French fashion and design. Recently, the President of Hermès was asked why his company's products (notably handbags, and their very distinctive silk scarves and ties) had become such status symbols, and his reply was both disarming and perceptive: "Well, it certainly has nothing to do with us. We do not have a policy of image, we have a policy of product.".

And when the product is of top quality workmanship and of a classic, long-lasting design, people will always buy, or if they cannot afford it, they will covet it, so that it will naturally become a sought-after status symbol.

Indeed, one of the problems facing the world of fashion has arisen, paradoxically, because of its own success and aura of expensive exclusivity. If you promote a longing for status symbols and price them too highly, then the inevitable happens – people copy, and people buy cheaper copies. There cannot be a street market anywhere in the world that does not sell "Louis Vuitton" and "Chanel" handbags, or "Lacoste" sports shirts. Highly publicized raids on forgers, and counterfeit shops certainly help, but as long as high fashion is seen to be desirable and expensive, people will always want to own the dress, or the scarf, or the bag that symbolizes that they have entered the world of the truly fashionable.

anywhere in the world, appear to be inhabited by people who are always in a hurry, the French are extremely kind and polite people, who will take the time to be welcoming to strangers, and who are genuinely pleased when visi-

tors can speak French, or even endeavour to learn a few words. The French rural lifestyle moves at a much slower pace than in the cities, villagers have much more time to stop and chat, and are less *blasé* about meeting foreigners. The village *café* plays an even more important *rôle* than its urban counterpart, for it is often the only meeting place, in tiny villages and *lieuxdits* (hamlets).

Although the majority of French people consider themselves as belonging to one single nation with a very distinct, unifying civilization, the country does, in fact, have several distinctive regional identities. The geographical position of France within the European land-mass had a direct impact on the country's racial mix, because before the discovery of America and the subsequent westward immigration there, France was the western-most point of continental Europe. Migratory groups, whether from northern Europe, the Middle East, Africa or southern Europe all ended up in France, and often settled down there, so that over the centuries, different groups slowly became assimilated into the population of France.

After a lapse of so many centuries, much of these diverse characteristics have naturally been absorbed and merged, but you will still find tall people in northern France, whose build and colouring owes something to their Germanic ancestors, whilst the inhabitants of the southern Midi will often bear a stronger resemblance to their Mediter-

A young François' slimy secret.

ranean neighbours.

Some of France's most diverse regional groups are to be found on her borders, especially the Bretons, the Corsicans and the Basques, all of whom have their own independent languages and customs, as well as small, but politi-

cally active independence movements.

Although the French government is totally opposed to any form of federalism, let alone independence, there is consistent pressure from these movements whose violent tactics alienate not only the French population at large, but

region of the Pyrenees, between France and Spain and speak a language that is one of the oldest in Europe. There are probably only 130,000 true French Basques, with more living in Spain and overseas. Despite much study of the origins of the Basque language, with attempts to link it to ancient, now defunct languages such as Iberian and Caucasian, the truth is that Basque is a language without any obvious linguistic relatives.

Brittany

Brittany is another region of France that has retained a strong sense of identity and its own language and has a recent legacy of political terrorism. Brittany owes much of its history to its geographical isolation and its difficult and dangerous coastline. Celts from Britain settled there in the AD5-6, and the Breton language is related to the Welsh and Cornish languages, which, like Basque, is struggling to survive, faced with the government's drive to ensure the uniformity of the French language all over France.

The island of Corsica, 170 miles off the south coast of France is most famous as the birthplace of France's dearest son, Napoléon Bonaparte.

But, today the island is one of France's most troublesome problem zones, for there is a small, but relentless, campaign of terrorism, bomb attacks and arson, all aimed at driving the

also any potential sympathizers among their compatriots.

Independence Movements

One of the still unsolved mysteries of Europe, is the precise origin of the Basque people and their language. The Basques live in the isolated mountainous border

mainland French out of the land.

Americanization

McDonalds® and Burger King® have encroached the Champs Elysées, and Mickey Mouse rules over the Magic Kingdom just outside Paris in the increasing Amerianisation which is happening all over France. There has always been an American love affair with France, especially *vis-à-vis* her artists and writers, but now the process is being reversed as French youngsters wear jeans, sneakers and sweatshirts. The arrival of Euro-Disney in France caused years of typically French controversy, much of it hinging on the cultural effects of middle-America on suburban France.

Many people feared that Mickey Mouse would bring about a "cultural Chernobyl", whereas amusement parks devoted to uniquely French themes have been miserable failures. In Paris in the 15th *arrondissement* (district), you can see a small version of the Statue of Liberty, which was donated by the American community living in Paris in 1885. On the Place de l'Alma is the Liberty Flame, commemorating the 200th anniversary of the French Revolution and standing as a recent monument to Franco-American friendship.

Colonial Immigrants

France in the closing years of the 20th

century is rapidly changing, largely through foreign influence. Second and third generation families from former colonies now regard France as home but the ties with their respective homelands still remain. Religious conformity is a major factor linking immigrants to their respective homelands, or separating them from their new home, depending how one views the issue. A growing

Making pals is child's play.

amount of conformity demanded of the large Muslim communities from North Africa and the Middle East has confused and angered many French people, for example, the issue of why young girls should cover their heads to go to school.

As you travel around France, you will meet many more exceptions than stereotypes, but occasionally, you will meet Frenchmen who really do say "*Oh là là*", or wear *berets*, kiss ladies' hands, and tell them they are looking *charmante* (charming), and you will realise why the French are so captivating.

Religion

Although a country with a long history of religious art, architecture and learning, modern France is not a country which moves to any one pronounced religious rhythm. The land of glorious Gothic cathedrals and breathtakingly beautiful religious works of art, of Protestant martyrs and the miraculous Lourdes pilgrimage, now lives according to its constitution and individual conscience, rather than any formalised dictates of organized religions. The day-to-day life of the majority of French people, in common with many western Europeans, is no longer governed by religious customs and beliefs. The Church and the State are legally separate, there is no religious instruction in state schools and marriages must be first registered with the civic authorities, and only then with the religious ones. This situation has evolved over the last 200 years, since the Revolution of 1789 which overthrew much of the existing struc-

Catholic finery in a Brittany Church.

The church of Sacré Coeur presides over Paris.

ture of society, and its institutions. In order to understand how the country that built the magnificent cathedrals of Notre Dame and Chartres has evolved into a secular state, the recent history of France since the Revolution must be examined.

Religion & the Revolution

Traditionally, the religious foundations of French society were Roman Catholic, and over the centuries both Jews and Protestants suffered at the hands of an

Stained glass at Notre Dame Cathedral, Paris, where this religious art form is seen to perfection.

often intolerant society. Many French Protestants, or Huguenots, fled from the country when the reasonably tolerant *Edict of Nantes* was revoked in 1685. However, during the violent upheavals of the French Revolution, much of the framework of the establishment was swept aside, including that of the Catholic Church.

Demands for the nationalization of Church lands met with very little opposition, but a proposal in July 1790, to impose the Civil Constitution on the Church produced a different reaction.

The new law stated that priests and bishops were to be democratically elected and that all religious orders would be dissolved with the exception of teaching orders and those involved in charity work. In the end, very few bishops and priests actually took the oath of loyalty to the new Constitution, and when, in March 1791, after much hesitation, the Vatican finally denounced the Constitution, many of the French clergy retracted their oaths. Despite a shortage of clergy, the Constitutional Church managed to survive for a decade.

The new Assembly did not confine its attentions to the Catholic Church as all offices were opened to Protestants in 1789, and despite opposition from the traditionally anti-semitic areas of Alsace and Lorraine, citizenship rights were granted to Jews.

In 1792, the secular registration of births, deaths, civil marriages and divorces were introduced.

Notre Dame Cathedral, Paris.

Napoléon Bonaparte

Curiously, despite religious persecution during the Revolution, the grip of the Catholic church on the French people did not weaken. On the contrary when Napoléon came to power, one of the administrative problems he faced was that of the status and role of the church in post-revolutionary France. Astute and ambitious politician as he was, he recognised that religion was a means to an end – in this case, the end was his own power. One of Napoléon's revealing statements on religion illustrates this: "The people must have a religion, and that religion must be in the hands of the government".

Although the Vatican had condemned the French Revolution, it was naturally keen to regain official recognition and influence in France. When Napoleon defeated the Austrians in 1801, thus gaining control over Northern Italy, the Vatican decided that it was necessary to come to terms with the French government and was even prepared to make considerable concessions to do so.

1801 Concordat

On 15th July, 1801, the First Consul, Napoléon Bonaparte, reached an agreement with the Roman Catholic Church in both Paris and Rome, which re-defined the status of the church in France, after the upheavals of the Revolution. This document, known as the *Concordat of 1801* was to remain in force, until it was denounced by the government in 1905 a century later.

According to the *Concordat*, Catholicism was described as "the religion of the great majority of citizens" and the practice of it was to be free, as long as police regulations were adhered to. Under the terms of the *Concordat*, which was not actually promulgated until Easter Sunday 1802, the First Consul was given the right to nominate bishops, a number of whom would come from the revolutionary Constitutional Church; parishes were redistributed; and the church was allowed to start building seminaries. Rome recognised the acqui-

The Virgin Mary and Jesus, are the focus of the Catholic faith.

sition and effective nationalization of church properties which had been seized during the Revolution. In a gesture of compensation, the French government undertook to pay salaries to priests and bishops and agreed that local authorities would pay for the upkeep of churches.

Having secured an agreement with the Church, Napoléon, in typical fashion, then drew up a series of supplementary provisions known as the "Organic Articles", by which he tried to distort the *Concordat* to his own ends. He did this by promoting Gallicanism, (a mixture of French political and religious beliefs) which he then used to restrict papal power. Under the *Organic Articles*, no Papal edict could be published, nor could any representative of the Pope function, without the permission of the government.

Bishops were placed under the control of prefects. To sweeten the pill, a few concessions to tradition were made: the revolutionary 10-day week was stopped, and Sunday once again became the official day of rest; the revolutionary calendar was replaced by the Gregorian; children were to be given names of saints or of major classical figures; clerical salaries were increased; religious orders were to be again allowed, and primary education was to come once more under church control.

Notwithstanding these concessions, Rome protested against the *Organic Articles* and manifested its displeasure by

Thousands of invalids faithfully visit Lourdes seeking miraculous cures.

delaying the consecration of Napoléon's nominees for bishoprics for two years. The *Concordat* when accepted represented a considerable victory for Napoléon, allowing him, effectively, to use the church as an instrument of government. Hence, his imperial statements were read out from the pulpit, and a national holiday was declared on the feast day of the Assumption (15 August), which happened – with no coincidence – to be Napoléon's birthday and also the day of reverence for the newly canonized – Saint Napoleon. Later, he

tained strong royalist tendencies and to some degree they undermined the republican loyalty of the people. Also, in part because of Napoléon's use of the *Concordat* for his own ends, the emphasis on Gallicanism backfired. This strengthened the hand of those in France who strongly believed in papal authority emanating from Rome. They were known as the ultra-*montane* party, derived from the Latin for "beyond the mountains" – beyond the Alps – namely, in Rome.

Napoleon also organized the country's Protestants and Jews. At that time, there were approximately 1 million French protestants who were organized into hierarchical "consistories", which came under state supervision and Protestant pastors who were paid by the state. The country's 60,000 Jews, who were mainly centred in Alsace and Lorraine were also organized into similar "consistories". But, although rabbis were supposed to promote obedience to the laws of the state, they were not paid by the government. Yet the anti-Semitic tendencies of France, which have always hovered near the surface, led to discriminatory laws. In 1808, a law, paradoxically aimed at the "social reformation of the Jews" cancelled any debts contracted by peasants to Jewish moneylenders.

would ask the church to teach a new Imperial Catechism, which would, among other things "bind the consciences of the young to the August person of the Emperor".

Anti-Gallicanism

Paradoxically, many of the clergy re-

Dreyfus Affair

The closing decade of the 19th century

Not everyone in France is Catholic.

was marred by the Dreyfus Affair in which a blatantly false accusation of treason was levelled against an army officer. The accompanying rabid anti-semitism polarized society and left scars which remained unhealed for decades. Prior to 1890, there were about 80,000 Jews in France, all of whom were fairly well assimilated, except in Alsace, from where Dreyfus himself came. Immigration from eastern Europe at the close of the century more than doubled these figures and provoked more wide-spread anti-semitism than ever before, espe-

A Catholic priest holds his ground in front of a poster protesting a restriction of freedom in Catholic schools.

cially in Alsace.

The ramifications of the Dreyfus Affair were many. At stake was not only the underlying issue of the fate of an innocent man, but the affair also became a forum for debate on the very nature of society and of the Republic.

Most of the people who called for a revision of the judgement on Dreyfus were writers, anti-clericals, Jews, Protestants and Freemasons, whilst those supporting the judgement were mainly Catholics, the Armed forces, monarchists and nationalists. These were hardline

Miracle At Lourdes

On Thursday 11 February 1858, a 14 year old illiterate peasant girl, Bernadette Soubirous, living in the southwest of France, was sent by her mother to gather wood near a rocky outcrop, called Massabielle, where there was a cave. She was accompanied by one of her sisters and a friend, when she had a vision of the Virgin Mary, whom she would later describe as a "beautiful lady" wearing a white dress, with yellow roses at her feet.

Over the next five months, there were 18 visions and as word of these apparitions spread, crowds of people would follow Bernadette to these meetings. During the ninth vision, the Virgin revealed to Bernadette the presence of an underground spring, which was later declared to have miraculous properties.

In 1862, the Pope declared that the visions were authentic, and a sanctuary was built close to the grotto. In 1866, Bernadette entered a convent as a novice, and took her vows the following year, while the cult of Our Lady of Lourdes was officially authorized by the Catholic Church and the site quickly became a major pilgrimage centre: today, Lourdes is the most visited place of pilgrimage in the world. In 1876, a basilica was built, and in 1958, an underground church made from pre-stressed concrete was constructed to accommodate the ever increasing numbers of pilgrims. Bernadette died in 1879, was beatified in 1925, and canonized in 1933, becoming Saint Bernadette.

Each year, 5 million pilgrims visit Lourdes – more than Rome, Jerusalem or Mecca. In the summer months between May and October, the normally quiet little town is invaded with visitors who stay in hotels boasting names in distinctly dubious taste, such as the Madonna Hotel, the Vatican Hotel and the Christ the King Hotel. In fact, other than Paris, Lourdes has more hotels than any other city in France! Since the water from the grotto at Lourdes is believed to have the power to heal the incurably sick, of the millions of pilgrims who visit Lourdes each year 50,000 are invalids, who pray for a cure – the elusive miracle. In 1991, for example, 400,000 pilgrims took a dip in one of the 17 grey marble pools, filled with "holy" water from the source.

The controls and documentation of cures from this holy water are stringent, both from the medical and religious point of view, with innate medical scepticism on the one hand, and the need for scrupulous verification of so-called miracles on the other.

Only 65 cures have been officially recognised as miracles by the Church, but unofficial "miraculous cures" run into the thousands and every invalid who makes his way to Lourdes prays that he or she will be the 66th miracle.

Hundreds of volunteers help lift the invalids from their beds or their wheelchairs, and carry them gently into the pools – six of which are reserved for men and 11 for women. Old pairs of crutches are hung on the walls of the grotto a poignant symbol of the hope engendered in the invalid, even though there has not been an officially recognised miracle since Delizia Cirolli a poor Sicilian, was cured of bone cancer in 1976. The case of Miss Cirolli was reviewed by international panels of doctors but even so, it took 12 years before her cure was officially recognised as a miracle.

divisions which took years to erode.

A Catholic religious order – the Assumptionist Order, took the Dreyfus issue a step further, raising the inflammatory question as to whether France was controlled by the Jews and Protestants and waging its own version of a holy war against both the Republic and the Jews in its publications.

Anti-semitism provided all the various factions of the political right with a rallying point and once the unhappy affair was legally over, it provided the opposite kind of focal point – uniting all the republican forces in the country. The incoming government of 1899 immediately set out to prosecute all those who had exploited the Dreyfus Affair (such as the Assumptionist Order) in the hope of a revolution. This order was later dissolved.

Separation of Church & State

The scars of the Dreyfus Affair were ever present, and the country became increasingly divided on the issue of anti-clericalism, tinged with some class hostility.

The Catholic church was identified with the aristocracy, and the wealthy middle classes. The lower middle classes and the lower levels of bureaucracy were anti-clerical, and the peasantry was divided on more regional lines.

The anti-clerical campaign, involving amongst other measures, the obligatory legal registration of religious orders, was conducted with its own degree of bigotry and unsavoury practices. In December 1905, a *Law of Separation* was passed, bringing about the separation of the church and state. Absolute liberty of religion was recognized, but the church was to have no special claims on the state.

Religious institutions could keep their property, but it had to be managed by a separate recognized association. Under this neat compromise, the state could not be said to be dealing directly with the church, whilst the latter would continue to function, although under a different corporate identity.

Predictably, the Vatican protested, with Pope Pius X opposing what appeared, in his eyes, as the formation of a godless state. In fact, the long-term repercussions were the strengthening of Rome's control over the French church.

For example, the Vatican could now appoint bishops without the need to consult the government. In the end, the legal separation of the church and state served to reduce tensions between the two institutions. Anti-clerical feeling inevitably died down, once there was less clerical involvement, or, depending on the point of view, interference in politics.

Modern Day Religion

What is the religious breakdown of the French today? Although three-quarters of the French population claim to belong to the Roman Catholic church, only a small percentage actually worships regularly.

Practising Catholics are more likely to be found in the west, in Brittany and La Vendée; in the eastern regions of Alsace-Lorraine; the Jura and the Vosges; in Flanders, to the north; the Basque country and south of the Massif Central, since these areas have all historically been Catholic. Protestants number over a million, and are found particularly in Alsace, the northern Jura, the south

Muslim Minority

In the fifth *arrondissement* (district) in Paris, in the quiet little Place du Puit-de-l'Ermite stands the main mosque of the city, with its minarets and its Arabic tile-work decoration adding a distinctly Middle Eastern flavour to a typical Parisian street.

The history of the pretty mosque, with its shaded courtyard and its crowded tea-room selling strong mint tea and delicious *baklava* pastries, in some way reflects the current dilemma which Islam is establishing in France. This mosque was constructed between 1922-1928, in memory of the 100,000 Muslims who died for France in W WI, yet 70 years later, many of the descendants of these brave men have still not been fully been assimilated into the country for which their ancestors died.

Even though they may be the third generation to have been born in France, and though most of them have never lived in North Africa, there is a growing disenchantment with their adopted country and a re-strengthening of their religious identity. And this is causing tensions within the avowedly secular structure of French society.

Poverty, unemployment, inner-city violence and a disturbing tide of racism are driving more and more young people to seek some form of unity and solidarity in Islam, which increasingly appears to offer a framework which is missing in mainstream French society. Traditionally strong links have always been maintained between the former French colony of Algeria and her large immigrant population in France with Algeria has supplied *imams* for French mosques. The increasingly fundamentalist approach to Islam among the North African and Arab countries has been mirrored in a growing number of active worshippers in France which has disturbed and antagonized the non-Muslim population.

The Gulf War further polarized Muslims, and French Muslims protested vehemently against the publication of Salman Rushdie's book ***The Satanic Verses***. The latest, simmering controversy to have surfaced in the country is the issue

The Paris Mosque.

of the *chador* – the veil with which traditional Muslim women are required to cover their heads.

A French law of 1937 forbids any display or outward manifestation of religious or political affiliations in schools. When, in 1989, against the background of an increasingly orthodox approach to their religion, a number of teenage schoolgirls insisted on wearing a *chador* to go to school, a crisis arose. Initially, only one school was involved, and after several warnings to the girls and their parents, the school banned the children from attending class – as long as their heads were veiled. Immediately, protests took place, and the *chador* quickly made its appearance in schools all over the country and the affair assumed national proportions, especially when Danielle Mitterrand, the wife of the French President, stated that she was in favour of allowing the *chador* to be worn. The government prevaricated, and the large majority of French people simply could not understand the intensity of feelings aroused amongst the Muslim populace and the issue went to court. Three years later, a court ruling ordered the girls back to school – with their *chadors* – stating, in a dissatisfyingly equivocal way, that they had been banned from school only for violating an internal school rule (namely, no outward display of religion) and not for any behavioural or discipline problem.

Neither side was happy with the ruling, for although it was immediately hailed as a victory for the traditionalists, in fact no real stance had been taken and the people were still uncertain. Is France still a secular society? Are French schools secular? Who makes the rules in schools, the teachers or the parents, the courts or public opinion? Is the *chador* the final stage, or is it only the first step in an increasingly strict Islamic approach to education, especially that of girls ?

The questions still persist as the country struggles with a recession, growing unemployment and increasing immigration, the position of both sides are hardening as Muslims and non-Muslims appear to be becoming less conciliatory to each other.

eastern Massif Central and the central Atlantic region.

Muslims are mainly drawn from the immigrant communities of North Africa, who have settled in large towns, especially Paris and the southern port city of Marseille.

The Jewish population today probably numbers about half a million, of which roughly half live in and around Paris; a-quarter in Marseille, with large communities in both Alsace and the east.

Sad to say, France still manifests religious intolerance, which is increasingly linked to racism. The shameful anti-semitism which led to the deportation of so many French Jews during WWII is still prevalent, fanned by an alarming rise in support for ultra right-wing groups.

There have been a small, but growing number of instances of Jewish cemeteries being desecrated.

France's large immigrant population, mainly from the north African countries of Algeria and Tunisia, have brought with them their own faith – Islam, and there are growing tensions in French society in the face of an increasing fundamentalist Muslim population. (see box story on p.112)

Extremist parties which seek to promote Gallic pride, are quick to criticize all immigrants, especially the Muslims. Religion, for centuries a problematic issue for the French, is still, after so many religious wars and so many attempts at reform, a contentious issue.

The French have an expression, "*faire le pont*", which translates literally as "to make the bridge". What this really means is taking off one of those days that are inconveniently sandwiched between a public holiday and a weekend. If Thursday is a holiday, Friday becomes a *jour de pont* (bridge day), and by taking it off, you *faire le pont*, thus gaining a nice long weekend. Planning all the year's *ponts* (bridges) is one of the first and most enjoyable activities of the New Year, and in a country with 11 legal holidays a year, there are always a couple of possibilities for long weekends.

French holidays are a mix of religious and civic holidays and in addition there are many regional celebrations. The French enjoy life, and any excuse to celebrate is welcomed, be it the feast day of your name-saint, or the arrival of the new local wine. In a country where food is a major topic of concern, conversation and interest, it is natural that many

Cannes Film Festival, excuse for colour, fun and gaiety.

Festivals

115

Belting it out at a small village festival.

holidays and family reunions involve food and drink.

Religious Holidays

The six religious public holidays com-memorate the major events in the Catholic calendar. *Pâques* (Easter), is a moveable feast-day, but always falls in the spring, followed 40 days later by **Ascension Day** and **Pentecost** 10 days later.

The **Feast of the Assumption** celebrated on 15th August, commemorates

The Champs Élysees at Christmas time.

the day the Virgin Mary was taken up to heaven. The feast of **Toussaint** (All Saints' Day) is celebrated on 1st November, when all the saints of the Church, known and unknown, well-loved or forgotten, are remembered. The religious year draws to a close with the commemoration of the birth of Christ, on 25th December.

On **Christmas Day**. French children, like children the world over, look forward to opening their presents in the morning, but for adults, much of the real celebration takes place on Christmas Eve. Midnight mass at church is preceded by an elaborate family dinner, at which the menu will traditionally include oysters, *foie gras* (fatted liver), a cooked goose, and a creamy cake called a *bûche de Noel* (yule-log). This menu, incidentally, will often be repeated a week later, on New Year's Eve.

Civic Holidays

Interspersed with these religious holidays are five civic holidays, of which two, **New Year's Day** on 1st January, and **Labour Day** on 1st May are internationally celebrated holidays. New Year's Day is generally a quiet day, after the parties of the previous night.

Armistice Day on 11th November is also celebrated in other European countries and marks the end of WW I in Europe in 1918. The other two holidays are uniquely French: **Victory in Europe**

Festivals of Cote d'Azur

In a country as regionally diverse as France, there will always be unique local festivals, and one part of France that has many such celebrations is the south. Perhaps it is the sunshine, or the beauty of the Mediterranean that encourages people to celebrate, but there seems to be something festive happening there in just about every season. Let us look at the calendar for a typical year on the Riviera.

January: In January, Monaco celebrates the memory of **St Dévote**, a third century martyr. In the Middle Ages, the relics of the saint were stolen by thieves, who tried to escape by ship. According to legend, they were caught, their ship burned, and with it, a tradition was born, because every year, on 26th January, a ship is burned on the square in front of the Église St Dévote, followed the next day by a procession.

February: February is the month when the mimosas flower, and every year there is a **Mimosa Festival** in Cannes, where the local farms and plantations send their floral contributions.

Depending when Easter falls, the date is fixed accordingly for the **Nice Carnival**, one of the biggest festivals in the south of France. His Majesty King Carnival makes his entry into Nice on the Saturday 10 days before Shrove Tuesday, when he will then be burnt in an effigy. The two Saturdays and Sundays between the King's entrance and Shrove Tuesday are given over to processions, masked balls, fireworks, and spectacular processions of floats.

Easter: At 9:00 pm on the night of Good Friday, in the pretty resort of Roquebrune-Cap-Martin, the **Procession of the Entombment of Christ** is held: people dress up as Roman centurions and as the disciples of Christ, and walk though illuminated streets.

May: May is when the season really begins. The month, and the entire Côte d'Azur, is dominated by the **Cannes Film Festival**, probably the best known film festival in the world. For two weeks, there is not a hotel room, a restaurant reservation, or a plane ticket to be had, unless, of course, you are a producer, a director, or, better still, a star. Cannes has its

Medieval fun, a provincial historical festival.

own tradition of *The Starlette*, usually young, usually unknown, and always female, who is happy to pose provocatively on La Croisette for the picture-hungry journalists who roam the place in packs. The Starlette is famous for a day, the photographers are happy, and tradition is maintained. Anyone who has any energy left after Cannes, heads straight off to Monaco, for the **Formula One Grand Prix**. Nice has its annual **Jazz Festival**, and St Tropez has its *bravade* (traditional festivity), when, on the 16th and 17th May, the statue of Saint Tropez is paraded around the town in a tradition going back to the late 15th century.

June: There is a second *bravade* again in Saint Tropez on 15th June, when the routing of a Spanish attack on the port in 1637, is commemorated.

July: On either the first or the second Sunday in July, the beautiful peninsula of Cap d'Antibes celebrates the **Festival of Our Lady of Safe Homecoming**. The statue of Our Lady, the patron of sailors, is taken from the tiny *Sanctuaire de la Garoupe* (Garoupe sanctuary) on the Thursday preceding the festival and is taken to the Cathedral in Antibes. On the Sunday of the festival, Our Lady is brought safely home again in a procession led by local sailors and fishermen. July also sees jazz festivals galore, notably in Antibes and Juan-les-Pins.

August: August is the month for arts festivals, be it the festival in Sisteron, or Fourcalquier. By mid-August, the crowds of French holidaymakers are heading home for *la rentrée scolaire* (the start of school), and the Côte d'Azur breathes easy again.

December: Christmas is a special time anywhere in the world, and midnight mass in the church of some of the little villages of Provence, can be a wonderful experience. Many of the villages have a *crèche vivante* (live crib) when cows, goats and sheep are brought by the local shepherds to church, in a happy, noisy procession to join the villagers who are representing Mary, Joseph, and the baby Jesus. Very often the baby starts crying, and the animals wander off around the church, exploring their unfamiliar surroundings. The tiny village of Lucéra has its own variation of the *crèche vivante*, when local shepherds offer lambs and fruit to the church, accompanied by musicians playing fifes and tambourines.

Day is celebrated on 8th May, and commemorates the end of WWII in Europe. **Bastille Day**, on the 14th July, is the most important French civic holiday: the storming of the Bastille prison on 14th July, 1789 marked the beginning of the revolution that would sweep away the monarchy, and turn France into a Republic. *Le quatorze juillet* (14 July) is celebrated by the French the world over, and tradition has it that a French citizen overseas can present himself at the French Embassy that day, without an invitation and join in the party. In France, on 14th July, local councils usu-ally organize outdoor dances and parties – in Paris, it will be done by the town hall of each *arrondissement* (district), and people party late into the night.

Festivals

As well as the public holidays, there are many festivals, which although working days, will still call for some form of celebration.

The feast of the **Epiphany** on 6th January commemorates the arrival of the Three Kings in Bethlehem to pay

Epiphany offerings.

their respects to the Infant Jesus. Traditionally, Epiphany, falls on the 12th day after Christmas marking the end of the Christmas celebrations. On that day, French families eat a special cake at dinner time, called *la galette des rois*, literally the kings' cake, but translatable as a Twelfth Night cake. It is made of flaky pastry and almond paste, and when you buy one, it comes supplied with a paper crown. Baked into the cake is a little token or charm, very often a small porcelain figure and whoever gets the piece of cake with the charm, is declared king, or queen, and can choose a partner who is then "crowned" with the paper crown.

Depending when Easter falls, sometime in the early spring French families will celebrate *Mardi Gras*, (Shrove Tuesday): tradition has it that you eat up all the rich food in the house, ready to start the 40 days of Lenten austerity which proceed Easter, so pancakes, consisting of the remaining butter, eggs and sugar are traditionally eaten. On the next day, **Ash Wednesday**, devout families will go to church were their foreheads are smeared with ash. They fast for the day. Easter Sunday and Monday are usually celebrated with big family meals, and children will often receive presents of little chocolate eggs or rabbits, which symbolize new life.

Like children the world over, French children like to play tricks on **1st April**, but unlike their English speaking counterparts, who shout "April fool!" at their hapless, adult victims, French children shout "*poisson d'avril*", meaning, somewhat inconsequentially "April fish".

The next few holidays such as **Ascension Thursday** (celebrating Christ's ascension into heaven) and Pentecost (the coming of the Holy Spirit) are days when, if the weather permits, the family will head out to the country or the beach, and if they can make a long weekend of it, so much the better. Since so much of French celebrations centre around food, a day like **Mother's Day** is often celebrated with a family lunch in a restaurant – the French believe in taking their children out to restaurants from a very early age, so a Mother's Day lunch in a smart restaurant, with grandparents, sons, daughters and a host of grandchildren is a common sight.

Hot Summer Fun

The French are great believers in the unwavering ritual of a long summer holiday and the country practically closes down during the months of July and August, while everyone heads off to the beaches in the south, or to the mountains, in search of cool, fresh air. The peak period for holidays is the month between Bastille Day and the Feast of the Assumption, otherwise known more prosaically as 14th July to 15th August. This is the time of the year when motorways are blocked solid with horrendous traffic jams, when the French driver loses his temper more often than usual, and when lucky visitors get to see Paris and the other major cities at their best as all the locals head for the "countryside". Paris during those four weeks is the perfect place to be, for the roads are empty, parking is free, and everyone is more casual and relaxed. It goes without saying, that the place not to go in the height of the summer is anywhere in the direction of the beaches of the Côte d'Azur in the south of France – unless you like crowds, frayed tempers, and traffic jams.

One of the features of summer in France, is the *festival estiraux* (summer festival). There are many arts festivals, ranging from small, local affairs to major festivals of international repute, such as the big festivals of the south – notably in **Aix-en-Provence**, **Avignon**, **Arles** and **Orange**. These festivals attract well-known international orchestras, dance and theatre groups, and take place outdoors, in the warm summer evenings, usually against a stunning backdrop,

Old traditions are kept up by villages in small towns.

such as the **Palais des Papes** in **Avignon**, or the Roman amphitheatres in Arles and Orange.

Another summer attraction in Provence is the spectacle of bull fighting: not usually as gory as the Spanish bullfights, although in Arles and **Nîmes**, some of the bulls are killed by the *picadors* (mounted bull fighter armed with a lance). For spectators who dislike the idea of watching a bull being killed, but who are still intrigued by the pageantry and atmosphere, there is another kind of bull-fight, called a *"course à la cocarde"*:

a *cocarde* (rosette) is placed between the bull's horns, and the young men endeavour to retrieve it – exciting but not as death-defying as the real thing.

Maudlin Memories

Just because there is no public holiday

there is still reason enough to celebrate, and if you party too long and too late, too bad, you will go to work the next morning with a hangover, picturesquely described in French slang as a *gueule de bois* (a wooden mouth or head)! A prime candidate for a *gueule de bois* is the celebration that accompanies the arrival of the new *beaujolais* wine in late November.

Cynics say that the popularity surrounding the arrival of what is often an undistinguished wine from the vineyards, is a triumph of marketing and public relations. Whatever it really tastes like, the British, the Japanese and the Americans have taken *le beaujolais nouveau* (the new beaujolais) well and truly to heart. There are races between restaurants to get the wine first; people fly the wine halfway across the world, or race through the night to reach the cross-Channel ferry to England with their *beaujolais* on board and with all the attendant media fanfare, of course. Such is the media hype about *beaujolais* that it has acquired a class in and prestige of its own. In France, the arrival of the *beaujolais nouveau* does not lead to such dramatics, but since the wine is only traditionally drunk in the month between its launching in late November and Christmas Day, it tends to be consumed in less than moderate amounts.

In a major wine-growing country like France, naturally enough, there are many *vendanges* (local wine festivals). A fascinating, but little-known wine festival takes place in Paris in early October,

Les Saintes – Maries-de-la Mer

The coastal village of **Les Saintes – Maries-de-la-Mer**, bordered on one side by the Mediterranean, and on the other by the Etang de Vaccares, surrounded by saltflats, quicksand and marshes, where bulls and horses roam wild, is the venue for one of France's most unusual and colourful festivals. Twice a year, thousands of gypsies converge on the Camargue, for a weekend of religious ceremonies and festivities.

But first of all, the legend behind the festival ... according to Provençal folklore, c. AD 40, a group of early Christians fled from Judea to escape persecution at the hands of the Jews. In the group were Mary Jacob who was the sister of the Virgin Mary; Mary Salomé who was the mother of Saint John and Saint James; Lazarus, whom Jesus had raised from the dead, and his two sisters Mary Magdalen and Martha.

They were put to sea in a flimsy boat, without a sail, oars and with no provisions. Sara, the black servant of the two Marys was left on shore, but wanted to go with her mistresses, so Mary Salomé tossed her cloak onto the waves, and miraculously it turned into a raft, enabling Sara to join them.

The group somehow managed to land their boat on a beach, at *Saintes-Maries-de-la-Mer* which means, the " Holy Marys from the sea". In gratitude they built a little oratory, where their relics would later be placed. In the mid-9th century, the church which had replaced the original oratory was fortified and in time, was itself replaced in the 12th century, by a fortified pre-Romanesque church, which is the village church today.

The oratory soon became a place of pilgrimage, especially for nomads and gypsies – the *gitans* of Spain and the Hungarian *tziganes*, who venerate Sara. Every year (the tradition still continues), gypsies from all over Europe converge on the village, to celebrate the Feast Days of Saint Mary Jacob in May, and of Saint Mary Salomé in October (on the weekend which falls closest to the 22nd of the month).

Saint Mary Jacob's Feast Day is celebrated over two days, the 24th and the 25th of May, and on the second day, the relics of the saint, accompanied by mounted *gardians*, (Camargue cow-boys), are carried in procession from the church, around the village, along the beach and finally, into the sea, before being blessed by the local bishop. After the two days of religious ceremonies are over, there are two more days of dancing, *farandoles* (branding), horse races and bull fights.

Bullfighting is unique to Provence and Languedoc-Roussillon, and in addition to the Camargue, can be seen in the Roman arenas of Nîmes and Arles.

---

for Paris actually has its own vineyard. In Montmartre, only a five minute walk away from the Church of Sacré Coeur, is a minuscule vineyard, growing white Thomery grapes.

Single's Day

November 25 is the **Feast Day of Saint Catherine of Alexandria**, and on that day any young woman who is 25 years old and unmarried, celebrates the day in a tradition going back to the late 19th century. The idea that at 25 a woman could still be unmarried was so horrifying to the seamstresses and milliners of 19th century Paris, that they determined to do their best for their unmarried friends. They would make especially elaborate hats, traditionally in green and yellow, which these "young maids" would wear, and even today, unmarried 25 year olds are referred to as *catherinettes* and the day is called "*coiffer sainte Catherine*" (Saint Catherine's hat).

Le Petit Journal
SUPPLÉMENT ILLUSTRÉ

LE MERCREDI DES CENDRES
A BAS LES MASQUES !!!

An 1893 newspaper reports Mardi Gras activities.

Begging Pardon

Brittany, with its huge pantheon of saints, many of them hardly known outside the region, is a natural venue for **regional festivals**, especially religious ones.

The most spectacular are the *pardons*, which take place throughout the year, all over Brittany, in little village chapels, and

The fruit of labour are exalted in a village festival.

in big churches.

A *pardon* is essentially a solemn, religious procession, in which people participate in order to fulfil a vow, or ask for a favour, or, simply, beg pardon for their sins. Although all *pardons* are interesting, two of the most impressive, and most popular take place in the little villages of **Sainte Anne la Palud**, and **Sainte Anne d'Auray**.

In **Sainte Anne la Palud**, the ceremonies take place on the last weekend of August: there is a torchlit procession along the beach to the chapel, followed by an outdoor Mass. The people wear colourful traditional Breton costumes, and the ceremony provides a fascinating glimpse into the cultural roots of Breton life.

The *pardons* of **Sainte Anne d'Auray** take place during much of the year, beginning 7th March, and lasting throughout the summer until early October. The two most spectacular days are the **Feast Day of St Anne**, on 26th July, and the **Feast of the Assumption**, on 15th August.

The Annual Paris Waiter's Race.

Balancing Acts

During late summer in Paris, waiters and waitresses take to the streets for the annual **Waiters' Race**. Dressed in their regular restaurant uniforms, they run through the streets balancing a tray, a bottle and a couple of glasses. The prize money increases every year, as does the number of international participants and international off-shoots, but it is still essentially a fun run. Crowds cheer the waiters on, groaning loudly when bottles or glasses fall from the tray, disqualifying the runners.

You can always celebrate your own name-day, or watch the annual big sporting events, which are part of the

social calendar. You can participate in any number of the hundreds of cultural festivals that are organised each year in every part of France. From *avant garde* cinema to modern dance, from painting to wind surfing, from marathons to

The Joker spreads his mischievous spirit at a village festival.

power boat racing on the Seine, there is always some kind of event taking place in France. After all, it was the French who coined the phrase "*joie de vivre*" (joy in life).

Amusez-vous bien (enjoy yourself)!

Art

The French are vigourously aware of art in all its manifestations, and are genuinely interested in it: they are unconcerned about voicing unconventional opinions, and are more than mere armchair connoisseurs. Wintery Sunday afternoons will find Parisians heading off to a small cinema hall to see **Casablanca** in its original English, or an early Satyajit Ray in Bengali, or queuing for hours for admission to the latest *exposition* (exhibition). Small wonder, then, that the arts in France are taken seriously and displayed with a flair and *panache* missing in many neighbouring European countries. Recent controversial architectural projects such as the **Pyramide du Louvre** – the startling entrance to the Louvre museum – or the **Opéra de la Bastille** – a new opera house in the unfashionable eastern side of Paris have aroused dissent, occasionally disapproval, but their very boldness has consistently stimulated debate and a large amount of respect.

Edouard Manet's "Argenteuil Les Canotiers".

Molière.

One of France's greatest playwrights, Moliére.

Historically, the roots of French culture lie in a complex mix of Celtic, Greco-Roman and Germanic elements. The Middle Ages saw the fostering of the arts by religious scholars, especially the monasteries and well into the 18th century the aristocracy and nobility continued to patronize artists. With the rise of the *bourgeoisie* (middle class) in the 18th century, culture became more accessible, and less exclusively centred on Paris. Great strides were made in the late 19th and the first half of the 20th centuries in the domain of compulsory education and the rising levels of literacy not only ensured that the general cultural level was raised, but more specifically it encouraged intellectual and social development within the lower income groups.

Architecture: Awesome & Avant-Garde

French architecture is a mirror of the country's historical development, from the well-preserved Roman arenas of Provence, to the sublime gothic cathedrals; the lavishly ornate royal palaces of Versailles and Fontainebleau, to the string of *châteaux* (castles) that follow the Loire valley. It was the Church that first required buildings, followed by the monarchy. Thus, their patronage at various stages in history influenced the development of a distinctly national architectural style.

Today, visitors throng the country's many *châteaux* and palaces, chiefly those in and around Paris, and those along the River Loire. With the brutal demise of the French monarchy in the 18th century, these monuments of unstinting luxury and opulence are the last vestiges of the aristocracy's patronage of the arts – henceforward it would be the task of the state to encourage and sponsor art and architecture and support new architectural styles.

Although the provinces have many superb museums, often traditionally reflecting their region's activities, inevitably Paris holds the lion's share of the country's principal museums, galleries and concert halls. **The Louvre**, with its vast array of artistic gems – the Mona Lisa to name only one of them – the 19th and early 20th centuries art collection of the **Musée d'Orsay**; and the 20th

That unmistakable smile.

The Citadel, opened in May 1992, in an underground warren of passages and galleries, and uses chillingly realistic holograms, with eerie sound effects. Visitors are seated in small carriages, which are automatically controlled and you are led inexorably from one scene of battle to another, to the final tableau – the selection of one coffin to become France's **Unknown Soldier**, which lies today under the **Arc de Triomphe** in central Paris.

Canvas Creations

French visual arts during the Middle Ages and the Renaissance, although undeniably important, were overshadowed by similar movements in Italy and the Low Countries (Netherlands). It was not until the 17th century that the paintings of Le Nain, Nicolas Poussin and Claude Lorrain started to give French art its own distinctive character.

A century later, François Boucher, Antoine Watteau and Jean-Honoré Fragonard were painting their idealized pastoral scenes, whilst Jacques-Louis David painted classical pictures, notably his celebrated canvas depicting the coronation of Emperor Napoleon I, displayed in the Louvre.

The French Academy had established certain conventions in painting, and in the 19th century painters sparked creativity by reacting against these same conventions. Eugène Delacroix, for example, indulged in exoticism, whilst

century paintings of the **Georges Pompidou Centre**, rank among some of the world's greatest art collections, and interestingly enough all are housed in provocative buildings. The Louvre's controversial steel and glass pyramid entrance, the Musée d'Orsay's renovation from a disused railway station and the external skeleton of the Pompidou Centre – these buildings have become infamous pieces of art themselves.

There are a couple of innovative museums that have recently opened in the French provinces that are monuments to technology which impress the visitor as much by their presentation as by the exhibits themselves. In Verdun, the scene of some of the most horrendous slaughter of WWI, a museum called

Picasso Museum, Antibes.

fluential figures in 20th-century art, spent most of his artistic life in France, bequeathing to her museums a major part of his collection.

132

Gustave Courbet and Honoré Daumier were exponents of realism. However the most far-reaching movement of the 19th century , was unquestionably Impressionism, which brought about a revolution not only in painting but also in music developments which well and truly established the French reputation in the arts.

The major figures of the Impressionist movement were Paul Cézanne, Édouard Manet, Claude Monet, Camille Pissarro, Alfred Sisley, and Edgar Degas, and they in turn influenced a generation of Post-Impressionists including Henri Matisse, Henri de Toulouse-Lautrec, Paul Gauguin, and Georges Seurat. Although not French, the artist Pablo Picasso, one of the most in-

Literary Lights

It is always difficult to accurately pinpoint when a country's literature began. But, in France, it is traditionally held to have begun in 842 with the *Oath of Strasbourg*.

The Middle Ages are known for epic poems such as *La Chanson de Roland (The Song of Roland)*, and the Arthurian romances of Chrétien de Troyes. The 16th century Renaissance provided such literary figures as the poet de Ronsard, the satirist and humorist Rabelais, and

Eugene Delacroix's revolutionary painting of Liberty Leading the People.

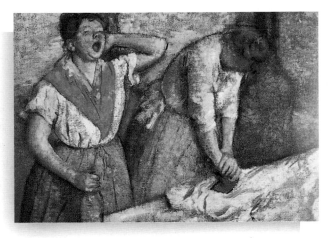

ART

133

French literature has carried on the dominance of the novel genre as a major literary form, beginning with the startling epic work of Marcel Proust, *À la Recherche du Temps Perdu* (*Remembrance of Things Passed*).

Montaigne – generally regarded as the inventor of the essay. Some of the country's better known playwrights wrote during the 17th century, with the tragedies of Pierre Corneille and Racine, and the comedies of Molière, which are often the first introduction foreigners have to French literature. What Shakespeare is to generations of English school-children, so Molière is to the French.

Major literary figures of the 18th century were the philosophers Voltaire, Diderot, and Jean-Jacques Rousseau, whilst the 19th century saw the predominance of the novel and writers such as Balzac, Stendhal, Flaubert, and Zola and the archetypal 19th century romantic writer Victor Hugo.

Twentieth century

The first half of the century was dominated by such writers as André Gide, François Mauriac, André Malraux, Albert Camus and Jean-Paul Sartre – a Marxist and the chief exponent of the philosophy of existentialism.

Philosophy and criticism have always played a central part in French intellectual and cultural life, enabling movements such as Surrealism, led by André Breton, to flourish in the 1920s and 1930s whilst existentialism was a powerful force in the mid-19th century.

One of Claude Monet's many paintings in the Impressionist Museum, Paris.

Works of anthropology, such as *Mythologiques and Tristes tropiques (A World on the Wane)* by Claude Lévi-Strauss, which at first glance appear to be aimed at a uniquely intellectual audience, have had a surprisingly major impact on French thinking.

The Twentieth Century – Crescendo

There is a parallel between the development of French classical music and that of painting, for it was not until the 19th and early 20th centuries that French music achieved high international status, via the works of composers such as Hector Berlioz, Maurice Ravel, Claude Debussy, and Frédéric Chopin, (although the latter was actually Polish by birth) who all created what can be called a distinctively French style.

On a popular level, although young French people are very much influenced by Anglo-Saxon modern music, just as they are by its cinema, there are still a number of very successful and long-standing French singers.

The songs of the late Edith Piaf and Jacques Brel remain popular, whilst someone like the fifty-something rock singer Johnny Hallyday is a past master at what the French call recycling a career, for he has been a star for well-nigh 30 years. Trends may come and songs may go, but Johnny and *"le rock"* remains.

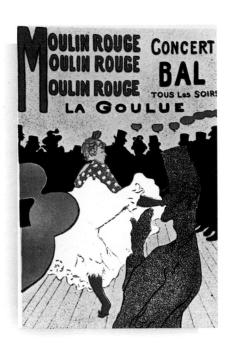

Moulin Rouge poster by Toulouse-Lautrec.

Figurines & the Flirtatious Dance

From the mid-17th century to the mid-18th century, one of the most popular dances in aristocratic circles was the *minuet*, an elegant derivative of a French folk dance.

The word *minuet* comes from the French word *menu* (small), and the dance reflected this origin in its use of very small dainty steps, which became more and more stylized over the years.

One of the dance forms linked in popular imagination with France, and especially with Paris during the years of the *Belle Époque*, is the *can-can*, a high-kicking dance, which made its debut in

Parisian dance halls in the 1830s, revealing lots of petticoat and, more scandalously, lots of leg. During the 1840s the *can-can* featured in many revues and variety shows, and composers such as Jacques Offenbach composed specific music for this boisterous dance, which was accompanied by raucous screams from the dancers, who often performed the splits. Other than seeing an Offenbach operetta, the only way to see the *can-can* today is at a revue such as the Lido, in Paris.

The two opera houses in Paris, and the main provincial theatres all have ballet companies. Paris, in particular, is regularly visited by the world's major dance companies, as well as small budget troupes, offering highly experimental fare.

The only problem with trying to go to the Opéra de Paris, or to the Bolshoi

French Impressionism

It was a journalist for the satirical magazine *Le Charivari*, Louis Leroy, who did it. In 1874, he wrote a review of the first exhibition by a group of painters whose work had been regularly refused by the official French Academy Salon. Monsieur Leroy used the derogatory term *impressioniste* to describe their work, especially one painting by a young painter called Claude Monet, *Impression du soleil levant* (Impression of the sunrise). If the now-forgotten M. Leroy could see the furore in the world art markets on the rare occasions that an Impressionist painting is put up for sale, perhaps he would rue his derisive words. Four hundred and thirty-two million francs were paid in May 1990 for a Renoir canvas, **Moulin de la Galette**. The figure speaks for itself – an Impressionist painting is currently one of the most *recherché* (sought after) acquisitions for an art collector, and the world's most spectacular collections, be they in private hands or in museums, all boast Impressionist masterpieces.

Exactly what did the hapless Leroy start, when he coined the term *impressioniste*? The Impressionist School was active during the late 19th and early 20th century, but the main corpus of the work was painted between 1867 and 1886.

The early, pivotal painters of the school were Manet, Monet, Renoir, Pissarro, Degas and Cézanne, though there were other followers of their style, whose works are perhaps not so well known, but are still acclaimed, such as Morisot and Guillaumin. The Impressionists were to have a major influence on later painters such as Gauguin, Seurat and Van Gogh.

These first Impressionist painters, all working in France, had begun to reject some traditional teaching concerning art. They rejected the emphasis on historical and mythological subjects, with their stylized and idealized treatment, and turned their attention in another direction, that of the senses. They tried to capture the fleeting effects of light, the movement of clouds, the play of colour such that the viewer was not merely looking at an object but entering into an experience of it. The Impressionist painters rejected the previously accepted practice of painting from sketches in a studio, preferring to paint the actual subject outdoors. Texture, colour and tone became ends in themselves – in a picture of his wife on the beach, painted by Monet in 1870, grains of sand embedded in the paint.

By the late 1860s, many of the painters were experimenting with their new approach to art: Manet aimed to make the viewer look more at the composition and texture rather than the subject *per se*. Renoir, Monet and Pissarro were trying to depict the effect of natural light on landscapes. Shadows, reflected light, ripples on water were represented not by blocks of colour, but by flecks of varying colour – a technique which would lead to a later school of "*Pointillisme*".

After the group's first show, they decided to adopt the ironic name provided by Monsieur Leroy, and so it was that the Impressionist group held a total of eight shows during the years 1874-86, while all the time continuing to develop their individual styles. It is undoubtedly Claude Monet (1840-1926) who is the major

---

during their eagerly awaited visits, is finding tickets, (which are very expensive), but if you draw a blank at the theatre box offices themselves, try the ticket desks at the major FNAC (a chain of photo shops) shops, where they often have tickets, and also lots of alternatives if your choice is unavailable.

Classic Cinema

France, and especially Paris, is a joy for cinema buffs, for the French love going to the cinema, seeing with equal interest a French film as well as an obscure, but well reviewed foreign film, which will

representative of both the philosophy and the practice of Impressionism. It was one of his canvases that coined the original term, and throughout his long and prolific life, he never wavered from what he considered to be the tenets of Impressionism.

Monet developed a system of painting several canvases of the same subject, showing the effects of changing light. His most famous "series" paintings are those of *Haystacks* painted in 1891, those of *Rouen Cathedral* (1894) and his last work, the wonderful *Décorations des Nymphéas*, (water-lilies), painted over 20 years, from 1906 until his death in 1926.

In 1883, Monet, his two sons by his late wife Camille, accompanied by his mistress, Alice Hoschedé and her six children from a previous marriage, all moved to a little village called Giverny, 84 kilometres from Paris. Not only would Giverny become Monet's home until his death, but it was the direct inspiration, indeed the cause, of the *Nymphéas* series, as well as *The Lily Pond* (1899-1906). Seven years after they moved to Giverny, Monet purchased a piece of marshy land across the road from the house, and by diverting the stream flowing through it, he constructed a pool, which became the water-lily garden he would immortalise in his canvases. The weeping willow, the bamboo, azaleas, wisterias, the Japanese bridge, and, of course, the water-lilies would be painted in varying moods and sizes. The first canvases were small, only about one yard square, but the last series of huge murals would later be installed in two 80-foot oval rooms in the Orangerie, in Paris's **Tuileries Gardens**.

Giverny went through a period of sad neglect, in the years following the death of Monet's daughter-in-law, Blanche Hoschedé-Monet, but 10 years of restoration, and large amounts of cash – $6.5 million, mainly from American donations – helped restore the house and gardens to their heyday when Monet had a special studio built to house his 6 by 12 foot *Nymphéas* canvases. In 1992, Giverny acquired a new addition, the **American Museum**, which aims to show the influence and the artistic contact between American and French painters, especially during the Impressionist years.

Although many of the Impressionist masterpieces are scattered all over the world's art galleries, there is a large body of their work displayed in the stunning **Musée d'Orsay** in Paris, a museum housed in a disaffected railway station. Monet, Cézanne, Renoir, Gauguin are all exhibited there, along with some of the most controversial paintings of another of their group, Édouard Manet.

Under the glass roof of a former station you can see Manet's 1863 painting, *Le Déjeuner sur l'herbe* (Luncheon on the Grass) rejected by the French Academy Salon, who were offended by the naked young woman amongst the clothed men; *Olympia*, 1863, which was also considered scandalous; and the charming study of a boy soldier, *The Fifer* 1866, also rejected by the Salon, this time for being "too flat" and too naked. Impressionism, however, endured these criticism and misunderstood painters of the 19th century have now achieved understanding, popularity and some of the highest prices in the world.

either be dubbed into French, or shown in the *version originale* (original language, usually referred to as VO) with French subtitles, though this does, inevitably, limit the options for visitors who speak neither English nor French.

If you want to see a classic old movie, or see long forgotten films of an obscure director, then Paris is the place for you: buy one of the two weekly magazines, **L'Officiel des Spectacles** or **Pariscope**, which give exhaustive listings of every show at every cinema in town and the immediate suburbs and watch out for the cheap tickets offered on Mondays and at the early afternoon

A question of art or a political statement at the Georges Pompidou Center.

shows. France has produced several internationally acclaimed film directors, notably François Truffaut, Jean-Luc Godard, Jacques Tati and Louis Malle.

Unexpected Art

As you explore France, you will frequently see works of art in the most unexpected places, in streets, in parks, half-way up the Champs Élysées, for the French do not hesitate to take art out to be seen and appreciated by the casual passer-by.

In 1985, for example, the controversial artist Christo "wrapped" the Pont Neuf (New Bridge) in Paris with hundreds of yards of buff coloured silk. People walked across it, touched it, criticized it, but everyone was involved. He thus succeeded in bringing art alive and beyond the connoisseur.

Similarly, in late 1992, the sculptor Botero was allowed to use the Champs Élysées as an open-air exhibition ground: groups of school-children were brought by the teachers for art classes, and they sat on the pavement, trying to draw the huge statues, oblivious to the traffic hurtling past them.

The French never underestimate art and its effect on our lives and much of its success today has been in being progressive and tangible, encouraging the young to be experimental, and thus for art to be a tangible and living expression of life.

Long term parking at the Foundation Cartier.

In the third century BC, the *Parisii* settled along the left bank of the River Seine, the first documented inhabitants of what is still the most atmospheric, artistic and stylish part of Paris.

But back in the third century BC, it was an inhospitable swamp, and the *Parisii* were forced to retreat to a tiny island in the middle of the Seine. That same island is now linked by bridges to the two banks of the river and is known as the **Ile de la Cité**. This is the very heart of Paris, from which all the subsequent urban development grew.

Terrace cafés are ideal for people watching.

Overview of the City

Look at a map of Paris: the city is divided by the River Seine, which flows in a gentle arc through the city. The area to the north is

143

Pigalle Métro, marks the beginning of Paris' red light district.

known as *la rive droite* (right bank), and that to the south as *la rive gauche* (the left bank).

The Seine is very much a part of Paris life. Many beautiful bridges cross it, people still live in houseboats along its length and there is a steady flow of river traffic sailing along it, from huge, glass-sided *bateaux mouches* (small passenger steamer) bearing camera-wielding visitors, to flat barges carrying prosaic loads of sand or cement.

You can go right down to the banks of the Seine, and walk along the cobbled quays, under the bridges, watching the slow barges, the old men quietly fishing and people sunbathing in the summer.

Those few families still lucky

enough to live on a houseboat may be lunching on deck, or watering their pots of plants, precariously balanced along the gangway, or collecting their mail from their shore-based letterbox. Meanwhile, on one of the bridges overhead, there will doubtless be an aspiring artist in place, easel set up, ready to paint his or her definitive view of Notre Dame.

Paris is divided into 20 *arrondissements* (districts), which spiral outwards from the first *arrondissement* situated at the historic heart of the city, forming an increasingly large circle – or, according to Parisians, the circular design on a snail's shell!

The second *arrondissement* is slightly to the north, the third round to the

Façade of Grecian grace at the La Madelaine Church, Paris.

east, the fourth down to the south and onwards, fanning out to the formerly working class districts of the 19th and 20th *arrondissements*. The city limit is marked by a circular ring road, the Péripherique.

To get around Paris in a hurry, you can take the efficient underground railway, le Métro, packed during rush hours and home to enterprising buskers during the rest of the day.

But the best way of experiencing the City of Lights is on foot – stop to lean over a bridge and gaze at the Seine, wander through the parks full of children playing, brave the insane traffic, or finally giving in to weariness, sit down at a pavement café to watch the world go by.

From Place de la Concorde to the Louvre

A good place to start your discovery of Paris is to stand on the **Pont** (bridge) **de la Concorde.** Ahead of you is the **Place (Square) de la Concorde** (with its crazy traffic hurtling across at great speed), its Egyptian obelisk and its elegant 18th century buildings. At the far side of the Square, you will see the Grecian façade of **La Madeleine Church.** Turn and look behind you and you will find a virtual mirror image of La Madeleine – **le Palais Bourbon,** or the **Assemblée Nationale,** the lower of the two French houses of Parliament. From here, look across the river. In every direction are

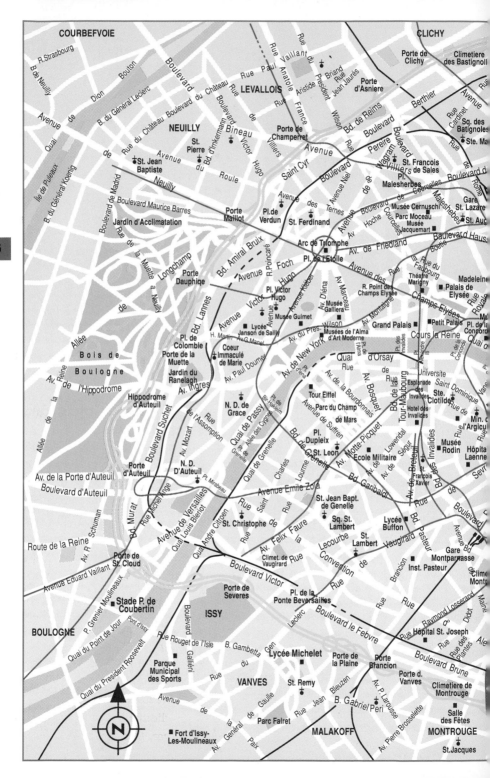

PARIS

int Quen

Porte de Clignancourt

SAINT DENIS

AUBERVILLIERS

Porte d'Aubervilliers

UEN   Boulevard Ney

Porte de la Chapelle

Boulevard MacDonald

Porte de la Villette

Championnet

Rue

PANTIN

Rue

Ordener

St. Jeanne d'Arc

Rue de la Chapelle

Rue d'Aubervilliers

Rue de Flandre

St. Christoph

Porte de Pantin

Av. Jean Lolive

Lamarck

Sacre Coeur

St. Pierre

St. Bernard

Rue de Clignancourt

St. Vincent de Paul

Rue du Meaux

Avenue Jean Jaurs

Crimée

Martin

Ste. Famille

Sq. St. Pierre

Moulin Rouge

St. Jean

rd de Glich   Bd. Rochechouart Boulevard de la Chapelle

Gare du Nord

Rue du Faubourg Saint Martin

Pl. de Stalingrad

St. Georges

Parc des Buttes Chaumont

Porte du Pré St. Gervais

LE PRÉ ST. GERVAIS

Ste. Marie Médiatrice

Notre Dame de Lorette

Rue de Maubeuge

Boulevard de Magenta

Gare du Nord

Valmy

Bd. de la Villette

Av. Simon

Ste. Marie Médiatrice

Bd. Serurier

Porte des Lilas

Faubourg

Fayette

Rue

Rue Poissonnière

St. Laurent

Jemmapes

Hôpital St. Louis

St. Jean Baptiste

Belleville

N. D. des Otages

Boulevard Mortier

Th. des Bd. Variétés

St. Eugene

Rue du Faubourg

Rue d'Hauteville

Porte St. Denis

Porte St. Martin

Quai de

N. D. de la Croix

St. Joseph

Belleville

Bolivar

Rue

Rue Ménilmontant

N. D. de Lourdes

Porte de Bagnolet

Bourse

Rue du 4 Septembre

Montmartre

Rue d'Aboukir

Bd. St. Martin

Pl. de la République

Rue de Turbigo

Avenue de la République

St. Ambroise

Av. Gambetta

Cimetière du Père Lachaise

St. Germain

Porte de Bagnolet

Boulevard Davout

liothèque ationale

Notre Dame des Victoires

Conserv. National des Arts Métiers

Rue Réaumur

Chemin Vert

Roquette

Egl. du Bon Pasteur

Porte de Montreuil

Palais Royal

Banque de France

Rue Saint Honoré

Halles Centres

Centre G. Pompidou

Rue de Sébastopol

Rue du Temple

Boulevard Beaumarchais

la Voltaire

Rollin

Charonne

St. Marguerite

Rue du Montreuil

Porte de Vincennes

MONTREUIL

Pyrenées

Rue d'Avron

Palais de Justice

Sainte Chapelle

St. Germain

Tour St. Jacques

Théatre du Châtelet

Quai de Gesvres

Musée Carnavalet

Archives Nationales

Pl. des Vosges

de

Rivoli

St. Paul

Colonn de Juillet

Pl. de la Bastille

Rue

Rue de Charenton

Hôpital St. Antoine

Pl. de la Nation Cours de Vincennes

Porte Mandé

Notre Dame

Quai St. Michel de la Tournelle

St. Louis

Pont Sully

Bd. Henri IV

St. Antoine

Boulevard Diderot

St. Elol

Av. de Saint Mandé

ST. MANDÉ

Musée St. Julien de Cluny le Pauvre

Germain

Ile St. Louis

Quai des Célestins

Bd. Bourdon

Avenue

Gare de Lyon

Avenue Daumesnil

Reuilly

Bd. de Reuilly

Bd. de Picpus

Michel

Bizot

Soult

Musée des Transport

St. Séverin

Sulpce

xembourg

Sorbonne

Quartier Latin

Ménagetie

Arenes de Lutèce

St. Etienne du Mont

Mosquée

Jardin des Plantes

Musée National d'Histoire Naturelle

Rue de Buffon

Quai St. Bernard

Pl. d' Austerlitz

Quai d'Austerlitz

Quai de la Rapée

Bd. de Bercy

Bd. de Bercy

St. Esprit

Av. du General

Porte Dorée

Daumesnil

St. Jacques de Haut Pas

Musée Pédagogique

St. Médard

Bd. du Port Royal

Gare d'Austerlitz

Hôp. d. l. Salpétrière

N. D. de Bercy

Quai de Bercy

Bois de Vincennes

oservatoire

Prison d. l. Santé

Manuf. d. Gobelins

Bd. St. Marcel

Rue de l'Hôpital

Hôp d. l. Pitié

Quai de la Gare

Carrefour de la Conservation

Boulevard

Arago

Pl. d'Italie

Bd. de la Gare

N. D. d. l. Gare

Velodrome Municipal

Bd. Auguste Blanqui

Bonillot

Jeanne d'Arc

Rue

Tolbiac

Nationale

Pl. de Bercy

CHARENTON

Alesia

arc de ntsouris

urdan

Rue

Rue d'Italy

de

Cité du Refuge

Porte de Bercy

St. Pierre

Boulevard Ke lemann

Porte d'Italie

Boulevard Masséna

Av. de la Libert

IVRY

Porte de Gentilly

Place de la Concorde, where often traffic, statuary and people merge.

Treasures of the Louvre

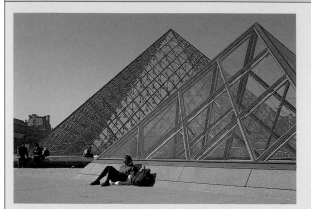

The Louvre Pyramid, a controversial art nouveau Statement.

Visitors to the Louvre always head for Leonardo da Vinci's painting of the *Mona Lisa*, arguably the most famous work of art in the world. Yet the Louvre's many different collections contain any number of equally impressive and famous masterpieces. In view of the work involved in the on-going, ambitious Great Louvre Project, the museum has been in a state of constant upheaval for well over a decade, during which time the Pyramid has been built, collections have been re-arranged, government offices have been transferred out of parts of the Louvre to provide more display space.

The work continues, with the Carousel project opposite. So when visiting the Louvre, bear in mind that it is a museum still in a state of flux, especially the exterior. Inside, the superb collections are, as with any other major museum, rotated, so your first port of call should be to the information desk in the entrance (right under the apex of the Pyramid), to get a plan of the collections, and find out which galleries are open and which are closed on any given day, information which you can easily get from any of the multilingual screens displayed around the entrance – the Louvre is decidedly technology-friendly.

The Louvre has several major collections: painting, sculpture, art objects and Mesopotamian, Egyptian, Greek, Etruscan and Roman antiquities.

Do not attempt to see everything in one visit: the result will only be exhaustion, confused impressions and cultural overkill. If you wish, make one preliminary visit, when you can see the really major items, such as the Mona Lisa and the *Venus de Milo*, and also decide which galleries to visit in depth on a subsequent visit –

some of the city's most famous landmarks – in one direction, the **Eiffel Tower** and **le Grand Palais** and in the other, the **Jeu de Paume**, the **Tuileries Gardens**, the **Louvre**, the **Musée d'Orsay** and further down the river, the Cathedral of **Notre Dame**.

Turn back to the Place de la Concorde, on a clear day, you will be able to see the white dome of the 19th century church of **Sacré Coeur**, way to the north of the city. You have witnessed a spectacular panorama of the best of Paris's architecture, palaces, museums – and traffic!

La Place de la Concorde is one of the focal points of revolutionary Paris, and thus modern Paris, for it was here, on 21st January, 1793, that King Louis XVI was guillotined. In a probable attempt at conciliation, the name of the square was later changed from Place de la Révolution to Place de la Concorde. The obelisk at the centre of the square is

or two.

The paintings cover European art from the 14th to the 19th century, and are usually displayed by "school", such as the French school and the Italian school. Although every visitor arrives with his or her own list of favourite paintings, there are many canvases that should not under any circumstance be missed, a few of which are, *David's Coronation of Napoleon*, *The Turkish Bath* by Ingres, *Fra Angelico's Coronation of the Virgin*, *Embarkation for the Island of Cythera* by Watteau, Van Dyck's portrait of *Charles I of England*, and, of course, the *Mona Lisa*.

The sculpture galleries trace the development of sculpture from the French Romanesque period through to the 19th century, and contain such masterpieces as the *Virgin of Isenheim*, a late Middle Age German statue; a Donatello *Virgin and Child*; Michelangelo's *The Slaves*; and *The Three Graces*.

Amongst the art objects displayed in the Louvre are mementos of the French royal family, including the crown jewels, and some spectacular tapestries, pottery and furniture.

The galleries devoted to the art of Mesopotamia trace its civilization from pre-history, through Iranian and Levantine art, to the art of Assyria.

There are remarkable steles and friezes, including the *Stele of the Vultures*, which dates from 2450 BC, the *Stele of Naram-Sin* (2250 BC), the Iranian *Frieze of the Archers*, dating from the sixth century BC, and from the Assyrian palaces of Nineveh, bas-reliefs and giant sculptures.

The Egyptian antiquities cover 30 dynasties, and a historical period from 3000 BC to the birth of Christ. There are sphinxes, mummies, jewellery, statues and bas-reliefs, including a beautiful one depicting King Seti I and the goddess Hathor, which comes from the Valley of the Kings.

In the galleries of Greek, Etruscan and Roman antiquities are some of the Louvre's most well-known sculptures – the *Venus de Milo* and the *Winged Victory of Samothrace*, but there are also fragments of the Parthenon marbles, the sixth century BC *Terracotta Cerveteri Sarcophagus* and one of the earliest examples of Greek sculpture, the rigid, simple statue of the Lady of Auxerre.

over 3,300 years old, and came from the Tomb of Ramses II at the Temple of Luxor. At the far side of the square are two elegant 18th century mansions: to the right, the **Admiralty Office** and to the left, the **Hotel Crillon**, one of the world's luxury hotels. It was at the Crillon, that a *Treaty of Friendship* was signed between the doomed Louis XVI and the 13 independent states of America (whereby France recognised their independence). The treaty was

The Louvre Museum houses some of the world's most precious treasures.

The graceful Notre Dame Cathedral on its own island on the Seine.

signed in 1778. Amongst the American signatories was a certain Mr. Benjamin Franklin.

To the east of the Place de la Concorde, are the **Tuileries Gardens**, now one of the refreshing green "lungs" of Paris, where children sail toy boats on the pond and joggers exercise amongst 19th century statues. Back in the 15th century this was a rubbish dump, and a source of *tuile* (clay) for making tiles – hence the name, Tuileries. As you stand at the entrance to the Tuileries, you can look across the Place de la Concorde, up

Biblical scenes on the west front
of the Notre Dame.

the Champs Élysées, to the Arc de Triomphe, and beyond that, to the new Arche de la Défense – the French sense of symmetry is clearly in evidence. Entering the gardens, there are two pavilions: to the left, the **Jeu de Paume**, and to the right, the **Orangerie**, whose most famous paintings are Monet's **Water-lilies**, displayed in two oval rooms.

The Jeu de Paume's former Impressionist collection has now been transferred across the river to the Musée d'Orsay, and it has become a gallery, housing temporary art exhibitions.

The **Louvre**, now home to one of the world's greatest art collections, is also the world's largest royal palace. The original fortress was built in 1200, and over the centuries, it became a palace. Although a succession of monarchs and heads of state augmented embellishments to the Louvre – *la Pyramide du Louvre,* a glass pyramid in the middle of the Cour Napoléon now serves as a spectacular entrance to the museum. Work still continues on the ambitious refurbishment of the whole Louvre complex.

View of Paris from the sculptured balconies and parapets of the Notre Dame.

Notre Dame & the Ile de la Cité

Continuing down the right bank of the Seine, and across the Pont Neuf, is the **Ile de la Cité**, where you can visit Marie Antoinette's last residence, the austere **Conciergerie** (caretaker's lodge), from where she and nearly 2,000 other prisoners left for the guillotine.

A stroll away from this grim reminder of the revolution is one of the jewels of French Gothic architecture, **La Sainte Chapelle**, consecrated in 1248, and today part of the complex now housing the Paris law courts. The chapel is an architectural masterpiece in its own right, but it is renowned for its

13th century stained glass windows, the oldest in Paris. The 1,134 scenes of the windows form a colourfully illustrated bible.

From La Sainte Chapelle, another short walk brings you to one of the major sights of Paris, the **Cathedral of Notre Dame**, a must for any visitor, and a worthwhile challenge for those who are fit enough to climb up the south tower and take in the panoramic view.

Over 2,000 years ago, a Gallo-Roman temple used to stand on what is now the site of Notre Dame and recent archeological excavations have unearthed Gallo-Roman remains which are exhibited in an underground museum, just in front of the main entrance to the church. Construction of the present cathedral began in 1163 where many royal marriages and ceremonies took place there.

Transformed into a storage depot after the Revolution, Notre Dame survived the onslaught of the 1871 Commune and WWII intact. The statues on the west face portal deserve close attention – they recount episodes from the bible and portray many saints, including Saint Denis, the first bishop of Paris, who is shown holding his own decapitated head.

The organ in the Cathedral, the largest in the country, has recently been restored, a feat of engineering prowess which took two and a half years, involving as it did the complete dismantling of the 8,000 pipes, which were re-fitted with the addition of computers to aid the organist in controlling the notes.

The square in front of the Cathedral, **la Place du Parvis**, is the point from which all road distances from central Paris are measured. Behind Notre Dame, at the tip of the Ile de la Cité is the chillingly stark **Deportation Memorial**, which boasts the tomb of the Unknown Deportee.

Marinas & Squares, the Parrots & the Unknown

Along the river banks, close by Notre Dame are *bouquinistes* (second-hand book-stalls) where you can pick up an antique, or a not-so-antique print, second-hand books and old postcards. Cross

The obelisk at Place de la Bastille.

over the tiny Pont Saint Louis to discover the **Ile Saint Louis**, the second of Paris's two islands and a gem of 17th century architecture with elegant townhouses and cobbled streets.

The **Place de la Bastille** no longer houses the notorious prison, which was stormed by an enraged mob on 14 July, 1789 and killed the seven prisoners inside being released. July 14 is France's national day. Called Bastille Day, it marks the symbolic start of the French Revolution.

The **Place de la Bastille** is now the site for Paris's second opera house, **L' Opéra de la Bastille**, yet another of President Mitterrand's monuments, inaugurated in 1989.

Just next to the Place de la Bastille

Catacombs

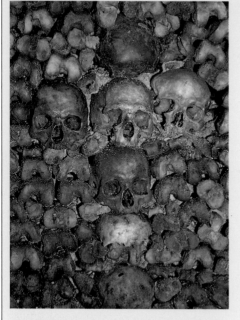

The Paris Catacombs are not for the fainthearted.

Twenty metres below the streets of Paris lies a parallel network of underground galleries filled with millions of skeletons. Macabre, but true. Back in the Gallo-Roman period, three of Paris's *monts* (mountains) were extensively quarried for building stone – Montrouge, Montsouris and Montparnasse. Initially, the mines were open-cast, but as demand for building stone increased, mining went underground to keep pace with the growth of the city. Over the

centuries, several successive levels of galleries were excavated, burrowing deep into yet another *mont* – La Montaigne Sainte Geneviève. Such intensive mining naturally affected the stability of the streets and houses on the surface, and during the Ancien Régime, several royal decrees were issued, aimed at controlling mining operations, but with little success.

In 1774, there was a major accident, when the Rue d'Enfers collapsed 30 metres, prompting the King to set up the office of *L'Inspection Générale des Carrières* (the Surveyor-General of Mines). Under the Empire, a decree banned underground mining in Paris proper. But the quarries of Montrouge, which were situated outside what were then the city limits, continued to be mined and it was not until 1860 that the Montrouge "catacombs" as they were known, came under the administrative control of Paris.

Meanwhile, the other Parisian quarries, which had been earlier abandoned had not been forgotten. The Paris city administration of the late 18th century found itself with another serious problem on its hands. One of the city's oldest cemeteries, **La Cimetière des Innocents**, had existed for over ten centuries, but by the 18th century, it was no longer large enough to cope with the number of corpses being sent there for burial from 20 parishes. It became a breeding ground for infection, so much so that in 1780 local residents complained to the police about the threat to public health. There were apparently so many corpses in the cemetery that its level had risen to over eight feet above the surrounding streets.

In the statement made by the residents, they

is one of Paris's more unusual sights – the **Arsenal Marina**. Walk down the stone steps from the busy Boulevard Bourdon and suddenly you are in a different world.

People are swabbing down their boats, or sitting out on deck gossiping, and only the muffled sound of the traffic

from the Boulevard reminds you that you are in a capital city and not a small coastal harbour.

You can take a boat ride, and follow the course of the Seine as it leaves the Marina and flows into the unexpectedly rural **Canal Saint Martin**, where lock keepers still operate the nine lock gates.

claimed that the air emanating from the cemetery was so foul that it curdled milk and turned wine sour! It took five years for a decision to be made: La Cimetière des Innocents would have to be evacuated, and a new location found to store the thousands of remains from the cemetery.

The place decided upon was the catacombs. So it was that on the 7th April, 1786, the catacombs were consecrated by Roman Catholic priests and the first remains from Les Innocents were transferred, a task that would take until January 1788.

Victims of the French Revolution were buried here, and the remains from other cemeteries which had closed down during the Empire were subsequently moved to the catacombs. It is thought that between six and seven million people are buried in these underground passages.

To visit the catacombs, take the metro to Denfert-Rocherau station, and then follow the signs to *Les Catacombes*, where you can wander at leisure along passages lined with skulls and bones, arranged into rather bizarre patterns. The skeletons are literally banked up on either side of the passageway, in some places to a depth of 30 metres. It is all curiously un-morbid, despite the dramatic sign over the entrance to the ossuary, "Stop! Here is the Empire of death".

As you wander around, reflect on the fact that guided tours of the catacombs began way back in 1812, when visitors were provided with a candle to light their way and told to follow the black line painted on the ceiling of the galleries – the line is still visible today, but you can dispense with the candle!

The Marais Museums & Multi-Culture

The **Marais** district is one of Paris's most beautiful *quartiers* (districts), for in this former *marais* (swamp) are some gems of Parisian architecture.

The Musée d'Orsay has an extensive collection of 19th and 20th century art.

The **Place des Vosges**, originally called the Place Royale, is the oldest square in Paris and in the early 17th century used to be one of the most elegant areas of the city, for Henri IV declared that all the houses should be "built to symmetry".

Nobility and courtiers in the 17th century built elegant townhouses, known as *hôtels*, in the Marais, but with the storming of nearby Bastille, the area was abandoned and fell into almost total neglect, to be restored to its current glory only in the 20th century.

An interesting street is the **Rue des Rosiers**, the heart of the Jewish quarter, where you can find *kosher* products, and delicious central European-style bread and pastries.

There are two major museums in the Marais, the **Musée Carnavalet**, a collection of 17th and 18th century furniture and Paris memorabilia, housed in the Renaissance Hôtel Carnavalet, and the excellent **Picasso Museum**, in the 17th century **Hôtel Salé**.

Modern Art

A short walk away from the elegant surroundings of these museums is a museum cast in a totally different mould – the **Centre Georges Pompidou**, housing the **Museum of Modern Art**. When the Centre was inaugurated in 1977, people were stunned, for this apparently inside-out structure had nothing in common with the surrounding architecture.

A glass building with all the pipes, conduits and even the escalators on the outside, initially shocked Parisians, but they were drawn by the quality of paintings on display in one of the world's most dynamic museums of modern art.

Today, the Centre Pompidou is one of the most visited sights in Paris. After you have admired the works of the *fauves* (wild beasts); the unconventional cu-

bists and the hyper-realists, take the escalator to the rooftop, from where you will see a panorama of typical grey Parisian rooftops and also the cobbled square in front of the museum, which is usually packed with entertainers of all kinds, jugglers, fire-eaters and mime artists – a real feast of street theatre.

Another museum which impresses as much by its architecture as by its collection is the **Musée d'Orsay**, on the left bank of the Seine, opposite the Tuileries Gardens.

The Orsay railway station was built for the 1900 Universal Exhibition, but with the electrification of the railways in 1935, it could no longer handle the longer trains and was closed down and transformed into a museum.

President Pompidou had the idea of transforming the station into a museum of 19th century art, President Giscard d'Estaing started the work, and President Mitterrand, yet again, inaugurated it in 1986. After visiting the collection of 19th and early 20th cen-

Les Halles, a huge modern shopping arcade.

tury art – paintings, sculpture, posters – visit the rooftop cafeteria, not only for its refreshments, but also for its view: you peer out from behind the former station clock, onto the Seine, the Tuileries and the Louvre.

controversial, but ultimately successful. It creates an undeniable impact, forcing people to talk about it.

Paris likes to juxtapose the old and the new, counter posing hallowed buildings with startling new aspects, such as the **Pyramide du Louvre**, and the black and white Buren columns placed in the courtyard of the 17th century **Palais Royal**.

The high-tech architecture of the Pompidou Centre regenerated a decaying district, and the half-subterranean **Forum des Halles** revitalised another. **Les Halles**, which used to be the central provisions market before operations were transferred to Rungis, near Orly Airport, has been given a new lease of life by the construction of the **Forum des Halles**, a huge shopping and entertainment complex.

Sad to say, one kind of insalubrious district has been replaced by another, for Les Halles has become a magnet for drifters, drunks and vice.

However, it is fun to visit. You descend four levels underground and the

Architectural Incongruity & Revival

Parisian architecture is a constant stimulus, often

The Arc De Triomphe dominates the Champs Elysee.

Pigalle

Montmartre attractions.

Pigalle. Le Moulin Rouge and le Moulin de la Galette; artists and cabaret dancers; Toulouse-Lautrec and Jane Avril; drinkers and *poseurs* (affected persons) … The very word "Pigalle" seems to sum up all that is naughty about Paris, or, at least, all that people think is naughty. Today, Pigalle tries hard to live up to the expectations of the hoards of visitors who come looking for traces of the Naughty Nineties (of the 1890s variety) and instead find naughtiness 1990s style.

Pigalle, with its dubious cinemas and peep-shows, is at the foot of probably the most famous of the hills in Paris – **Montmartre**, home to innumerable artists and writers, briefly an independent commune in the 19th century and the site of the only vineyard in Paris.

In the late 18th century, the gypsum and flint mines under Montmartre were closed, but their existence lives on in the name of one of Pigalle's squares, **Place Blanche** (white), whose name refers to the white plaster from the quarries. In the early 19th century, Montmartre was a pretty country village way outside Paris. Since Baron Haussmann had not yet built the wide streets and avenues that would so alter the physiognomy of Paris, access to Montmartre was difficult and land was consequently cheap. Artists gradually settled there, and the inhabitants of *la Butte* (the knoll) read like a roll call of the French literary and artistic scene of the 19th century – Berlioz, Heinrich Heine, Toulouse-

shopping is good – but you need to be on your guard as you walk around the area.

The futuristic glass and steel architecture of the Forum is offset by the Gothic lines of the neighbouring church

Lautrec, Renoir, Van Gogh, Utrillo. The artists congregated in cafés and bars, or at the Moulin Rouge nightclub, whose singers and dancers such as Jane Avril and La Goulue were immortalised by Toulouse-Lautrec.

Today, coachloads of visitors follow in the artistic steps of these 19th century bohemians, gravitating to the pretty **Place du Tertre**, which still manages to retain a charming, village atmosphere about it, especially in the mornings, before Montmartre has welcomed its day's quota of visitors. Later in the day, artists of varying kinds, skill and price set up their easels on the cobbled stones of Place du Tertre, and visitors stroll, sit and have their portrait sketched, or sip a drink at a pavement café. Dominating Montmartre is the striking, white basilica of **Sacré Coeur** (Sacred Heart), an integral part of the Paris skyline, with its 19th century Romano-Byzantine inspired cupolas and dome. From the dome there is a superb view of the city and on the steps in front of the church you can sit and listen to folk musicians, gospel singers and would-be rock stars. On sunny weekend afternoons, the steps are packed with spectators, and you can hear the singing and applause from the unexpectedly quiet residential streets that still exist on La Butte.

One of the surprises of this admittedly major tourist area is the existence of a tiny vineyard: the **Montmartre Vineyard.** The vineyard celebrates the start of its grape harvest on the first Saturday of October, and if you ask for it in local restaurants, you can taste the wine which is usually consumed exclusively in the cafés and restaurants around the Butte. Around the vineyard are pretty ivy-covered houses, little flights of steps, and the famous, rustic-looking *Au Lapin Agile* Bar, the haunt of well-known writers and artists in the early 20th century, which is now haunted by late-20th century hopefuls. This area has a picturesque charm, making it hard to believe that a short distance down the hill are the sex shops and tourist bars of the

of **Saint Eustache** and the 19th century circular **Commercial Exchange** building.

Boulevard de Clichy.

At the beginning of this century, there were still many windmills on Montmartre, but only a couple are still in existence today. The picturesque **Moulin de la Galette** and on the corner of Rue Lepic, the **Radet windmill**. The history of this latter mill is interesting, for it originally stood in the city, on a hillock which was demolished in 1668. The windmill was preserved and transferred to Montmartre, and only the name Rue des Moulins (Windmill Street) indicates that a street near the Louvre was its earlier home.

As befits its bohemian neighbourhood, Montmartre Cemetery is the last resting place of many artists, amongst them the Russian dancer Nijinsky, the Impressionist painter Degas, some former residents of the area, such as Berlioz and Heine and the artist Poulbot, whose line drawings of local, wide-eyed children, which are now sold in scores of souvenir shops, have come to epitomise the spirit of Pigalle.

The Moulin Rouge, was immortalized by artist Toulouse-Lautrec.

The futuristic architecture at La Défense.

Promenades along Les Grands Boulevards

North of Les Halles are those wide 19th century streets known collectively as **Les Grands Boulevards**: Boulevard des Italiens, now home to many cinema halls and corporate headquarters, Boulevard Haussmann, home to many of Paris's best known department stores (for more details see the chapter on Shopping) and named in honour of the 19th century Prefect of Paris, Baron

everyday. Just before the Avenue de l'Opéra meets the Rue de Rivoli and the Louvre, is the **Comédie Française** one of the best known theatres in Paris, where you can see performances penned by such classical playwrights as Molière, Corneille and Racine.

Next to the Comédie Française is the 17th century **Palais Royal**, the former residence of Cardinal Richelieu, which he willed to King Louis XIII in 1642. The gardens of the Palais Royal are a favourite place for a lunch-time stroll for many of the people who work in the Banque de France, the antique shops of the **Louvre des Antiquaires** shopping complex opposite, or the countless souvenir shops on the Rue de Rivoli nearby.

Arc de Triomphe

From the western side of Place de la Concorde, the **Avenue des Champs Elysées** leads to one of Napoléon's architectural projects, the **Arc de Triomphe** (Arch of Triumph) designed to commemorate Napoleonic victories. Initially there were only five roads leading off from the Arc de Triomphe, but 20 years after its delayed inauguration in 1836, Baron Haussmann redesigned the surrounding square, creating another seven roads, which is why, today, most Parisians refer to the Place around the Arc de Triomphe as – *L'Étoile*, (the star). On 11th November, 1920, the body of an unknown soldier was placed under

Haussmann, who was responsible for much of the modernization of the city. At the junction of Boulevard des Italiens and Boulevard des Capucines is the **Opéra**, designed by Charles Garnier and inaugurated in 1875.

Even if you are unable to attend a performance at the Opéra, you can always visit the theatre, which is open

The Eiffel Tower as seen from the Trocadero.

the arch and three years later, to the day, the flame of remembrance was lit. If you wish to see Paris driving at its worst, (or best, depending on your loyalties), stand at the Arc de Triomphe, and watch 12 streams of traffic doing battle.

The view from the top of the Arc de Triomphe is superb, for not only can you appreciate the symmetry of Haussmann's construction, but you can also see two of President Mitterrand's architectural additions – the Pyramide du Louvre in one direction, and diametrically opposite, the **Grande Arch de la Défense**, just over the western boundary of Paris. On the horizon, you will be able to see the distinctive white dome of the church of **Sacré Coeur**, on the hill of Montmartre. To get to Mont-

martre, take the metro to either Pigalle, Abbesses or Anvers Station, and then take the only funicular railway in Paris to the base of the church. (see box story on Pigalle p 160).

Eiffel Tower

Another Paris landmark that is clearly visible from the top of the Arc de Triomphe is the **Eiffel Tower**, probably the city's most famous symbol. Like any piece of innovative Parisian architecture, the Tower came in for a lot of initial opposition when it was completed in 1889 from a design executed by Gustave Eiffel. Garnier, who designed the Opéra, signed a letter of protest, as did the writers Dumas the Younger and Guy de Maupassant.

In 1909 it was nearly dismantled, but was saved simply because its huge antenna was essential for French radio telegraphy. If you ascend only one monument in Paris, make it the Eiffel Tower: the amazing view from the third platform extends for 65 kilometres on a really clear day.

Lesser Known Sites

Exploring Paris is a constant journey of discovery, which includes less famous, but equally fascinating places. For example, there is the **Jardin des Plantes**, (Botanical Gardens), surrounded by an intriguingly diverse potpourri of places

If you haven't lost your breath walking up the Eiffel Tower, you will at the view from above.

reasons.

You can visit the **Panthéon**, a monument built in the 18th century, to honour France's great men – or go to **Père Lachaise Cemetery** and pay your respects to more bohemian souls, such as Oscar Wilde, Jim Morrison and Edith Piaf, or even visit the **Animal Cemetery** in Asnières, just outside the Péripherique, where family pets are remembered with elaborate statues. See Paris' very own, but smaller version of the **Statue of Liberty**, on a pretty little island called the Allée des Cygnes, in the 15th *arrondissement* (district); the **Russian Orthodox Cathedral**; and the **statue of the Zouave soldier** on the Pont de l'Alma, the popular Paris highwater marker.

– the **Paris Mosque**, the Gallo-Roman **Lutetia Arena** and the recently constructed **Institute of the Arab World**, with its innovative architecture. You can visit the **Gobelins Tapestry Factory**, where carpets, made exclusively for the use of the French state, are still woven by hand using 17th century methods.

A very different but intriguing trip is to visit the 2,100 kilometre long Paris **sewer system**, complete with high-tech audio-visual displays – but remember, there are no visits when the Seine is in flood, or after heavy rains, for obvious

You can watch the annual waiters' race, when hundreds of waiters and waitresses run through the streets, balancing bottles and glasses on trays, to the cheers of thousands of spectators, or join in the Montmartre wine festival; ride on the open platform of the #29 bus, or watch dazzling displays of skateboarding at the **Palais de Chaillot** – the City of Lights is made up of an elaborate patchwork of museums, galleries, gardens, churches, fountains, shops, cafés and Paris has something to captivate everyone, any time of the year.

The Ile de France, whose name means Island of France, is, along with Paris, one of the most historic parts of the country, and houses an impressive number of palaces, abbeys, fortresses and forests. Sprawling suburbs have spread outwards from the city, creeper-like, surrounding the palaces and the abbeys and encircling the city.

However, there are still large tracts of forest, which were formerly the favourite hunting grounds of the French monarchy, who built country residences outside Paris. Today, these forests are a vital breathing space for urban families, who flock there on weekends to picnic, to ride, to walk, and to relax.

Today, the Ile de France is a compromise between urbanisation and history, between development and the environment. There are new towns such as Saint Quentin-en-Yvelines, which are less than 20 years old and churches such as the Basilica of

Ile de France

167

The grandeur of Versailles' March Hall.

The stunning Gothic interior of the Basilica of Saint Denis, burial place for many a French king.

Saint Denis, which are over 800 years old. There are three airports – Roissy, Orly and Le Bourget, one of the country's leading universities – HEC and one of Europe's leading business schools – INSEAD. There are also small country towns whose names are immortalised by their products, such as Brie and Coulommiers, some of France's best known cheeses, and Pithiviers whose speciality is a delicious almond cake of the same name.

Holy Places

Journeying north from Paris on the A1 auto-route, before you reach Roissy Airport, you will see the **Basilica of Saint Denis** towering above the rows of suburban homes. The backdrop may be uninspiring, but the magnificent Basilica, the first major Gothic building and the inspiration for Notre Dame and Chartres Cathedral, is impressive.

The origins of what would later become the burial place of the French monarchy for 12 centuries, goes back to Saint Denis himself, the first bishop of Paris. In AD250 Saint Denis was tortured and beheaded, but legend has it that he picked up his severed head, and walked north, finally collapsing at the site of the Basilica that now bears his name. Further north, surrounded by woods and lakes, is another important religious monument, the **Abbey of Royaumont**, founded in 1228 by Saint Louis.

Statue of Louis XIV at Versailles.

The Abbey, 37 kilometres from Paris, was favoured by the French monarchs, who financed most of its construction, and who were later buried there, before being transferred years later to Saint Denis. Although in ruins, you can see the impressive Gothic architecture of the cloisters and the refectory, where Saint Louis himself served the monks.

Chateaux

A few kilometres further north, driving through the Forest of Chantilly is the **Château de Chantilly**, seat of the Montmorency family and today home to **Le Musée Condé**, a museum housing the superb family collections. Although the château and its gardens suffered during the Revolution, the family restored it, and today you can visit not only the château and its museum, but also its formal gardens and an equestrian museum, housed in the 18th century stables.

A few kilometres from Chantilly is the historic little town of **Senlis**, where, in AD987, Hugues Capet succeeded to the French throne, after the accidental death of Louis V put an end to the Carolingan Dynasty. You can still see traces of the Gallo-Roman city wall, and visit the only museum to commemorate staghunting in Europe. The museum is housed in an 18th century priory. The Cathedral, dating from 1153, is crowned with a 13th century spire.

Thirty-two kilometres to the northwest is the **Château of Compiègne**, whose origins go back to 1374, but which was the favourite of later kings and emperors. Louis XIV used to regularly visit Compiègne, but found it too small for his entourage, and complained "At Versailles, I am lodged like a king, at Fontainebleau like a prince, and at Compiègne like a peasant". He had new wings built, and Louis XV began further construction work, which was continued under Louis XVI. After the Revolution, in 1806, Compiègne was restored, and became the residence of the Emperor Napoléon. Compiègne has been the backdrop for many momentous events, from engagements to peace treaties. The palace witnessed the engagement ceremonies of the future Louis XVI

ILE DE FRANCE

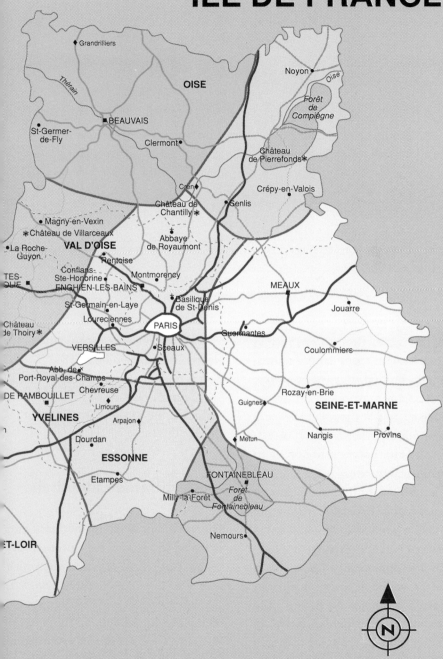

Grandrilliers

Thérain

OISE

Noyon

Oise

Forêt de Compiègne

BEAUVAIS

St-Germer-de-Fly

Clermont

Château de Pierrefonds ✳

Creil

Crépy-en-Valois

Château de Chantilly ✳

Senlis

Magny-en-Vexin

✳ Château de Villarceaux

Abbaye de Royaumont

VAL D'OISE

La Roche-Guyon

Pontoise

TES-
QUE

Conflans-Ste-Honorine

Montmorency

MEAUX

ENGHIEN-LES-BAINS

St-Germain-en-Laye

Basilique de St-Denis

Jouarre

Château de Thoiry ✳

Louveciennes

PARIS

Guermantes

VERSAILLES

Sceaux

Coulommiers

Abb. de Port-Royal-des-Champs

DE RAMBOUILLET

Chevreuse

Rozay-en-Brie

SEINE-ET-MARNE

Limours

Guignes

YVELINES

Arpajon

ESSONNE

Dourdan

Melun

Nangis

Provins

Etampes

FONTAINEBLEAU

Milly-la-Forêt

Forêt de Fontainebleau

ET-LOIR

Nemours

N

The Queen's Hamlet, Versailles.

and Marie-Antoinette; the first meeting of Napoléon with Marie-Louise of Austria, whom he had married by proxy; and in 1832, the marriage of Louise, the daughter of Louis-Philippe with Léopold of Saxe-Cobourg, the first King of Belgium. Part of the palace now houses an excellent car museum.

The treaties signalling the formal ending of both WWI and WWII were signed in the forest of Compiègne, at the "*Clairière de l'Armistice*" (glade of the armistice) in a railway carriage. Just a couple of kilometres southwest of Compiègne, through the forest, is the **Château of Pierrefonds**, a 19th century restoration of a 12th century castle. In 1617, the castle of Pierrefonds was destroyed, after the lord of the castle un-

successfully rebelled against the king. Nearly 200 years later, in 1813, Napoléon I bought the ruins for less than 3,000 francs, and in 1857 Napoléon III entrusted the restoration to Viollet-le-Duc.

Celebrated Cathedrals

The last major site in the northern part of the Ile de France is the extraordinary Gothic **Cathedral of Beauvais**, which rises over the totally ordinary modern city which was rebuilt after being badly bombed in June 1940.

The construction of the Cathedral was very long and very eventful. In 1247, construction of the chancel was

Euro Disney

On 12th April, 1992, a theme park in the flat countryside to the east of Paris was opened, and the controversial Euro Disney finally opened its doors to what the owners hoped would be the first of millions of visitors. With the arrival of Mickey Mouse and the Magic Kingdom just a short train ride from Paris, a decade of wrangling and dissent moved to a different, higher gear.

The French view, both official and unofficial, of Euro Disney has long been confused, for although they vociferously criticise the dominance of American culture, the French government did everything it could to attract Disney to the country, giving them a prime site close to Paris at derisory rates. This, not surprisingly, provoked the anger of the French agricultural lobby, who resented such good land being given over to a theme park. The plot sold to Euro Disney in 1987 was one-fifth the size of Paris itself, and given the then-prevalent boom in property prices, big profits were predicted. Land concessions were not the government's only ploy to secure the arrival of Mickey Mouse, they also offered loans at concessionary rates and agreed to finance the extension of the high-speed TGV train from Paris, to the land of Mickey Mouse.

Once construction of the theme park got underway, French criticism moved on from material issues like land and interest rates, to the cultural impact of middle America on suburban France. Mickey was lambasted as bringing about a "cultural Chernobyl", with his alien language and his alien culture. The Americans compromised – signs in the park would be in French as well as in English, and, to everyone's surprise, even Walt Disney suddenly acquired French ancestors, his name apparently originally coming from the little Norman town of Isigny.

Euro Disney opened, the spring and early summer crowds came, but paradoxically, there were criticisms of over-crowding and the resulting long queues. The farmers, still angered by this alien presence, took to blocking access to the park in the early weeks of the school holidays and by early August, just 100 days after its opening, Euro Disney itself was predicting a loss in its first year of operation. There were various facts to be faced up to. First, the weather in northern France is not that of Florida or California, where Mickey also has his Kingdoms. In France it rains, often in the summer, and no one likes to queue in the rain. Also, officials quickly realized that although British and German visitors were coming in higher than expected numbers, the French, on the other hand, were failing to come. As to why this was so, hypothetical answers abounded: theme parks are just not part of the French way of life, the French are some of the world's worst queuers, unlike the more disciplined Anglo-Saxons and language is a barrier. Perhaps it was none of these, and speculation began that paradoxically, Euro Disney's proximity to Paris was actually a possible disadvantage, for, faced with an abundance of things to do in the capital itself, many holidaymakers simply do not reckon that Mickey deserves a whole day away from the charms of Mona Lisa or the Eiffel Tower.

Unfortunately for Euro Disney, the downturn in the global economy has not helped its prospects, and the expected property gains have not materialized, which have had a negative impact on its medium-term financing. People are also travelling less, spending less, and by the time Euro Disney entered its first winter season, ticket prices were being reduced, in an effort to attract the crucial local French visitors in this bleak vacation time.

By the time the park celebrates the first anniversary of its opening, it will no longer be run by an American, but by a Frenchman. Now, all Mickey and his friends can do is pray for an upswing in the economy and lots of good weather.

started, but the plans required a height of 48 metres at the keystone of the arches, and an internal roof height of 68 metres. To build such a high ceiling was technically extremely demanding, and it took 25 years for the chancel to be built. But, in 1284, it collapsed, and it was to take another 40 years and vast

Fontainebleau Palace, the Cour des Adieux (Courtyard of the Farewell) from where Napoléon took leave of his troops.

sums of money to reconstruct it.

The Hundred Years War put an end to any further work and it was not until 1500, that construction was restarted. But, once again, money was lacking. After an appeal to Pope Léon X, who himself was struggling to raise money to build Saint Peter's in Rome, the Bishop of Beauvais was authorised to sell indulgences – licences from the Pope which granted remission from purgatorial penance, for confessed sin – which raised enough money so that construction work was able to restart. In 1550, the transept

The southern half of the Ile de France has a Cathedral that cannot boast such a troubled history as Beauvais, but which dazzles by its beauty – **Chartres**, whose 12th and 13th century stained glass windows are among the finest in the country. On the site of the Cathedral was originally a Roman temple, and later, five successive Christian churches, which were later destroyed by fire. Most of the current structure was built after the fire of 1194, and Chartres somehow managed to emerge unscathed from the Hundred Years War, the Revolution, and two World Wars.

The carvings on the *Portail Royal* (Royal Portal), were originally columns which were later carved into statues, which explains the rigidity of the bodies, although the faces of the statues are amazingly alive. The *chef d'oeuvre* (masterpiece), of Chartres is its stained glass, which was donated not only by the royal family and nobility, but also by the craft guilds, whose daily life is represented amongst the saints and the scenes from the Bible. The royal palace of **Fontainebleau** is situated east of Chartres in a forest where, from the 12th century onwards, the kings of France used to hunt. A manor house was built, to be replaced by a 16th century palace, during the reign of François I. Successive kings embellished the palace, which is an interesting combination of a relatively sober exterior and a very exuberant interior, executed by a team of Italian artists. The courtyard in front of the principal façade of the palace is known

was finally completed.

The drama of Beauvais was however, far from over, for instead of constructing the nave of the church, a tower topped by a spire was built. In 1573, without the necessary buttressing, the tower inevitably collapsed, and the Cathedral was to remain forever without a spire and nave.

Versailles "A Garden For a Great Child"

Marie Antoinette, wife of Louis XVI.

In 1739, long before the Revolution swept away the French nobility, Horace Walpole had several fairly trenchant comments to make about Versailles: "… The garden is littered with statues and fountains…There are avenues of waterpots, which (sic) disport themselves much in squirting up…In short, 'tis a garden for a great child. Such was Louis *quatorze*…"

Perhaps some of this description was justifiable – Versailles even had its own imitation village, a group of 12 thatched cottages, where Marie-Antoinette, used to dress up and pretend at being a peasant – but it was also the scene of momentous events in real history, invaded by live peasants and Parisians who in the name of the Republic put an end to this dream chapter in French history.

The palace that today symbolizes the opulence of pre-revolutionary France, began life as a farm on a hillock, surrounded by game-filled marshes. Louis XIII used to hunt in the area. In 1624 he bought land, in order to build himself

a *pied à terre* (temporary lodging for this purpose). After more than 50 years of major construction, ambitious landscaping and even the damming of rivers to feed the ornamental fountains so belittled by Walpole, the *pied à terre* had become the Palace of Versailles, the glittering centrepiece of the French court.

In 1682, Louis XIV moved into Versailles, with his entourage of 20,000 courtiers, servants and soldiers. Louis, (also known as the Sun King), encouraged the nobility to spend time, and money, at Versailles – that way, he could keep control over any opposition to his rule, and could slowly ruin his aristocrats by their own lavish spending. After his death, the court moved back to Paris and it was not until 1722 that Louis XV moved again to Versailles. Lack of money prevented Louis from undertaking any major construction work at Versailles, other than the Palace of the Petit Trianon, so beloved by his ill-fated daughter-in-law, Marie Antoinette. Marie-Antoinette and her husband, Louis XVI were the last monarchs to live at Versailles.

Versailles is a vast complex, set amidst gardens and woods, and even today is dazzling and resplendent. The château's most famous room is the *Galerie des Glaces* (Gallery of Mirrors) where 578 mirrors reflect the light from the large picture windows. This gallery was the social centre of the palace, where the balls, *soirées* (parties) and the reception of ambassadors took place, the guests no doubt suitably impressed by the solid silver furniture Louis XIV had made. The château had separate suites for the king, queen, *dauphin* (the eldest son of the King), dauphin's wife and even for the royal mistresses. There are suites for Madame de Maintenon, Louis XIV's mistress of over 30 years and for two of Louis XV's mistresses, La Marquise de Pompadour and Madame du Barry. But since so much pomp and opulence inevitably palled, the kings needed smaller retreats, (especially to be alone with their mistresses), the solution was a small palace which was built on the grounds of Versailles, called **Le Grand Trianon**. The first palace, which dated from 1670, was only used for Louis XIV's *tête à têtes* with Madame de Montespan, but the building

The Grand Trianon, Versailles.

du Barry, who entertained the king there. Louis XVI gave it to his wife, Marie-Antoinette, and it became her favourite retreat. She went there almost everyday, with her children and her maids, to escape from palace etiquette, and to play in the village.

This delightful retreat was however interrupted forever on 5th October, 1789, when a courtier ran into the gardens of the Petit Trianon, to inform the Queen that a mob was marching from Paris to Versailles. Marie-Antoinette left the Trianon for the last time, and the following day the royal family left Versailles for Paris, imprisonment and execution four years later.

became unsafe, and Madame fell from royal favour, so a new palace was built, a new mistress found, and Louis continued his *tête à têtes* – this time with Madame de Maintenon.

Louis XV also wanted a hideaway, and so he built **Le Petit Trianon** at the instigation of the Marquise de Pompadour. But, she died before it was finished, so it was her successor, Madame

Louis XVI held many intimate tête á têtes at the Grand Trianon.

Statue of Apollo and horses in the Gardens of Versailles.

either as the *"Cour du Cheval-Blanc"* (White Horse Courtyard), or as the *Cour des Adieux* (Courtyard of the Farewell) since it was here that Napoléon Bonaparte took farewell of his weeping sol-diers, before leaving for exile on the island of Elba in 1814.

Close to Fontainebleau is the pretty little town of **Moret-sur-Loing**, immortalised in the paintings of the Impres-

Between Fontainebleau and Paris is the beautiful 17th century **Château of Vaux-le-Vicomte**, a palace that was built to be ostentatious, but which proved to be its ambitious owner's undoing. Fouquet, the Finance Secretary under Louis XIV, built Vaux-le-Vicomte using the finest artists of the day – the architect Le Vau, the designer Le Brun, and the landscape gardener Le Nôtre.

On 17th August, 1661, Fouquet invited the king to a reception given in his honour in the newly completed château, but the lavishness of the evening only succeeded in making Louis so jealous that he was ready to arrest his host that very night. The queen persuaded him otherwise, but Louis was infuriated by an opulence that outdid his own – 500 dozen silver plates were used to serve dinner, and particularly galling, a solid gold dinner service was provided for the king's use – Louis had been obliged to have his own service melted down, to defray some of the expenses of the Thirty Years War.

Nineteen days after the fateful party, Fouquet was arrested, his goods confiscated, and after a trial, he was sentenced to banishment, a verdict subsequently changed to life imprisonment. Louis XIV used the same artists and ordered them to build a palace even more beautiful than Vaux-le-Vicomte, by the name of Versailles (see box story page 176).

East of Vaux-le-Vicomte, is the pretty little town of **Provins**, whose old section seems to have little changed since its

sionist painter Sisley, who spent the last 20 years of his life there. Nine and a-half kilometres to the northwest of Fontainebleau is the village of **Barbizon** which was the focal point of a 19th century group of artists and writers, amongst them the painters Corot, Rousseau, Millet and Daumier.

The celebrated Hall of Mirrors, Versailles, where the WWI Peace Treaty was signed.

heyday in the 12th and 13th century. The ramparts still stand, as does the 12th century keep, the *Tour de César*, from where a superb view over the town can be enjoyed. The **Château of**

Rambouillet has been the summer residence of the Presidents of France since 1897. Thus, it can only be visited when the President is not in residence.

Rambouillet was built in 1375 and

leon spent his last night as Emperor in Rambouillet, before his departure to Saint Helena, and in 1830, Charles X fled to Rambouillet, from where he announced his abdication.

Among the more interesting of the smaller *châteaux* in the Ile de France are Anet, Saint Germain-en Laye and Thoiry. The 16th century **Château of Anet** was the residence of Diane de Poitiers, mistress of Henri II and rival of Queen Catherine de Medicis.

On the death of Henri, the Queen took her revenge on the mistress, Diane's beloved Château de Chenonceau was taken from her and Diane retired to Anet, where she died. (For more details, see Loire Valley chapter p 183).

The château of **St Germain-en-Laye** is easily reached from Paris on the commuter train network, the RER, and in addition to the 16th century fort, houses the **Museum of National Antiquities**, an excellent museum of artefacts ranging from pre-history to the Merovingan period. Very few people visit **Thoiry** for its 16th century buildings. Instead they came to visit the **African Game Park**, in the grounds of the château, where they can see the very un-French sight of lions, elephants and tigers, all a mere 45 kilometres away from Paris.

At the **Fondation Cartier**, in the little town of **Jouy-en-Josas**, 21 kilometres southwest of Paris, you can visit an open-air museum of modern sculpture, and a fascinating display of counterfeit goods – ranging from Cartier watches to spare automobile parts.

was considerably enlarged and improved in the early 18th century, after which it passed into the hands of the royal family.

Queen Marie-Antoinette disliked Rambouillet, which she found dull, despite the little dairy built along the same lines as the hamlet in Versailles. Napo-

Loire Valley

D riving south from Paris along the A10, you arrive at Orléans, situated on the banks of the Loire River. Leaving the *autoroute* (motorway), follow the course of the Loire, France's longest river, as it heads west towards Angers. But be warned, it can take you days, even weeks to cover these 214 kilometres, for along the bank of the Loire are the greatest concentration of palaces and *châteaux* to be found anywhere in France. From the grandeur of the royal palace of Chambord, to the relative simplicity of a small *château* like Saché, from the fortified castle of Amboise, to the elegant gardens of Villandry, the Loire Valley has a range of sites that make a quick drive along the river impossible.

During the 17th and 18th centuries, the river was a major highway for the movement of goods, and a system of canals linked it to the River

■ ■ ■ ■ ■ ■

The grand fortress Chateau of Saumur houses two museums.

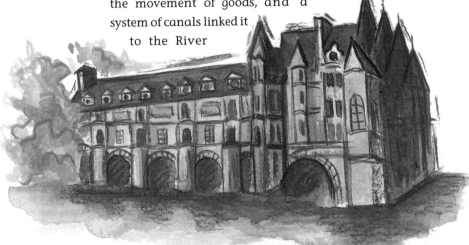

Chambord, the largest chateau in the Loire.

Seine, allowing goods to be transported directly to Paris. Now, it is a major tourist route.

Chambord

West of Orléans, the first *château* on the itinerary should be **Chambord**, the largest of the Loire *châteaux*. A massive, turreted vision, which dazzles not only by its architecture, but by its statistics – a façade 128 metres long, 440 rooms, 365 chimneys – one for every day of the year – and a famous double staircase, that allows people to both ascend and descend without ever meeting. The whole building is also surrounded by the longest wall in France, 32 kilometres long.

Chambord is indeed a fitting introduction to the extravagant and colourful royal history of the Loire.

King François I started the construction of Chambord in 1519, allegedly accordingly to plans drawn up by Leonardo da Vinci. Chambord rapidly became an obsession even when the Treasury ran out of money and he was unable to pay the King of Spain the ransom demanded for the release of his own two sons, François continued the construction of Chambord, appropriating church treasures to finance his dream.

Molière wrote some of his plays there, which were later premiered for Louis XIV. Louis XV later gave Chambord to the Maréchal de Saxe, the illegiti-

Cheverny Chateau, a supreme example of the architectural style of Louis XII.

mate son of a Polish ruler and a larger-than-life military figure, who installed two regiments in the grounds and had wrong-doers hanged from a tree.

Blois

Blois, which began life as a feudal castle, is a showcase of the best of the architectural styles from the 13th to the 17th centuries. Its most celebrated feature is the Renaissance façade, with the *escalier François I* (Francis I's staircase), a five-storey spiral staircase housed in an octagonal case. Blois was the seat of one of the most powerful French families in the Middle Ages, the counts of Blois, from whom the Capetian kings of France

were descended.

In 1429, Joan of Arc set out from Blois, to raise the siege of Orléans. In 1498 Louis XII ascended the throne, and, deeply attached to his birthplace of Blois, he made it virtually the second capital of France, a pre-eminence that would continue until the end of the 16th century.

On 23 December, 1588, a violent murder took place on the second floor of the château when the Duc de Guise (Duke of Guise), who had been plotting with Spain to usurp the French throne and depose King Henri III, was murdered. The next day, the Duc's brother, the Cardinal de Lorraine was also assassinated, and the corpses of the two brothers were burned, and their ashes thrown

LOIRE VALLEY

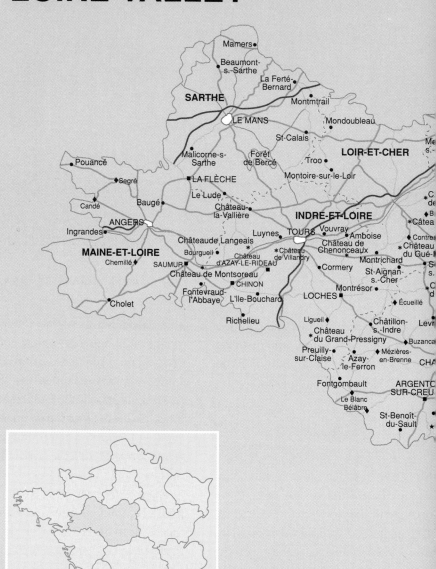

Mamers

Beaumont-
s.-Sarthe

La Ferté-
Bernard

Montmtrail

SARTHE

Mondoubleau

LE MANS

St-Calais

Me
s.-

LOIR-ET-CHER

Pouancé

Malicorne-s-
Sarthe

Forêt
de Bercé

Troo

Segré

LA FLÈCHE

Montoire-sur-le-Loir

C
de

Candé

Baugé

Le Lude

B

INDRE-ET-LOIRE

Câtea

Ingrandes

ANGERS

Château-
la-Vallière

Luynes

TOURS

Vouvray

C

Châteaude Langeais

Amboise

Contre

MAINE-ET-LOIRE

Bourgueil

Château
de Villandry

Château

Château de
Chenonceaux

Château
du Gué-

Chemillé

SAUMUR

Château
d'AZAY-LE-RIDEAU

Montrichard

S

Château de Montsoreau

CHINON

Cormery

St-Aignan-
s.-Cher

s.

Fontevraud-
l'Abbaye

L'Ile-Bouchard

Montrésor

C
d

Cholet

LOCHES

Écueillé

Richelieu

Ligueil

Châtillon-
s.-Indre

Levr

Château
du Grand-Pressigny

Buzanca

Preuilly-
sur-Claise

Azay-
le-Ferron

Mézières-
en-Brenne

CHA

Fontgombault

**ARGENTO
SUR-CREU**

Le Blanc

Bélâbre

St-Benoît-
du-Sault

Emblems come in all shapes
and forms.

into the Loire. A few days later, the
Queen Mother, Catherine de Medici died
in a room just below the spot where the
Duc was killed.

In 1617, Louis XIII had his mother,
Marie de Medici imprisoned in Blois,
where she spent two comfortable years,
before making a dramatic escape down
a rope ladder into the moat – her large
girth notwithstanding. Possibly her gym-
nastic exploits impressed her son, for
they were soon reconciled!

Cheverny, Chaumont &
Chenonceau

Cheverny, a little to the south of the
river, is a haven of peace and sobriety

The Chateau of Chenonceau, "The Castle of Six Women".

after the exuberances of Chambord and Blois. It was built in a relatively short period of time, between 1604 and 1634, and as a result is a particularly harmonious example of the architectural style of Louis XII and is of a much simpler style than that of other neighbouring châteaux. The interior of Cheverny is much more opulent than the exterior – for example, the ceiling and panelling

bridge lends a distinctly military air to the castle. One of Chaumont's most notorious residents was the Florentine astrologer, Cosimo Ruggieri, a protégé of Catherine de Medicis. Catherine allowed Ruggieri to install his laboratory in a tower, from where, legend has it, he would conjure up the faces of Catherine's sons and the destiny that awaited them. Catherine acquired Chaumont in 1560, with the avowed aim of seeking revenge on Diane de Poitiers, the mistress of her late husband, King Henri II. Knowing how attached her rival was to the Palace of Chenonceau, Catherine bought Chaumont and then forced Diane to exchange Chenonceau for Chaumont. Catherine was exultant, but Diane stopped only fleetingly at Chaumont, retiring to Anet, where she died seven years later.

Amboise

Only part of the fortifications of the **Château d'Amboise** remain today, situated high on a rocky outcrop, towering over the town. The site was fortified during the Gallo-Roman period and modified many times over the centuries. In the 11th century, there were even two fortresses on the rock and a third in the town below. The three constantly fought amongst themselves.

Amboise was at the height of its influence in the 15th century, under Louis XI and Charles VIII, who was born there. Charles was impressed by the

of the *Grand Salon* (Grand Drawing Room) are painted in gold, as is the King's bedroom which is the most dazzling room in the *château*.

Chaumont was built between 1445 and 1510, on the site of two earlier fortresses, and the entrance over a draw-

Chenonceau

Chenonceau is often described as "the castle of six women", for over a period of 400 years, six women had a major influence on the castle's history.

The castle originally belonged to the de Marques family, who, by the late 15th century, were financially ruined with the family fortunes squandered. Thomas Bohier, a district tax collector under Charles VIII, Louis XII and François I, had long had designs on the property and as the impoverished family sold off their lands, piece by piece, he bought them all.

The de Marques family struggled to keep Thomas Bohier at bay, but after 20 years, in 1512, the fight was over, Bohier bought the castle for 12,500 francs, and immediately razed it to the ground, sparing only the keep. The current structure was built between 1513 and 1521.

Bohier gave the responsibility for much of the construction of the new castle to his wife, Catherine Briçonnet, the first of Chenonceau's "six women". Catherine had a lasting influence on the castle, for she envisaged things with a practical, feminine eye. For example, rooms were constructed around a central hall, making the serving of meals much easier.

After so many years spent scheming for Chenonceau, ultimately Thomas Bohier did not live long enough to enjoy his triumph, for he died in 1524, followed two years later by Catherine. After Bohier's death, King François I had the accounts examined and discovered that large sums of money were owing to the richness and elegance of contemporary Italy so he decorated Amboise with Italian furniture and paintings and had the gardens landscaped by an Italian gardener.

On the afternoon of 7th April, 1498, Charles accompanied his wife to a game of tennis and hit his head on a low doorway. He sat through the game, chatting normally, until he suddenly collapsed, unconscious. By 11 pm, he was dead.

In 1560, Amboise again figured in history, with the mass execution of the Huguenots, who wanted to petition the King at Blois for the freedom to practise their religion. The court abandoned Blois, for the more defensible fortress of Amboise and as the Huguenots arrived they were systematically executed – some were hanged from the balcony of the castle, others from the battlements, or tied in sacks and thrown in the Loire, whilst those who were of a higher class were beheaded and their bodies quartered.

Chenonceau, on the banks of the Cher, a tributary of the River Loire is one

crown. In 1535, Bohier's son Antoine handed over the castle to the King, to settle his late father's debts.

The next of Chenonceau's six women was the beautiful Diane de Poitiers, mistress of Henri II. Although Diane, a widow, was 20 years older than Henri, she held the king totally in her power. He gave her Chenonceau, which she loved, staying there often. She designed a large garden, still known today as *Diane's Garden*, and built a bridge, linking the castle to the far bank of the River Cher. When Henri was killed in 1559 during a tournament, his widow, Queen Catherine de Medici became the Regent, and decided to extract revenge from Diane. She "suggested" to Diane that she exchanged Chenonceau for the Chateau de Chaumont. Poor Diane, of course, had no choice.

Catherine was as delighted with Chenonceau as her predecessor had been, and her new acquisition became the backdrop for many of the sumptuous *soirées* (gatherings) for which she was famous. Catherine also laid out a garden, and constructed what is undoubtedly the most famous feature of the castle – the double gallery on the bridge.

Nearly 400 years later, this beautiful gallery would play a small part in history: during the German occupation, from 1940 to 1942, the castle was situated in occupied France, whereas the south door of the gallery gave direct access into free France. Catherine de Medici willed Chenonceau to her daughter-in-law, Louise de Lorraine. After the assassination of her husband, Henri III in 1589, Louise retired to Chenonceau, where she dressed in white, the colour of royal mourning, for the rest of her life.

The castle then went through a period of neglect, until it became the property of the Dupin family in the 18th century. Madame Dupin hosted literary salons here, one of her regular visitors being Jean-Jacques Rousseau, her son's tutor, who had nothing but happy memories of Chenonceau, "We enjoyed ourselves alot in that beautiful place, we lived well, and I became as fat as a monk". Madame Dupin was popular amongst the local people, and so Chenonceau survived the French Revolution intact, protected by the loyal villagers.

The last of the castle's "six women" was Madame Pelouze, who bought the castle in 1864 and devoted her life to its restoration. She restored it to the state in which Thomas Bohier had had it built, altering some of Catherine de Medicis' construction, but leaving in place the bridge and the gallery, built by a royal mistress and a royal wife – the temporary symbol of a divided France.

of the prettiest and most visited of the Loire castles, its feminine prettiness a direct reflection of the influence of six women in its construction and decoration.

The Playthings of Kings

Tours makes a good base for exploring the Loire Valley. It is also a delightful town in its own right, with a charming old quarter and the Cathedral of Saint Gatien.

Construction of the Cathedral took from the 13th to the 16th century, and so the finished product offers a panorama of the evolution of Gothic style. The fine stained glass windows are from the 13th, 14th and 15th centuries.

Villandry is famous for its gardens, which, frankly, outshines the 16th century castle, built by Jean le Breton, the Secretary of State to François I. The gardens are situated on three levels, and are the only surviving example of a 16th century garden in France.

Each of the three terraces, which

The maze at the Chateau of Villandry is a fun reprieve from sightseeing.

are separated by high hedges, has a different character. The highest terrace is devoted to *le jardin d'eau* (water garden), with an ornamental lake, moat, and fountains.

On the next level is the ornamental garden, planted with box trees and yews to shield the flowerbeds from the wind. The flowerbeds are laid out in symbolic designs, each one representing an aspect of love. The third and lowest level is a vegetable garden, planted in a colourful and imaginative display.

As with Chenonceau, water is an integral feature of the pretty **Château of Azay-le-Rideau**, which was partly built on pilings sunk in the bed of the River Indre. But Azay-le-Rideau's peaceful beauty hides an eventful past. In 1418, the Dauphin, Charles VII was staying at Azay, and because he felt that he had been insulted by the castle's soldiers, he had the castle burned down, and the captain of the garrison and his 350 soldiers executed. Until the 16th century, the village was called *Azay-le-Brûlé* (Burned Azay) to commemorate this gruesome episode.

A hundred years later, Gilles Bertholet, an important financier, built a new castle on the site of the burned ruins. The work lasted from 1518 to 1529, and in another parallel with Chenonceau, it was Bertholet's wife who supervised the work, giving Azay a hospitable, feminine touch.

The *château* was eventually confiscated by François I and after a succession of owners, was almost pulled down again for retribution. In 1870, Prince Frédéric-Charles of Prussia was staying at Azay, when one day a chandelier fell onto the table where he was dining. Suspecting an assassination attempt, the Prince wanted to raze Azay to the ground, but luckily, wiser counsel prevailed.

When you first see the **Château of Ussé**, its fortified turrets outlined against the backdrop of the dark forest of Chinon, it looks like an illustration from the pages of a storybook. This fairytale image is only strengthened when you are told that legend has it that Charles Perrault used Ussé as his model for the setting of his story, ***Sleeping Beauty***. Ussé is pretty, romantic, and has a history singularly unmarked by the bloodthirstiness or scandal of many of its neighbours.

On the opposite bank of the river from Ussé is the oldest *château* in France, **Langeais**, whose ruined keep dates back to the 10th century.

The castle was built in a very short time, (1465 – 1469), making the architecture particularly homogeneous. It has remained virtually untouched and undamaged over the centuries and provides a wonderfully evocative example of a 15th century nobleman's residence. The exterior of Langeais is that of a typical medieval fortress – turrets, battlements, and a drawbridge – and the interior is furnished with Flemish tapestries and period furniture.

Another medieval fortress, on the banks of the River Vienne, is **Chinon**, which towers over the old city, with its maze of narrow cobbled streets and old wooden houses. Parts of the ruined fortress were constructed by Henri Plantagenet, who later became the King of England, and who later died in Chinon in 1189. During the Hundred Years War, the English King Henry VI controlled large tracts of France while the Dauphin, the future Charles VII, only controlled the part of France around the Loire Valley.

Charles made Chinon his headquarters, and it was there, in 1429, that Joan of Arc picked out a disguised Charles from among his courtiers, and told him, in her simple peasant language, that she had been sent by God to escort him to Reims, where he would be crowned king. (See box story on Joan of Arc.)

Just 12 kilometres away from the old district of Chinon with its Middle

A young lad on a farm.

Ages ambience, is a 20th century intrusion – the nuclear power-station of **Avoine-Chinon**, the first one constructed in France. The two oldest reactors are no longer in service and can be visited.

Of Horses & Wine

Saumur is a charming town, known to different people for different reasons. To riding enthusiasts, Saumur is the home of the *École Nationale d'équitation* (National Riding School), famed for its *Cadre Noir* team.

To wine lovers, Saumur is the home of a delightful red wine – Saumur-Champigny, which, contrary to usual practice, is drunk chilled. WWII history

buffs will know Saumur as the site of the courageous defence of the Loire by officers and cadets of the Riding School, who held the German troops at bay for three days in June 1940. And do not forget to see the largest carnival mask factory in Europe also in Saumur.

The castle, built during the second half of the 14th century, was one of the inspirations for the early 15th century illustrated manuscript **Les Très Riches Heures du Duc de Berry** (*The Richest Hours of the Duke of Berry*). At the end of the 16th century, fortifications were added and during the rule of Louis XIV and Louis XV, it became the residence of the Governor of Saumur.

Today, the fortress houses two museums – one devoted to the art of the Middle Ages and the Renaissance, and the other, not surprisingly, to horses.

Historic Retreats

The last of the major *châteaux* along this historic valley is the 13th century fortress **Angers**, situated on the River Maine, a tributary of the Loire, only 10 kilometres long. Angers was formerly the capital of Anjou and is today the centre for the production of Anjou wines.

If you imagine Angers and Tours as the bottom of a triangle, the top corner is **Le Mans**, a historic town, with a 20th century profile. There is the magnificent Gothic Cathedral of Saint Julien, with its superb 13th century stained glass windows, the old quarter of town with

Village square of Alexander Calder.

15th century wooden houses and 18th century *hôtels* (hotels). Le Mans is however also the venue for a decidedly modern event – one of the best known automobile races, the 24-hour race.

South of the Loire is an area which can best be described as a geographically diverse region, for each one of the boundaries of **Poitou-Charentes** is different. The two great rivers of the Loire and the Gironde form its northern and southern boundaries, the Atlantic coast lies to the east, and to the west are the mountains of the Auvergne.

Immediately south of the town of Nantes is **Vendée**, an area of marshy landscapes and offshore islands. On the coast is the attractive port town of **Les Sables d'Olonne**, with its 18th century promenade **Le Remblai**, built to protect the town behind it, but which has now become a favourite place for an evening stroll.

The town's good, sandy beach stretches for more than three kilometres, there is a harbour for fishing boats, another for yachts and a wet dock. There are oyster beds and fish farming in the former salt marshes, just outside the town.

Ninety kilometres southwards is the historic port of **La Rochelle** which was a centre for the Protestant religion during the 16th century. It underwent two major sieges; one in 1573, at the hands of the Catholic Duke of Anjou, the future Henri III; the second from 1627 to 1628, when La Rochelle sided with the Eng-

A meditative afternoon on the banks of the Loire.

lish, who had invaded the pretty Island of Ré, (now linked by a road-bridge to the mainland).

La Rochelle has an extensive harbour complex, which is well worth a visit. It comprises an outer harbour, two wet docks, and a *Vieux Port* (old harbour) where both sardine-fishing vessels and pleasure craft can moor. Every morning a fish auction is held next to the larger of the two docks, where trawlers moor.

From Poitiers to Cognac

Poitiers is the regional capital of Poitou-Charentes, a town which straddles 16 centuries of history, for it is home to both the oldest Christian building in France, the 4th century Baptistry of Saint Jean as well as the Futuroscope Park, where research into many high-technology developments (especially in connection with audio-visual material) is being carried out.

Saint Jean's Baptistry is an amalgam of early Christian architecture, as it contains the 4th century pool where the early Christians were baptised by immersion, 6th and 7th century additions, a 10th century narthex and 12th and 13th century frescoes. Land subsidence has resulted in Saint Jean's Baptistry now being four metres below ground level.

The huge Cathedral of Saint Pierre was built at the instigation of Queen Eleanor of Aquitaine and its construc-

Sixteenth century woodcarvings in the Church of Notre Dame la Grande, Poitiers.

tion dates from the end of the 12th century, although it was not completed for another two centuries.

The **Church of Notre Dame la Grande**, also dates from the 12th century and has an exceptionally beautiful carved façade, one of the best examples of Romanesque workmanship in the country.

In 1429, Saint Joan of Arc was sent to Poitiers, to be cross-examined by a panel of academics, a meeting which took place in the Palais de Justice.

Angoulême has an impressive location, for the town is perched high on a plateau, surrounded by the city's ramparts, with the commercial and business districts below. Starting from the **Place des Halles**, visitors can walk all

the way around the city's ramparts, which offers good views of the surrounding countryside and the River Charente. Towards the north, the older parts of town have narrow streets, whilst the area to the south has many beautiful 18th and 19th century houses, with large gardens.

At one point on the rampart walls is a plaque commemorating the test flight made by a General Resnier (a local man) in 1806, of a plane of his own invention, with which he was planning an airborne invasion of England. Luckily for England, the General broke his leg when he landed, and gave up the whole idea in disgust!

The 12th century Cathedral of Saint Pierre was partly destroyed in the 16th

Atlantic Islands

They may not perhaps be the sunniest of islands, but the islands off the western Atlantic Coast are interesting to visit, with much history attached to them, and beautiful scenery.

Northwest of the coastal town of Les Sables d'Olonne is the tiny **Ile d'Yeu**, whose rugged cliffs remind one of Brittany. The name of the island is thought to have derived from *Ile Dieu* (God's Island), but since, over the years, there have been 31 successive names for this little speck of land, separating fact from fiction tends to be somewhat difficult. Yeu was peopled by the Celts, then by the Bretons, it was later invaded by the British, occupied by the Spanish and became a prison for political prisoners, the most notorious of whom was Maréchal Pétain, the head of the French collaborationist state during WWII. The 90-year old Pétain arrived on the island in November 1945, and was imprisoned in the Citadel just outside the island's main town, Port-Joinville. He died on the island in July 1951, where he was buried.

The southern coastline of Yeu is called the Côte Sauvage (Savage Coast), and is an impressive sight, with its bizarrely shaped rocks, its Trembling Stone – an enormous boulder that can be made to move by touching one specific point – and its lighthouse, which offers a good view of the island, and, on a clear day, of the Atlantic Coast.

North of Yeu is the pretty Ile de Noirmoutier, which is now attached to the mainland by a road-bridge. The island's topography is often reminiscent of the flat Dutch countryside, for there are marshes, dykes, windmills and also fields full of flowers – not the typical Dutch tulips, however, but fragrant mimosas, reminding visitors more of the south of France than of the Atlantic coast. The painter Renoir stayed on the island and later said of it, "It is a pretty place, as beautiful as the Midi, but the sea there is beautiful in a different way from the Mediterranean".

On the island, there is farming, and off its shores, fishing and oyster beds. Noirmoutier's salt marshes are an important contributor to the island's economy, producing several hundred tons of salt each year. The capital of the island is the attractive little town of **Noirmoutier-en-L'Ile**, with its 11th century castle keep surrounded by 15th century fortifications. One of the floors of the castle is devoted to an excellent collection of 18th and 19th English Staffordshire pottery.

Off the coast of La Rochelle is the sunny **Ile de Ré**, which is also linked to the mainland by a road-bridge. The island is nearly 30 kilometres long, and is nick-named *L'Ile blanche* (White Island) partly because of its white rocky landscape as well as its stretches of salt marshes. Ré was originally a series of even smaller islands, which are now joined together, but the western section of the island, around the Bay of Fiers d'Ars is only connected by a dyke and a narrow isthmus. The marshes here have been turned into a bird sanctuary, and further west, on the tip of the island is a lighthouse called the *Phare des Baleines* (Whales' Lighthouse), because, according to legend, 300 whales were beached here during Roman times.

The main town on the island is the pretty port of **St-Martin-de-Ré**, with its narrow, cobbled streets, low houses, its city walls and its 17th century fortress. **St-Martin-de-Ré** used to be a busy commercial port, but is now mainly given over to pleasure craft, although there is

century and was restored in the 17th and later in the mid-19th century. The Cathedrals' impressive façade with over 70 carved statues tells the story of the Last Judgement, although there are a couple of interspersed battlescenes which are episodes from the epic poem of the Middle Ages *La Chanson de Roland* (The Song of Roland).

Saintes was a major town on the pilgrimage route south through France to Santiago de Compostela in Spain. It boasts an 11th century **Abbey** and **Cathedral of Saint Pierre**, built on a Rostill some fishing. The old *quartier des marins* (sailors' district), is itself a tiny island in the middle of the harbour, today surrounded by yachts and dinghies, rather than trading ships, but the old houses, the tiny streets, and the quays paved with ballast from old ships give the area a nostalgic atmosphere.

The viaduct bridge linking the Ile d'Oléron with the coast is the longest in France, a little over three kilometres long. Oléron is the second largest of the French islands (after Corsica) and, like the other Atlantic Islands, oyster-farming is a major industry. Many of the salt marshes have been drained and turned into oyster beds, and there is also commercial mussel and fish farming. On the western tip of the island, at Chassiron Point, the locals have a unique way of fishing: there is a system of sluice-gates in the fish farms, which function according to the tides, and at low tide, the fishermen spear the fish with a local type of harpoon called a *fouëne*.

The main town on the island is **St-Pierre-d'Oléron**, which has a surprising variety of architecture for such a small place, ranging from the 30 metre high Lantern of the Dead, erected in the 13th century, during the English occupation of the island, to the 17th century church with its octagonal tower, which offers an excellent view of the island and the nearby coastline.

The novelist Pierre Loti (1850 to 1923) who was elected to the prestigious Académie Française at the young age of 41, spent many childhood holidays in St-Pierre-d'Oléron, where his grandparents lived. The writer was buried in the family garden there, and, according to his wishes, his childhood bucket and spade were also buried with him.

man foundation. The Town's picturesque streets and its Roman arena are further reflections of the town's historical ambience.

The drive between Angoulême and Saintes is a pretty one, following the course of the River Charente, and going

Orléans Cathedral, captured by Joan of Arc.

through the town of **Cognac**, whose name is famous the world over. The Cognac vineyards stretch from La Rochefoucauld in the east right across to La Rochelle on the west coast. Cognac is a distillation of the local white wines. In the 17th century the local people began to burn these local white wines to obtain longer-lasting spirits which were principally exported to Northern Europe.

The Dutch and the English had a monopoly over this trade, and the Dutch word *brandewijn*, meaning burned wine, became the English word brandy. The English still hold a kind of monopoly over the brandy business – they are a major importer and consumer of it!

If France has a mystic heart, it is to be found in Brittany, a beautiful region of dramatic coastlines, misty weather and legends, which has preserved its distinctive character, with its own language and dress, though the latter two are sadly under threat from the increasing uniformity of 20th century society.

The rhythm of Breton life is regulated by the sea, which sculpts its deeply jagged coastlines, and whose tides control access to tiny offshore islands. Deep sea fishing, shipbuilding and fish farming provide jobs, many of Brittany's major towns are seaports, and the local cuisine is famed for its excellent seafood.

Brittany abounds in legends, most famously, King Arthur and his Knights of the Round Table, Merlin, Tristan and Isolde, but the peninsula's proven historical roots lie somewhere between 5,000 and 2,000 BC, when

Harbour at Concarneau.

Brittany & Normandy

201

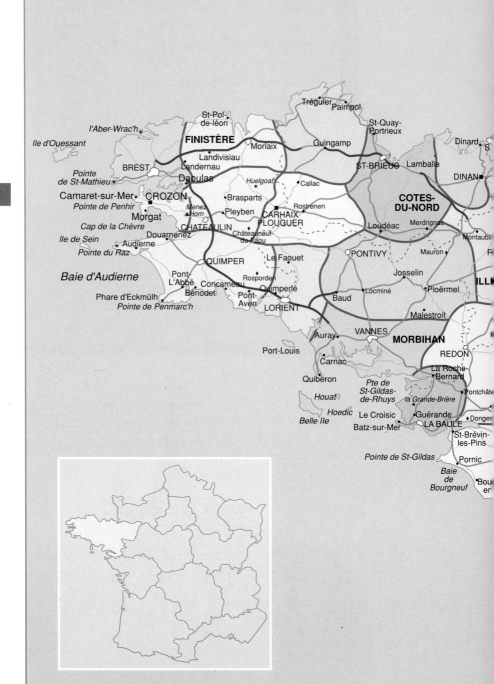

Ile d'Ouessant

l'Aber-Wrac'h

St-Pol-de-léon

FINISTÈRE

Tréguier
Paimpol

St-Quay-Portrieux

Dinard
S

Morlaix

Guingamp

Landivisiau

BREST

Landernau

ST-BRIEUC
Lamballe

DINAN

Pointe de St-Mathieu

Daoulas

Huelgoat

Callac

Camaret-sur-Mer
Pointe de Penhir

CROZON

Brasparts

Rostrenen

COTES-DU-NORD

Morgat

*Menez
Hom*

Pleyben

CARHAIX

Loudéac
Merdrignac

Cap de la Chèvre

CHATEAULIN

PLOUGUER

Montauba

Ile de Sein

Douarnenez

Châteauneuf-du-Faou

QUIMPER

Le Faouet

PONTIVY

Mauron

F

Audierne

Pointe du Raz

Baie d'Audierne

Pont-L'Abbé

Rosporden

Josselin

ILL

Concarneau

Quimperlé

Locminé

Ploërmel

Phare d'Eckmülh

Bénodet

Pont-Aven

Baud

Pointe de Penmarc'h

LORIENT

Malestroit

VANNES

Auray

MORBIHAN

Port-Louis

REDON

Carnac

La Roche-Bernard

Quiberon

Pte de
St-Gildas-de-Rhuys

Pontchât

Houat

la Grande-Brière

Guérande
Donges

*Hoedic
Belle Ile*

Le Croisic

LA BAULE

St-Brévin-les-Pins

Batz-sur-Mer

Pointe de St-Gildas

Pornic

*Baie
de
Bourgneuf*

Bou
er

BRITTANY

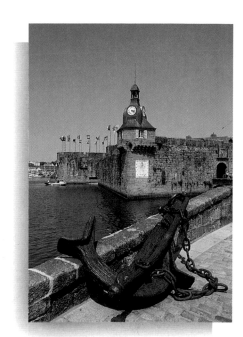

The ramparts of Concarneau, Brittany.

the predecessors of the Gauls erected thousands of megaliths, menhirs and dolmens. Over 3,000 of these structures still survive today, and some of the more spectacular alignments of menhirs are to be found near the town of **Carnac**, on the southern coast.

Mont Saint Michel

Much of the character of Breton architecture, as well as its customs and society, has been formed by religion, for in this traditionally Catholic part of France, churches abound – every village has its cross, its statues, its patron saint or its festivals.

Probably the most spectacular ex-

The imposing abbey of Mont Saint Michel.

ample of religious architecture is the **Mont Saint Michel**, an 11th century abbey built on a tiny, fortified island off the north Breton coast. Although one of the most visited monuments in the country, there is still a magic about the island, especially in the quiet of the early morning or late evening, after the crowds have left and the cobbled streets leading up to the abbey are deserted.

Chic Resorts

A little further down the coast is the fortified town of **Saint Malo**, whose original foundations were also on an island. Saint Malo's history dates back to the sixth century AD, its ramparts were built by the town's bishops in the 12th century, but centuries of history were wiped out during two weeks of desperate fighting in August 1944, when much of the city was left in ruins.

However, the towering walls of the fortified city survived the destruction of the war, and the town's buildings have since been restored, so visitors can walk around the ramparts, with their spectacular views of the offshore islands on one side and maze of tiny streets on the other.

Dinard, is another high-class resort situated next to Saint Malo on the Rance estuary with its dramatic cliffs and sandy beaches. There is an interesting **Marine Amusement and Aquarium**, displaying a variety of

Breton species and a picturesque harbour. At La Baule in the south, smart 19th century villas line the long flat, sandy beaches in this old-fashioned upmarket resort. However, the most characteristic feature of the Breton coastline comes not from such pleasantly relaxing beaches, but rather from the wilder, craggy headlands, crashing waves, and enormous rocks often eroded by the climate into bizarre shapes.

Ploumanach, a little fishing village on the north coast, has piles of curiously shaped rocks, and **Trégastel-Plage**, a short distance away has equally intriguing rocks and a cluster of tiny islands. The **Crozon Peninsula** on the west coast and **Raz Point**, further south-west boast some of Brittany's most spectacular coastal scenery.

Fishing Towns & Villages

Brest is a major maritime city, home to a large commercial port and an important naval base. Yet, sadly for Brest, it was precisely these activities and the city's strategic importance, that made it such a prize for the Germans during WWII.

The city was heavily bombed during the four years of German occupation and when the city was liberated by the Americans in September 1944, Brest lay in ruins. The city was rebuilt, and the shipyards are once again flourishing.

Quimper is a pretty cathedral town

Collecting oysters in Cancale, is a satisfying and lucrative occupation.

at the junction of two small rivers, from where it derives its name, for *kemper* means junction in Breton. Quimper is one of Brittany's more traditional towns, and its cobbled old town surrounds the Gothic **Cathedral of St Corentin**, which has some beautiful 15th century stained glass windows. Quimper produces attractive handpainted pottery, a local craft dating back to the 17th century.

One of Brittany's most charming towns is the southern fishing port of **Concarneau**, with its tiny fortified islet, **La Ville Close**, whose massive ramparts were built in the 14th century.

Although Concarneau is the third-largest fishing port in France and one of the biggest markets for tuna fish, it has a charm and relaxed feel about it. A

Watching over the waves and the clear blue sky, Quiberon Castle
stands alone, but not lonely.

Druidical ceremonies continue ancient rituals amongst believers.

good view of the trawlers in the harbour can be enjoyed from the **Porte au Vin** (Wine Gate) on the islet.

Vannes, at the head of the Gulf of Morbihan, has a beautiful old section of town, with half-timbered houses, washhouses with unusual sloping roofs, and 13th century ramparts.

Rennes is the capital of Brittany and has a different atmosphere from the windy port towns. Rennes is a busy, industrial town, whose population has doubled since WWII, yet there is still a distinct sense of history in the city centre. There are cobbled medieval streets with half-timbered houses, which escaped unscathed from a disastrous fire in 1720, which otherwise ravaged the city. The centre was rebuilt in a classical style, the most impressive example being the focal **Place de la Mairie** (Town Hall Square).

The Province of Brittany, has a very distinct feeling about it, notably different from the rest of France; it has its own language, with roots linking it to the Welsh and Irish languages, rather than to French. It has a huge pantheon of saints, not all of whom have necessarily been recognised by the Vatican authorities, but who are fêted in unique, local festivals called *pardons* (pilgrimages). Breton women wear extravagant lace headdresses, especially for such religious celebrations; even the traditional food is different, for Bretons love to eat crêpes and *galettes* (pancakes) which are washed down with cider.

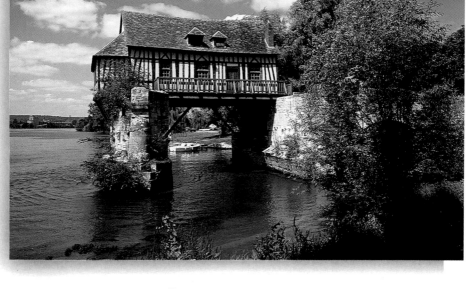

Precarious serenity.

Normandy

Normandy is a land of peaceful rolling, countryside, with green fields and grazing cows, half-timbered cottages, small unpretentious *châteaux*, and apple orchards. It is also a land of cliffs and sand dunes, of picturesque fishing villages and major ports, of elegant summer resorts and WWII memorials.

It was from Normandy that invaders sailed for England in the 11th century, while nine centuries later, the pattern was reversed, as the D-Day liberation forces sailed from England back to Normandy to bring the prisoners to liberty.

The coastline, its harbours and its port towns have all played a very important part in the region's history, and today play a major economic role.

Normandy has several industrial ports such as **Le Havre**, **Dieppe** and **Cherbourg**. The latter two are major ferry ports, connecting France and England. They are also holiday towns, especially Dieppe, which has the closest beach to Paris.

The **Chateau de Dieppe** overlooks Dieppe from a cliff above the town. The Chateau contains a large selection of ivories. Cherbourg has a fine square dominated by the **Municipal Theatre** and several fine beaches.

In 1945, immediately after WWII, **Le Havre** had the unenviable title of the most damaged port in Europe.

Brittany's Parish Closes

Catholicism and centuries-old intervillage rivalries gave rise to one of the most distinctive forms of Breton architecture, the *Enclos Paroissial* (Parish Close), an art form unique to Brittany.

Essentially the heart of the close was the village church and the cemetery, around which, over the centuries an array of religious monuments were built – the main ones being: a triumphal arch, a charnel house, a little square and a calvary. Every parish close is different, both in terms of size and in the wealth of its decoration, and they do not necessarily have all of these monuments, each of which did play a practical as well as symbolic role.

Next to the village church is a small square, known as a *placître*, and the cemetery. The lack of space in these tiny cemeteries often meant that bodies had to be exhumed, so charnel houses were built to receive the bones. Initially these charnel houses were little more than shelters leaning against the church wall, but over the years they evolved into separate buildings, gradually becoming larger and more elaborate. Access to the cemetery was often through a decorated monumental gate, a triumphal archway meant to symbolize the accession of the Just and the Good to immortality.

The calvary, the most impressive element in most village *enclos* (closes) was not only a decorative monument, upon which were carved religious scenes, but it was also a valuable teaching device, for the priest would preach to the illiterate villagers, using the scenes on the calvary as visual aides to his sermon. Generally the sculpture on the calvaries is not sophisticated, for they were carved by local stonemasons, but they usually have a lifelike vigour, with many of the figures dressed in 16th or 17th century dress.

The two most impressive Breton *enclos* (closes) are the direct result of a two century long fierce rivalry, between the villages of Guimiliau and Saint Thégonnec. As each village tried to outshine the other, the churches were the direct beneficiaries, getting even more elaborate statues, porches, fonts and pulpits.

The calvary of Saint Thégonnec dates from 1610, and has some charming details – the saint himself, harnessing a wolf to his cart, after wolves had eaten his donkey and angels standing under the crucified Christ, collecting his blood as it runs down.

The calvary of Guimiliau was built between 1581–1588, and with over 200 figures, is one of the largest in Brittany. Amongst the conventional Biblical scenes depicted, is one with a difference, the story of Catherine the Lost, wayward servant, whose journey to hell begins with not telling the priest everything during confession!

MARIÉE DE QUIMPER

Brittany's scarfs are a local tradition of handicraft.

Today, it is the second most important port in the country (after Marseilles), and the third most important in Europe. It handles huge quantities of imports and exports, as well as passenger ships sailing to England and Ireland.

Honfleur a quaint Normandy town, was a favourite with the Impressionists.

Upmarket Holiday Towns

Dotted along the coast, are many pretty little fishing and holiday towns, amongst them Deauville, Trouville, Honfleur and Étretat. Of these, **Deauville** is without doubt the most fashionable and expensive of them all, and boasts all the necessary jet-set amenities – a casino, a yachting marina, regattas and horse-racing, with the Grand Prix de Deauville, which always takes place on the last Sunday of August being a major society

NORMANDY

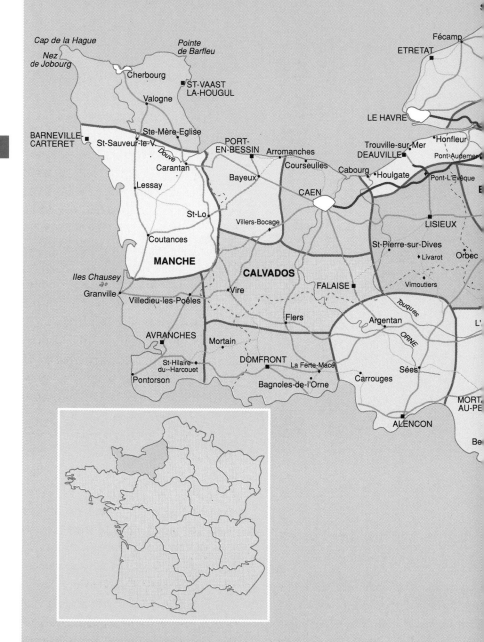

Cap de la Hague

Nez
de Jobourg

Cherbourg

Valogne

Pointe
de Barfleu

ST-VAAST
LA-HOUGUL

Ste-Mère-Eglise

BARNEVILLE-
CARTERET   St-Sauveur-le-V.

Carantan

Lessay

Douve

St-Lo

Coutances

MANCHE

Iles Chausey

Granville

Villedieu-les-Poêles

AVRANCHES

Mortain

St-Hilaire-
du--Harcouet

Pontorson

PORT-
EN-BESSIN   Arromanches

Courseulles

Bayeux

CAEN

Villers-Bocage

CALVADOS

Vire

FALAISE

Flers

DOMFRONT   La Ferte-Macé

Bagnoles-de-l'Orne

Fécamp

ETRETAT

LE HAVRE

Trouville-sur-Mer   Honfleur
DEAUVILLE   Pont-Audemer

Cabourg   Houlgate   Pont-L'Evêque

LISIEUX

St-Pierre-sur-Dives
                    Livarot   Orbec

Vimoutiers

Touques

Argentan

ORNE

Sées

Carrouges

MORT.
AU-PE

ALENCON

Be

event. During the brief summer season, everyone strolls along the *Promenade des Planches* (boardwalk), celebrity-spotting. **Trouville** is virtually an extension of Deauville, which it faces, immediately across the mouth of the River Touques. It is every bit as elegant, every bit as popular and its own casino and *Promenade des Planches* are just as crowded.

Honfleur has a totally different feel to it, centred as it is around its old harbour, its 14th century church and its tiny, gabled houses. Honfleur does not have a beach, unlike its more sophisticated neighbours, but it is still one of the most popular towns on the Normandy coast, especially amongst artists, who come here in search of the same inspiration that so marked the 19th century Impressionist painters. It was at the **Ferme St-Siméon**, today the most expensive hotel in town, that the Impressionists lodged, whilst they tried to do justice to the changing light of the Norman skies, inspired by a Honfleur-born painter, Eugène Boudin.

Étretat only 28 kilometres away from the major industrial town of Le Havre, was also immortalised by the Impressionists, who painted the town's extraordinary cliffs, which rise out of the sea to a height of 85 metres.

Battle Beaches

The **Normandy battlefields**, stretching along the coast from south of Cherbourg

Montfort Chateau offers accommodation for would-be lords and ladies.

to Caen, were the scene of the Allied invasion of occupied France, an invasion that was many years in the planning and which culminated in Operation Overlord when British and Canadian troops landed on D-Day, 6th June, 1944 (the legendary bad weather over the Channel had forced the postponement of the invasion by a day) and established contact with the beach–heads on Juno Beach, Gold Beach and Sword Beach, while the American troops faced a more difficult landing on the beaches of Omaha and Utah. The battle for Normandy continued until the night of 21st August, when the German troops were finally defeated. Today, the five invasion beaches commemorate their thousands of dead with simple memorials.

After the War

Inland, **Rouen**, is the regional capital of Upper Normandy, a historic town which suffered badly during WWII. Much of the old town, squashed between the banks of the River Seine and the Cathedral, was destroyed, but some streets survived the bombing and fires. Today, 700 houses have been restored, and the whole area has been made into a charming pedestrian precinct. Rouen's 12th century **Notre Dame Cathedral** is one of the marvels of French Gothic architecture. It inspired the Impressionist painter Monet to create one of his masterpieces, a series of canvases, simply

The quaint old town of Honfleur.

called **Cathédrales de Rouen**, which depict the same façade of the Cathedral capturing the changing light from dawn through dusk. There is a legend surrounding one of the towers of the cathedral, called the Butter Tower which was reputedly built in the 14th century using money given to the church, in exchange for permission to eat butter during Lent – usually forbidden during this customary time of frugality.

On 30th May, 1431, Joan of Arc was burned at the scaffold in what is now the **Place du Vieux Marché** (Old Market

The Castle of Carroliges.

place) and the exact spot where she died s marked by a 20 metre high cross.

Caen, is also a regional capital, of Lower Normandy, an old town which also suffered badly from bombing raids during WWII. Paradoxically, the liberation of the town, which took over two months, left much of it in ruins. On D-Day, 6th June, 1944, bombs literally rained down on the town, which caught fire, and it was 11 days before the fires could be brought under control.

During the battle for Caen, over 1,500 citizens took refuge in the **Church of Saint Étienne**, whose foundation dates back to 1066, though the present building dates from the early 17th century. Saint Étienne was mercifully spared from the mass destruction that occured around it, and is today one of the town's more historic vestiges which remain amidst much new architecture.

Lisieux & Bayeux

Lisieux was the birthplace of one of the most popular and best-loved Catholic saints, Saint Theresa of Lisieux, and is an important place of pilgrimage. Saint Theresa was born in 1873, became a Carmelite nun at the age of 15, and died in 1897, when she was only 24. She was canonised a saint in 1925, and nearly 30 years later, in 1954, a basilica was consecrated in her honour. It is here that pilgrims now flock.

Bayeux is a pretty cathedral town,

Timbered houses and quaint restaurants of Rouen.

which owes its notoriety to two dates in history: 1065, and, nearly 900 years later, 7th June, 1944. In 1065, William the Conqueror decided to invade England, which he did the following year, defeating the English King Harold at the Battle of Hastings. The invasion and the preparations for it are recorded on the Bayeux Tapestry, a 70 metre long masterpiece of embroidery. No one knows exactly when the tapestry was made, but almost certainly it was ordered by the Bishop of Bayeux, William's half-brother, very soon after the Norman conquest of England – probably sometime between 1070 and 1077.

The tapestry records the momentous battle, in 58 different scenes, which are filled with many lively details. It is displayed in a specially designed room in an 18th century building housing the town's Cultural Centre. The other major date in Bayeux's history, 7th June, 1944, was the date of its liberation from the Germans during WWII. It was also the first town in France to be liberated.

Norman Cuisine

People in Normandy enjoy their food, and there is a tradition of excellent local cuisine – cream is used liberally in Norman cooking, so much so that a simple cream sauce is usually referred to as a *sauce normande* (Normandy sauce). Cheese is one of the specialities of Normandy, and among the better-known cal cheeses are the widely popular Camembert and two delicious, but much stronger ones, Pont l'Évêque and Livarot. With so many apple orchards in Normandy, it is not surprising that its two most famous drinks are both apple-based, cider and calvados – a liqueur made from apples.

When a Norman pauses for a while during a rich meal, he may well drink a quick glass of calvados, to aid his digestion, something the French refer to as *le trou Normand* (the Norman hole).

North-western France

The north-west corner of France, covering two *départements* (administrative provinces) known as the Pas de Calais and the Somme, is an area also greatly influenced by the sea and its coastal towns, and also by war, though this time the area bears scars and memories from both World Wars.

The coast between Normandy and the Belgian border is dominated by the smart resort town of Le Touquet, and the Channel ports of **Boulogne-sur-Mer**, **Calais** and **Dunkerque**, from which there are frequent ferries and hover-

crafts to England. Le Touquet was a famous Victorian seaside resort, with an upmarket image that is still evident, as can be seen by its pricy shops, casino, racetrack and golf course.

The town also has a pleasant sandy beach and a number of good hotels. Paradoxically, much of **Calais'** importance is due to its proximity to England, which lies just 38 kilometres across the Channel – on clear days, you can see Dover's white cliffs.

It is from Calais that the long-awaited, much-discussed, often reviled **Channel Tunnel** will connect France and England. The emotional impact of the *Chunnel* as the French call it, may well be more than its eventual economic effect, for two neighbours with a tradition of a love-hate relationship will at long last be physically linked.

In the town itself, you can see Rodin's sculpture of the **Monument des Bourgeois de Calais** (Monument to Calais Bourgeois), erected in memory of the townsmen who sacrificed themselves to the English crown in 1347 in order to spare the common people of Calais from

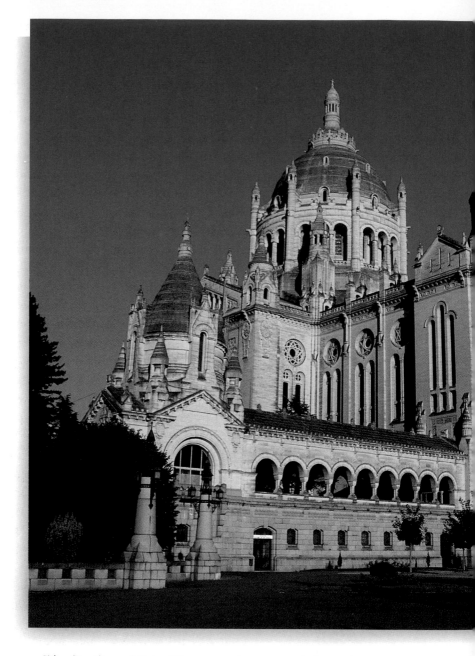

The Basilica of Saint Theresa in Lisieux, is dedicated to a local girl.

retribution for their revolt against the English occupation. The **Musée des Beaux-Arts et de la Dentelle** (Museum of Art and Lace) is also worth seeing. Boulogne-Sur-Mer, 27 kilometres from Le Touquet along the coast is well worth

taking a look around before embarking or disembarking the cross-channel ferries.

Napoléon indeed chose this town as his base from which to invade England. However, his plans never solidi-

fied, but a monument – **Colonne de la Grand Armee** still bears witness to the venture.

Boulogne is divided into the new town with its vast port extensions and concrete houses and a quaint old town with cobbled streets and buildings dating from the 13th century. Take some time to explore these streets.

Flanders and the area around the River Somme saw much horrific fighting during WWI, with huge losses of life in the trenches. The area again suffered during WWII, when the German Panzer divisions invaded France through its northwestern borders, sweeping down to Paris.

Lille is only a few kilometres from the Belgian border and is closer to Brussels than to Paris. The old city centre has been beautifully renovated over recent years, not only the magnificent 17th and 18th century buildings, such as the **Vieille Bourse** (Old Stock Exchange), and the **Place du Théâtre** (Theatre Square) with its 19th century architecture, but also the maze of tiny surrounding streets, which are now occupied by smart shops, art galleries and restaurants.

Lille is a town that is rapidly coming to terms with the harsh economic realities of the area, for the traditional industries of the north, such as textiles and coal mining are moribund. Lille is therefore facing its future innovatively evolving as a major commercial, conference and transport centre for the region.

The Eastern Wine Region

If you were to draw an admittedly rather wavy line down France's eastern frontier, from north to south, in one sweep you would link up four of the country's major wine producing regions. From the northeastern the **Champagne** district; then slightly east to **Lorraine** and **Alsace** on the German border; south to **Burgundy**, the show-case of French wine; down to the south-eastern **Rhône Valley** – it is easy to see why the eastern side of France is so famous for its wines and champagnes. A judicious combination of climate, soil and terrain has made this area one of the principal wine growing areas of the country.

■ ■ ■ ■ ■

The small town of Riquewihr in Alsace has a distinctly Germanic influence.

Champagne

The champagne district is centred around the cathedral city of **Reims**, 142 kilometres northeast of Paris; the former regional capital, **Troyes** and the smaller town of **Épernay**. The sparkling champagne comes from the rolling valleys and

Strasbourg Cathedral is a gigantic edifice of Gothic art.

chalky soil of the region of Champagne, an area with its own micro-climate. The western part of the lowlands are known as *sèche* (dry) Champagne, since the chalky soil absorbs water, making it good agricultural land. The eastern part is known as *humide* (damp) Champagne, its soil is a mixture of sand and clay and the farms here are devoted to cattle farming.

The 13th century **Notre Dame Cathedral** in **Reims** is one of the most important churches in France, not only for its age and impressive architecture, but also because of the special place it has in French history. From the 12th century onwards, successive kings went to Reims on the day of their coronation, to be anointed by the bishops. Without

doubt, the most famous *cérémonial de sacre* (sacred ceremony) of all was that of Charles VII, whose coronation, witnessed by Joan of Arc, symbolised more than simply a rite of passage. It was the culmination of a campaign led by her to oust the English from French soil.

The Cathedral suffered badly during WWI, with the 13th century stained glass windows and many of the statues on the façade bearing the brunt of the damage. The windows were restored after the war and over the decades the damaged statues have gradually been replaced with copies – sad, but necessary, for pollution was also eroding the original sculptures. Restoration work is still under way.

In **Épernay**, on and around the appropriately named Avenue de Champagne are many of the main champagne houses, some of which can be visited. One of the most interesting parts of any visit, is to walk through the extensive networks of galleries running underneath the 18th century champagne houses. Here, in a constantly cool temperature, deep inside the chalky cliff, champagne is stored for several years. Champagne is synonymous with celebration and romance, and although it is an expensive drink, it is always in demand, whenever there is something to celebrate. From births to weddings, from engagements to New Year's Eve, everyone loves to have an excuse for drinking champagne, a sparkling wine produced by the *méthode champenoise* (champagne method).

Hundreds of treasure troves of wine are hidden away in the Alsace countryside.

Wine has been produced in the area since the days of the Gauls and the Romans, but champagne, as we know it today, dates from the 17th century, when a Benedictine monk named Dom Pérignon perfected the process of making the local wine sparkle. He introduced the use of corks to stop the bottles, and experimented with the blending of wines from different vineyards. The fame of this knowledgeable monk lives on, since one of the finest champagnes is called Dom Pérignon.

Another important figure in the history of champagne was a young woman, Nicole Barbe Cliquot who became head of one of the champagne firms in 1805 when she was widowed at the age of 27. Cliquot devised a system for removing the sediment from champagne and her fame, too, lives on. **La Veuve Cliquot** (the widow cliquot) is another excellent champagne.

One of the reasons champagne is so expensive is that the wine must be kept for a stipulated number of years in the producers' cellars before being sold. The quality of the grapes used must also be excellent and skilled labour is required to supervise the infinitesimal turning of each bottle every day. After all this it makes sense to open the bottle carefully! Leave the dramatic popping of corks and spraying of champagne over the crowds to racing drivers, the correct way to open a bottle of champagne is slowly and carefully, gently using the cork to stem the escaping gas.

Yet despite its timeless, festive connotations, all is not well in the town of Champagne, because the world economic crisis has hit sales of champagne. Since the 1980s, the champagne industry has seen a marked downturn in both domestic and export sales, and 1992 was the third bad year in succession. Paradoxically, the very strength of the French Franc has not helped, making French champagne more expensive overseas, especially in the face of competition from the much improved California sparkling wines.

The champagne industry directly employs 6,500 people with many thousands more indirectly employed. The recent 1980s tendency for big industrial houses to buy up smaller players in the business, a scenario that has affected the world of fashion and luxury goods, is also prevalent in the champagne industry. Although three of the biggest champagne companies are still in family hands, groups such as Seagram and LVMH now control most of the business.

Lorraine

The eastern regions of **Alsace** and **Lorraine** are areas of France that have had an eventful and often troubled history, and were the subject of many disputes, especially between 1871 and 1945, during which time they vacillated between French and German ownership. The further you journey towards the German border, the less French the villages and countryside seem.

The pretty little black and white houses are half-timbered, with geranium-filled window boxes of Germanic influence and the village names reflect their proximity to the Rhine, with many names ending in "-heim" or "-wihr". Both Alsace and Lorraine are now aggressively European in their outlook and geographically much closer to Germany, Switzerland and Belgium than they are to Paris, consequently these areas have exploited their geographical position and have been quick to seize on the new economic and business potential of the EEC.

Metz is the capital of **Lorraine**, an old and rather austere city, with one of the most important gothic cathedrals in France, **Saint Étienne**, which has been affectionately nicknamed "God's lantern" because of its superb stained glass windows which covered an area of over 6,000 square metres.

One of the fascinating things about these windows is that they cover seven centuries, forming a virtual museum of stained glass. The oldest glass is 13th century, the most recent is the work of 20th century artists, amongst them Marc Chagall.

Verdun

Verdun 65 kilometres west of Metz, is one of the places that tragically symbolizes the Franco-German dissent that was so prevalent in this part of the country,

A monument to Andre Maginot who was Minister of War
during WWJ, Verdun.

and to visit it, is to understand something of the desolation of the WWI. The town was virtually destroyed during the war, and both the town and the surrounding countryside saw horrendous slaughter, a fact chillingly illustrated by one simple statistic – there are more than 70 cemeteries in the area.

The battle for Verdun raged for 18 months, from 21st February, 1916 to 20th August, 1917 and was one of the turning points in the war. Hundreds of thousands of men died, no one knows exactly how many, but probably close

The perfect elegance of 18th century French architecture can be seen in Stanislas Square, Nancy.

to 400,000 Frenchmen, the same number of Germans, and thousands more Americans. Small wonder that Winston Churchill said of Verdun that it was "the anvil upon which French manhood was to be hammered to death".

There are many sites to visit, including the various battlefields, the Maginot Monument and the **Douaumont Ossuary**, which contains the remains of 130,000 unidentified French and German soldiers and is surrounded by a peaceful cemetery containing 15,000 plain white crosses.

One of the most poignant memorials is that to the village of **Fleury** that was entirely wiped out during the war. On a grassy slope, simple little markers indicate where the former streets and

shops used to exist, the signs being written in French, German and English.

In the underground passages beneath the **Citadel of Verdun** are seven kilometres of galleries, which were used as both shelters and command posts during the WWI. A high-tech museum, using holograms and sound effects has recently opened in the galleries, to illustrate the horrors of the trenches and the way men lived in this subterranean world. (See the chapter on Flourishing Arts, for more information about the Citadel Museum). It is cold inside the Citadel, the statistics of death and suffering are sobering and visitors emerge with a feeling of disbelief, that what is now a comfortable, attractive town could have endured so much suffering.

Stanislas, a deposed king of Poland adored Nancy, for which he built this beautiful square.

Nancy

In the heart of Lorraine is the beautiful and elegant 18th century city of **Nancy**, the former capital of the powerful Dukes of Lorraine, which in the mid 18th century was an independent kingdom with Stanislas, the deposed King of Poland on the throne.

Nancy owes its current elegant appearance to Stanislas, whose love for his adopted capital was equalled by his love for construction. During the 30 years of his rule over Nancy, Stanislas oversaw the construction of many of the city's most beautiful buildings.

The **Place Stanislas** (Stanislas Square) is his ultimate tribute to the city

– an ensemble of elegant buildings, two ornate fountains and spectacular, golden-painted iron grilles, that have made Nancy one of the most perfect examples of 18th century French architecture.

Not only is the Place Stanislas at the administrative heart of the city, it is also the emotional heart of Nancy – the square is bordered with cafés, whose chairs spill over onto the pavements in the summer.

People sit out in the sun enjoying a morning coffee while reading a newspaper or a guidebook, depending on whether they are locals or visitors, many of the latter are from France and just as many from neighbouring Germany. On one side of the square is the **Hôtel de**

How To Appreciate Fine Wine

The Alsace region is famous for its wines.

For the French, wine is an integral part of their very serious enjoyment of food and a necessary complement to the art of cooking. Menus are just as easily planned around good wines, and vice versa. For the uninitiated, though, a restaurant wine list can appear daunting and a visit to a winemerchant can be a confusing experience. Yet, with just a little knowledge, much of the mystery can be solved.

There are a couple of generally accepted conventions governing which wine to drink with which food, namely red wine with red meat and game, white wine with fish and white meat and a sweet wine with dessert.

However, while people will happily break these rules at home, or at an informal dinner with friends, at any formal dinner, tradition is usually respected. White and rosé wines are usually served chilled, while red wine is served at room temperature, and in both cases, extremes should be avoided, white wine should not be frozen, nor should the red be warm.

Red wine improves by being opened an hour or so before it is to be drunk – the technical term is allowing the wine to "breathe". You can simply uncork the bottle, or if you wish, pour the wine into another glass container – known as "decanting" the wine.

Decanting allows air to get to the wine and is a way of getting rid of the sediment which will be found at the bottom of the bottle – especially with vintage wines and port.

The next stage in the process is choosing the right glass and there are, of course, different shaped glasses for different kinds of wine. Although it is certainly more aesthetically pleasing to serve champagne in a champagne flute, and burgundy in an over-sized balloon glass, do

Ville (Town Hall), built in the middle of the 18th century and on another is the Museum of Fine Arts containing art ranging from the Impressionists to Rubens, other old masters and art nouveau.

You leave the Place Stanislas, with its statue of Louis XV in the middle, via an Arc de Triomphe, built in honour of the same king, who was none other than Stanislas's son-in-law. Close by is the Palais Ducal, whose original foundations date back to the 13th century, though it was largely rebuilt in the 19th century. Today, the Palace houses the Historical Museum of Lorraine where exhibits trace Lorraine's history from the stone age up to WWI.

Although much of Nancy's architectural glory dates from the 18th century, the city was also the focal point of a major artistic movement in the mid-

remember that the shape or colour of a glass does not substantially affect the taste of a wine. The choice of a particular glass is more a question of aesthetics and ritual. Just ensure that the glass is always clean and that it is not over-filled, fill the glass between a-third and to half-full.

Before serving wine to your guests, you should taste it, to ensure that it is indeed as good as you think, so aim to have a clean palate – no chillies or peppermints before tasting – and pour just two or three mouthfuls into your glass. First, examine the colour of the wine. Lift the glass up to, preferably, natural light, and always hold the glass by the stem, so as not to smear it. Essentially, the wine should be clear, and, as a general rule of thumb, the better the vintage, the more colour it will have.

After colour, the next quality to check is the smell, or "nose", of the wine (barring an unfortunate bottle that has turned sour and therefore tastes vinegary), the reaction to the "nose" of a wine is very subjective. You will hear descriptions of wines varying from woody to melony to spicy, but the essential thing is that it must be pleasant – to you, the drinker.

Finally, you taste the wine, not by gulping it, but by taking only a mouthful, which you swirl around in your mouth, savouring both its taste and density.

Purists and professional wine-tasters will spit out the wine at this point, but we will avoid stretching a point this time, so sit back, and enjoy your glass of wine. *Salut* (cheers)!

19th century, still known by its original name, *Art Nouveau* (New Art). Artists such as Émile Gallé and the Daum brothers, although specialists in glass-making, aimed, through their *École de Nancy* (Nancy School), at promoting and enhancing all aspects of decorative art. As you explore Nancy, you will come across many examples of Art Nouveau houses, dating from the beginning of this century.

Industries

Vittel and **Contrexéville** are two spa towns whose springs produce mineral water, both of the same name, which are extremely popular in France, a country where people drink mineral water in preference to tap water. In Vittel, you can visit the bottling factory.

The Lorraine region has undergone profound social and industrial changes over the past 25 years, having seen its former traditional industries of coal, steel, iron ore and textiles suffer from a massive slump.

In the past quarter of a century, Lorraine has lost 75,000 jobs in the steel and iron ore sector, 16,000 in coal mining, and 26,000 in textiles – yet, overall, there has not been undue upheaval or social unrest.

Part of the reason for this was foresight – the Saar coalfields in the northeast of Lorraine have planned all their pit closures, spreading them evenly over a period of 25 years.

By the year 2005, there will be no coal mining in Lorraine, and another 14,000 jobs will have disappeared as a consequence. The region has received massive state-aid, generous incentives are offered to foreign investors and there have been successful local initiatives, such as the creation of Technopole at Nancy. This complex serves as the headquarters for 100 small businesses, offering them cheap office space, advice and start-up capital facilities.

The charming sign outside the Alsace Museum, Strasbourg.

Strasbourg

Alsace, according to the young mayor of Strasbourg is "at a crossroads, not just of motorways but of cultures...we are no longer at a frontier. We are in front of a new region that links France and Germany. Paris is no longer at the heart of Europe." Strong, forward-looking words, and one glance at a map indicates that Alsace is looking in the right direction when it looks towards Europe. What other solution could the region have, linked as it is by such a long common border with Germany and Switzerland? Alsace is struggling to create a new destiny for itself, less tied to Paris, and more geared towards its eastern neighbours. For example, the region desperately wants the French express train, the TGV, to link up with the German Inter-City Express network and on into eastern Europe.

Little surprise, therefore, that **Strasbourg** is today one of the most affirmatively "European" cities of Europe, situated on the border of two of the largest European Community powers, France and Germany. Strasbourg confirmed its European credentials, when, in the autumn of 1992, it turned in the highest "yes" vote in France on the referendum on European political and monetary union. Historically, Strasbourg has been a most European city, influenced by the alternating identities of the French and the Germans, due to the constant changing of national boundaries around this periphery town.

The Romans turned it into a garrison town, in the 5th century the Franks captured it and called the town *Strateburgum* (the city of roads). Standing as it did in the direct path of German invasions, Strasbourg has been attacked, destroyed and rebuilt many times. During the Franco-German War (1870-1871), Strasbourg surrendered to the Germans, after a seige of 50 days, during which the city was repeatedly shelled. After the end of the WWI, the city became French again, only to be occupied

Cathedral of Notre Dame, Reims.

by the Germans between 1940 and 1944, during WWII.

All this political turbulence is now part of history, for the Strasbourg of the late 20th century is vociferously European. The modern buildings of the **Palais d'Europe** house the Council of Ministers, the European Assembly and the International Secretariat of the EEC, as well as some of the sessions of the European Parliament. In January 1993, the French government, affirming its confidence in the future and dynamism of Strasbourg, chose to relocate one of France's most prestigious colleges, the **École Nationale d'Administration,** (the breeding ground for most of the top bureaucrats in the country) here.

Dominating the city is the single

The quaint timbered houses of Riquewihr, Alsace.

tower of the **Cathedral of Notre Dame**, which was built and re-built from the 11th to the 15th centuries. Notre Dame has suffered over the centuries: a 12th century fire destroyed the original building; the Revolution saw the destruction of 230 of the Cathedral's statues; the roof was burned down by Prussian shells in 1870 and Allied bombing in 1944 damaged parts of the structure. Careful restoration work has been carried out, and those statues that were saved from revolutionary fervour are now on display in the **Maison de l'Oeuvre de Notre**

Dame (Museum of the Work of Notre Dame) which is located next door to the Cathedral.

The 18th century neoclassical **Palais Rohan**, formerly the Bishop's Palace, houses three excellent museums – the **Museum of Fine Arts**, the **Archaeological Museum** and the **Museum of Decorative Arts** which has a good display of ceramics.

One of the most charming areas of Strasbourg is the old district of **Petite France**, with its small neat canals lined with timbered and gabled houses.

Over the centuries Strasbourg has been home to many famous people: Gutenberg lived there in the early 15th century; Goethe studied at Strasbourg University (where as part of his campaign of rigourous self-control, he used to climb up to the top of the Cathedral, despite his vertigo) and a young poet and soldier called Rouget de Lisle, the composer of the French national anthem, the mis-named "Marseillaise", composed this stirring anthem in Strasbourg, working all through the night in a fit of feverish creative genius.

Alsace Region – Wine Routers

One excellent way of seeing the Alsace countryside and experiencing first hand some of the region's wine culture – and, in moderation, the wine – is to drive south from the little town of Marlenheim, 20 kilometres west of Strasbourg, along

The 10th century crypt of Saint Benigne Cathedral, Dijon.

a picturesque route that has been designated the **Route du Vin** (Wine Route). For 180 kilometres, down to the town of Thann, the road winds through vineyards, picturesque villages, with ruined castles and towers perched on the hillside – all in all the perfect way to experience Alsace. During the time of the grape harvest, one will not miss the sight of the bustle and activity of little villages, whose economy largely depends on the vineyards.

The proximity of Alsace to both France and Germany has had an impact on its vineyards and the white wine of Alsace bears characteristics of both countries, although the names of some of the most famous Alsatian wines definitely sound more German than French

– Riesling, Tokay and Gewürztraminer. Although wine has been produced in the region since the 3rd century, the Alsatian white wines do not possess, it must be admitted, the same *cachet* (prestige) as the great burgundies of France, but they are very high quality wines, and the local producers have consistently worked to update technology, to improve the grapes, and, above all to publicize the merits of their wines. They even trade on the difficulty of some of their names: one recent advertising campaign, after showing pretty pictures of Alsatian vineyards, claims "And now, when someone asks you to spell Gueberschwihr or Mittelbergheim, perhaps you won't be quite so lost".

Driving down the Route du Vin, the pretty town of **Obernai** seems to be just waiting to be used as a backdrop for a play or a light-hearted operetta. Twisting streets, gabled houses, painted houses, half-timbered houses, full-timbered houses – Obernai looks exactly the way a typical Alsatian town should look. A short distance outside town is the **Mont Sainte Odile** mound 763 metres high. At its summit is a 17th century convent which boasts a breathtaking view over the surrounding countryside, forests and vineyards. The convent was formed during the eighth century by Odile, Duke Etichon of Obernais' daughter who after being born blind recovered her sight upon baptism. Today, the mound is a major pilgrim and tourist sight, with over one million visitors a year.

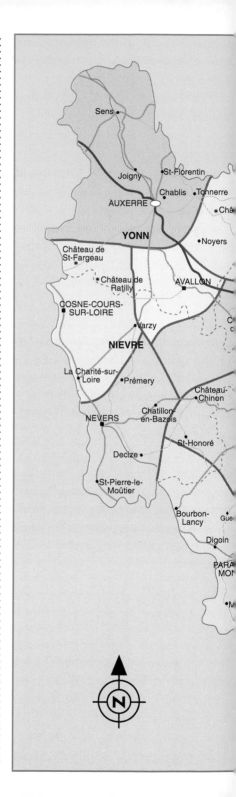

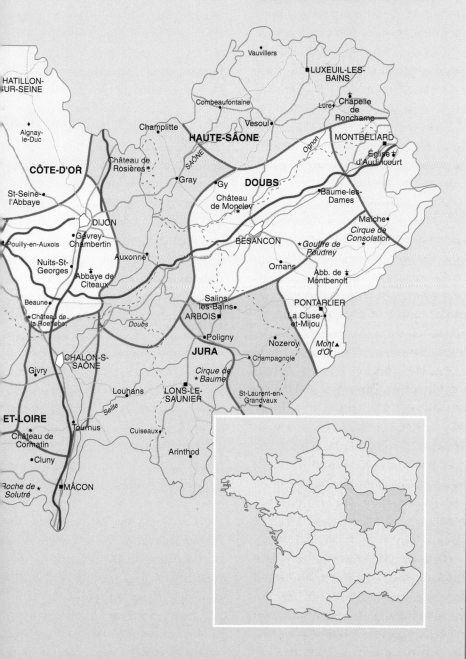

BURGUNDY

Vauvillers

■LUXEUIL-LES-
BAINS

HATILLON-
UR-SEINE

Combeaufontaine

Lure• Chapelle
de
Ronchamp

Aignay-
le-Duc

Champlitte

Vesoul•

HAUTE-SÂONE

MONTBÉLIARD■

Église ✝
d'Audincourt

CÔTE-D'OR

Château de
Rosières ✳

SAÔNE

•Gray

•Gy

DOUBS

Baume-les-
Dames

St-Seine-•
l'Abbaye

Château
de Moncley
✳

Ognon

Marche•

Cirque de
Consolation

DIJON

•Pouilly-en-Auxois

•Gevrey-
Chambertin

Auxonne•

BESANCON

•Gouffre de
Poudrey
✳

Nuits-St-
Georges

Abbaye de ✝
Citeaux

Ornans•

Abb. de ✝
Montbenoit

Beaune•

•Château de
la Rochepot

Doubs

Salins-
les-Bains•

ARBOIS■

PONTARLIER

La Cluse-•
et-Mijou

•Poligny

Nozeroy•

Mont▲
d'Or

CHALON-S-
SAÔNE

JURA

•Champagnole

Givry•

Cirque de
✳ Baume

Louhans•

LONS-LE-
SAUNIER

St-Laurent-en-•
Grandvaux

ET-LOIRE

Seille

Cuiseaux•

✳
Château de
Cormatin

Tournus•

Arinthod•

•Cluny

Roche de ✳
Solutré

■MÂCON

Continuing south, through the village which possesses the difficult name, **Mittelbergheim**, you arrive at **Ribeauvillé**, yet another picture postcard little town, with the added attraction of holding one of the last remaining traditional Alsatian festivals, the equally unpronounceable *Pfifferdaj* (Day of the Fifes), which takes place on the first Sunday of September. It offers one an opportunity to see the local costumes, and to share in the *Fontaine du Vin* (Fountain of Wine), which is set up in front of the Town Hall.

A few kilometres further south, is the village of **Riquewihr**, famous not only for its excellent Riesling wine, but also for being one of the most beautiful villages in Alsace, no mean achievement in an area so crowded with picturesque towns and villages. Riquewihr managed to escape unscathed from the ravages of war, and today appears to still possess much of the original 16th century architecture which is both still in place and very much in use. The village is not a museum-piece, far from it, for over a thousand people live there. Apart from the usual sprinkling of cafés, there is a **National Necropolis**, erected in memory of the 1,684 soldiers of the First French Army, who were killed in 1944.

Colmar, 68 kilometres southwest of Strasbourg, is a beautiful town, whose old city centre is filled with cobbled streets, brightly painted, timbered houses and canals bordered with neat houses. One section of town is called **Little Ven-**

ice, and as you follow the course of the River Lauch, as it wanders through town, you will see old houses with rowing boats moored outside, overhanging weeping willow trees and pretty bridges. One of the most attractive houses in the old town is the **Maison Pfister**, whose highly decorated façade dates from 1537. The **Unterlinden Museum**, which justly deserves its place on a list of must-see French museums, is housed in a 13th century convent. It holds the record for being the most visited of all French provincial museums, with some 350,000 visitors each year. The museum houses an impressive collection of paintings, but the undisputed showpiece is a stunning early 16th century altar piece, called the **Issenheim Altar**. It is a highly complex work of art, in which successive layers of painted wooden panels open out, giving different compositions as the various panels are opened with a group of carved statues at the heart. Each panel represents a different religious scene or saint, painted by the artist Mathias Grünewald.

In 1854, Frédéric-Auguste Bartholdi was born in Colmar. He later gained fame as the sculptor of New York's ultimate monument, the Statue of Liberty.

The Route du Vin continues on southwards, with more complicated names such as Gueberschwihr and Pfaffenheim, and from Thann it is only 20 kilometres to **Mulhouse**, the industrial heart of Alsace. Mulhouse has a solidly European history, having been variously French, Swiss and German, and even now it shares its airport with Basel, in Switzerland, the local newspapers are in both French and German, and everyday 35,000 people cross over into Germany to work.

Dijon

South of Champagne, and southwest of Lorraine is **Burgundy**, the area that produces much of France's most prestigious wines and good food. The beef, especially *boeuf à la bourguignonne* (Burgundian beef) is wonderful, and so is the other local speciality, snails. Do not be put off by the idea of the snail itself – just tell yourself, the object of the exercise is to eat all the creamy garlic butter in which the snails are cooked! In addition to its gastronomic reputation, Burgundy is also one of the most historic areas of France.

Dijon was the former capital of the Dukes of Burgundy, and during its heyday in the 15th century, the country's best artists and craftsmen were attracted here. They left behind stunning works of art, beautiful buildings and gave the historic heart of Dijon a grace and charm which the 20th century visitor immediately feels. The line

of the Dukes of Burgundy began in 1364, when Philippe le Hardi (the Bold), the fourth son of the King of France, was endowed with the title at birth. Three dukes succeeded him, all with equally inspiring names: Jean *sans Peur* (the Fearless), Philippe *le Bon* (the Good) and Charles *le Téméraire* (the Reckless).

The focal point of the town is the impressive **Palais des Ducs et des États de Bourgogne** (Palace of the Dukes and the States of Burgundy). The palace was abandoned by Charles, the last duke and in the 17th century, whatever was left of the original palace was incorporated into a new, classical style building. The Palace houses the city's **Musée des Beaux Arts** (Art Museum), an excellent collection of painting and sculpture, and, not to be missed, the stunningly beautiful tombs of the Dukes of Burgundy. The Dukes were originally buried in a monastery outside the city, called the **Chartreuse de Champmol** (Carthusian Monastery of Champmol), founded by the first Duke Philippe in 1383. The funerary monuments have now been transferred to the Museum, and are extraordinarily beautiful, with a wealth of carving and detailed frescoes of weeping mourners. The statue of Philippe on his own tomb

Folk art in Dijon.

is protected by two pretty angels, with sad, serious faces and delicate golden wings. In front of the palace is a semicircular **Place de la Libération** (Liberation Square), formerly Place Royale, which was designed by Mansart, the architect of Versailles.

The 13th century **St Bénigne Cathedral** was built on top of the 10th century Romanesque basilica, which is now the crypt. Among the 86 pillars of the impressive rotunda, you can see traces of the early carved decorations. One of the city's other major collections

and votive offerings and if you want to know how the ancestors of the food-loving French used to eat, a table has been set with 1,800-year old recipes, amongst them dishes of snails and oysters!

Burgundian Countryside & Wines

One of the pleasantest ways of discovering Burgundy is to drive through the countryside and the hilly vineyards, one very pretty drive being the 60 kilometre trip south from Dijon to Chagny, driving through the **Côte d'Or Vineyards**, and stopping at the historic town of **Beaune** en route. In the 19th century, there was an outbreak of Phylloxera, an insect related to the green-fly, which destroyed almost all the vines in Burgundy. These were then reconstituted by imported cuttings from the US. As you follow the main road, the N74, or better still, the smaller, quieter D122, the village names are a roll-call of the best of French wines: **Gevrey-Chambertin**, **Nuits-St-George**, and after **Beaune**, **Meursault** and **Puligny-Montrachet**. One of the reasons that burgundy is so expensive is that the actual area producing any one of the 114 *appellations* (types of wine) is very small. Some of the vineyards would probably be described as large gardens, anywhere else in the world. For example, when a top wine like Romanée-Conti is produced from a mere 4.5 acres,

is the **Musée Archéologique** (Archaeological Museum), housed in the former Benedictine Abbey of St Bénigne. There are some fascinating exhibits, including a bracelet dating from the 9th century BC which is made of solid gold and weighs an impressive 3 pounds. In the 11th century cellars of the monastery, is a collection of Gallo-Roman sculptures

Saint Fargeau Chateau in Burgundy.

the risk of bad weather ruining an entire crop, or reducing the final yield, is considerable.

The narrow strip of hillside which constitutes the Côte d'Or (Golden Hillside), produces both red and white wines of a very high quality which are usually classified as Côte de Nuits, north of Beaune and Côte de Beaune to the south. The Pinot Noir grapes that are grown in the **Côte de Nuits** vineyards produce excellent red burgundies, as well as a small quantity of equally excellent white wine. Some of the *grand cru* (great wines)

perfection! These wines are sold in Côte de Nuits villages.

South of Beaune lie the **Côte de Beaune** vineyards, famous for their white wines, though high quality red wine is also produced. White wine makes up less than a-quarter of the area's total output. The two best known names are possibly those of two small villages, which produce the Montrachet grape: each village has, in local Burgundian style, tacked on the name of the wine to its own name, and thus came about Pouligny-Montrachet and Chassagne-Montrachet, wonderful, expensive wines.

Slightly to the north of Pouligny-Montrachet, is Mersault, an equally prestigious white wine and further north again, but still south of Beaune, are the vineyards producing the red Côtes de Beaune – Volnay, Pommard and Beaune.

Wine Sales

The picture-postcard pretty town of **Beaune**, which used to be the residence of the Dukes of Burgundy, before they moved to Dijon, is the administrative centre of the Burgundy wine industry. Each November it is also home to the prestigious **Hospices de Beaune** wine auction.

The history behind this hospice, a charity hospital for the elderly, is intimately linked to the history of Burgundy and wine. The hospice received its first bequest in the 15th century, and over

of the red variety are grown here, such as Gevrey-Chambertin and Romanée-Conti.

Both very expensive wines, though thankfully for the wallets of the not so rich wine lover, this area also produces what are generally referred to as inferior wines – but do not forget that "inferior" is a relative term, when discussing near

the ensuing decades, owners of the local vineyards have traditionally bequeathed more land. So, now the hospice owns plots of vine all over the Côte de Beaune, for example, 58 hectares between Aloxe-Corton and Mersault.

Since the annual winter auction is still part of a charitable tradition, the bids are usually high, but the wine is also of an excellent quality. The money raised through what has been termed the biggest charity sale in the world is used for both the acquisition of new medical equipment, as well as the up-keep of the Hôtel Dieu, which is the building housing the hospice.

The **Hôtel Dieu**, with its highly decorated, brightly coloured tiled roof, is one of the classic images of Burgundy, appropriate for an institution so closely linked with the region's principal trade.

Autun was a Roman settlement, and the Emperor Augustus himself gave the town its name, *Augustodonum*. The town served as an important stop on the Lyon-Boulogne road, but only traces of the former Roman grandeur survive – the **Roman theatre**, which could seat 15,000, and the two city gates, the **Porte d'Arroux** and the **Porte St André**.

The **Cathedral of St Lazare** was built between 1120 and 1146, specifically to house the remains of its name saint. But, later additions, such as the 15th century bell-tower and the 19th century doors, have broken the harmony of the Romanesque façade. The tympanum positioned over the main entrance, is a masterpiece of Roman-esque sculpture.

It was sculpted in record time between 1130 and 1135 by Gislebertus whose signature can be read just under the feet of the centre statue of Christ. Southwest of Autun, is the 18th century **Château de Plaige**, surrounded by a park. The park is pretty, but not wholly unexpected in a country dotted with so many pretty *châteaux*. What is totally unexpected is that within the *château* is a Tibetan Monastery – **Kagyu-Ling**. The monastery, with its stupa, white prayer flags and temple, has been in Burgundy since 1974 where it is both completely integrated and accepted by the local community.

Lyon

Surrounded by Burgundy to the north, the Massif Central to the west, the Alps to the East and Provence to the south, is the **Rhône Valley**, whose lifeblood is the River Rhône.

Lyon not only dominates the Rhône Valley, but as the second largest urban area in France, it dominates the whole of the southern half of the country. The city has a beautiful setting, straddling the two major regional rivers, the Rhône and the Saône and surrounded by two hills, the Fourvière and Croix Rousse.

The peninsula between the rivers lies at the heart of the modern city and is home to some of Lyon's most impor-tant museums – the **Palais St Pierre**, the **Fine Arts Museum** and the excellent

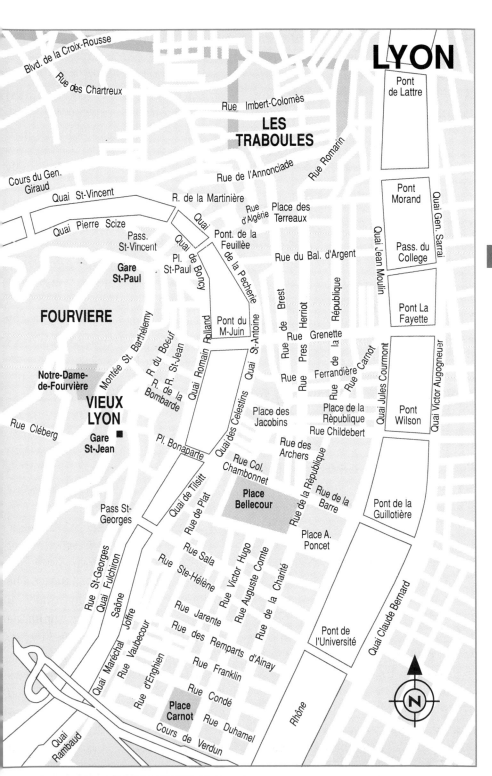

LYON

Pont de Lattre

Pont Morand

Pass. du College

Pont La Fayette

Quai Gen. Sarrai

Quai Jean Moulin

Rue Imbert-Colomès

LES TRABOULES

Rue Romarin

Rue de l'Annonciade

Blvd. de la Croix-Rousse

Rue des Chartreux

Cours du Gen. Giraud

Quai St-Vincent

R. de la Martinière

Rue d'Algérie

Place des Terreaux

Quai Pierre Scize

Quai

Pont. de la Feuillèe

Rue du Bal. d'Argent

Pass. St-Vincent

Quai de Boncy

de la Pecherie

Pl. St-Paul

Gare St-Paul

Rue de Brest

République

FOURVIERE

Rolland

Pont du M-Juin

Quai St-Antoine

Rue Herriot

Rue du Pres

Grenette

Montée St. Barthélemy

R. du Boeuf

R. R. St-Jean

Quai Romain

Quai Celestins

Rue de la Ferrandière

Rue Carnot

Quai Jules Courmont

Notre-Dame-de-Fourvière

R. de la Bombarde

Rue

Rue

Place des Jacobins

Place de la Règublique

Pont Wilson

Quai Victor Augogneur

VIEUX LYON

Gare St-Jean

Pl. Bonaparte

Quai des Celestins

Rue Childebert

Rue Cléberg

Rue Col. Chambonnet

Rue des Archers

Rue de la République

Pont de la Guillotière

Rue de la Barre

Pass St-Georges

Quai de Tilsitt

Rue de Plat

Place Bellecour

Place A. Poncet

Rue St-Georges

Quai Fulchiron

Rue Sala

Rue Victor Hugo

Rue Auguste Comte

Rue Ste-Hélène

Rue de la Charité

Saône

Joffre

Rue Jarente

Quai Claude Bernard

Rue des Remparts d'Ainay

Quai Maréchal

Rue Vaubecour

Rue Franklin

Pont de l'Université

Rue d'Enghien

Rue Condé

Rhône

Place Carnot

Rue Duhamel

Quai Rambaud

Cours de Verdun

N

Musée Historique de Tissus (History of Textiles Museum), where the city's past as the centre of the French silk industry is illustrated with exquisite examples of fabrics dating back to the 17th century.

The heart of Lyon is the **Place Bellecour**, one of the largest squares in the country, dominated by a statue of Louis XIV.

The current statue, which dates from 1828, replaces the original, which was considered a symbol of the hated monarchy and thus was melted down during the Revolution.

The city's long history, dating back to the Gauls and the Romans, is still very much in evidence, in the well-preserved archaeological sites on **Fourvière Hills**. In addition to the **Museum of Gallo-Roman Civilization**, are two **Roman theatres**: the small **Odeon**, which was reserved for the exclusive use of the elite, who would listen to musical recitals there, and the larger **Theatre**, the oldest in France which is comparable in size to the theatres in Arles and Orange. You can see the remains and trace the outlines of an aqueduct, a temple, and some of the streets that formerly surrounded this area.

Today, the Roman remains overlook the modern city, across the River Sâone and are themselves overshadowed by the late 19th century **Basilica of Notre Dame**.

The basilica with its statue of the Virgin Mary, dominates the city's skyline and its little chapel with a 16th century statue of Mary (which is reput-edly miraculous), is a major pilgrimage site.

Sadly, pollution has taken its toll on the basilica and at least 3 million French Francs are urgently needed to restore the upper parts of the church, especially the towers. In keeping with 20th century money-making tactics, the basilica sells *pins* (souvenir badges) to raise the money needed.

Other than the super-fit, who can cope with walking all the way up to the top of Fourvière, an interesting and easy way up, is to take the funicular from the bottom of the hill.

Then, of course, when you have visited the basilica and enjoyed the panoramic view of Lyon, you can walk back down the hill to town. Leaving the church grounds, you set off down a pretty path that zig-zags its way through the woods clustered at the bottom of the basilica, which are carpeted with chestnuts in autumn.

From the woods, you then have a choice of how you continue on down to the old town, as there are several paths. You can either opt to walk down one of the very steep narrow streets, or you can walk down the equally steep flights of steps.

On your walk, you will see glimpses of the old town, with its high Renaissance buildings, many of them the former homes of silk merchants, who formed the backbone of Lyon's industrial prominence in the 16th century.

One of the most interesting streets is Rue Juiverie (Street of the Jews), lined with beautiful homes, built by the city's wealthy bankers. The Jews were all expelled from Lyon in the late 14th century.

Lyon is acknowledged by most French people to be the gastronomic centre of their country, an accolade partly due to its geographical position and the consequent availability of produce from the Rhône Valley, Savoy and Bresse, and also partly due to the unwavering simplicity of Lyonnaise cooking: no frills, no fads, but consistently good, everyday food.

There is a saying about Lyon: "Lyon is washed by three rivers – the Rhône, the Saône ... and the Beaujolais", for, to the north of the city, on the west bank of the River Saône, is the **Beaujolais** region.

Beaujolais is famous for its excellent red wines, and, since the 1980s, for one of its not-quite-so-distinguished wines, the Beaujolais Nouveau, which has been one of the great marketing successes of the last decade. As you drive in a wide arc around the town of Villefranche-sur-Saône, the vineyards and villages bear the names of some of the country's best wines, tiny hamlets whose names are known the world over.

Rhône Valley Wines

To the north of Villefranche, the vineyards that produce the 10 most recognized wines are called **Beaujolais Villages**, namely Moulin-à-vent (or wind-mill), Brouilly, Côte de Brouilly, Chénas, Fleurie, Juliénas, Saint Amour, Morgon, Chiroubles, and the most recent addition to this classification, Régnié, which was only admitted in 1988.

South of Villefranche and along the valley of the little River Azregues is the prettily named region "**Le Pays des Pierres Dorées**" (Land of the Golden Stones), a name derived from the ochre colour of the stone used to build the houses and *châteaux*. The wine from this region is simply called **Beaujolais** or **Beaujolais Supérieur** (superior Beaujolais).

The vineyards of the Rhône Valley stretch to the south of Lyon, following the course of the river valley for 200 kilometres and stretching on into Provence.

The town of **Montélimar**, the centre of the nougat industry, marks the theoretical division between the northern **Côte du Rhône** wines, such as the Hermitage and Saint Joseph, and the southern Côte du Rhône, whose most famous name is Châteauneuf-du-Pape. Currently, 160,000 hectares along the valley are used for vineyards.

All along the Rhône Valley are orchards, where a wide variety of fruit is grown – peaches, pears, apricots, cherries, some apples and even chestnuts. A combination of different ripening times, and varying amounts of sun received (depending on the direction and the height of the orchards) means that this area alone can produce one-third of the country's fruit.

La Loire

The River Loire runs parallel to the Rhône, to the west – but this is not Le Loire, the river famous for its royal *châteaux*, but **La Loire**, whose twisting course flows through gorges, with ruined fortresses and castles on the peaks. A drive along La Loire, through the many dramatic gorges, should include a visit to the extraordinary **Puy-en-Velay**.

The town sits on a fertile plain, out of which suddenly rise two volcanic peaks: the largest is called **le Rocher Corneille** or le Mont d'Anis, and the most sharply pointed is called the **Rocher Saint Michel**, or le Mont d'Aiguilhe. The Rocher Saint Michel is 80 metres high, and is crowned, by a 10th century Romanesque chapel, which replaced an earlier Roman temple dedicated to the god Mercury.

Two hundred and sixty-eight steps lead up to the summit – well worth the climb, not only for the view, but also for the unusual chapel itself, with its pseudo-oriental exterior and its irregular interior, which follows the shape of the rock.

Roman & Romanesque

South of Lyon, at the start of the Rhône Valley is the historic town of **Vienne**, a town that was destined to be the Rome of France, that is until her northerly neighbour Lugdunum (Lyon) outpaced

her. Vienne boasts an impressive array of Roman monuments and a superb Romanesque-Gothic Cathedral. Remember, Romanesque is not the same as Roman; Roman architecture, generally refers, to ancient Rome, whilst Romanesque refers to the transitional period between Roman and Gothic. If you think it is difficult to remember which is which in English, just try it in French: the French distinguish *Romain* (Roman) and *Roman* (Romanesque); *Roman* is also known, as the Norman style of architecture by the English.

Vienne's Roman monuments include the **Temple of Augustus and Livia**, a well-preserved temple, only slightly smaller than the Maison Carrée in Nîmes; the large **Roman Theatre** and as in Lyon, a smaller, accompanying theatre or **Odeon**, as well as a fragment of a Roman road, and **Pyramide**. In the Middle Ages, it was thought that Pontius Pilat, the man who condemned Jesus Christ to death, was buried there. According to legend, Pontius Pilat travelled from Jerusalem to Vienne, where, overcome with remorse at having caused the death of Christ, he committed suicide, by throwing himself into the River Rhône.

Further south, at **Valence**, the visitor begins to feel that he is entering the Midi, the sunny south of the country, for the prettily named **Auto-route du Soleil** (Highway to the Sun), passes through Valence, which has an impressive communications network. It was doubtless the ease of access that made the Ro-

Basilica of Saint Reni, Reims.

mans settle there, and "Valentia" as the Romans called it was one of the largest Roman settlements in Gaul. The pretty old town clusters round the Roman-esque **Saint Apollinaire Cathedral**, which was added to in the 17th and 19th centuries.

The **Musée des Beaux Arts**, features local sculpture and furniture and the beautiful **Parc Jouvet** has 14 acres of gardens and a pool. In 1785, a 16 year old army cadet was sent to study at the Artillery School in Valence – his name, Napoléon Bonaparte.

Heartland

Auvergne, covering 26,013 square kilometres, is at the geographical heart of France, and is dominated by the **Massif Central**, a region of extinct volcanos and mountains. This mountainous terrain is a crucial factor not only in influencing the geography of the region but also the character of the inhabitants. Auvergne is sparsely populated, for life in the mountains is difficult, and there has been considerable emigration towards an easier urban life, leaving behind an ageing population, with a not entirely justified reputation for being taciturn.

Auvergne has never been at the forefront of history, no armies have fought over it, as they did in Bordeaux and Périgord, and time seems to have moved more slowly here than elsewhere in France. But, even though major history was never made in Auvergne, it has, on occasions, been made by the men of Auvergne. The Marquis de la

251

■ ■ ■ ■ ■

Intricate stained glass windows of the Cathedral of Saint Étienne, Bourges.

Highly decorated doorway of Bourges' Cathedral, St Etienne.

Fayette, the French hero of the American War of Independence was an Auvergnat, as were two recent French Presidents, President Pompidou and President Giscard d'Estaing.

Therefore to understand the Auvergne, the best thing the visitor can do is to explore the rugged countryside, shaped by volcanic activity which has so influenced its people. The best place to start is the **Parc Naturel Régional des Volcans d'Auvergne** (Auvergne Regional Natural Volcano Park).

This impressive sounding natural park, the largest in France, was set up in 1984, and covers 350,000 hectares, and a distance of over 120 kilometres. It contains a series of volcanic mountains which are universally unique. The three

most spectacular volcanic areas are the Monts Dômes, close to Clermont-Ferrand, the Monts Dore further south, and the Monts du Cantal even further south.

The Challenge of the Puy-de-Dômes

The Monts Dômes, also known as the **Chaîne des Puys**, is a series of 112 extinct volcanos, the "youngest" in Auvergne. The highest of the *puys* (peaks) is the **Puy de Dôme** (Dôme Peak) at 1,465 metres, which is crowned by the ruins of a Gallo-Roman temple and a television tower. It has now become a favourite launching-off point for hang-gliders. It takes about an hour to walk to the summit of the *puy* (peak) and back, though you will almost certainly spend a long time just enjoying the view and remembering the exploits that have taken place here.

In 1648, the Clermont-Ferrand – a town at the foot of the Puy-de-Dôme was the site where mathematician and physicist, Blaise Pascal proved his theory of air pressure. Actually it was his brother-in-law who climbed up to the summit, carrying a barometer, to observe the change in the level of mercury.

In 1908, the Michelin brothers offered a prize of 100,000 Francs to any pilot who could fly from Paris, carrying a passenger weighing 75 kilogrammes, and land on the summit of the Puy de Dôme, less than six hours later.

They threw in an extra condition: the pilot first had to fly 1,500 metres to the right of the Cathedral of Clermont Ferrand.

Three years later, on 7th March, 1911, Eugène Renaux and his suitably heavy passenger, Senouque, managed it, in exactly 5 hours 11 minutes.

Dore & Cantal Mountains

The **Monts Dore** (Dore Mountains), to the south, are much older than the Monts Dôme, for they are the remains of a three million year old volcano, later sculpted by glacial erosion. The highest point is the **Puy** (Peak) **de Sancy** at 1,885 metres, it requires much more time and stamina to climb this peak than the Puy de Dôme. Remember, as you walk or drive around this region, that there is a risk that the roads might be blocked by snow from December to April.

The southern **Monts du Cantal** are far older than the other two major volcanic groups, since they are 20 million years old, and were formed by the streams of lava which flowed from a huge volcano, estimated to measure 3,000 metres. The layers of lava from this volcano eventually covered a surface 70 kilometres in diameter.

The two highest points are **Puy**

Ready and waiting for festivities in a small heartland village.

Mary (Peak Mary) at 1,785 metres, and **le Plomb de Cantal** at 1,855 metres. It is a rough walk up Puy Mary, though it does not take more than an hour, but it is imperative to stay on the marked-out path. You can take a *téléphérique* (cable car) up the Plomb de Cantal.

Famous Mineral Spas

One of the results of such intensive volcanic activity is the presence of mineral water springs and thermal spas, with the thick layers of volcanic rock acting as a filter. **Volvic** is one of the most popular mineral waters in France, a country where the drinking of mineral water is a serious activity. It is interest-

ing to visit the bottling plant – with a free tasting session at the end, of course! The medical benefits of thermal baths were known to the Romans, but they were not rediscovered until the 18th and 19th centuries, when it became distinctly fashionable to "take the waters".

Royat was launched by the visit of the Empress Eugénie in 1862, and **Vichy** was well-known for curing rheumatism, long before the 17th century writer Madame de Sévigné described Vichy water, in a letter to her daughter: "I took the waters this morning ... Ah, how horrible they are! You go at 6 am, everybody is there, you drink, and pull a face, because, if you can believe it, the water is boiling and it has an unpleasant taste of saltpetre."

Bordeaux and its glorious monuments.

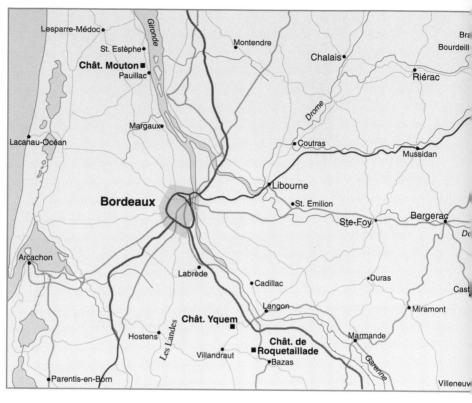

Unpleasant tasting or not, the waters of Vichy have always attracted the leaders of society; the daughters of King Louis XV who gave their name to a spring, the **Source Mesdames**; the mother of Napoleon Bonaparte; and the Emperor Napoleon III, who had a chalet built in the Parc de l'Allier. When the Germans invaded France in WWII, the government first fled to Bordeaux and then to Vichy, where it stayed from 12th July, 1940 to 20th August 1944.

Michelin's Home

Clermont-Ferrand is the capital of the Auvergne, a town born of the union of the two close but rival towns of Clermont and Montferrand in 1731. Today, it is a prosperous town due to the rubber industry, for Clermont-Ferrand is, to most people, the city of Michelin, the manufacturer of rubber tyres.

The Michelin brothers, André and Édouard, founded their tyre company in 1888, first manufacturing tyres for bicycles and horse-drawn carriages. They moved on to automobile tyres in 1895. And, in 1946, Michelin was the first company to introduce radial tyres.

Most of the houses in the old part of town, as well as the 13th century Cathedral are built of dark, volcanic rock. Thus, this section of town which stands on the remnants of a volcanic cone, is

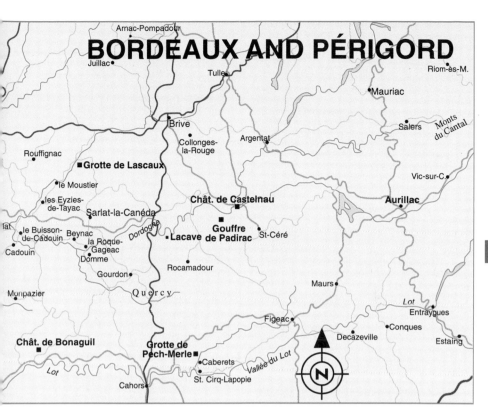

BORDEAUX AND PÉRIGORD

Arnac-Pompadour
Juillac
Tulle
Riom-ès-M.
Mauriac
Brive
Salers
Monts du Cantal
Collonges-la-Rouge
Argentat
Rouffignac
■Grotte de Lascaux
Vic-sur-C.
le Moustier
les Eyzies-de-Tayac
Sarlat-la-Canéda
Chât. de Castelnau
Aurillac
lat
le Buisson-de-Cadouin
Beynac
la Roque-Gageac
Dordogne
Gouffre
Lacave de Padirac
St-Céré
Cadouin
Domme
Rocamadour
Gourdon
Maurs
Monpazier
Quercy
Lot
Entraygues
Figeac
Conques
Chât. de Bonaguil
Decazeville
Estaing
Lot
Grotte de Pech-Merle
Caberets
Vallée du Lot
N
Cahors
St. Cirq-Lapopie

known as "ville noire".

The Gothic **Cathedral of Notre Dame de l'Assomption** contains some superb 12th and 13th century stained glass. The **Basilica of Notre Dame du Port**, dating from the 11th and 12th century, is a fine example of Romanesque Auvergne architecture. Seven kilometres south of Clermont-Ferrand is the **Plateau de Gergovia** where the leader of the Gauls, Vercingetorix, defeated Julius Caesar in March 52BC.

Berry & Limousin

To the west of Auvergne are the two regions of **Berry** and **Limousin**.

Limousin was one of the many subjects of dispute from the 12th to the 15th century, between the French and the English. But, unlike Bordeaux, which remained under unbroken English rule for 300 years, control over Limousin went back and forth between the two countries. Limousin was French, until it passed to the English as part of Eleanor of Aquitaine's dowry in 1152 (see the section on Bordeaux). It was retaken by the French in the early 13th century, only to be handed back to the English under the *Treaty of Calais* in 1360, and was recaptured 10 years later by Charles V, in a campaign lasting from 1370 to 1374. In the 20th century, the mass emigration from the agricultural coun-

Jacques Coeur – A Role Model for the *Bourgeoisie*?

In the early 15th century, the town of Bourges, in Berry, was the effective capital of Charles VII, the *Dauphin* (eldest son of the king), who was the claimant to the French throne but was virtually powerless, since the English controlled much of the country. Charles himself was a weak, suspicious, fearful person, whose sense of destiny would not be shaken out of its apathy until his encounter with a young peasant girl called Joan of Arc.

Jacques Coeur was born in Bourges c.1395, the son of a furrier, and he acquired his training in the financial dealings that would later be of such importance, notably through a business trip he took to the Middle East.

When the *Dauphin* was brought by Joan of Arc to be crowned King, Coeur became his banker and later a member of his council. His fortunes rose in-line with his increasing responsibilities – tax collector, Inspector-General of salt taxes, diplomatic representative of the King, and by 1441, he was given a title.

He set about improving the social status of his family, marrying his daughter to a nobleman, making his son the Archbishop of Bourges, and his brother the Bishop of Luçon. He also acquired land, lots of it, including some 40 manors, and he built a palace for himself in Bourges.

History has been divided in its judgement on Jacques Coeur, some seeing him as nothing more than an adventurer who on his on account, exploited public money for his own good. In the 18th century, history saw him as a victim of jealous despotism, whilst the 19th century looked at him in a less romantic light, seeing him as the first successful precursor of the *bourgeoisie*. However, when the facts are presented, the truth is that Jacques Coeur was an extremely astute businessman, who used every opportunity that presented itself for making money, managing at the same time to serve the state as well as himself. As the King's *argentier*, (steward and banker), he had access to the King himself, to the court and to the suppliers and used this to make much capital. He dealt in a wide variety of merchandise, from salt to Scottish wool, he built an early form of stock exchange in Montpellier, owned a silk factory in Florence, had a staff of travelling salesmen and set up individual companies for each branch of his diversified business empire.

Although he had wealth in the form of real estate, the amount of liquidity he actually had at his disposal is questionable, for much of his capital was in the form of jewellery and low-yielding farm-lands.

However, he loaned a great deal of money including the funding of the King's 1450 campaign to recapture Normandy from the English, and he also extended credit to much of the aristocracy.

Under these circumstances, it was hardly surprising that he aroused a great deal of jealousy and envy. He was arrested on 31st July, 1451 on charges of having poisoned the pretty young Agnès Sorel, the King's mistress, and of engaging in dishonest speculation. At the time of his arrest, his immense fortune was estimated to be in the region of 500,000 écus, and after his goods were seized, 100,000 écus were immediately taken to finance the expenses of the war in Guyenne. Charles VII was harsher on Coeur than his predecessors and did nothing to help his financier, in just the same way as he had done nothing to save Joan of Arc.

tryside has left behind an ageing population and there is widespread absentee ownership of farms.

Limoges is the capital of Limousin and is the only town in the region of any industrial importance. The manufacture of porcelain was introduced to the town in the second half of the 18th century and the first factory was opened in 1771.

Today, porcelain manufacture is still the economic mainstay of the town. Limoges is especially known for its table ware which accounts for more than half

Coeur's trial began a year later, and given the blatant falseness of the poisoning charges, the court had to dig deep in his past to find material to support their accusations. Not that Coeur was aware of any of the charges for he was held in secret and did not hear any of the testimony. On 29th May, 1453, he was found guilty of all the charges, except that of poisoning Sorel, and was sentenced to death.

This sentence was quickly commuted to banishment and the confiscation of all his possessions, in view of the services he had rendered to the country. In addition, he would have to pay a fine of 400,000 écus if he wished to be freed.

Ironically, as Coeur was being imprisoned, the decisive victory of the French over the English took place on 12th July, 1453 – the French troops having been paid from the confiscation of Coeur's property.

The resourceful Coeur managed to escape, and in 1455, he was in Rome, doubtless benefiting from the support he had earlier received from the Pope, who had previously authorized his trade with Egyptian Muslims as a reward for commanding a naval expedition to Turkey, on behalf of the Pope. He died on 25th November, 1456, probably on the Aegean island of Chios. Charles VII's son, Louis XI, made amends to Coeur's sons, for the treatment meted out to their father, by returning some of their father's properties to them.

Jacques Coeur stands out from his contemporaries for his flair and business acumen, and for the volume of trading of his highly diversified companies. He was a worthy model for the middle-class merchants and traders who would rise to prominence over the next generation.

of the total French production.

Berry located north of Limousin, was yet another bone of contention between the English and the French, but unlike Limousin, it did not change hands so often. After 1360, Berry was held on behalf of the French Crown, usually by

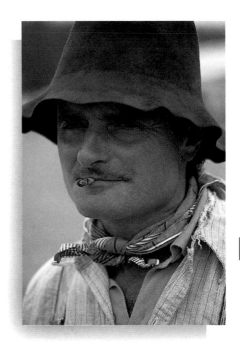

A country farmer.

a prince of the royal family. The Duchy became an integral part of the French Crown on the death of Louise de Lorraine, in 1601. Of all the Dukes of Berry, the most famous is Jean de France (1340-1416), whose patronage of the arts resulted in a number of exquisite illuminated manuscripts, of which the most renowned is the **Très Riches Heures du Duc de Berry** (Richest Hours of the Duke of Berry).

The regional capital of Berry is the attractive town of **Bourges**, which is situated almost in the exact centre of France. A very early commentary on the city, written by Julius Caesar in 52 BC, still exists. Bourges was formerly called Avaricum and was the capital of a Celtic tribe known as the Bituriges, who allied

Sunflowers in the lush fields of the Heartlands.

themselves with Vercingetorix in his campaign to oust the Roman invaders. The Bituriges pleaded with Vercinge-torix to exempt their city from his policy of destroying towns to deprive the Roman invaders of resources. Vercingetorix accepted the pleas of the Bituriges, but the Romans won the city, in spite of a valiant defence. Caesar states that every one of the 40,000 inhabitants were massacred, but he also notes that it was "one of the most beautiful cities in Gaul".

Bourges quickly started again. Saint Ursin introduced Christianity here in the 3rd century and Charlemagne later made it the capital of a unified Berry. It was the residence of Charles VII for 15 years during the Hundred Years War and Joan of Arc spent the winter of 1429 there. At the outset of Charles VII's campaign to reclaim the French throne, the English were masters of large parts of the country, and they derisively described Charles as the "King of Bourges", since that is where much of the royal court and administration was based. Bourges was also the home town of an enterprising merchant by the name of Jacques

Office buildings in Bordeaux.

Coeur, who would later become the king's banker, and is regarded by many historians as the prototype of the rich bourgeoisie. Coeur's palace is one of the most attractive examples of Gothic civil architecture in France, and cost the then astronomical sum of 100,000 écus to build. The city's beautiful Gothic **Cathedral of Saint Étienne** boasts one of the finest collections of stained glass windows in the country, many of which were made between 1215 and 1225 and are predominantly red and blue in colour.

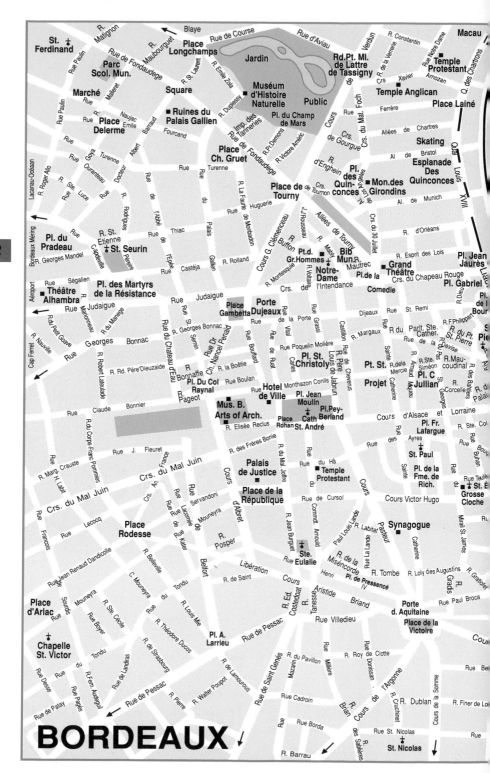

Macau

St. Ferdinand

Blaye

R. Matignon

Rue de Course

Rue d'Aviau

R. Constantin

R. Notre Dame

Verdun

Place Longchamps

R. Maubourguet

R. St. Laurent

R. Emile Zola

Jardin

Rue d'Aviau

R. de la Verrerie

Temple Protestant

Q. des Chartrons

Rue de Fondaudege

Parc Scol. Mun.

Rd.Pt. Ml. de Lattre de Tassigny

Rue Paulin

Rue Mallerat

Square

Muséum d'Histoire Naturelle

Public

Crs

Xavier

Amozan

Rue du Mal. Foch

Crs. de Gourgue

Temple Anglican

Place Lainé

Marché

Rue

R. Duplessy

Pl. du Champ de Mars

Cours

Rue

Ferrère

Rue Paulin

Rue Naujac

Ruines du Palais Gallien

Allées de Chartres

Place Delerme

Emile

Barraud

Imp. des Tanneries

R. Pt. Demons

Skating

R. Georg Albert

Fourcand

Rue de Fondaudege

R. Victoire Americ

Esplanade Des Quinconces

Turenne

Rue Ste. Luce

Docteur

Place Ch. Gruet

Turenne

R. d'Enghien

Pl. des Quin- conces

Mon. des Girondins

Al. de Munich

Lacanau-Océan

R. Roger Allo

Rue

Ouranteau

Rue de l'Abbé

Rue du

Huguerie

Place de la Tourny

Crs. Tournon

Crs. du 30 Juillet

R. d'Orléans

Rue

Rodrigues

R. St. Etienne

Rue

Thiac

Palais

Allées de Tourny

J.J.Rousseau

R. Mably

R. Esprit des Lois

Pl. du Pradeau

Capdeville

St. Seurin

Castéja

Gallien

R. Rolland

Cours G. Clémenceau

R. Buffon

Pt.d. Gr.Hommes

Bib Mun.

Grand Théâtre

Crs. du Chapeau Rouge

Pl. Jean Jaurès

Bordeaux Méring

R. Georges Mandel

Pérera

R. Montesquieu

R. Voltaire

Mautrec

Pl.de la Comedie

Pl. Gabriel

Ségalien

Pl. des Martyrs de la Résistance

Rue Castéja

Notre- Dame l'Intendance

Pl. Die

Aéroport

Théâtre Alhambra

Judaigue

Crs. de

Rue St. Remi

R.Die

R.F.Philippart

Pl. de l Bour

Rue Judaigue

Place Gambetta

Porte Dujeaux

Dijeaux

R. du Parlt. Ste. Cather.

St. Pierre

R. du Pt. Pie

Cap-Ferret

R. Nauville

R.d.du Petit Goave

R. Mariormeau

Rue St Bonnac

Georges Bonnac

Rue de la Porte

Castillon

R. Margaux

Rue de la Devise

Georges

Bonnac

R. Georges Bonnac

Semin

Rue de Ruat

Rue Poquelin Molière

Sante

R.dela Mercie

Ste. Siméon

R.Mau- coudinal

R. Robert Lateuilade

R. Dr. Nancel Penard

R. la Boëtie

Pl. St. Christoly

Pt. St. Projet

Catherine

Pl. C Jullian

R. Corcelles

R. d. Palai

R. Rd. Père'Dieuzaide

Pl. Du Col Raynal

Rue Boulan

Hotel de Ville

Monthazon Conils

Pl. Jean Moulin

Cours d'Alsace et

Lorraine

Pl. Fr. Lafargue

Bonnaffe

Pageot

Mus. B. Arts of Arch.

Place Rohan

Pl.Pey- Berland

St. André

des Ayres

St. Ste. Ste. Paul

Claude

Bonnier

R. Elisée Reclus

R. des Frères Bonie

Pl. de la Fme. de Rich.

Rue Teule

St. E

R. du Corps-Franc Pommies

J. Fleuret

Crs. du Mal Juin

R. du Mal. Joffre

Palais de Justice

Rue du Hâ

Temple Protestant

Cours Victor Hugo

Grosse Cloche

R. Marg. Crauste

R. H. Labit

Crs. Av. France

Rue Servandoni

Cours d'Albret

Rue de Cursol

Synagogue

Mirail St. James

Crs. du Mal Juin

Rue

Lecocq

Place Rodesse

R. Posper

Place de la République

R. Jean Burguet

R. Labitat

Pasteur

Catherine

R. Gradis

R. Graitiol

Francois

Rue Jean Renaud Dandicolle

C. Mouneyra

Belfort

Ste. Eulalie

R. de la Miséncorde

Pl. de Pressencé

R. Tombe

R. Loly des Augustins

Place d'Arlac

Mouneyra

Ste. Cécile

Libération

R. de Saint

Cours

Henri

Porte d. Aquitaine

Rue Paul Broca

Chapelle St. Victor

Tondu

R. Louis Mie

Pl. A. Larrieu

Rue de Pessac

Aristide

Briand

Place de la Victoire

Rue de Patay

R. Desse

R. Pagès

R. Fern. Audeguil

Rue de Strasbourg

R. Pierre

R. Walter Poupot

Rue de Lamourous

Rue de Saint Genés

R. du Pavillon

Mazarin

Millière

R. Roy de Clotte

R. Dublan

R. Finer de Lo

BORDEAUX

R. Barrau

Rue Borda

Rue St. Nicolas

St. Nicolas

Rue

Bordeaux: A History of Trade & Occupation

A little inland from the Bay of Biscay, on France's western coast, **Bordeaux** is a city whose history and destiny have always been intricately linked to the wine trade. It was once much fought over by the French and the English invaders. In 1137, Eleanor of Aquitaine married Prince Louis, the son of the King of France and the future King Louis VII.

Part of her rich dowry included the Duchies of Périgord, Limousin, Poitou, and the already important port city of Bordeaux. The marriage was not a success, and after 15 unhappy years, they were divorced in 1152, with Eleanor regaining control over her extensive dowry.

Within two months, Eleanor had remarried, and her husband was Henri Plantagenêt, Count of Anjou and lord of large areas of land in Normandy.

The combined land-holdings of the newly married couple were as large as those of the King of France, and as if this were not a worrying enough situation for the King, two months after the wedding, Henri inherited the throne of England, becoming King Henry II. The stage was set for three centuries of Anglo-French political and acquisition struggles.

During the time of their occupation the English developed Bordeaux, though they had some difficulty pronouncing the name of their Duchy, and "Aqui-

Celebrating the season's best.

taine" was mis-pronounced "Guyenne", a name that would be used right up to the French Revolution.

The English also managed to distort the pronunciation of one of the major regional products, wine. The local Gascons called their wine *clairet*, a reference to its light colour, and the English (mis-) pronounced it as "claret". The British still call Bordeaux wines claret.

Since Bordeaux was English, the local exporters of wine to England received preferential treatment, and so it was that claret got a 300 year head start on international competition, and even today, there is still a markedly British affection for red Bordeaux, or claret.

In the 14th century, Bordeaux was the capital of Edward the Black Prince, the son of King Edward III of England whose son Richard II was born there. Bordeaux did not revert to France until 1453, when the English were defeated in the Hundred Years War.

After the downturn in trade during the Wars of Religion, commerce again improved in the 18th century, thanks to the so-called "triangular" trade : wine and arms were shipped from Bordeaux to Africa, where slaves were taken on board and shipped to the West Indies, from where coffee and sugar were shipped back to Bordeaux.

It was during this time that much of the city was laid out, solid stone buildings replacing the twisting, unhealthy alleys of the old town. Trade had always been vitally important to the city and who better to manipulate this knowledge than the British, who blockaded the port during the Napoleonic Wars. When the French Government fled Paris in 1870, 1914 and 1940, they all took refuge in Bordeaux.

Late 20th century Bordeaux is a busy, attractive town, which has preserved its history at the same time as developing its traditional port activities, especially the new container terminal of Bordeaux-LeVerdon. Whole stretches of the historic city centre have been made into pedestrian precincts, which makes exploring the city on foot a pleasure.

Richelieu, the then Governor of Guyenne, ordered the construction of the **Grand Théâtre**, which was inaugurated in 1780, and which is one of the most beautiful theatres in France.

It has a colonnade topped with classical statues, and inside, its double stairway and cupola were copied by Garnier, when he designed the Opéra in Paris. The **Esplanade des Quinconces** is a huge square on the banks of the River Garonne and has a remarkable **Monument aux Girondins** (Monument to the Girondins).

The Girondins were a local revolutionary party who were denounced by other parties, as being enemies of the Revolution. Twenty-two of them were beheaded in 1792. The monument consists of a 50 metre high column and two impressive bronze fountains.

Bordeaux Wines

Bordeaux is surrounded by vineyards, and the 50,000 wine growers produce some of the country's finest wines. Unlike the wines of Burgundy, which are made from only one grape, Bordeaux wines are made from a blend of three main types: Cabernet Sauvignon, Cabernet Franc and Merlot.

Bordeaux wines cover a wide range; reds, whites and sweet dessert wines. Beware of one thing when buying Bordeaux: just because the label says "Château", it does not necessarily mean very much, (unless, of course, it is a particularly famous *château*) since there are nearly 10,000 *châteaux* in Bordeaux, many of them consisting of little more than a vineyard and a cellar.

North of Bordeaux is the **Médoc** region, which produces the best quality

Market Day in the Heartlands is a banquet of nature.

and the best known wines. The most northerly part of Médoc, Bas-Médoc, produces good, reasonably priced wines, whilst the southern part, Haut-Médoc produces such famous and expensive wines as Château Margaux, Château Lafite, Château Mouton-Rothschild, Saint Julien and Pauillac.

Vineyards spread in a virtually unbroken sweep east across to **Saint Émilion**, an attractive little town, built on a plateau overlooking the Valley of the Dordogne and enclosed by 13th century ramparts.

Red wine is produced in the surrounding countryside; a glass of Saint Émilion wine is halfway between a Bordeaux and a Burgundy, since it has a richer taste and a redder colour.

Périgord & The Dordogne Valley

The River Dordogne rises in the Massif Central, at the foot of the highest peak, and flows west towards Bordeaux, to join the Garonne and flow out to sea. At various stages along its winding course there are gorges, prehistoric caves, *châteaux* galore and a succession of spectacular scenery, all of which makes this one of the most interesting parts of France to visit. Although people refer, in rather general terms, to the "Dordogne", this description actually covers the former historical province of **Périgord**, a region which was disputed over by both the French and the English, and which

The rustle of trees reminds one of the liberating beauty of the country.

was not united with the French Crown until 1607. It is situated on the south-west of the Massif Central and is traditionally seen as a four-piece jigsaw, each "piece" of Périgord being identified by the predominant colour of its landscape. Thus, you have *le Périgord blanc* (white Périgord); *le Périgord noir* (black Périgord); *le Périgord vert* (green périgord) and *le Périgord pourpre* (purple Périgord).

A Drive Along The Dordogne Valley

There are a large number of different drives you can make along the River

Wine resting and maturing in caskets in Bordeaux cellars.

Dordogne itself, or its tributaries, and any one itinerary will provide a perfect mix of scenery and history. One such drive (and it is literally only one out of many, it must be emphasized) is the 180 kilometre drive from Bergerac to Souillac through the **Vallée de la Dordogne** (Dordogne Valley).

You start this drive at **Bergerac**, a pleasant little town, 88 kilometres from Bordeaux, surrounded by vineyards, and fields growing tobacco and corn. In the restored old town, you can see houses dating from the 15th and 16th century. This is the part of the countryside referred to as le Périgord pourpre (Purple Périgord), in reference to the colour of the vineyards.

Twenty kilometres east of Bergerac,

is the **Château de Lanquais**, the construction of which was started in the 15th century, when it was destined to be a fortress, but it was not finished till decades later, by which time plans had changed it into an Italianate, Renaissance-style palace.

Further east is the charming village of **Trémolat**, with its curiously fortified 12th century church and the beautiful **Cingle de Trémolat**, a semi-circle of white cliffs going down to the river. **Limeuil** is one of the many pretty villages of the Dordogne – perched on a cliff, topped by a fortress and a church, with tiny streets and two bridges standing at right angles to each other.

At Limeuil, you can either branch off towards the north, following the course of the River Vézère and the Vallée de la Vézère, or you can continue along the Dordogne Valley.

The 12th century church in the village of **Cadouin** has a particularly beautiful cloister, which was built from the 15th to mid-16th century. Cadouin is famous for housing an interesting religious relic – interesting not so much in itself, but because of its history. From the 13th century onwards, a linen cloth originally thought to belong to Saint Suaire, and reputed to be the Shroud of Christ came into the Church's possession. The Saint Suaire became the focal point of pilgrimages: Richard the Lionheart, Saint Louis and King Charles V, all journeyed to the village to worship the so-called shroud. During the Hundred Years War, it was given for safekeeping to Toulouse and Cadouin did not regain possession of it until the end of the 15th century, and even then after the personal intervention of the Pope and King Louis XI. It was not until 1934 that the relic was declared to only date from the 11th century. After which the pilgrimages were stopped. The "Saint Suaire" is now on display in a little museum attached to the church.

Chateaux Galore

This stretch of the river valley seems to have a *château*, or a picturesque village at every bend, and you drive through a succession of stunning views, and historic sites. The **Château of Beynac-en-Cazenac**, perched on a rocky outcrop 150 metres above the Dordogne River changed hands during the Hundred Years War, passing from the English to the French. Its former strategic position now offers superb views over the surrounding countryside. Immediately across the river are two other *châteaux*; the 16th century **Château de Fayrac**, with its mass of watch-turrets, two drawbridges and a 19th century pseudo-keep and, the **Château de Castelnaud**, a one-time bitter rival of Beynac during the incessant conflicts that raged in this region during the Middle Ages. The medieval fortifications are interesting to visit, but above all, it is the view from the battlements that is stunning – one of the most beautiful in the whole of Dordogne.

There is plenty of grape picking to do in this wine producing region.

After the pretty village of **La Roque-Gageac**, with its abundance of craft shops and pretty views over the countryside, is the Romanesque church of **Cénac**, and the 13th century **Bastide de Domme**, a fortified village built in 1281, which offers one of the Dordogne's many famous views. The **Cingle de Montfort**, the **Château de Montfort**, and the pretty village church of **Carsac-Aillac**, come in close succession, before the road turns north, to **Sarlat-la-Canéda**.

Black Périgord: The Land of Truffles

Sarlat-la-Canéda is at the heart of **le Périgord noir** (Black Périgord), a market town specialising in the most famous food products of Périgord, *foie gras* and truffles. Incidentally, *Le Périgord noir* derives its name from its dark forests of oak and chestnut and from the colour of its most famous speciality – truffles.

La Maison de la Boétie

The 16th century writer, Étienne de la Boétie was born in Sarlat and his home, **La Maison de la Boétie**, built in 1525, still stands today – an attractive stone house, with large square windows and a decorated roof. Sarlat is full of winding streets lined with houses with medieval ground floors but with Gothic or Renaissance top floors.

Thanks to its distance from a main axis of communication, Sarlat was saved from the dubious process of "modernization" in the 19th and 20th centuries, which survived it almost untouched. In 1962, the French Government chose Sarlat as one of the first towns in the country to be restored.

Further east is one of the jewels of the Dordogne Valley, the village of **Rocamadour**, which "climbs up" the steep cliff. Rocamadour is known for a stunning collection of churches, fortress, ramparts, and for a long time it was a place of pilgrimage.

During the 13th century it was rumoured that pardons (forgiveness for sins) could be obtained here, even if they had been refused by other higher church authorities. A donation helped,

of course and the village and her seven sanctuaries flourished.

Inevitably, quarrels broke out, as neighbouring abbeys struggled to gain control over the incoming wealth, and during the Hundred Years War, the village was ransacked several times.

The Wars of Religion and the French Revolution seemed to sound the death-knell for Rocamadour, which fell into disrepair. It was not until the 19th century that the Bishops of Cahors spearheaded the restoration of the village, and religious pilgrims returned to this beautiful site.

Green & White Périgord: Valley Lakes and Plateaux

Le Périgord vert (Green Périgord) takes its name from the green landscape, from the lakes and rivers that make this such a tranquil part of the country. At its heart is the pretty little town of **Brantôme**, the Venice of Périgord.

The River Dronne flows through the town, in a curve, with a cluster of red-roofed houses on one bank and the abbey across a little bridge, on the other. The history of the **Abbey** dates back to its foundation in AD769 by Charlemagne, who presented the relics of Saint Sicaire to the new abbey. South of Brantôme is the equally pretty village of **Bourdeilles** and its well-preserved medieval fortress.

Périgueux is the centre of le Périgord blanc, which derives its name from the

Different grapes for different wines.

surrounding white limestone plateaux and cliffs.

The town has two 12th century churches, both remarkable for their excess of cupolas, the **Church of Saint Étienne-de-la-Cité**, and the **Cathédrale Saint Front**, which was "redesigned" in the 19th century by Abadie, who later used it as a blueprint for the Sacré Coeur in Paris.

Forty-eight kilometres east of Périgeuex, in the Vézère Valley, is the **Lascaux Cave**, which contains one of the most outstanding examples of prehistoric art in Europe. The cave was discovered on 12th September, 1940, when four young men were out looking for their dog which had fallen down a hole.

A main cave and a series of galleries are decorated with a variety of drawings of many different animals, an analysis of the types of animals depicted, as well as carbon-14 tests, the date of the cave was fixed as 15,000-13,000 BC.

Lascaux quickly became the victim of its own popularity, for soon after it was opened to visitors, there was a frighteningly rapid deterioration in the paintings. The colours faded and fungus began to grow, to such an alarming extent that the cave was closed to the public in 1963. Visitors now visit **Lascaux II**, a facsimile cave, 200 metres from the original site.

The last word on Périgord goes to the writer André Maurois, who said, with only the faintest touch of irony, "You were born Parisian, or Belgian, or American ... after all, that is not your fault, we will forgive you, if you can prove that you love Périgord".

The southwestern corner of France, bordering Spain, is known for many things – rugby and *pelota*; the Basque language, whose linguistic roots are still a mystery; its food and excellent "vins de pays" (regional wine); the Pyrenean mountain passes that torture the cyclists participating in the annual Tour de France race and its sunny weather. Yes, sunny weather, for, surprisingly, Languedoc Roussillon statistically out performs the better known Côte d'Azur for sunshine.

Southwest

273

■　■　■　■　■　■

Biarritz is a pretty town with excellent beaches.

The **Pays Basque** (Basque Country) exists on both sides of the Pyrenees, which means that the Basque people live in seven provinces, three of which are in France and the remainder on the Spanish side of the Pyrenees. The Basques say about themselves *"Zaspiak-bat"*, which translates roughly as

Rock formations at Biarritz.

"the seven make only one" and they proudly preserve their traditions, especially *euskara* – the Basque language.

Over the past 20 years, both sides of the border have suffered at the hands of Basque extremists who want to set up an independent Basque homeland, a claim unsupported by the majority of the Basques.

Basque Resorts

Biarritz, a pretty town with good beaches, a rocky headland, a casino and flower-filled gardens, owes its current status as a major holiday resort to Eugénie, the Empress of France, who used to visit it every year as a young girl.

She later persuaded her husband, Napoléon III, (whose uncle was Napoléon Bonaparte) to visit Biarritz, in 1854. The Emperor was so impressed that he had a villa built there the very next year, and the destiny of Biarritz as a smart, expensive holiday town was launched. Today the former "Villa Eugénie" (Eugénie Villa) is the **Hôtel du Palais**, and the beaches are frequented by surfers.

Saint Jean de Luz is a picturesque fishing town, a major holiday town, and probably the most Basque of the French Basque towns. The town's most famous moment in history took place in 1660, when Louis XIV and Marie-Thérèse, the Spanish Infanta, were married here, in a sumptuous ceremony. You can visit the pretty 15th century **Church of Saint Jean-Baptiste** where the ceremony took place and the houses where the King and the Infanta lodged. Today, Saint Jean de Luz is a major centre for sardine, tuna and anchovy fishing. For anyone who wishes to learn more about the Basque country and its people, **Bayonne** has an excellent **Musée Basque** (Basque Museum), which covers the history and ethnography of the area. There is even a section especially devoted to one of the most popular regional sports, *pelota* (a Spanish related court game).

The Pyrénées Mountain Area

The mountain chain of the **Pyrénées**

Still life on the Pyrénées road from Carcassone to Albi.

forms a natural barrier between France and Spain, and its 430 kilometre length can be roughly divided into three geographic areas, namely from west to east of the Atlantic, or Basque Pyrenees; the central Pyrenees; and the Mediterranean Pyrenees to the east.

Tucked away in the central Pyrenees, bordered by Spain to the south, is one of Europe's smallest, and least-known countries, **Andorra**. The principality only covers 464 square kilometres, and until this century remained virtually cut-off from its two large neighbours. The first motorable road linking it to Spain was not opened until 1913, and that linking Andorra to France was only opened in 1931.

By an interesting quirk of history, Andorra is under the political leadership of a Spanish bishop and the President of France, an arrangement dating back to a treaty signed in 1278, which conferred dual control over the principality on the Bishop of Urgel and the Count of Foix. The Bishop of Urgel still exercises this authority, but the vagaries of history have given the French responsibility of the country's President.

The spa town of **Pau** in central Pyrénées, perched on a plateau 40 metres above the river valley, is also a centre for winter sports. The spectacular **Boulevard des Pyrénées** which is over one mile long, and is high above the valley stretches from the 14th century castle to the Parc Beaumont.

From the Boulevard, is a superb

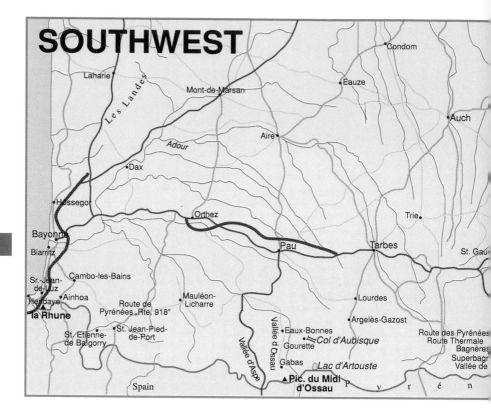

SOUTHWEST

Condom
Eauze
Auch
Laharie
Mont-de-Marsan
Les Landes
Adour
Aire
Dax
Hossegor
Orthez
Trie
Bayonne
Pau
Tarbes
St. Gau
Biarritz
Sr.-Jean-de-Luz
Cambo-les-Bains
Hendaye
Ainhoa
Mauléon-Licharre
Lourdes
la Rhune
Route de Pyrénées „Rte. 918"
Argelès-Gazost
St. Etienne-de Baïgorry
St. Jean-Pied-de-Port
Vallée d'Ossau
Eaux-Bonnes
Col d'Aubisque
Route des Pyrénées
Route Thermale
Gourette
Bagnères
Vallée d'Aspe
Gabas
Lac d'Artouste
Superbagr
Vallée de
Spain
Pic. du Midi d'Ossau
P y r é n

panorama of the Pyrenees, and amongst the visible peaks, you can clearly identify the Pic du Midi de Bigorre (2,865 metres), the Pic d'Anie (2,504 metres) and the Pic du Midi d'Ossau (2,884 metres).

Lourdes is one of the world's most celebrated pilgrimage places, site of the appearance of the Virgin Mary to Saint Bernadette in the mid-19th century, and visited every year by thousands of invalids who pray for a miraculous cure.

Fifty kilometres south of Lourdes, virtually on the Spanish border, is the sparsely populated village of **Gavarnie**, a hamlet which marks the end of the motorable road and which has less than 200 residents. For most of the year, the village is quiet, devoting itself to farming, but during the summer, it is the busy departure point for trips to a beautiful natural amphitheatre, called the **Cirque de Gavernie**.

The Cirque de Gavarnie is formed out of glacially-eroded rocks, and its mountainous "walls" rise up to a height of 5,000 feet. You can either walk the two and a half kilometres from the village to the foot of the Cirque, or go on horseback.

Villagers rent out donkeys or horses, and accompany you on the trek. This is an exciting way to travel, and even if you have never ridden, the horses know

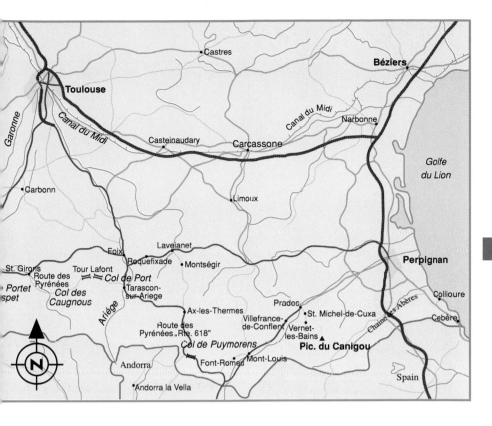

the way by heart, but be warned – some of the horses have a slightly alarming habit of rushing off without warning in the direction of food and drink stands, where they know they will usually get something to eat, so hold on tight! If you are only intending to go to the base of the Cirque, no special equipment is needed, other than strong shoes.

Bagnères de Bigorre is in itself a pleasant enough spa town, with thermal springs, but it is especially popular as a base for exploring the high mountain passes and peaks of the nearby region called **La Bigorre**. La Bigorre has some of the highest peaks of the Pyrenees, including Mount Balaïtous (3,142 metres) and Mount Vignemale (3,192 metres), high altitude lakes and impressive waterfalls. From November to June some of the mountain passes are blocked by snow.

Languedoc-Roussillon

The word "yes" in French is *oui*, or *oïl* in old French, whereas in the south the local word was *oc* and sometime around the 13th century, the areas where this southern language was spoken came to be known as the "langue d'oc", or **Languedoc**. Today, Languedoc-Roussillon refers to a large area, from

The banks of the River Garonne in Toulouse.

the eastern part of the Pyrenees to the lowlands that extend along the shore of the Mediterranean, and 200 kilometres east, to the right bank of the River Rhône. Although Languedoc and Roussillon have different historical backgrounds, today they share one thing in common, wine, which is an important element in the local economy.

The wines from this area, although not of the burgundy class, are good, not ruinously expensive, well marketed and very popular. One of the distinctive features of the landscape, is the ever present

sixth largest town in France and a major industrial base, especially for the aeronautics industry. The factories producing the European consortium plane, the Airbus, are well outside the city centre, which is extremely attractive, with its distinctive red brick architecture, its friendly citizens and its historic old town.

The clay from the alluvial plain of the River Garonne, which flows through Toulouse, supplied bricks, out of which much of the city was built, giving it a distinctive character and an even more distinctive pink colour. There is a saying about Toulouse, "A pink city at dawn, a red city in the glare of the sun, a mauve city at dusk".

The centre of the city is the **Capitole**, a rather splendid name for the Town Hall, which has a large, busy square in front of it, bordered with cafés and restaurants, which always seem to be full, especially those with outside terraces. The major historic sights of Toulouse are all within easy walking distance of the **Place du Capitole** (Capitol Square): the Saint Sernin Basilica, the Church of the Jacobins and the Musée des Augustins – all religious buildings.

The construction of the **Basilica of Saint Sernin** which started towards 1080, was finished by the middle of the 14th century and has several claims to fame; it is the largest Romanesque basilica in Europe, it is the church in France with the most relics and it was an important staging post for pilgrims going to Santiago de Compostela in Spain.

The brick **Church of Les Jacobins** is

vineyard, often clinging to a hillside, or overlooking the sea, or at the foot of a fort.

Toulouse

Toulouse was historically the capital of the Languedoc region and is today the

Foie Gras – Cuisine or Cruelty

Good food is almost an established fact of life in France: there is probably some little village, somewhere, that serves perfectly unappetising fare, but happily for most visitors, no one has yet found it.

What is also a fact of life is that some of the ways food is obtained may not be as palatable as the final product. A case in point is *foie gras*. *Foie gras* is a delicacy in France, expensive, delicious, and served on special occasions. The southwest is a major producer, and although the people of Strasbourg may well claim that their *foie gras* is, in fact, the best in the country it is still very much a speciality of the southwest.

To obtain the delicious texture of the liver, which should be firm and smooth and a creamy white colour, tinged with pink, the geese and ducks are force fed. The *gavage* (force) feeding takes place three times a day, when a funnel is put into the bird's throat and maize is poured down. If the goose refuses to swallow, the grain is simply pushed down its throat with a little stick. At the end of a month, the bird is so fat that it can hardly walk, and when it is incapable of standing up, the liver is ready.

Although the method may be unpleasant, the end product is delicious (if you can stomach the idea of eating force fed animal). *Foie gras* is usually eaten with thin toast and is served with jelly. Sometimes a truffle is added, making it even more expensive. There are also more elaborate ways of preparing it, including baking it in a pastry crust.

The French are not unnaturally very protective of their food, and recently an organisation was formed to protect the *foie gras* producers (not the birds).

This Comité Renaissance is made up of producers who, between them, account for nearly 3 million *foies* a year, and their aim is to protect French producers against foreign products, some of which are considered to be of an inferior standard.

a stunning example of the Mediterranean – Gothic style, its soaring interior divided into two naves by seven pillars, whose design makes them look like thin, elegant palm trees. The calm, cool interior of the church has a simple, almost stark feeling giving one a feeling of peace and it has a pretty, quiet cloister.

The **Musée des Augustins** is in a disaffected Augustinian convent, to which it owes its name. The museum boasts a superb collection of Romanesque sculptures, which are displayed with flair and originality. Toulouse is an attractive town to explore on-foot, especially the pretty and elegant red-brick **Place du President Wilson** (President Wilson Square) and the walk along the bank of the River Garonne.

Birthplace of Toulouse-Lautrec

Albi is dominated by the dramatic outline of its 13th century, red-brick **Cathedral of Saint Cécile**, a massive building which resembles a fortress more than a church, and which took more than a century to build. It is an amazing, almost overwhelming building when you are close to it and to appreciate its unusual architecture, you have to see it from a distance – a good vantage point is from the 22nd August 1944 Bridge. Next to the Cathedral is the **Palais de la Berbie** built in 1265 as a Bishop's Palace. It later became a fortress and houses an excellent museum dedicated to the

Symbols of the Republic stand guard over the Capitole in Toulouse.

19th century painter Toulouse-Lautrec, who was born in Albi in 1864.

The painter Toulouse-Lautrec was the son of a nobleman. He settled in the raffish district of Montmartre in Paris, which he immortalised in some of his most famous paintings. The Museum contains pictures, posters, and such personal items as his cane (his legs were permanently deformed due to two childhood accidents). In fact, when he was put in a clinic to try and combat his alcoholism, he would walk round the gardens of the clinic and take a quick drink from his secret supplies concealed within the hollowed-out cane. More personal exhibits of the artist can be seen in the **Maison Natale de Toulouse-Lautrec** (Birthplace of Toulouse Lautrec) on Boulevard Sibille.

North of Toulouse: Fortresses & Castle

Twenty-five kilometres northwest of Albi is the 13th century village of **Cordes**, perched dramatically on a ridge, dominating the valley. On the Grande Rue of the village, are some beautiful, sculpted 13th and 14th century houses, and pretty cobbled streets which lead to the various gates of this fortified village.

Sixty-nine kilometres north of Toulouse is the town of **Moissac** with an 11th century church. The south portal of the church is one of the masterpieces of Romanesque sculpture, and was

Albi's Cathedral of Saint Cécile dominates the town.

carved between 1100 and 1130.

Before the re-conquest of Roussillon by Richelieu in 1659, the French border with Spain was formed by **Les Corbières** – a natural barrier of rocky outcrops which are now crowned with the ruins of medieval castles that formerly guarded the approach roads from Spain to France for five centuries. The medieval fortress of **Carcassonne**, the largest in Europe, was the central element in this defensive system, along with the so-called "five sons of Carcassonne", the fortresses of **Puilaurens, Peyrepertuse,**

Trencavel was imprisoned and his title given away to Simon de Montfort. Twenty years later, in 1240, Trencavel's son failed in an attempt to wrest control of the city from royal occupiers. In retribution for having supported the rebellion, the town was razed to the ground and its inhabitants forced into a seven year exile. At the end of their exile, the citizens of Carcassonne were allowed to rebuild their town, which today still stands as *la ville basse* (within the walls of the fortress).

The fortress was so successfully strengthened that it was henceforth regarded as impregnable – the central **Château Comtal** which now contains a Museum of Stone relics is surrounded by a double fortification, an outer wall with 14 towers and an inner wall with 24. By the late 17th century, Carcassonne despite its strong fortification was considered to be too far from the Spanish border, and Perpignan replaced it as a key defensive location.

The huge medieval fortress began a slow drift into decline and disuse, only to be saved 150 years later by two men, Prosper Mérimée, the Inspector-General for historical monuments who was determined to save the ruins of Carcassonne and the architect Viollet-le-Duc who undertook the restoration of the massive fortress.

Today, visitors can walk along the ramparts and through the watch towers of the impressive fortress, which still has a small resident population, a school and a bank, giving it a life beyond mere

Quéribus, Termes and **Aguilar**, which formed a medieval Maginot line.

The site of **Carcassonne** was considered both important and strategic since Roman days, and for four centuries it was the capital of a regional kingdom. In 1209, during a turbulent period of civil war, Carcassonne was besieged; the 24-year-old Viscount

The medieval fortress of Carcassone is the largest of its kind in Europe.

tourism. Carassonne is also believed to be the setting for Perrault's story, ***Puss in Boots***. **Perpignan**, the town that superseded Carcassonne, has historically always been a Spanish outpost in France – or, more specifically, a Catalonian outpost, an affiliation dating back to the 14th century. The Catalonian "Corts" was centred around Barcelona, but they sent a deputation to Perpignan, which did not officially come under French control until 1659, when the *Treaty of the Pyrenees* was signed.

The massive **Palace of the Kings of Majorca** is a reminder of the town's historical links with Spain. On Good Friday, the day on which Christians remember the death of Christ, a quasimystic ceremony takes place, the pro-cession of the Sanch, which dates back to 1416. A group of religious penitents, covered in red or black robes and hoods, walk in a barefoot procession through the streets of Perpignan.

Salses Fort, to the north of Perpignan is surrounded by vineyards and dominates the surrounding countryside. During the battle to recapture Roussillon from the Spanish, Salses was a key element, changing hands as the tide of success flowed back and forth between the Spanish and the French.

Border Territory

Inland, dominating the Roussillon vineyards is **Mount Canigou**, whose snowy summit stands at a height of 2,784 me-

The medieval village of Conques is set amidst wooded scenery.

Rope-marking is a meticulous craft needing the patience of fishermen.

tres. Part of the way up the mountain, at an altitude of 1,094 metres and with a breathtaking view of the mountains, is the 11th century abbey of **Saint Martin du Canigou** and two churches, one from the same period and one dating from the 10th century. At the foot of Mount Canigou, is another beautiful abbey, the 10th century **St Michel de Cuxa**.

Collioure, almost on the Spanish border, is a charming little town, built along a sheltered bay and apparently blessed with all the requirements for success and popularity – a beautiful view, two picturesque little harbours, a good beach, a pretty church, a *château*, and a tiny islet, now linked by a causeway. Small wonder that over the years artists, both famous and unknown from Bracque, Matisse and Picasso, to scores of enthusiastic amateurs have been attracted to Collioure.

The town is crowded in the summer and peaceful in the winter, when the 17th century church is decorated for Christmas, and café owners are happy to gossip with out-of-season visitors. The drive south from Collioure towards the Spanish border passes through the beautiful port of **Port Vendres** and the charming resort of **Banyuls**, known for the locally grown sweet aperitif wine.

Cerbère is the last town before the border, and for a tiny fishing village, it has an extraordinarily large railway station and marshalling yards, as it is an important station on the Paris-Barcelona line.

French Alps

I f there was anyone who harboured any doubts about the beauty
and the facilities of the French
Alps, then February 1992 must
have settled the issue once and
for all. For this was when the
French Alps played host to the 1992
Winter Olympic Games and for any fan
of winter sports, **Albertville** was the
place to be.

The French Alps represent the largest skiing area in the world and the
challenge of the Ol-
ympics was actu-
ally to utilize as
many of these fa-
cilities as possible.

So, Albertville was made the focal
point, because of its geographically strategic position, whilst 13 of the many
surrounding ski
stations and re-
sorts were used
to stage indi-
vidual events.

It is im-
possible to say
that any win-
ter sports'
resort,
is "the
best",
f o r
popu-
larity
a n d
prestige

■ ■ ■ ■ ■ ■

Barcelonette Valley in the Southern
Alps.

Breathtaking suspension above the mountains in Chamonix.

depend on many things – the facilities themselves, the level of ski instruction offered, the prettiness of the village, the *après ski* (after skiing) life – and of course, how much snow the resort receives.

During winter in France, especially in the Alps, everyone watches anxiously to see how much snow is falling, because even though artificial snow can be sprayed onto the slopes in very extreme cases, everyone naturally wants to ski in real, fresh snow.

For *off-piste* (skiing) enthusiasts (when you ski off the well-known, marked-out trails) there is nothing quite so marvellous as being the first person, early in the morning, to ski through an overnight fall of fresh, powdery snow.

Ski Resorts

The French Alps have many excellent ski resorts, some more suited to beginners and some offering challenging high-altitude skiing. The ski slopes in **Val d'Isère** range from an altitude of 1,800 metres up to 3,750 metres. **Tignes**, which at 2,100 metres is one of the highest ski resorts in the country, is a relatively new resort.

A village called Tignes was drowned by a dam project in 1952 and the villagers moved up to a new settlement, 1,000 metres higher up the valley, which they also called Tignes and set about developing it into a ski resort.

Within five years the resort was

Ski-jumping in the Barcelonette Valley, Southern Alps.

completed – a new complex with good facilities and lots of accommodation, and now, as a result of the Olympic Games, Tignes has a 3.4 kilometre long underground funicular, which takes visitors and skiers, close to the summit of La Grande Motte Mountain (3,656 metres). Visitors can enjoy the stunning views from a panoramic terrace, whilst skiers continue a little higher up, to the summit and defy more challenging conditions as they ski down·to the village.

The Three Valleys comprise the 500 kilometres of ski-friendly slopes that surround the four resorts of Les Menuires, Val-Thorens, Méribel and Courchevel. A resort like **Les Menuires** is symptomatic of the problems facing the Alpine region, which is essentially that of rec-

onciling the pristine beauty of the environment, with the need for more resorts, and certainly a lot more accommodation, to satisfy an ever increasing number of skiers. Although Les Menuires has superb skiing, its purpose-built modern apartment blocks might be considered totally unaesthetic by some.

The neighbouring **Val-Thorens** has the same problem, but recently celebrated its 20th anniversary in a positive way by building a pretty pink alpine-style village church, which was finished on Christmas Eve, 1992.

At 2,300 metres, Val-Thorens is the highest resort in Europe and has a giant cable car, designed to hold 150 people. It carries visitors and skiers up to the summit of la Cime de Caron (3,200

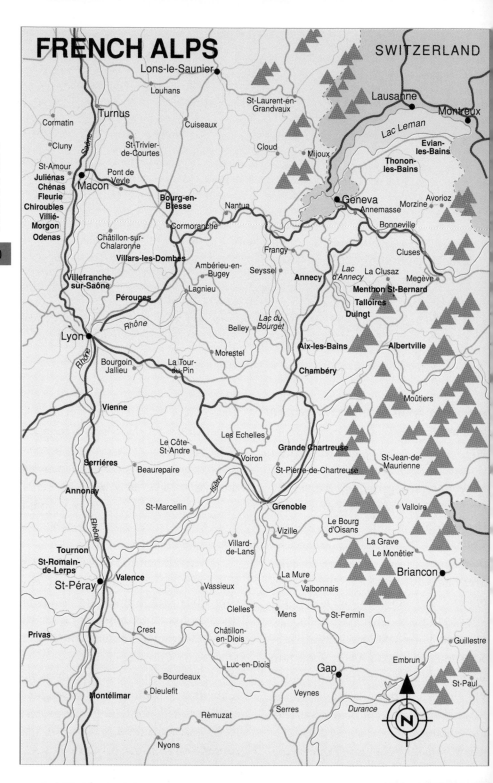

FRENCH ALPS

SWITZERLAND

Lons-le-Saunier

Louhans

St-Laurent-en-Grandvaux

Lausanne

Montreux

Cormatin

Turnus

Cuiseaux

Lac Leman

Cluny

St-Trivier-de-Courtes

Cloud

Mijoux

Evian-les-Bains

St-Amour

Juliénas

Chénas

Pont de Veyle

Thonon-les-Bains

Fleurie

Macon

Bourg-en-Bresse

Nantua

Geneva

Morzine

Avorioz

Chiroubles

Villié-

Annemasse

Morgon

Cormoranche

Bonneville

Odenas

Châtillon-sur-Chalaronne

Frangy

Cluses

Villars-les-Dombes

Ambérieu-en-Bugey

Seyssel

Lac
d'Annecy

La Clusaz

Villefranche-sur-Saône

Annecy

Megève

Lagnieu

Menthon St-Bernard

Pérouges

Talloires

Rhône

Belley

Lac du
Bourget

Duingt

Lyon

Aix-les-Bains

Albertville

Morestel

Bourgoin
Jallieu

La Tour-du-Pin

Chambéry

Rhône

Vienne

Moûtiers

Le Côte-St-Andre

Les Echelles

Grande Chartreuse

Serriéres

Beaurepaire

Voiron

St-Pierre-de-Chartreuse

St-Jean-de-Maurienne

Annonay

St-Marcellin

Grenoble

Valloire

Isère

Vizille

Le Bourg
d'Oisans

Tournon

Villard-de-Lans

La Grave

St-Romain-de-Lerps

Le Monêtier

Rhône

Valence

La Mure

Briancon

St-Péray

Vassieux

Valbonnais

Privas

Clelles

Mens

St-Fermin

Crest

Châtillon-en-Diois

Guillestre

Luc-en-Diois

Embrun

Gap

St-Paul

Bourdeaux

Veynes

Dieulefit

Durance

Montélimar

Serres

Rèmuzat

N

Nyons

Mont Blanc is the tallest mountain in France.

metres). From the top of this mountain, you can see the Italian Alps in the distance, as well as the many excellent ski runs down the Three Valleys.

Courchevel actually consists of four resorts, Le Praz at 1,300 metres, Courchevel 1550, Courchevel 1650, and Courchevel 1850 metres – the figures refer to their altitude. It is Courchevel 1850 that is far and away the most *chic* of them all, for in addition to its excellent sports facilities, there are all kinds of unexpected facilities, such as discotheques, cinemas, piano bars, top-class hotels and restaurants. With its elegant, affluent and very high-profile visitors, Courchevel 1850 has a somewhat Parisian ambience.

A resort that can challenge Courchevel's *chic*, high-society image is **Megève**, further north in Savoy, closer to Mont Blanc. The streets of this attractive little village are filled with elegant shops, expensive restaurants and lots of well-dressed people strolling up and down looking at all the other well turned-out people.

Megève is definitely a place to be seen in, preferably dressed in the latest fashions – and never forget, that in fashion conscious France, and especially in smart resorts like Megève, what you wear whilst you are skiing is just as important as what you wear *après ski* (after skiing). Ski clothes have their trends and fashions, just like any other form of clothing, be it the colour of the anorak, the design of the trousers, and,

Taking to the hills in Chamonix.

of course, the style and make of the ski-boots. It is not enough to be sporty, you must be smart as well.

Chamonix, which is dominated by Mont Blanc, is another very popular resort and since it is linked with Italy via the **Tunnel du Mont Blanc**, skiers can benefit from quick and easy access to the excellent slopes of the Val d'Aoste, and the resort of Courmayeur, just across the border. The tunnel is 11.6 kilometres long, and for many years, was the longest road tunnel in the world. It only takes 25 minutes to drive through the

enjoy the cold, try not to miss the pristine beauty of the Alps by visiting them in the summer.

When the snow on the lower slopes has melted, the valleys are filled with grazing cattle and masses of flowers and you can use the ski-lifts and chair-cars unencumbered by skis, poles and wet gloves.

There will always be fanatics who ski even in the height of summer – bikinis, sunglasses and ski boots make for an interesting fashion statement – but for those who want to enjoy the mountains in the summer rather than in the winter, the Alps hold a wealth of attractions.

Beautiful Drive

There are beautiful drives to be taken up into the mountains through spectacular countryside, there are old abbeys and *chartreuses* (monasteries) to visit, and there are the towns with their museums and galleries.

For mountain drives, one of the most impressive is a circuit you can take along the foot of **Mont Blanc**, the highest mountain in Europe, with an altitude of 4,807 metres. From the beautiful spa-town of **Saint Gervais-les-Bains**, drive south along the winding D902 to the little chapel of **Notre Dame de la Gorge**, with its early 18th century altar. Another drive from Saint Gervais-les-Bains also has a little church at the end, the 18th century **Saint Nicholas-de-**

tunnel, to Courmayeur only 20 kilometres away. Why not breakfast in France, have lunch in Italy, and be back in Chamonix in time for dinner?

Summertime Beauty

For those who are non-sporty and do not

Grenoble seen from the téléphérique.

Véroce. You can enjoy wonderful views of Mont Blanc all the way along this drive.

For those who enjoy mountain walking, and who are in very good physical condition, it is possible to trek up to the base of Mont Blanc. A short trek which takes you just to the base of the mountain will take four days, but if you choose to trek round the entire perimeter of the mountain, you will need at least 10 to 12 days.

Even a four day expedition should not be undertaken without proper planning, advice and equipment, so consult the local tourist offices – and remember your passport, since Courmayer, which is an overnight halt on even the shorter treks, is just over the border in Italy.

Grenoble & Environs

Grenoble is a modern city set in a timeless setting, and its tower-blocks and residential districts, many of them built to cater for the 1968 Winter Olympics are set against the backdrop of the surrounding peaks. A *téléphérique* (cable-car) takes visitors across the River Isère and up to the Fort de la Bastille, from where there are beautiful panoramic views of the town and the mountains beyond. The city's **Museum of Painting and Sculptur**e has a very good collection of both the Old Masters and 20th century artists.

Grenoble is the birthplace of the novelist Henri Beyle (1783-1842) who is

The Liqueurs of La Grande Chartreuse

In bars all the world over, you will find bottles of liqueurs bearing the name Chartreuse. From the silent, monastic world of Carthusian monks in Savoy, it is a long way to the liqueur cabinets. How did the monks, who lead solitary, contemplative lives, only eating one meal a week together and only going for a walk in the monastery gardens once a week, develop their thriving business?

No one knows for sure, but it probably all began somewhere back in the 16th century, when an alchemist, was trying to find, as was currently fashionable, the Elixir of Life. Using his extensive knowledge of herbs, the unknown alchemist combined 130 of them to produce his own elixir.

In 1605, a French nobleman by the name of le Maréchal d'Estrées, presented a Carthusian monastery on the outskirts of Paris with the original manuscript, containing the recipe.

A century later, this manuscript found its way to Savoy, where it was handed over to La Grande Chartreuse Monastery. One of the monks – Brother Jérome Maubec, was a skilled apothecary. After studying the document for years, he finally managed to perfect the process for making an elixir which he named the Elixir Végétal de la Grande Chartreuse in 1737.

Another monk, Brother Antoine, completed Maubec's work, by writing down the recipe with all the secret ingredients, and began making the elixir, and the most famous of the monastery's liqueurs, the Green Chartreuse. In 1838, Brother Bruno Jacquet, modified the original formula to produce yet another drink, the sweet after-dinner liqueur, Yellow Chartreuse.

The exact composition of these liqueurs has always been a well-kept secret. Even today, only three Brothers from the Monastery are entrusted with the exact details of the recipes, and the 130 herbal plants that are still used. In 1903, the Brothers were expelled from France, finally settling in Spain, where they continued production and where a factory still stands today. Once back in France, the production of the Chartreuse liqueurs were transferred from the monastery's pharmacy to a site at Voiron, near Grenoble in 1935.

The Voiron distillery can be visited. Here visitors can see the monks at work in the distilling rooms and in the 164 metres of cellars, where the casks of liqueurs are aged. The laboratory where Brother Jérome Maubec worked has been reconstructed and holds a superb collection of china pots and vessels from the monastery.

The original Elixir Végétal de la Grande Chartreuse, over the years has been complemented with an array of different drinks: the Green and Yellow Chartreuse, a Génépi Liqueur, l'Eau de Noix des Pères Chartreux (Walnut Liqueur), as well as a range of fruit liqueurs – Blackberry, Bilberry, Raspberry and Blackcurrant.

One pleasant way to drink Green Chartreuse is as a long drink. To make a Chartreuse Tonic, fill a tall glass with crushed ice, pour in 1.5 cl of liqueur and fill the glass with tonic water. And for those who are out skiing, sledging, or just watching other people getting cold in the snow, try adding a teaspoonful of Green Chartreuse to a cup of hot chocolate for a rich and warming drink.

---

better known as Stendhal (well-known writer of the classic *Le Rouge et Le Noir* or its translation *The Red and the Black*). You can not only visit his birthplace, but also the **Musée Stendhal** to learn more about this great man.

Chambéry, which was the capital of an independent state until the 16th century, is a peaceful pretty old town. It makes a good base for a trip south to the **Massif de la Chartreuse**, and the well-known Monastery, the **Convent de la Grande Chartreuse**. The Carthusian order whose members lead a solitary, silent life, was founded in 1084 by Saint Bruno. The current monastery was built

The misty slopes of Savoy.

in 1676 on the site where earlier buildings had successively been constructed
and destroyed, some by fire, and one, in
1132, by an avalanche. The fame of the
monastery resides, to a great extent, on
the liqueur that bears its name. (See box
story "The Liqueurs of La Grande Chartreuse" p 295.)

Situated on the shores of Lake
Annecy, the attractive town of **Annecy**
combines the beauty of its old town with
its new-found 20th century dynamism.
Since 1976, the town has had a nuclear
research station, and since 1980, it has

been the base for the National Institute of Underwater Archaeology.

The town has an interesting factory which produces and exports church bells, an old *château*, and a range of excellent hotels and highly rated restaurants, which ensures that Annecy is not only a popular destination for French visitors, but also for the many weekenders and holiday makers who cross over from Geneva, a mere 43 kilometres away.

A drive around Lake Annecy is an excellent day's excursion, during which you can visit the surrounding villages, the 17th century *château* at Duingt, the Ermitage de Saint Germain, a local pilgrimage spot, and drive through the surrounding mountain passes.

Chamonix is a popular resort dominated by Mont Blanc.

Post-Olympic Worries

And finally, back to Albertville and the Olympics. The area is taking stock of things now that the Games are over, and visitors are no longer buying the leftover stocks of souvenir sweatshirts and key-chains, even with hefty reductions. The cost of staging such a huge event is being estimated in terms of its long-lasting effects. Hosting an event on the scale of the Olympic Games is no simple matter, and 11 years of planning

went into the Albertville Games. The Games came and went, well organized, blessed with good weather, and, produced a good haul of medals for the home crowd. It is only now that an economic analysis of the cost of the games, both in real and in environmental terms is taking place.

Basically, now that the euphoria has worn off, and the first post-Olympics winter season has come and gone, the villages and resorts are examining their balance sheets and finding grim news. Overall, the Olympic Organizing Committee left behind a deficit of US$ 57 million, of which the French Government has paid 75 percent. But, that still leaves huge amounts to be paid off by the villages, saddled with very expensive equipment that is not necessarily going to be profitable enough to reimburse their debts. For example, the tiny village of **Brides-les-Bains** with a total population of 618, is a thermal resort, whose waters are used in slimming treatments and for health reasons. It was used as the athletes' village, and is now burdened with a debt of US$13.2 million.

The equally tiny village of **Pralognan-la-Valoise**, with a population of 634, now has a curling stadium it could not, and still can not, afford. The cost for them is US$1 million. There are also expensive maintenance charges for the new equipment, such as the US$754,000 it will cost each year just to maintain the bobsled run in La Plagne.

Even though there will be an inevitable increase in visitors coming to practise a whole host of winter sports besides skiing due to the area's extensive facilities, for Savoy locals there is a bitter end to the Olympic story – now that the Games are over, construction companies have laid-off many workers, and in the Albertville Basin alone, unemployment rose by 33 percent in 1992.

Theast

T he 350-mile stretch of southern coastline from the Spanish border to the Italian border is one of the most pictur-esque, sunny, and popular regions of France. When Pa-risians are shivering in winter rain, they dream of escaping to the *midi* (midday) – that part of their country where the sun is always shining at midday or any part of the day.

Southeast

Today, the **Côte d'Azur** is one of the country's major tourist destina-tions, for French as well as foreign visi-

■　■　■　■　■　■

Juan Les Pins is a little bustling resort.

tors. But, this seemingly charmed land of beaches, azure seas (hence the name, la Cote d'Azur) and picturesque har-bours, for centuries was poor, sparsely populated and isolated from the main-stream of French life.

Prestigious Resorts

Cannes, which is today the epitome of el-egance and wealth, with its marinas housing some of the world's most expensive yachts, and which is home for two weeks

Place Masséna, Nice built in Genoese style.

every year to the world's most prestigious film festival, was nothing but a small fishing village in 1834, when the Lord Chancellor of England, Lord Brougham and Vaux stopped there due to the eruption of a cholera epidemic at his final destination of Nice. He decided to wait in Cannes for the lifting of quarantine, lodging at the village's only hotel, the Hotel de la Poste aux Chevaux. Today, the site of the modest hotel is occupied by the much smarter Sofitel.

Like future generations of his fellow countrymen, Lord Brougham fell in love with Cannes, built himself a villa, and, for the next 34 years, spent his winters in the south of France, as did growing numbers of the British aristocracy. The village rapidly developed, its future as a

magnet for the rich and famous assured, though today's jet-setters have broken with the fashion of wintering in Cannes. Today, paradoxically, the town is packed during its hottest summer months, and is largely neglected during the time of its perfect winter weather.

The main boulevard, **La Croisette**, is the place to see and be seen. Flanked by beaches on one side, (some private and some public) and luxury hotels and apartments on the other, it is one and a half miles of status symbols and trend-setters, with the **Palm Beach Casino** at one end and the picturesque harbour at the other. The **Palais des Congres**, home to the annual film festival, towers over the little wooden fishing boats, and the ferries that sail to the two islands off the

The Riviera beaches at Nice are chic and populated.

coast of Cannes: the **Ile Saint Honorat** named after a 5th century hermit-monk who founded an old monstery there (the old fortified monastery can still be seen) and the **Ile Sainte Marguerite**, a lovely wooded hilly island whose **Fort Royal** housed the mysterious 17th century prisoner, called the "Man in the Iron Mask".

Nice can trace its history back to the Greeks, who founded a small trading post there in 350 BC, and who probably gave it its name, (*"nike"* in Greek means victory). It was neglected under the Romans who turned away from the small seaport, preferring instead to build a provincial capital on the other side of the river, on the hill of **Cimiez**, one of Nice's smartest districts today. In 1388, a civil war over succession was tearing

Provence apart, and Nice, led by its Governor Jean Grimaldi, seceded from Provence and joined Savoy (to which it continued to belong, barring a few interruptions) until 1860.

In the alignment of 18th century politics, the British were allies of the King of Sardinia, (the new title of the Duke of Savoy), and so were welcome in Nice, to which they flocked. When a bad frost killed all the orange trees in 1822, and many people were thrown out of work, it was the English community in Nice who undertook and financed the construction of a coastal road, partly to create jobs, and partly to facilitate access to the beach. Their work and their name still live on in Nice's most famous boulevard, the four kilometre long

COTE D'AZUR

Chartreuse de ‡
Valbonne

Bagn
C

Alès•

GARD

Anduze•

Uzès•

Le Vigan•

Remc

Le Caylar ★ *Cirque de*   *Grotte des*
   Navacelles   *Demoiselles*

Po
B

NIMES

Grotte de
★ *Clamouze*

A

Bédareux ♦   MONTPELLIER

Signac   ♦

•Aigues
Mortes

St-Pons-de-
Thomières ♦

Lamalou-
les-Bains

La
Grande *CAMARGUE*

•Frontignan Motte

Stes-Marie
de-la-Me

Pic de Nore ▲

St. Chinian ♦

Sète

Casteinaudary   Caunes-•.   Minerve ♦ •   **BEZIERS**
   Minervois

Fanjeaux•   **CARCASSONNE**   **NARBONNE**■

Abbaye de ‡   Gruissan
Fontfroide

Limoux♦

AUDE

Couiza

Château de
Peyrepertuse ★

Leucate-
Plage

Quillan

•Port
Barcares

St-Paul-de-
Fenouillet

PYRENEES   **PERPIGNAN**

•Canet
Plage

**Col de
Puymorens**

Villefranche-de-
Conflent •

‡St-Michel-
de-Cuxa

Cloitre
♦ d'Elne

Font-
Romeu •

ATLANTIQUES

•Collioure

le Canigou ▲

Céret ♦

Col du Banyuia-
Perthus sur-Mer

Bourg
Madame

Col d'Ares

Prats-de-Mollo-
la-Preste

ESPAGNE

Promenade des Anglais.

Today, Nice is a prosperous, booming, all-year-round city, with a very busy
international airport, an opera house,
and an enviable position: a beach town
just a couple of hours drive away from
the ski slopes of the Maritime Alps, close
to the northern industrial centres of Italy,

and with excellent transport and communication links to Paris.

Place Masséna (Masséna Square)
is at the heart of modern Nice. It is a
busy square, constructed in the 19th
century, in typical 18th century Genoese
style. The square is the focal point for
the annual festival which takes place 10

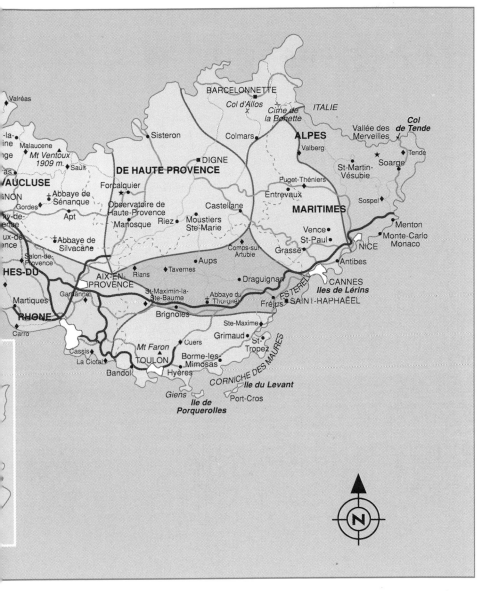

Valréas

-la-
ine
ge   Malaucene
      Mt Ventoux
      1909 m.   Sault
as.
VAUCLUSE   Forcalquier
NON   Abbaye de
      Sénanque
Gordes
-de-   Apt
se
ux-de-   Abbaye de
nce   Silvacane
       Salon-de-
       Provence
HES-DU

Martiques   Gardanne
RHONE
Carro

BARCELONNETTE
       Col d'Allos   x
              Cime de   ITALIE
              la Bonette
Sisteron   Colmars   ALPES   Vallée des   de Tende
                         Valberg   Merveilles   Tende
DIGNE
DE HAUTE-PROVENCE   St-Martin-   Soarge
                                 Vésubie
                    Puget-Théniers
Observatoire de   Entrevaux   Sospel
Haute-Provence
             Castellane   MARITIMES
Manosque   Riez   Moustiers
                  Ste-Marie   Vence
                                         St-Paul   Menton
             Comps-sur-   Grasse   NICE Monte-Carlo
             Artubie   Monaco
      Aups   Antibes

AIX-EN-   Rians   Tavernes   Draguignan   ESTEREL   CANNES
PROVENCE   Iles de Lérins
        St-Maximin-la-   Abbaye du
        Ste-Baume   Thoronet   Fréjus SAINT-HAPHAËEL
        Brignoles
                    Ste-Maxime
Cassis   Grimaud   St-
La Ciotat   Mt Faron   Cuers Tropez
Bandol   TOULON   Borme-les-
          Hyères   Mimosas   CORNICHE DES MAURES
       Giens   Ile du Levant
       Ile de   Port-Cros
       Porquerolles

Col
de Tende

N

days before Shrove Tuesday. The Promenade des Anglais, although not quite
as *chic* as La Croisette in Cannes, is
definitely more bustling, and Nice also
has a fascinating old town. The old
town is centred around **Place Grimaldi**,
the castle (which is actually only a 300
foot high hill where a fortress once stood),
and the picturesque little port, from
where you can take an overnight ferry
to Corsica. The ruins of the former Roman town of Cemenelum, on **Cimiez
Hill**, (especially the baths and the arena)
are easily visited. Cimiez is home to two
important art collections, the **Matisse
Museum**, and the splendid **Chagall Mu-**

The old quarter of Antibes is quaint and charmant.

The Picasso Museum in Antibes overlooks a beautiful boating harbour.

seum which displays the 20th century paintings of the artist of the same name, most of the paintings are of old testament subjects.

Antibes, dominated by its 12th century castle which overlooks a beautiful yachting harbour, was originally a Greek settlement. Its Greek name, Antipolis, meaning "the city opposite", refers to Nice, which it faces, across the prettily-named *Baie des Anges* (Bay of Angels).

In 1794, a young, impecunious general by the name of Napoléon Bonaparte installed his family in Antibes, where his mother did the family washing in a nearby stream and his sisters, future princesses of Napoléonic Europe, raided the neighbouring fig and artichoke plantations. Pablo Picasso spent several months in Antibes, immediately after the WWII, where he was given studio space in the museum which now houses the work left to the town by the grateful painter.

Four kilometres inland from Antibes is the pretty village of **Biot**, a haven for craftsmen, especially potters and basket-weavers, and the site of the **Fernand Léger Museum**. Léger (and his neighbour Picasso) was one of the pioneers of Cubism.

"Villages" of the Riviera

Despite massive real estate development along the whole of the coastline, you can still find quiet, totally unspoilt

The quiet harbour of Saint Tropez belies the town's racy reputation.

Provençal villages like **Gassin** and **Ramatuelle**, as well as an architect's idea of a Provençal village, in the port and marina complex of **Port Grimaud**. Port Grimaud is a delightful but expensive complex of prettily-painted houses linked by bridges and cobbled alleys.

Saint Tropez is one of the most famous (perhaps infamous) villages in France, its name redolent of the hedonistic south – topless sunbathing on the beaches, palatial yachts and rich jetsetters. From being an unknown fishing village at the turn of the century, Saint Tropez was "discovered" by painters such as Signac, who settled there in 1892, and his friends Matisse and Bonnard.

The writer Colette wintered in Saint Tropez between the two world wars,

bringing with her, as always, a whiff of scandal. But it was in the 1950s that the village really entered folklore, as the favourite haunt of film stars such as Brigitte Bardot. At the height of the season, the cafés bordering the harbour are crammed with people ardently people-watching for well-known faces.

Once you leave the beautiful, crowded beaches, and head into the *arrière pays* (inland countryside), the whole pace of life changes. Little villages cling precariously to rocky hills, there are miles of mimosa and jasmine fields, and spectacular gorges, like the **Gorges de Verdon.**

Grasse owes its important perfume industry to a 16th century fashion for perfumed gloves, launched by none other than Catherine de Medici. Today, the town produces many of the essences which are sent to the perfume houses in Paris for blending. One-third of the city's jasmine crop and one-sixth of its rose harvest go to the laboratories of Jean Patou, to be distilled into the most expensive perfume in the world – Joy.

The "Little Rome" of Provence

If the Côte d'Azur is principally oriented towards the sea and beach-life, much of the character of Provence is determined by its rich history and its monument-crammed inland towns. The Romans took the waters at **Aix-en-Provence**, whose very name comes from the Latin word *aqua* (water). They built towns such as **Vaison-la-Romaine**, and constructed spectacular arenas for gladiatorial combats and triumphal arches in celebration of their victories in battle. Nîmes, Orange, Saint Rémy, Arles and the Pont du Gard, all located within a fairly small area, form an impressive "little Rome", as the Romans called Arles.

Arles is an eclectic place – the bull-

Lhe Roman Arena at Arles.

fighting capital of Provence; the inspiration for some of Van Gogh's most memorable paintings and home to some of France's best Roman monuments. The two most impressive Roman buildings in Arles are the **arena**, built in 46 BC, and the **theatre**, of which only some remnants stand today, the bulk of the theatre having been used as building material for the town's churches and ramparts.

The 19th century Dutch painter,

The Arena at Arles has a distinctly Spanish flavour.

Van Gogh, lived in Arles in 1888, immortalising its cafés in canvases such as *Café du Soir* (Evening Café) and *Café de Nuit* (Night Café), but when he cut off his ear in December 1888, handing it to a woman with an order to "Look after this carefully" – the time had come to commit him to an asylum. He left Arles the next day for **Saint Rémy de Provence**, where he died 18 months later. Arles is an ideal centre from which to visit much of Provence and the neighbouring towns.

To the south stretch the salt marshes and lagoons of the **Camargue**, home to bulls and wild horses and France's *les gardiens* (cowboys). The Camargue is a fascinating, often lonely region – flat, wind-swept, a pilgrimage centre for gypsies, and its huge **Étang de Vaccarès** is another place of pilgrimage, this time, for thousands of migratory birds.

Rising out of the flat, salty landscape is **Aigues Mortes**, a perfectly preserved medieval town, whose **Tower of Constance** can be seen for miles as you drive towards it through the marshes. The tower was used in the 18th century as a prison for Protestants who refused to convert to the official Catholic religion.

Aigues Mortes, the City of the Dead Waters, was built as France's first Mediterranean port in the 13th century by Saint Louis. This was his port of departure when he sailed off to the Crusades. The prosperity of Aigues Mortes was shortlived, for, by the middle of the 14th

Avignon is a city with a rich and dramatic history.

century, the sea had receded, the canals silted up and the town remained virtually untouched, forgotten and inaccessible.

To the west of Arles is **Nîmes**, the oldest of the towns that the Romans constructed in France. Its huge amphitheatre, seating 20,000 spectators, is in excellent condition, as is **La Maison Carrée** (the Square House), a temple built as a perfect example of Roman architecture in the first century BC. Louis XIV wanted La Maison Carrée to be dismantled and reerected in his beloved Versailles – a project which, luckily, proved too difficult.

North of Nîmes is the **Pont du Gard**, the surviving part of the Roman aqueduct, which provided Nîmes with its drinking water. The aqueduct, built in 19 BC by Agrippa, consists of three levels of arches with the water channel running along the topmost tier.

Nineteen kilometres to the north of Arles, on a hill overlooking a harsh landscape, is the mysterious, ruined village of **Les Baux de Provence**, formerly the seat of the warring and powerful Lords of Baux. During the 13th century, Les Baux was famous for its Courts of Love, where troubadours met to sing their tributes to the high-born ladies who were invited to the Court. Over the centuries, Les Baux became notorious as a bandits' hideout, and in the late 16th century at the time of the Wars of Religion, it was a Protestant stronghold. These Protestants, offered shelter to rebels

Monaco

Monte Carlo, Monaco is a gambling and nightlife paradise.

The principality of Monaco might be small, but what it lacks in square miles, it makes up for in notoriety. Say "Monaco" to most people, and chances are they will immediately reply "Princess Grace", or "the casino", or "the Grand Prix". Ask a French person, however, for his impressions of Monaco, and you will almost certainly be regaled with titbits from whichever headlines one of the two princesses has been making, for France's adopted royal family certainly makes tabloid gossip.

Monaco is an independent, sovereign state, covering just under a square mile, situated on the southeastern coast, between the ultra-expensive Saint-Jean-Cap Ferrat and the quiet town of Menton. Beyond it lies Italy, the country from where the Grimaldi ruling family originated. The principality consists geographically of four areas – the **old town of Monaco** on the rocky headland; the new town of Monte Carlo, centred around the casino, the man-made beaches and hotels; the residential and business area, **La Condamine**, and the industrial area of **Fontvieille**, where land is still being reclaimed from the sea.

The history of the principality is exactly as it should be for such a high-profile place – a family dynasty, foreign overlords, wealth, beautiful people, and, of late, tragedy. The Grimaldi family bought Monaco in 1308 from the Genoese, and it has since remained in possession of the family.

From 1524 to 1641, Monaco was occupied by the Spaniards, then from 1641-1814 by the French and in 1815 it passed briefly under the control of the King of Sardinia. The principality used to own the towns of Menton and Roquebrune, but they were sold to Napoléon III in 1861.

In 1856, desperately in need of funds to run the principality, Prince Charles III decided to set up a casino, emulating the Grand Duke of Baden, whose sucasino in Baden-Baden provided him with a healthy income.

and sympathizers to their cause. In 1632, Cardinal Richelieu had the fortified village demolished, at the inhabitants' own expense and thus Les Baux remains today, abandoned, its dramatic ruins on a windy hill. However, the name Les Baux still lives on, in the mineral bauxite, discovered there in 1822.

Continuing north from Les Baux is **Avignon**, a gracious city that has been immortalised in the childrens' song *Sur Le Pont d'Avignon* (On the Bridge at

Within a few years Monaco became the smartest and the most fashionable casino in Europe, and by the time the new casino designed by Charles Garnier was built in 1878, Monaco was transformed. It had become the haunt of the rich, the royal, the famous and the infamous. This image was only strengthened by the1956 marriage of the current ruler, Prince Rainier III with the beautiful American film star, the late Grace Kelly. You can visit the casino as a tourist even if you do not wish to place a bet (bring your passport with you). The main gambling hall is the American Room whilst the most serious gambling goes on in adjoining private rooms.

The **old part of town** is built on a rock, about 200 feet above the shore-line, which is crowned by a *Jardin Exotique* (tropical garden). On the rocky headland, are **Prince Rainier's Palace**, parts of which date back to the 13th century; the **Cathedral**, built between 1875 and 1903 of neo-Romanesque design; the much older **Misericord Chapel**, built in 1646, and the **Oceanographic Museum**, founded in 1910 by Prince Rainier's uncle. Everyday, in the **Place du Palais** (Palace Square), you can watch the changing of the guard, which involves a large percentage of the Monegasque army.

Native Monegasques, as the citizens of Monaco are called, are exempt from military service and from income tax, as are the principality's foreign residents. Because of the tax concessions, many foreigners have chosen to live there, or at least, own property there, to establish residency. Real estate prices are as high as the high-rise apartment blocks that predominate and land reclamation continues. Monaco is visited all year round – after all, there is never a closed season for gambling away your

money or for saving it from the tax-man – but it is especially popular in the summer. The season really gets under way with an international tennis tournament in April, the flower festival in May, ballet at Easter, and, each May, the **Formula One Grand Prix,** when the roads of the principality are converted into a challenging, twisting race-track 3,145 kilometres long.

The French press, especially the glossy magazines, bored with local politics, and probably a little piqued by the non-stop dramas of Britain's royal family, has transformed the Monegasque princely family into their own royal family. Their every move, romance, or *faux-pas* is reported with great glee, be it "Steph's" (as HRH Princess Stephanie is known) latest boyfriend, or their despair over Prince Albert's continued bachelor status. The life of the Monaco royal family is a continued saga which the French people enjoy watching.

Avignon), probably the first French song most foreign schoolchildren learn. The bridge is now nothing more than a ruin, jutting out into the river. Avignon has a rich and dramatic history, for in the 14th century it was the focal point of a

Sauntering through Monaco's old town.

The dramatic ruins of Les Baux en Provence rests on a windy hill over the town.

bitter religious controversy. Rome had become so anarchic and dangerous, that Pope Clement V decided to move the seat of the papacy to Avignon in 1305. Seven successive French popes governed from the city, which was fortified with ramparts.

During the 14th century, the glory, wealth and reputation of the town grew, people and money poured into the city, and many palatial homes were built – the most famous amongst them being the 15,000 square metre **Palais des Papes** (Papal Palace).

In 1377, Saint Catherine of Siena persuaded the Pope to return to Rome, but a faction in Avignon, seeing the imminent demise of their wealth and authority, decided to elect their own Pope, leading to a major conflict within the Church, known as the Great Schism. The Pope and the Anti-Pope, based in Avignon, both tried to gain supremacy by excommunicating each other. The Great Schism was solved in 1449. Although Avignon suffered much at the hands of the mob during the Revolution, the Papal Palace escaped to remain one of the most imposing and important medieval buildings in Europe. It serves as a stunning backdrop during the city's summer arts festival.

Orange, 30 kilometres north of Avignon, was another important Roman settlement. The theatre is the only one in Europe which still sports the Roman façade. The city would have had many more such monuments today, were it not for a 17th century ruler, Prince Maurice of Nassau, who used the Roman buildings as a quarry.

By one of the quirks of marriage and succession that make up so much of history, Orange passed into the hands of William the Silent, founder of the Dutch Republic in 1559. The city did not return to French control until 1713, but even today the Dutch Royal family is known as the House of Orange!

Aix-en-Provence is a pleasant town that seems to have been blessed by nature. Pretty, with a good climate, thermal springs, a university and even a flourishing local industry which consists of the preparation of almonds.

The city's earlier history was overshadowed by Arles, but in the late Middle Ages, *Le Bon Roi René* (Good King René), the exiled King of Naples who governed over Provence, ruled from Aix-en-Provence.

Less than two years after the death of René in 1480, Provence was reunited with France, but Aix retained a large degree of autonomy. During the 17th and 18th centuries the elegant *hôtels* (mansion houses), squares and fountains that make up the character of today's city were constructed.

The main avenue, the **Cours Mirabeau**, was named after the city's adopted son, Mirabeau, one of the major figures in the French Revolution. Although Mirabeau was not born in Aix, he lived, married, divorced and later represented it in the States General.

Flower market at Aix-en-Provence.

Marseille

Marseille, the third largest town in France and the most important port in the country, has 2,500 years of history behind it, most of it maritime and commercial.

Founded in c.600 BC, by Phoenician Greeks from Asia Minor, Marseille quickly acquired a commercial hinterland, as the Greeks set up trading posts along the coast, from Spain across to Nice, Antibes and the Hyères Islands, and inland at Arles.

The city's fortunes rose and fell, very much in rhythm with maritime history and developments. Marseille had a second period of wealth and influence

The Basilica of Notre Dame de la Garde is a monument to Romanesque – Byzantine architecture.

during the Crusades, when trading posts were established in Asia Minor; suffered a decline with the discovery of America, when the Atlantic ports prospered and flourished once again with the opening of the Suez Canal in 1869.

The French national anthem is known to everyone as *La Marseillaise*, yet this stirring, revolutionary-era song is actually a misnomer. Since the song was composed in Strasbourg, its original title was, appropriately enough, *Battle Hymn of the Army of the Rhine*. News of the song, and its text arrived in

One of Marseille's best known landmarks is the Basilica of Notre Dame de la Garde.

Marseille, and at the farewell banquet for 500 Paris-bound volunteers, someone sung the new song, which was greeted with much success. As they marched through the country towards Paris, these soldiers from Marseille sang the song, which quickly acquired its erroneous name, La Marseillaise.

The city's best-known landmark is the 19th century Basilica of Notre Dame de la Garde, a monument of the then fashionable Romanesque-Byzantine architectural style. It is well worth visiting for the panoramic view it offers over

Megalithic menhir in Corsica, looks out over the Île de Beauté
(Beautiful Isle).

the city, the harbour and the islands. On one of these small off-shore islands is the Château d'If, where, like the Île Ste Marguerite off Cannes, the "Man in the Iron Mask" was imprisoned and immortalised in Dumas', *The Count of Monte Cristo*.

Although it is one of the oldest cities in the country, Marseille does not have conventional "sights". Rather, it is a city to be explored on foot, its main attraction lying more in the rich mix of people, the crowded streets of the picturesque **Vieux Port**, old port area, and the

Eroded cliffs of Bonifacio, Corsica.

animation of its best-known street, **La Canebière**. There is a saying in Marseille: "If only Paris had La Canebière then it would be a little Marseille". Proud words for this important historical city. The Palais de la Bourse (Stock Exchange) on La Canebière contains an interesting **Musée de la Marine** (Maritime Museum), where displays of model ships recount the history of the port.

Corsica: Beauty Bespoiled

The island of **Corsica** is different from the rest of Mediterranean France. Geographically separate and politically potentially explosive, home to much mindless terrorism, it is nonetheless an island of such great beauty that it is referred to as, simply, *Ile de Beauté* (Beautiful Isle).

Sadly for the island, its reputation has been tarnished by the continuing terrorism, carried out in the name of independence. But, for non-French visitors, the welcome is genuine and spontaneously warm.

Corsica's most famous son was Napoléon Bonaparte, who was born in **Ajaccio.** You can visit the Maison Bonaparte (Bonaparte's House) containing several of Napoleon's momentoes and the cathedral where Napoleon was baptized. **Bastia** to the north is a busy port town where the **Corsican Cultural Museum**, relates the story of life and history in Corsica.

Inherent in the French is a certain *joie de vivre* (the joy of living), which expresses itself through their instinctive, unashamed love of good food and good wine, of clothing and perfumes. In addition, they are a people who firmly believe in the wisdom of recreation and sports and if the latter can tie in with their very strong sense of national pride, then *tant mieux* (so much the better).

Like most people, the French like to win, so they obviously like winners and they have little understanding of the rather genteel English notion of supporting the underdog, or playing a game only for glory and not for victory. The French aim to win, they are openly partisan, and they are vociferous in their support of their national teams.

Cross country racing.

Sports & Recreation

Le Mans 24-hour motor race draws crowds from all over France.

Team & Spectator Sports

The most popular team sports are football and rugby, though other sports where the French excel in competition, such as skiing, tennis and cycling, are also keenly followed.

Football is one of the national passions and now that France is hosting the World Cup in 1998, interest is likely to increase even more. The country is committed to a massive building programme, involving both the modernization of existing stadiums and the construction of new ones. All of this involves a huge financial outlay of more than 8,000 million French Francs, of which roughly half will be for the stadiums alone. Two of the country's favourite spectator sports are the annual **Le Mans Car Race**, and the **Tour de France** cycling competition, and interestingly, both of them are long events, Le Mans lasting for 24 hours, and the Tour de France for three weeks.

The Le Mans race is 70 years old, and since it began in 1923, it has become one of the world's major motor races, along with the Formula One championships and the Indianapolis 500. (See box story on the Tour de France p 327).

Formula One

Like many countries, France hosts one

La pêche (fishing) is an ideal way to wind down.

of the annual races in motor racing's Formula One world championships, but a recent legal battle between the anti-smoking lobby, who invoked new legislation banning the advertising of tobacco, and the tobacco companies, who are the principal sponsors of Formula One racing, threatens the future of this French championship.

Every dawn on January 1st, when most Parisians are sleeping off the festivities of the night before, scores of rally drivers, bikers and their supporters gather at the Trocadéro, opposite the Eiffel Tower, for the departure of one of the most challenging races, the Paris-Dakar race.

The annual competition is less than 20 years old, but has a large following,

enjoys extensive television coverage, but is not without its share of opposition and controversy. Increasingly, people are questioning the ecological impact of scores of polluting vehicles thundering through African villages, as well as the danger to both contestant and spectator.

Individual Sports & Hobbies

Individual sports such as golf, skiing, tennis and cycling are also very popular in France, and anything to do with aerobics and health clubs in general has recently become fashionable. Winter sports have always been important for the French and most people try and

Old regattas make a picturesque scene.

enjoy at least a week or two skiing a year. Many schools arrange for the whole class to go to the mountains, where the children can combine skiing with academic work. France hosted the 1992 Winter Olympics, which means that the region around the core town of Albert-ville now enjoys top-class facilities.

Golf has only recently become popular in France and is still not played with the same passion as it is in Japan, nor with the same quietly discerning enthusiasm as in Britain. But, golf is gaining in popularity as more and more people

Boules is one of the most traditional of French sports.

pick up in the sport and the country hosts several major tournaments, including the **Trophée Lancôme**, which is played on one of the country's most beautiful courses, **Saint-Nom-la-Bretèche golf course**, just outside Paris.

There are very few uniquely "French" popular hobbies, and the country probably has its average share of stamp collectors, mountain climbers, bird watchers and crossword addicts, much like any other Western European country. Incidentally, if you are a stamp, coin, or postcard collector, head off to the informal, outdoor **stamp market on Avenue Gabriel** in Paris, which takes place on Thursdays, Saturdays and Sundays. Over the years, the scope of the market has been extended so, aside from stamps you can browse through stalls selling old bond certificates, coins, old postcards, and the latest craze, telephone cards.

Museums

France has hundreds of museums, ranging from small provincial galleries to the major Paris collections and the museum-going public is rapidly growing. Over the last 10 years, attendance at the state-run National Museums has increased by over 60 percent. Between 1989 and 1990, the Louvre registered a 40 percent increase in the number of visitors – many, no doubt, lured by the fascinating and controversial construc-

It may not be the Tour de France, but cycling is a perennial past-time for all ages.

tion of the Pyramid at the entrance to the museum.

Although Paris undoubtedly has the lion's share of the country's museums, every city will have its municipal museum or art gallery. Many of the provincial collections are outstanding either in terms of the works of art on display, or in the innovative ways of presenting them. The **Musée de la Paix** (Peace Museum) in Caen or the newly opened **Citadel** in Verdun are examples of high-tech museums, where audio-visual techniques and holograms are used. And in Marseille, a beautiful 17th century hospice has been converted into an exhibition complex, housing the city's permanent collection of Mediterranean archaeology as well as temporary exhibitions.

France tries to encourage people to go to museums, so very often they stay open late once or twice a week in major cities. There is usually also one day a week with reduced tariffs, and every year admission to all museums in the country is free on a certain weekend.

French Theatre

For non-French-speaking visitors to the country, the theatre will almost certainly remain inaccessible. But, for those who speak French, a visit to one of the major Paris theatres, such as the **Comédie Française**, or the **Odéon**, is a must. Find out what is happening in Paris from one of the two weekly "What's

Tour De France

The discussion of the chances of success of the 180 participants in France's annual country-wide cycle competition begins about eight months before the actual start of the race.

In the late autumn, the exact details of the 3,800 kilometre route are given out, with a day-by-day programme – and then the speculation starts in earnest. Newspapers, even ultra-serious ones like *Le Monde*, devote columns to analyzing the structure of the race, and the strengths of the likely contestants – particularly the French cyclists.

Every year the race changes its route, and in 1992, supposedly in keeping with the spirit of European unity, the race visited seven European countries.

The 1993 race, which will be the 80th in the life of the Tour de France, is decidedly French, keeping within the country's borders, except for a brief incursion into the principality of Andorra, tucked high up in the Pyrénées.

The Tour de France is anything but predictable. The race is broken into 21 stages or laps, there are days off during the competition and participants even fly between some stages. In addition to the combination of team and individual time trials, flat stretches and arduous mountain climbs, it is easy to understand why the Tour de France commands so much press analysis – you need expert help just to understand the complicated scoring system.

What can one say of a race that has twice been won by cyclists who never actually won a single lap? Consistent performance is the key in this ultimate test of stamina and endurance.

The history of the Tour de France mirrors in part the country's social development. It began in 1903 and although initially popular, it never really generated much enthusiasm outside the poorer sections of the population – the prize money was small, and there was virtually no international interest in it.

Recently, though, the bicycle has become thoroughly middle-class, a non-polluting, environmentally sound form of transport, a trend not limited to France. Sponsorship is now corporate, the prize money is big, though still not on the scale of tennis or football winnings, the participants are international and interest in what is now perceived to be a major "green" sporting event is widespread.

Limited Participation

Participation in the Tour de France is limited to 20 teams, each comprising six riders. Teams are often headed up by one star cyclist, and the rest of his team mates will act as his *domestiques*, which literally means servants; surrounding him, to protect him from collisions (accidental or otherwise), to set the pace and to act as blocks against rival teams. Protected by their *domestiques*, the stars all keep an eye on each other, ready to make a dash, to break away from the pack and become an *échappé* (fugitive) or at least pretend to do so.

Often the winner of the Tour de France is a strong all-rounder, equally able to tackle the gruelling mountain climbs as well as the individual (against the clock) sprints.

At the end of each day's race, the day's winner receives, *le maillot jaune* (yellow tee-shirt), usually emblazoned with the name of one of the major corporate sponsors. There are cyclists who have entered sporting history such as the Belgian Eddie Mercx who won four times in a row, from 1969 to 1972, and then again in 1974, and the popular French cyclist Bernard Hinault, also a five-time winner. And, all because of the Tour de France.

There are also cyclists who enter sporting history without ever winning the Tour de France, such as the immensely popular Raymond Polidor, who was a serious challenger all through the early 1960s, without ever being successful.

Routes may change, cyclists may come and go, the Tour de France may wander into neighbouring countries, but one thing never changes, the final lap of the race is always a sprint up the most famous street in Paris, the Champs Elysées. Cheered on by thousands of spectators, the exhausted cyclists hurl themselves and their bikes up the last few metres of the race, desperately reaching for the *maillot jaune* (yellow tee-shirt) and, the hope of spraying the crowd with a magnum of champagne.

The Spanish influence of La Corrida is only found in Arles.

on" magazines, ***L'Officiel des Specta-cles*** or ***Pariscope***. Check out ticket availability at the theatre itself or at outlets like FNAC (a chain of camera and video stores), or the half-price ticket booths (there is one in the Châtelet Les Halles metro station). In a city like Paris, the theatre will often offer a mix of the classics, translations of foreign plays, as well as an intellectually undemanding range of comedies, variety shows and farces, and usually some form of experimental theatre.

A tiny, uncomfortable little theatre called **Les Bouffes du Nord**, in the unfashionable north of Paris, stages some exceptionally good productions. A few years ago, they staged a nine-hour French version of the Indian classic ***The Mahabharata***, with every show sold-out. **Théâtre Guignol** is a form of puppet theatre unique to France. It originated in Lyon. (See box story p.329.)

Theme Parks

France's recent, and indeed, current experience with theme parks has not turned out to be a particularly happy one. Of all these parks, **Euro Disney** which opened in April 1992 is proving to be the most controversial, and financial viability is, as yet, far from guaranteed. Although the French are intrigued by many aspects of the American way of life, Euro Disney, with its transplant of Mickey Mouse and Main Street USA,

Guignol Puppet Theatre

One of France's traditional forms of entertainment, the *guignol* puppet theatre, was born out of an 18th century economic crisis.

Laurent Mourguet, born in Lyon in 1769 was a silk-worker. But, in 1795, he lost his job during the widespread industrial crisis and was forced into a succession of insecure jobs, including that of an itinerant pedlar and later a tooth-extractor. It was to attract customers to this latter business, that he set up a small puppet theatre next to his "dental" stall. Initially Mourguet entertained his prospective patients with the classic plays about Punchinello and other characters from the Italian *Comedia del Arte*, but he gradually invented new characters which were drawn from real life. His associate, Pere Thomas was the role model for Gnafron, his wife was the inspiration for Madelon, and he himself became Guignol le Canut, or Guignol the Silk-worker. Guignol, Gnafron and Madelon are hand-puppets, with wooden heads and cloth bodies.

Physically, Guignol is represented as being round-eyed, snub-nosed and with a shock of hair peeping out from under his black hat. He has an air of being perpetually surprised and is easily duped by his friends. As befits a hero (of sorts) though, he always manages to extricate himself from trouble and come to the rescue of his friends and drinking companions, especially the tall, truculent Gnafron, from whom he is inseparable. Gnafron's weakness for a bottle of *beaujolais* is shown by his red nose, and his raucous voice. Madelon is portrayed as a model wife, though not above grumbling a lot, which often leads to quarrels with her husband. A *guignol* puppet show requires lots of audience participation, and audiences (mainly children), are expected to respond and react to questions posed by the puppets.

Laurent Mourguet had 16 children, who were all trained in this new art form, and in association with his son Etienne and his son-in-law Louis Josserand, he established the first permanent *guignol* theatre, at the **Caveau des Celestins**. Mourguet left for Vienne in 1840, where he died in 1844. Originally, *guignol* theatre was performed in regional dialect, and the puppets wore traditional peasant dress. Today, one of Mourguet's descendants, Jean-Guy Mourguet, runs a puppet theatre at the **Nouveau Guignol de Lyon** where he has adapted and up-dated some of the traditional plays, and set them in a modern context.

aroused passions in France from all sectors of the population. The local farmers around Marne-la-Vallée, 32 kilometres east of Paris, were outraged, not only at the building of the park on prime agricultural land, but also at the derisory rates at which the government sold the land to Euro-Disney. As a result they instigated many well-publicized blockades. French intellectuals, on the other hand, criticized the potential dangers of a "cultural Chernobyl" with the influx of commercial American culture at the expense of the French. Although it is still too early to speak with any certainty on the long-term success of Euro Disney, one fact is clear – in a depressed economic climate, the park employs over 12,500 people, mainly youngsters, and has quickly become part of the tourist circuit for foreign visitors. (See box story on Euro Disney p.173).

As for the other French theme parks, there is the **Parc Astérix**, located 20 kilometres north of Paris's Charles de Gaulle (Roissy) Airport, which brings to life the incredibly successful Astérix the Gaul cartoon books. But, 1991 saw the closure of Mirapolis, just outside of Paris, of Zygofolis in Nice and the Paris-based

Despite the protests of wildlife groups, hunting is still an upper class sport and recreation.

Parc Océanique Cousteau. A couple of theme parks, now owned by a Belgian company, are, however, operating successfully – **The Big Bang Schtroumpf** in eastern France and **Babyland**, located 25 kilometres away from the troubled Euro Disney.

Summer Holidays

It is always a mistake to generalise about any race too much, but one generalization about the French that is permitted, is in connection with their holidaying

and 15 August, Ascension Day.

Travel within France at your peril over those periods, especially in the south, for the roads will be blocked with traffic jams, the hotels and restaurants fully booked and tempers will be frayed. The obvious thing to do at this time is, of course, to visit Paris, which completely relaxes in the summer because of the exodus of residents to the south.

The city is suddenly free of traffic jams, there is even free parking during the month of August. True, some restaurants are either closed in July or August, but that is a small price to pay for a calmer, quieter, friendlier city.

Truly French Sport

Wherever you go in France, be it a remote village in the Midi, or Montmartre in Paris, you will certainly come across men playing – one of the country's more typical games – bowls.

Boules

Known in most of France as *boules*, it has slightly different rules and a different name in the south, where it is called *pétanque*, and where it is something of an obsession.

The game is played on any sandy patch of land (a far cry from the manicured lawns of the English game), and whenever you see a group of men, huddled together, staring at the ground,

habits.

Vacations are sacrosanct to the French, who are firm believers in the unvarying ritual of *les grandes vacances* (summer holidays).

Summer holidays are usually for a month and are nearly always taken in July or August, with the peak month being between the 14 July, Bastille Day

If your ambitions are high, start young.

there is almost certainly a *partie de boules* (a game of *boules*) taking place.

Pelota is to the Basques (both on the Spanish and French sides of the Pyrénées) what cricket is to the English, a much loved game, but one that is difficult to

Pelota

Long-court *pelota*, where players wear a curved wicker basket strapped to their wrist and hurl a hard leather ball, (slightly bigger than an orange), at the wall of the court, is the fastest ball game in the world. Professional players have been known to record throwing speeds of 160 mph. Thus, the court walls have to be built in marble, since concrete crumbles under the impact. A *pelota* ball is made of either box-wood or rubber, surrounded by wool and covered in either kid or calf-skin.

The ball is thrown at the court wall, and caught on the rebound, at high speeds and within certain lines traced on the court floor. It is a very fast game, and the two teams of three players, have to leap into the air to catch the high-speed projectile.

There are variants of the game, one of which is played with a wooden bat and another with the bare hand. For matches, the two teams wear white trousers and white shirts, with different coloured waist sashes – either red or blue.

The Basques have another unique sport, which, it must be admitted, is hardly known outside the Basque country, but which is keenly followed there – Basque lifting. This local version of weight-lifting involves lifting traditionally cut stones, but if you feel the urge to have a go, just remember that the Basques classify any stone under 200 kilogrammes as small!

explain to the uninitiated. Firstly, there is not one unique way to play *pelota*, but 10, and the *pelota* court can vary, according to which type of *pelota* is played there.

Cuisine

In France, to state the obvious, food is important. That does not mean merely eating to appease hunger, but the ritualistic enjoyment of food, the savouring of skills that are highly ranked and highly regarded. Interestingly enough, it was not a Frenchman, but an Italian, Luigi Barzini, who said of French cooking: "French cuisine is a challenge to Nature, it subverts Nature, it creates a new Nature of its own. It is an art".

Unlike some European countries which lack anything but the most basic of cuisines – such as English roast beef and Yorkshire pudding or Hungarian goulash – France has a rich and varied range of foods and a cuisine which is slowly adapting not only to health concerns, but also to the influence of its immigrant communities. Just about every town in France boasts a Vietnamese and a Chinese restaurant, and many others will have Moroccan or Tunisian restaurants too.

The French not only enjoy their food, they

■ ■ ■ ■ ■

Dining out is a favourite French form of recreation.

335

An offering of Loire cuisine.

enjoy shopping for it, preparing it, going out to eat it, and, very importantly, they love talking about it.

Classic dinner party conversation in France, whilst savouring one delicious meal, will be to discuss other good meals, or bad meals, or new restaurants. The French see no incongruity in describing the *plat du jour* (dish of the day) they had at lunch, whilst eating dinner. It is this passionate interest in all things culinary and gastronomic that has given French cuisine such an international reputation.

Culinary Brotherhoods

Hardly surprisingly, the French have institutionalized some aspects of their passion for food, albeit in a purely celebratory way, via their *grandes confréries* (brotherhoods). Over 150 food societies exist in France, honouring everything from the sublime to the virtually ridiculous from Saint Emilion wine to tripe, sausages and snails – there is even a Tea Drinkers' Club, where members drink their tea with much more aplomb than even the British do.

Although these societies take themselves and their food seriously, with elaborate rituals and even more elaborate robes, their purpose is essentially the celebration, enjoyment and promotion of publicity for their chosen food – be it the Order of the Stuffed Chicken based near Albi, in Southwest France, or

Wining and dining in an elegant setting.

the Brotherhood of the Golden Sword, honouring the art of opening a champagne bottle with a sabre.

Cynics might suggest that all this is nothing more than a slick 20th century public relations exercise. True, the Brotherhood of the Muscadet Sausage only dates back to 1990, but the Jurade de Saint Emilion dates back to 1199, proving that the French have taken their food seriously for centuries! Some of the world's best cooks and restaurants are French, and with the closely followed annual culinary awards of such companies as Michelin and Gault-Millault, everyone knows which restaurants are currently the best, which have slipped in the ratings, and how many weeks in advance you need to reserve a table.

As in any country, there is nothing to compare with home cooking, but as the visitor to France will quickly realise, the French eat out regularly, be it for breakfast, lunch or dinner, so there is nothing easier than hunting out the busiest *café*, the noisiest *bistro*, or the longest queue outside the *pâtisserie*, to discover where the locals eat and shop for their food.

Haute Cuisine & Recent Trends

France is justly famed for her *haute cuisine*, for her classic, excellent food, painstakingly prepared, impeccably served and more often than not, ruinously ex-

Black Diamonds – Truffles

Do you fancy tasting an edible subterranean fungus, that has been "hunted" by a pig? Absolutely not? Well, let us put it another way – would you like to eat one of the most prized and expensive foods in France? *Le diamant noir de l'hiver* (the black winter diamond) – a pretty and poetic name for a legendary delicacy, the truffle.

Part of the mystique surrounding truffles lies in their harvesting, for, in what could well be the opening of a children's story, to go truffle-hunting, you need a farmer, a dog and a pig.

Sometimes, truffles grow just under the surface of the ground, cracking it as they reach maturity, but usually they are found up to 30 centimetres below ground-level, which makes detection that much more difficult. Although there are some clues that indicate where the truffles may be found, such as "burn marks", which are in fact round, bare spots at the base of an oak tree, truffle-hunting is usually done with trained dogs and trained pigs, whose keen sense of smell leads then directly to the underground treasure trove.

Pigs actually have a more highly developed sense of smell than dogs, but since they are partial to truffles themselves, the "hunt" can sometimes end in disaster, as the pigs eat up all the harvest, which is why farmers are beginning to use dogs more and more.

Truffles have been popular in France since the 15th century, and the most valued of the 30 or so kinds that exist is the Périgord variety, found, naturally enough, in the Périgord region.

Although truffles can be found in many parts of the country, wherever there is a suitable combination of open woodland, the correct soil type (calcareous) and tree roots, especially oak, the main *truffières* (truffle grounds) are in Périgord and Vaucluse. Before WWI, the Périgord truffle harvest was in the region of 1,800 tons a year. Nowadays, the annual harvest is barely 200 tons.

Truffles are harvested between November and February, and are often sold immediately, the peak supply months being January and February.

There are a few professional truffle markets, the most famous of which are in Carpentras and Lalbenque, where the "black winter diamonds" are sold, straight from the earth, still wrapped in their muddy covering. Commercial cultivation of truffles is both difficult and long, with a time lag of at least 10 years before it becomes profitable.

You can eat truffles in a number of ways: raw, peeled and with a sprinkling of salt; or in omelettes, scrambled eggs or coddled eggs, when the truffle enhances the taste of the food; or you find thin slivers of it in such delicacies as goose liver *pâté*. To accompany such a delicacy, you should ideally drink one of France's great wines – either one of the good wines from Burgundy, such as a Puligny-Montrachet or a Chambertin, or, if you prefer Bordeaux wines, a Pomerol or a first-class Médoc.

The last word must go to the 19th century writer, Jules de Goncourt, who wrote in his *journal* (diary): "And to think that we still don't know the name of the first pig to have discovered a truffle!"

Go to Maxim's for a celebrated taste of some of France's best.

pensive. If you can afford such luxuries, then dinner at one of the truly great Parisian restaurants such as **La Tour d' Argent**, with its breathtaking view of Notre Dame Cathedral is an unforgettable experience. But, do not forget that in France although good food is undoubtedly found in the country's top-ranked restaurants, it is not exclusive to them, you can eat extremely well in tiny family-run restaurants in out-of-the-way little towns.

In France, cooking, is not seen as a set of fixed rules, but as something that develops, adapting itself to local conventions and current thinking. Thus, in the 1980s, with a new awareness of healthy living and lifestyles, French chefs pioneered *nouvelle cuisine*, (new cooking), with the emphasis on smaller portions, lighter foods and fewer rich sauces. The rest of the world eagerly jumped on the *nouvelle cuisine* bandwagon, inevitably distorting it, debasing it and finally pushing it to ridiculous extremes – ultra-large plates, ultra-small but aesthetically presented portions, kiwis and raspberry vinegar with everything. So the French rapidly veered away from such clichés, preferring to call their lighter, less calorific cuisine *cuisine minceur* (lean cuisine). Many restaurants will now feature a dish that is particularly low in calories. Although without a doubt there is an increased awareness of health and dietary concerns, there is no way that the French will ever totally abandon such traditionally rich foods

Rillettes (minced pork), is the local speciality of Provence.

such as *boeuf bourguignon* (Burgundy beef) or *coq au vin* (chicken in wine), nor their love of cheese, wine and *pâtisseries* (pastries). People may drink more mineral water with their meals than formerly, but food is still sacrosanct, cholesterol-packed or cholesterol-free!

Famous Regional Cuisine

It would not only be ridiculous to try and nominate one dish as "quintessentially French", it would be far too time-consuming, for one of the joys of travelling around the country is the variety of its regional cooking. So much of what is termed regional food, is, at heart, simple peasant food, using only locally available produce, often leaving the ingredients to cook for a long time, and usually served in hearty portions. *Fondue, cassoulet, pot au feu* (stock-pot or beef stew), *crêpes, coq au vin* (chicken in wine), *bouillabaisse* (fish soup, see recipe p.346) and *choucroute* (sauerkraut) are all favourite dishes that originated from the need to use up left-overs and satisfy healthy appetites amongst country folk.

Burgundy has given France its love of snails and *boeuf à la bourguignon* (Burgundy beef), whilst the mountainous Savoy area has provided the *fondue savoyarde* (cheese fondue).

Périgord is the home of truffles (see box p.338), whilst Toulouse is famous for *cassoulet* which is essentially a bean and pork hot-pot, although such a bland

A man dressed in François I costume makes an offering of baguettes.

description does no justice to the delicious end result. Provence has given the superb fish stews, such as *bouillabaisse, bourride* and *brandade de morue* (cod fish), which are still best eaten locally because of the availability of so many types of Mediterranean fish, but also *daube à la provençale* (Provence stew) which is a variation of the general *pot au feu* (stock-pot). One of the most copied and most mishandled of French dishes is the *quiche lorraine*, a superb feast when made locally in eastern France.

The food of the southwest, espe-

A shop for epicures.

cially the Basque country utilizes fish and ham, especially *jambon de Bayonne* (Bayonne ham). A local speciality is *la piperade,* an omelette with lots of peppers, onions and tomatoes. One thing to bear in mind when tasting regional food, is that very often it goes best with the local wine.

Bread & Cheese: Vignettes of French Life

As befits a country with a large agricultural base, France has excellent dairy products with a wide variety of butter, yoghurt, cream, and, of course, cheese. Particularly delicious are little cream cheeses called *Petit Suisse*. When mixed

with a little sugar they make a simple, sweet dessert. Amidst all the political controversy aroused by the European Community (Common Market), one of the many issues that has seriously upset the French has been the threat to their beloved cheese. It was General de Gaulle who neatly summed up his fellow countrymen thus: "You can only unite the French through fear. You cannot simply bring together a country that has 265 kinds of cheese." And sure enough, when the French were threatened with European rules on how to make their cheese, they were united in their outrage.

The mere idea of foreign technocrats pronouncing judgement on their beloved *Camembert* provoked an outburst of articles and letters to the press.

The storm within the Common Market over the making of cheese from non-pasteurised versus pasteurised milk, which set traditional French methods against Scandinavian and German health concerns, has now been settled but the indignation aroused is typical of the French attitude to their food – proud and protective.

French cheese comes in all shapes, sizes and strengths, from the bland but cutely named, foil-wrapped triangles of *La vache qui rit* (the laughing cow), which can be found just about anywhere in the world except on a Frenchman's dinner table, to the strong cheeses such as *Roquefort* and *Reblochon* which are more popular with the French but often difficult for foreigners to eat. Actually, de Gaulle under-estimated the number of cheeses, the total is closer to 400 than 265.

What better accompaniment for *Camembert* or *Brie* cheese, than a *baguette* (a long stick-shaped loaf of bread) which is another of the simple things in life that the French do so successfully.

Watch any *boulangerie* (bakery), and you will see a typical vignette of French life: someone comes out of the *boulangerie*, child or adult, with a freshly baked *baguette* under their arm, and

proceeds to break off a bit of crust, nibble away at it, then a little more, and so it goes on, and yet another half-eaten loaf of bread is delivered home. Fresh French bread is so irresistible that it is imitated all over the world, but it never tastes the same as it does fresh from the *boulangerie* in France.

Wine: Contentment for Connoisseurs

To wash down the cheese and the freshly baked *baguette*, a glass of wine is surely called for, and in a country like France, the only problem is deciding which one of the many superb wines to drink, and which colour - red, white, *rosé* or *gris* (grey wine from the south). Although France is not the world's largest producer of wines, it does produce more quality wines than any other country in the world, and it is the reputation of the wines of Bordeaux and Burgundy which are pre-eminent.

Wine has been grown in France since Roman times, so there is a long tradition of expertise, which, combined with a fortuitously ideal combination of soil and sunshine, makes for a wide range of successful vintages and types of wine. For top class wines, many of which were classed as *grand cru* (vintage wine)

French cheese comes in all shapes, sizes and strengths.

in an 1855 classification of 62 *crus classés* (classes of wine), look no further than Bordeaux, in the southwest of the country, which produces wines whose names are a roll-call of the most distinguished *châteaux:* Médoc, Haut-Médoc, Pomerol, Saint-Emilion, Margaux, Château Lafite, Château Yquem. These are the kinds of wines that wine-lovers dream of owning (and drinking), laying them down in their wine cellars for special occasions.

For everyday drinking, France has another category of wines – *vin de pays* (country wines), a classification which was introduced in 1973. Basically, a *vin de pays* is a table wine with a geographical origin and currently, 85 percent of this category of wine comes from the south of France, from Languedoc, Roussillon and Provence, areas of the country where the greatest improvements in French wines are taking place. *Vins de pays* are reasonably inexpensive and highly effective in the constant struggle to maintain good export levels in the face of competition from inexpensive Italian, Californian and Australian wines. People do not buy a *vin du pays* as a long-term investment, but as a wine to be drunk almost immediately (although some of these wines can be kept for up to 10 years). French people drink wine with almost every meal – except breakfast – and it is even an essential ingredient for a successful family picnic.

Bistros and *brasseries*, which translate rather inadequately as pubs are

A gastronomic spread.

essentially restaurants with a bar, but in fact are much more since they are an integral part of the French eating scene. Basically, a *bistro* or a *brasserie* will be noisier and less formal than a restaurant, which is not to say that the food will be less impressive, for some of Paris's turn-of-the-century *brasseries* are very highly rated.

Possibly one of the greatest of French institutions is the *café*. *Café* is an all-encompassing term that covers the grand and famous Parisian literary *cafés* such as Le Dôme, La Coupole, and La Rotonde – once the haunt of Cocteau and Hemingway and now haunted by would-be writers, as well as the neighbourhood *café du coin* (corner *café*). One of the joys of French *cafés* is that they

cater to many tastes and many needs, from a rushed croissant and coffee in the morning on the way to work, through to a beer or a glass of wine on the way home from a late movie.

Cafés offer food, drink, the conversation of a garrulous *patron* (proprietor), pinball machines and if they are *café-tabacs*, you can buy cigarettes, stamps, fiscal stamps, and metro tickets. *Café-tabacs* are always particularly crowded on the last day for sending in one's tax returns, or when paying one's road tax when everyone realizes they desperately need a fiscal stamp and a cup of coffee.

Café etiquette offers a choice of standing at the bar, sipping your coffee, beer or wine, or paying a little more and

La Bouillabaisse

La bouillabaisse is one of the great show-pieces of Mediterranean cuisine. It translates prosaically as Provençal fish soup, but a bouillabaisse served in a restaurant in Marseille or by the vieux port (old port) in Cannes has as much relation to fish soup as table wine does to a grand cru classé (vintage wine).

It is an expensive, luxurious, complicated, and delicious dish. Each chef will have his own version of bouillabaisse, which will depend on both personal taste on the availability of fish and also on cost – for a less expensive version, you can always omit the lobster !

Ingredients:
For 6 people you need :
2 kg of fish – choose a selection of saint-pierre (John Dory), merlan (whiting), vive (weever or stingray), and congre (conger eel);
3 leeks;
3 tomatoes;
salt;
pepper;
one piece of dried orange peel;
$^{1}/_{2}$ a glass of olive oil;
potatoes (optional).

To make le fumet (the flavour) you need:
600 g of rock fish – rouquier, sarans, rascasse (scorpion fish), girelle;
2 onions;
3 carrots;
2 pinches of mixed herbs;
1 piece of parsley;
1 stick of celery;
$^{1}/_{2}$ a litre of good white wine;

30 g of butter;
2 soup spoons of oil.

To make the marinade :
A large pinch of saffron;
a pinch of thyme;
a pinch of rosemary;
a soup spoon of pastis;
$^{1}/_{2}$ a glass of olive oil;
2 pinches of salt;
2 pinches of white pepper;
1 pinch of black pepper.

To make la rouille which literally means rust but for bouillabaisse is a marvellous, pungent, rust-coloured sauce, you need:
2 small red peppers;
1 clove of garlic;
2 livers from the scorpion fish;
1 small potato;
1 coffee spoon of olive oil (optional).

Method:
To make the fumet: Cook the vegetables, the mixed herbs, the parsley and the celery together gently in a pan, with a little oil and melted butter and then add the wine. Add the fish, cook on a high flame for 15 minutes, then strain, so you are left with a purée.

To make the bouillabaisse: Cut the fish into medium-sized pieces, mix together all the marinade ingredients, cover the fish and put aside to marinade in a cool place for one hour. From time to time, gently move the fish to check that all the pieces are covered with the marinade.
Cut the leeks into thin strips. Peel and de-

sitting down to be served – and if the weather is good, the café may put its chairs and tables outside on the street, then you also get to indulge in a favourite French past-time, people watching. Do not be shy, French cafés are designed that way, for the chairs are always put in rows, facing out towards the pave-

ment, so sit back, sip your aperitif, and enjoy café life.

Yet, although the local café is an integral part of French life, especially in the provinces, where the village café is often a major focal point for social life, in the cities it is facing stiff competition and fighting to exist. The famous cafés

seed the tomatoes, then purée them. If you want to add potatoes (a question of individual taste), then peel and cut into thin slices, roughly 1 centimetre thick.

Gently heat a little oil in a cast-iron pan with an enamel-bottom, brown the leeks, stirring constantly with a wooden spoon.

Add the fish and the marinade, and cover with the *fumet*. Add salt, pepper, the dried orange peel, and the tomato purée.

Bring to the boil and let it continue to boil, uncovered, on a high flame for 15 minutes, after which the bouillabaisse will be ready, (if you have omitted the potatoes). If you included the potatoes, then let the *bouillabaisse* continue boiling until they are cooked, since they will require a little more time than the fish.

To make *la rouille*: Grind the garlic and chillies, adding olive oil if you so wish, but only a little, since its powerful taste will alter that of the sauce.

Cook the potato in a small portion of either the *bouillabaisse* or the *fumet* sauce, then blend it with the fish liver, the garlic and chillies. When the mixture appears smooth, strain off some of the *bouillabaisse* stock and gradually add it to the liver and potato.

To Serve: Place several pieces of stale bread at the bottom of a warm soup tureen and pour the *bouillabaisse* over. Serve the *rouille* in a separate sauce dish, and taste a little spread on a piece of fresh bread. That wonderful taste alone justifies such a long and complicated recipe.

will always survive, but for many, the news that a fast food outlet is opening in the neighbourhood can sound the death knell.

It is a sad reflection on the evolution of French eating habits, but a recent survey disclosed that a typical café loses 30 percent of business if a McDonald's opens nearby.

To combat this attrition, some cafés change their image, such as the wildly trendy **Café Costas** in Paris's off-beat Les Halles district, while others change their name, preferring to call themselves wine bars, in the hope of retaining customers with a more trendy image.

French Eating Habits

The French do not eat noticeably more often than other nationalities, but since they enjoy eating out, it can often seem as though they are eating throughout the day. They are not, they are simply relishing one of the pleasures in life. A French breakfast is simple usually a cup of coffee and a *croissant* (a crescent-shaped roll of flaky bread), or for children a *pain au chocolat* (another flaky roll, with chocolate inside).

In French homes, the breakfast coffee will often be served in large bowls, rather than cups, into which the *croissant* is often dipped.

Although time-saving devices like coffee machines in offices are prevalent, everyone still prefers to call into a *café* close to the office for a pre-work coffee, or a mid-morning coffee-break, often accompanied by a *tartine* (half a baguette, opened and buttered).

Lunch is taken seriously in France, so seriously, in fact, that the notion of working business lunches is anathema to a French businessman. The Anglo-Saxon style of settling down to discuss

Brasseries are an integral part of the everyday French eating scene.

work immediately is just not done in France.

In France, the rule of thumb is as follows: either you are lunching to build up relations in general, without really expecting anything specific immediately; or you are lunching to discuss an on-going deal, or to celebrate a successful conclusion to a deal. But, whatever happens, never try and clinch a deal over lunch – leave that for the office. A word of warning, in France business lunches are long, anything from two to three hours, and as with all French meals, remember that cheese precedes dessert.

Although tea is not as institutionalized as in England, there are some well-known Parisian haunts for France's growing number of *théophiles* (tea lovers), ranging from the conventional, bordering on the bourgeois, such as **Angelina's** on the Rue de Rivoli, so

table, especially for the better known restaurants.

By law, all restaurants must offer a fixed price menu, which is a good idea if you are unsure of what to order. In Paris, waiters may well seem rushed and off-hand with hesitant customers, but in provincial towns, especially in the south, they will be only too happy to explain the meaning of unfamiliar dishes on the menu.

The French do not eat out very late at night, and even in Paris, you may find it difficult to walk into a restaurant without a reservation after 10:00 pm at night. So, if you are planning on eating after the theatre or cinema, find out which are the restaurants which stay open late (usually *brasseries*) and reserve a table.

Since late 1992, all restaurants must by-law have separate non-smoking sections, but as the French are not as virulently anti-smoking as many other countries, nor do they necessarily obey laws just because they exist, the application of this rule tends to depend very much on the individual *patron* (proprietor).

Never feel guilty about eating too much good food and drinking too much good wine in France, instead, tell yourself that not only will you walk it all off whilst exploring, but that you are also entering into the spirit of the country and participating in one of the national passions – food. It is truly a waste not to go out and enjoy this marvellous cuisine, so *Bon appetit*!

well known that you might have to queue to get in, to the distinctly off-the-beaten-track **Paris Mosque**, where you can sit outside in the shady garden, drink mint tea and eat North African pastries.

Dinner is an important meal in France, and when it comes to choosing a restaurant the guiding factor will be what kind of food you like, price, and how many other people want to eat in the same restaurant that night – it always pays to call ahead and reserve a

351

Shopping in France is blissfully easy, for faced with merchandise of such a high quality, and the total acceptability of credit cards, travellers' cheques and Euro-cheques, it is fatally easy to shop till you drop. France is world famous for its perfumes and jewellery, for designer clothes, handbags, silk scarves and other fashion accessories, as well as its food and wine – and if you should just happen to overshop, you can easily find excellent luggage, too!

Galleries Lafayette.

Beyond Shopping

If Paris is the acknowledged shopping centre of France, then the **Avenue Montaigne** is the undisputed place of pilgrimage for every shopper in search of France's best offerings – luxury goods and *haute couture* (high fashion). A stroll along Avenue Montaigne is a severe temptation for the serious dresser, with its continuous line of well-known names: Chanel, Christian Dior, Nina Ricci, Scherrer, Ungaro, Thierry Mugler, and the

Yves Saint Laurent is one of a succession of Parisian couture boutiques.

ruin of all handbag-lovers, Louis Vuitton. Here, and in the streets around **Avenue George V** and **Avenue Montaigne** is a "golden triangle" for shoppers, where designers create exclusive clothes for the few thousand women in the world still willing and able to pay for made-to-measure *haute couture* (high fashion) clothes each season.

Close rivals to the Avenue Montaigne are the Rue du Faubourg-St-Honoré and Place Vendôme. In Place Vendôme are found some of the capital's most famous jewellers, such as Van Cleef and Arples, Boucheron, Chaumet and Cartier and some of the famous parfumeries such as Guerlain, Schiaparelli and Payot.

Take a stroll from la Place de la Concorde towards the church of La Madeleine, passing **Maxim's Restaurant** – yes, *the* Maxim's, where the rich and famous allow themselves to be refused admittance, or relegated to a bad table, depending on which richer and more famous person is dining there that night.

Turn left into the **Rue du Faubourg-St-Honoré**, and begin your *lèche vitrine* (window shopping) at any of the elegant windows of Hermès, Yves Saint Laurent, Karl Lagerfeld, Lancôme, Revillon, Lanvin and Gucci (not French, admittedly, but European at least). Hermès has recently moved its workshops, which were occupying prime real estate, out to the suburbs, so their shop will soon be enlarged with yet more

A great many second-hand book stores sprawl along the banks of the River Seine.

wonderful silk scarfs and ties on display.

For the less fabulously wealthy, there are always the *prêt à porter* (ready-to-wear) lines, or the *soldes* (sales), or a trip to some of the less expensive areas, the **Marais District**, **Boulevard Saint Germain** and the **Rue Saint Sulpice** which are now home to new, smaller boutiques, so do not confine your shopping to only the more prestigious streets.

Food & Wine

Not surprisingly, food and wine figure prominently on the shopping lists of visitors to France, for the selection of wines, cheese, *pâtés* and *saucissons* (sausages) are superb.

Buying wine is largely a matter of taste, white or red, *beaujolais* or *burgundy,* and if you are holidaying in one of the wine regions of the country (see the chapter on Eastern Wine region), a visit to a wine producer's *château* is recommended. Here you can taste, talk to an expert and buy directly from them.

If you do not have the time to visit a *château*, then a less romantic option is to head for one of the many hyper-markets which proliferate in France, often on the outskirts of cities. There you can choose from amongst hundreds of bottles and a selection of wines from all over the country though without the benefit of tasting them.

Mid-way between the wine-producer and the hyper-market would be a

The Economics of Luxury

Nina Ricci on Avenue Montaigne, Paris.

During the prosperous decade of the 1980s, when money appeared to be no problem and the ethics of conspicuous consumption troubled few people, the French fashion industry experienced almost uninterrupted growth. Wealthy Americans and Arabs shopped freely, and the booming Japanese market was a major source of sales and profit.

The worldwide recession that heralded the opening of the 1990s has had and is still having, obvious and dramatic repercussions for the world of luxury goods. Clearly, in times of economic downturn, people buy less of what are, after all, non-essential items. Currency fluctuations and their effect on costs and profits are an additional short-term headache. The internal economics of the industry are in-turn having an effect on individual designers and small-scale manufacturers of luxury goods.

What is of more long-term importance is the growing trend towards luxury goods conglomerates, such as Dunhill, Orcofi, and LVMH: the latter, for example, owns not only the Louis Vuitton luggage and Moët et Chandon cham-

pagne, but also the houses of Christian Dior, Christian Lacroix and Givenchy. These conglomerates have a huge spending power, which they use on advertising campaigns, expensive catwalk displays, and the launching of new products. LVMH's launching several years ago of the designer Christian Lacroix is thought to have cost in the region of 150 million French Francs; Lacroix's recently ill-fated perfume *C'est La Vie* is thought to have cost £17.5 million to launch; whilst the recent re-launch of the classic 1947 Dior perfume *Miss Dior*, cost close to 45 million French Francs on European advertising in one financial quarter alone. Such budgets are way beyond the means of smaller, independent fashion houses, who at worst are forced out of business, or at best into the arms of a conglomerate. The spectre of individual creativity being priced out of the market hangs over the mind of any small-scale entrepreneur.

Put simply, all is not well in the world of fashion and luxury. According to the *Chambre Syndical de la Couture*, the representative body of the French fashion houses, combined sales of the Paris designers fell by 11 percent in 1991. The year 1992 was even worse, for with the bursting of the Japanese economic bubble, one of the major markets of the last decade dried up.

The extraordinary aspect of the world of couture, is that it centres around a very small

visit to a wine-merchant. France has a country-wide chain of wine-merchants called Nicolas. These are small wine shops, often run by a husband and wife team, who will be happy to advise you and who will often hold promotions of lesser known regional wines.

There are certain statements one can make about France, without fear of contradiction, such as every French town and village will have a good *boulangerie* (bakery). You will almost always find a good *charcuterie* (meat delicatessen) selling *pâté* and *saucisson* (sausages) and a

Annual fur sale.

number of seriously rich women who can afford to pay the high prices for individually made-to-measure clothes.

The couture houses are happy to provide statistics (but never names) of their mega-rich customers. For example, Dior has about 200 ready-to-wear clients a year, only 28 percent of whom are European. So with the cost of *haute couture* (high fashion) way beyond the reach of most people anyway and even *prêt à porter* (ready-to-wear) looking expensive in an economic crisis, the bulk of sales are currently being made in accessories – perfumes, luggage and scarfs.

Perfume, especially, is a major earner for the fashion houses. For example, Christian Dior enjoyed a turnover of 3.13 million French Francs, half of which came from the perfume industry. Classic fragrances such as *Chanel No.5* and Guerlain's *Shalimar* both generate sales of approximately 500 million French Francs a year.

Despite the recession, perfumes still sell, so much so that the perfume houses are not only re-launching and re-packaging old fragrances, as in the case of *Miss Dior*, but are also launching new fragrances. The family-owned House of Patou has just launched a new perfume, called *Sublime* aimed at those women who find its perfume *Joy*, labelled as "the most expensive perfume in the world", a little too pricey.

Guerlain has also recently launched a new fragrance for men, called *Héritage*, which is the 323rd perfume to be launched by the company since 1828.

Yet even the buoyant fragrance market does have its expensive failures. The first perfume launched by Christian Lacroix, whose clothes were one of the fashion successes of the 1980s, failed badly. With the advent of the single European Market, cutting down on duty-free shopping, trade within Europe may be affected, and since a large percentage of perfume purchases are made by holiday-makers, this will have an impact on the industry.

The whole fashion and luxury goods business is in a state of flux, for as long as the economic outlook remains gloomy, people will not buy, nor will financiers feel inclined to further invest in the industry. As people become more ecologically aware, the instant obsolescence of fashion, with its pressure to buy new clothes and accessories every season, begins to appear unacceptable.

good *fromagerie* selling cheese.

In Paris, visit one of the high temples of food shopping, **Fauchon** at the corner of Place de la Madeleine where some of the food on sale is breathtakingly expensive, but the whole shop is gastronomically tempting.

Books & Films

Although books are an expensive buy in France, most visitors to Paris head for the *bouquinistes* (book-stalls) lining the River Seine. Here, in tiny, metal trunk-

The great department store of Au Printemps should meet most shopping needs.

like stalls, you can browse through second-hand books, old magazines, prints and maps (some, sadly, have clearly been ripped out of old books), old fashion plates and turn-of-the century postcards. At the *bouquinistes* you can pick up attractive presents and souvenirs at very reasonable prices.

If you do want to buy books, records, compact discs, any kind of hi-fi and photographic material, including film, check out a store called FNAC, which is found in major cities all over the country. They offer good prices and an enormous selection of their items for sale and they are serviced by knowledgeable staff. In Paris, there is a huge FNAC in the underground **Forum des Halles**, and smaller ones on Avenue Wagram,

just off the Arc de Triomphe and Rue de Rennes.

Table Ware

France is reputed for its porcelain, silver tableware and glassware, so if you want to give your dining table a face lift, now is the time. Personal taste is obviously the prime factor in this domain, but with such prestigious French names as Limoges, Christofle, Baccarat, Lalique and Daum, there is a luxury of choice.

The town of Limoges, in the centre of the country, is a major producer of porcelain, and one of the country's most reputed crystal companies, **Daum**, is based in Nancy, eastern France. But,

Searching out antiques can be most interesting near the St Germain district.

most large department stores all over the country will sell a wide range of tableware. In Paris, you can get excellent reductions on glass, china and cutlery in any of the many shops along the **Rue du Paradis**, in the definitely unfashionable 10th *arrondissement* (district). Canny about-to-be-newly-weds leave their wedding present lists with a shop in the Rue de Paradis, rather than with a chic department store. Since the shops in the Rue du Paradis do a lot of export trade, it is very simple to have your purchases shipped for you.

Handicrafts make most representative souvenirs.

Department Stores

Although department stores are by no means unique to France, some of Paris's *grands magasins* (department stores) are worth a visit. Two of the better known stores are on **Boulevard Haussmann – Galeries Lafayette** with its spectacular Art Déco glass dome, and **Au Printemps**, which has a superb view from its terrace. Opposite the flamboyant pseudo-*château* housing the Paris Town Hall (Hôtel de Ville) in the first *arrondissement*

number of tools, hooks, widgets and gadgets that you never knew existed, and that you never knew until now that you needed!

Many of the major Paris department stores not only have leaflets and plans in various foreign languages, but also an information desk, staffed by foreign language speakers.

As an overseas visitor to France, you will be entitled to a refund of the Value Added Tax (VAT) you have paid, so before making a major purchase, or even many smaller purchases in one department store, ask for information about VAT – which is called TVA in French. Be it in Paris or in smaller country towns, new shops open and old ones close, so it is difficult to give an up-to-date list of specific *boutiques* (shops), but one shop that is currently making headlines in Paris is, of all things, a shop selling wrist watches.

The Swiss success story of Swatch watches, has caught on in such a big way in Paris, that although their newly opened shop, on Rue Royale, only opens at 9:30 am, people start queueing outside from 8:00 am. To mollify these ardent "swatchers", who, to add insult to injury are then limited to only one purchase each, the shop serves coffee and croissants on the pavement outside.

(district), is a department store called the **Bazaar de l'Hôtel de Ville**, but known universally by its initials, **BHV**. Although **BHV** is not the most chic of stores, it is worth a visit just for its basement – it has a mind-numbing array of do-it-yourself gadgets, with miles of counters specializing exclusively in plugs, washers, picture hooks, and any

Antique Appeal

Even if you do not intend to buy an-

Bargains along the Seine!

tiques in Paris, there are two places which are well worth a visit and if you then succumb to temptation, so much the better.

On **Rue de Rivoli**, a stone's throw from the Louvre, is what could be called an antiques' department store, the **Lou-**vre des Antiquaires**, where you can wander from one floor full of antique shops to another.

In the antique market in the 15th *arrondissement*, known as the **Village Suisse** (a two minute walk away from La Motte-Picquet-Grenelle metro station)

Museum Shopping

If you feel like combining the two apparently unrelated activities of shopping and visiting museums, French museums have discovered that there is more to a museum shop than postcards, and have gone into artefact merchandizing in a big way. The shopping area under the **Pyramide du Louvre** is the best example of this, for there you can find dozens of shops, selling everything from glossy, arty coffee-table books, to tableware and reproductions of Egyptian jewellery.

Many of the Paris museums now have well-stocked shops, including the **Musée d'Orsay**, the **Pompidou Centre**, the **Picasso Museum**, and, most recently, the Asiatic collections of the **Musée Guimet**. Theatres were not slow to join in this trend, and at the respectable **Comédie Française**, you can now buy videos of their plays, or T-shirts emblazoned with Molière quotations.

Customs

...are streets full of antique shops. If you have any energy left after wandering round there, you are only a minute away from the Champ de Mars and the Eiffel Tower.

One of Paris's best known flea-markets is held at the **Porte de Clignancourt**, on the northern periphery of the city, every Saturday and Sunday morning.

Finally, bear in mind the maxim *Caveat emptor*: Be aware of the customs' regulations in your own home country, so that you will not find yourself facing problems over your holiday purchases. Countries which are signatories to various wildlife protection treaties may well look unfavourably on the import of items such as ostrich-skin handbags, or ivory.

T R A V E L   T I P S

ARRIVAL

By Air

Paris is a major airline hub, and its two airports, Roissy to the north and Orly to the south, handle hundreds of flights a day. There is a large domestic network.

By Sea

Other than cruise ships, very few people arrive these days by sea (other than the British). In peak season, there are many daily ferry and Hovercraft crossings between the English and French channel ports of Calais, Boulogne and Cherbourg, but at the height of the summer, places for cars on the ferries get booked up quickly, though foot passengers should not usually have a problem. Things will be very different once the Channel Tunnel opens which at the time of writing, is supposed to be in late1993/early 1994.

By Road

Good road connections exist from France to all her neighbours, so your only problem might be traffic jams at the frontier posts if you travel at peak times. Otherwise you can, for example, drive almost without stopping from the Netherlands, through Belgium and on into France, on excellent motorways.

By Rail

Regular, efficient train services exist between France and her neighbours, and for longer journeys, such as Paris-Milan, or Paris-Madrid, you can take comfortable overnight sleepers.

BUSINESS HOURS

Cafés and local shops, such as the *patisserie* (pastry shop) selling bread, open very early, around 6:00 am, and will also stay open late. Regular shops and department stores open at 9:00 am and some will stay open until 10:00 pm.

Offices and banks are open from 9:00 am until 5:00 pm.

CLIMATE

You can usually count on good weather all year round in the extreme south. But, for the rest of the country, remember that winters are cold and damp, but that museums, restaurants and shops will be well-heated. Summer can get hot, even in the north of the country, but very few places are air-conditioned. Spring and autumn are extremely variable.

CULTURE & ETIQUETTE

The French are a polite race in a slightly formalized sense, which means that on being introduced you should shake hands, and, if you do not speak French, at least say *Bonjour* (Good day), with a smile. If you are invited to a French home, which will usually only happen if you already know someone, or have a good business contact, you should arrive only five to ten minutes after the stipulated time, and it will be appreciated if you offer a bunch of flowers, or take a bottle of wine.

Remember to use the polite *vous* form of address when talking French.

CUSTOMS

There are different allowances for visitors arriving from an EEC country – though these rules are likely to change with the revised rules for almost frontierless travel within Europe – so before buying any duty free items, check. Currently, the duty-free allowances for Community travellers are 300 cigarettes, or 150 cigarillos, or 75 cigars or 400 grammes of tobacco; 5 litres of table wine plus 1.5 litres of alcohol over 22 proof or 3 litres of alcohol under 22 proof; 75 grammes of perfume and 37.5 centilitres of eau de toilette. For non-Community travellers, the allowances are

200 cigarettes, or 100 cigarillos, or 50 cigars or 250 grammes of tobacco; 2 litres of table wine plus 1 litre of alcohol over 22 proof or 2 litres of alcohol under 22 proof; 50 grammes of perfume and 25 centilitres of eau de toilette.

ELECTRICITY
220 volts.

FESTIVALS
There are festivals for the main religious events – Easter, Christmas, and the beginning of Lent – but these are generally celebrated more in the countryside than in large towns. If you are travelling in Brittany or along the Côte d'Azur, where there are many more purely local celebrations, check with the tourist office first. Bastille Day, 14 July, is celebrated all over the country.

HEALTH
Health certificates are only necessary if you are arriving from an area where yellow fever is present.

HOLIDAYS
There are 11 public holidays, plus the occasional regional holiday a year. All banks, offices, post offices and most shops and department stores are closed on Sundays and public holidays, though food shops usually stay open until noon and restaurants are open.

MEDIA
The main television stations are good, with regular news, though only in French, with many dubbed American soap-operas and quiz shows. The BBC and CNN are available in the better hotels. All radio programmes are in French, but if you are travelling in the north of the country, the BBC broadcast from London is available.
French newspapers range from the ultra-serious *Le Monde* which is suitable for visitors with a good knowledge of the language, through *Le Figaro* which has a wonderful array of glossy magazines on a Saturday, to the investigative *Le Canard Enchaîné* and the absolute bottom-of-the-line scandal sheets, which appear to exist on a constant diet of the British Royal Family. The *International Herald Tribune* is printed in Paris, and can be found in most large towns in France (try the railway station kiosks). In Paris you can find newspapers and magazines in just about any language you wish.

MEDICAL ASSISTANCE
Should any problem arise, first visit a *pharmacie* (chemist). They should be able to give you basic medicine, or if the problem is more urgent, direct you to a doctor or hospital. Every town, and in Paris, each *arrondissement* (district) will have a 24 hour *pharmacie de garde* (chemist) so if a problem arises, and your local chemist is closed, look on the chemist shop door, where the name, address and phone number of the *pharmacie de garde* should usually be displayed.

MONEY & CURRENCY
The French Franc is divided into 100 centimes. Foreign currency and travellers' cheques can be changed at banks, major hotels and exchange booths. Credit cards are widely used.

ON FOOT
The best way to see any town in detail is on foot. To prevent aching feet, avoid high heels and new shoes. All streets are very clearly marked, and larger towns will have large street plans displayed at regular intervals, in the major tourist areas. If you get really lost, and cannot speak French, just stop someone with a *S'il vous plaît* (Please) and show them where you want to go on the map – after that, sign language is universal.

PASSPORTS & VISAS
All visitors need current passports, as well as a French visa. Nationals of the following countries do not require a visa to enter France:
Andorra, Austria, Belgium, Canada, Czechoslovakia, Cyprus, Denmark, Finland, Germany, Great Britain, Greece, Hungary, Iceland, Ireland, Italy, Japan, Leichtenstein, Luxembourg, Malta, Monaco, Netherlands, Norway, New Zealand, Poland, Portugal, San Marino, Slovenia, South Korea, Spain, Sweden, Switzerland, USA, Vatican City.

PHOTOGRAPHY
You can photograph without any problems in France, except where it is expressly forbidden – for example in certain museums. Nobody really objects to your taking pictures of their children, though a smile always helps, but if you intend taking pictures of adults, it does help to ask permission first.
Film is widely available and can be processed with no problem anywhere in the country. France is one of the few countries in the world where

Kodachrome is processed. The country-wide chain of FNAC stores stocks everything for the photographer, the staff is knowledgeable and film can be processed very quickly.

POSTAL SERVICES

Post offices are called PTT, and are open during standard business hours, which means on weekdays from 8:00 am to 7:00 pm and until 12:00 pm on Saturday, and closed on Sundays. There is a 24-hour post office at 52 Rue du Louvre in Paris. There are usually separate counters for every kind of transaction and staff rarely speak any English. However, routine transactions such as mailing letters and cards should not present any problem. Once you know the amount of postage required, you can always buy a stock of stamps in advance.

PRIVATE TRANSPORT

All the major car rental companies are present in France, and it is easy to reserve cars in advance. Very often, the rental companies have offices at the railway stations and airports, so you can walk straight off a train or a plane and hire a car. You will need your driving licence, an international licence, and, ideally, a credit card with which to pay the deposit.

PUBLIC TRANSPORT

Ask at the local tourist office for details of the buses, trams or underground trains. Urban transport systems have fewer conductors these days, so you will need to purchase tickets before boarding, usually from automatic ticket dispensers, which require coins. Try and get route maps from the tourist office.

France has a large and efficient train network, but there are a bewildering number of prices, depending on the day you travel and even the time (to discourage peak season congestion) so ask – by travelling just one hour later, you might benefit from a reduction. The larger railway stations often have an information desk (as opposed to a ticket counter) so go there first, especially if language is a problem. *Warning*: For longer train journeys, you have to get your ticket punched on the platform *before* boarding the train, you will see rows of orange coloured machines just before you go onto the platform, marked *composter* (puncher). Just push the ticket in, and it will be automatically punched by the machine. If you do forget to get your ticket punched, or do not understand how to do it, most inspectors on the trains are tolerant of visitors! For details of long-distance buses, ask at the tourist office, or at the bus station.

Taxis are clearly marked and metered.

TELEPHONES

More and more French telephone booths will accept telephone cards rather than coins, so buy a card, called *une carte téléphonique* (telephone card) from a post office, or wherever you see the sign – usually in large newsagents and *café tabacs*. Telephone booths will almost certainly have information panels, giving you the access codes for both domestic and overseas dialling.

TIME ZONES

The whole of France is GMT + 1 hour

TIPPING

A 15 percent service charge in restaurants and hotels is now included in the bill, so there is no need to tip in addition – just leave the small, loose change. Bell boys and porters in hotels will expect tips – a couple of French Francs per piece of luggage.

TOURS

Available in abundance in Paris, and in a range of languages, prices, and length – from half a day to a week's trip along the Loire Valley. Ask for details from the local tourist office, for both Paris and the rest of the country.

WEIGHTS & MEASURES

France is fully metric, so expect litres, centimetres, metres, ounces and kilometres.

WHAT TO WEAR

Although Paris is the fashion capital of the world, do not worry too much about dressing for sightseeing, when comfort should be your main priority. Wear comfortable shoes for all the city walking. Beachwear is only appropriate for the beach and certainly not for visiting churches. If you intend to go to a good restaurant, or show or if you are invited to a French person's house, you should have at least one smart outfit.

For men this means a jacket and tie. Anoraks and sunglasses are for the Alps while shorts and sunglasses are for the beach. Essentially, pack clothing to cover a range of weather conditions and always remember an umbrella or raincoat.

DIRECTORY

ACCOMMODATION

The price quoted is the minimum rate for a single room. Not all hotels necessarily have restaurants. Where there is no address given, that is because the place is so small that the hotel should be well-known. Not all these hotels will necessarily be open 365 days a year so make sure to call before arriving.

Paris
Holiday Inn
10 Place de la République
Paris 11
Tel: 43 55 44 34
FF 1080

Hôtel Angleterre
44 Rue Jacob
Paris 6
Tel: 42 60 34 72
FF 450

Hôtel Astoria
42 Rue de Moscou
Paris 8
Tel: 42 93 63 53
FF 500

Hôtel Atlantic
44 Rue de Londres
Paris 8
Tel: 43 87 45 40
FF 334

Hôtel Cambon
3 Rue Cambon
Paris 1
Tel: 42 60 38 09
FF 780

Hôtel Caumartin
27 Rue Caumartin
Paris 9
Tel: 47 42 95 95
FF 530

Hôtel Charing Cross
39 Rue Pasquier
Paris 8
Tel: 43 87 41 04
FF 307

Hôtel de l'Odéon
13 Rue St Sulpice
Paris 6
Tel: 43 25 70 11
FF 460

Hôtel des Arts
8 Rue Coypel
Paris 13
Tel: 47 07 76 32
FF 135

Hôtel des Saints-Pères
65 Rue des Saints-Pères
Paris 6
Tel: 45 44 50 00
FF 400

Hôtel Deux Iles
59 Rue St-Louis-en-L'Ile
Paris 4
Tel: 43 26 13 35
FF 530

Hôtel Eden
90 Rue Ordener
Paris 18
Tel: 42 64 61 63
FF 190

Hôtel Fénélon
23 Rue Buffault
Paris 9
Tel: 48 78 32 18
FF 180

Hôtel Gare du Nord
33 Rue St Quentin
Paris 10
Tel: 48 78 02 92
FF 230

Hôtel Ibis Paris Bercy
77 Rue Bercy
Paris 12
Tel: 43 42 91 91
FF 390

Hôtel Lutétia
45 Boulevard Raspail
Paris 6
Tel: 45 44 38 10
FF 900

Hôtel Meurice
228 Rue de Rivoli
Paris 1
Tel: 42 60 38 60
FF 2150

Hôtel Muséum
9 Rue Buffon
Paris 5

Tel: 43 31 51 90
FF 250

Hôtel Solférino
91 Rue de Lille
Paris 7
Tel: 47 05 85 54
FF 198

Hôtel St-Germain
88 Rue du Bac
Paris 7
Tel: 45 48 69 92
FF 275

Hôtel Tour Eiffel
17 Rue Exposition
Paris 7
Tel: 47 05 14 75
FF 300

Hôtel Université
22 Rue Université
Paris 7
Tel: 42 61 09 39
FF 480

Inter-Continental
3 Rue Castiglione
Paris 1
Tel: 42 60 37 80
FF 1700

Lotti
7 Rue Castiglione
Paris 1
Tel: 42 60 37 34
FF 1400

Relais Christine
3 Rue Christine
Paris 6
Tel: 43 26 71 80
FF 1080

Ritz
15 Place Vendôme
Paris 1
Tel: 42 60 38 30
FF 1995

Terminus Montparnasse
59 Boulevard Montparnasse
Paris 6

Tel: 45 48 99 10
FF 395

Aix-en-Provence
Hôtel Le Manoir
8 Rue Entrecasteaux
Tel: 42 26 27 20
FF 281

Hôtel Mozart
49 Cours Gambetta
Tel: 42 21 62 86
FF 273

Hôtel Pullman Roi René
24 Boulevard Roi René
Tel: 42 37 61 00
FF 660

Albertville
Hôtel Ibis
Route de Chambéry
Tel: 79 37 89 99
FF 285

Hôtel Million
8 Place Liberté
Tel: 79 32 25 15
FF 400

Albi
Hôtel La Réserve
Route de Cordes
Tel: 63 47 60 22
FF 480

Hôtel St Clair
Rue St Clair
Tel: 63 54 25 66
FF 190

Angers
Hôtel Concorde
18 Boulevard Maréchal Foch
Tel: 41 87 37 20
FF 470

Hôtel Royal
8 Bis Place Visitation
Tel: 41 88 30 25
FF 106

Annecy
Hôtel Ibis
12 Rue de la Gare
Tel: 50 45 43 21
FF 310

Hôtel Imperial Palace
32 Avenue Albigny
Tel: 50 09 30 00
FF 880

Splendid Hôtel
4 Quai E. Chappuis
Tel: 50 45 20 00
FF 420

Antibes
Hôtel du Cap
Boulevard Kennedy, Cap
d'Antibes
Tel: 93 61 39 01
FF 2300

Hôtel Royal
Boulevard Maréchal Leclerc
Tel: 93 34 03 09
FF 390

Arles
Hôtel Jules César
Boulevard Lices
Tel: 90 93 43 20
FF 500

Hôtel St Trophime
16 Rue Calade
Tel: 90 96 88 38
FF 175

Avignon
Hôtel Angleterre
29 Boulevard Raspail
Tel: 90 86 34 31
FF 190

Hôtel Europe
12 Place Crillon
Tel: 90 82 66 92
FF 550

Hôtel Garlande
20 Rue Galante
Tel: 90 85 08 85
FF 220

Azay-le-Rideau
Hôtel de Biencourt
Tel: 47 45 20 75
FF 195

Bayeux
Hôtel Lion d'Or
71 Rue St. Jean
Tel: 31 92 06 90
FF 150

Hôtel Reine Mathilde
23 Rue Larcher
Tel: 31 92 08 13
FF 230

Beaune
Hôtel de la Poste
3 Boulevard Clémenceau
Tel: 80 22 08 11
FF 750

Hôtel Le Home
138 Route de Dijon
Tel: 80 22 16 43
FF 285

Beauvais
Hôtel Bristol
60 Rue Madeleine
Tel: 44 45 01 31
FF 100

Bergerac
Hôtel Bordeaux
38 Place Gambetta
Tel: 53 57 12 83
FF 265

Hôtel France
18 Place Gambetta
Tel: 53 57 11 61
FF 230

Biarritz
Hôtel Central
8 Rue Maison Suisse
Tel: 59 22 02 06
FF 190

Hôtel Palais
1 Avenue Impératrice
Tel: 59 41 64 00
FF 1300

Hôtel Plaza
Avenue Edouard VII
Tel: 59 24 74 00
FF 300

Blois
Hôtel Le Lys
3 Rue Cordeliers
Tel: 54 74 66 08
FF 180

Hôtel Savoie
6 Rue Ducoux
Tel: 54 74 32 21
FF 180

Bordeaux
Hôtel Alliance
30 Rue de Tauzia
Tel: 56 92 21 21
FF 450

Hôtel Atlantic
69 Rue E. Leroy
Tel: 56 92 92 22
FF 190

Hôtel Château Chartron
81 Cours St. Louis
Tel: 56 43 15 00
FF 650

Hôtel Gambetta
66 Rue Porte Dijeaux
Tel: 56 51 21 83
FF 245

Boulogne-sur-Mer
Hôtel Ibis
Boulevard Diderot
Tel: 21 30 12 40
FF 275

Hôtel Londres
22 Place France
Tel: 21 31 35 63
FF 120

Bourges
Hôtel Bourbon
Boulevard République
Tel: 48 70 70 00
FF 460

Hôtel Christina
5 Rue Halle
Tel: 48 70 56 50
FF 195

Hôtel Ibis
Quartier Prado
Tel: 48 65 89 99
FF 285

Brest
Hôtel Bellevue
53 Rue Victor Hugo
Tel: 98 80 51 78
FF 170

Hôtel Océania
82 Rue Siam
Tel: 98 80 66 66
FF 460

Caen
Hôtel Central
23 Place J Letellier
Tel: 31 86 18 52
FF 150

Hôtel Mercure
1 Rue Courtonne
Tel: 31 47 24 24
FF 450

Calais
Hôtel Pacary
Avenue de Lattre-de-Tassigny
Tel: 21 96 68 00
FF 310

Hôtel Windsor
2 Rue Commandant Bonningue
Tel: 21 34 59 40
FF 130

Cannes
Hotel Arcade
8 Rue Marceau
Tel: 92 98 96 96
FF 378

Hôtel Carlton Intercontinental
58 Boulevard de la Croisette
Tel: 93 68 91 68
FF 2000

Hôtel France
85 Rue d'Antibes
Tel: 93 39 23 34
FF 370

Hôtel Majestic
14 Boulevard de la Croisette
Tel: 92 98 77 00
FF 1070

Hôtel Martinez
73 Boulevard de la Croisette
Tel: 93 94 30 30
FF 1250

Hôtel Sofitel Méditerranée
2 Boulevard J Hibert
Tel: 92 99 73 00
FF 850

Carcassonne
Hôtel Arcade
5 Square Gambetta
Tel: 68 72 37 37
FF 275

Hôtel Cité
Place de l'Eglise
Tel: 68 25 03 34
FF 780

Hôtel Terminus
2 Avenue Maréchal Joffre
Tel: 68 25 25 00
FF 250

Chalon-Sur-Saône
Hôtel St Georges
32 Avenue J Jaurès   Tel : 85 48
27 07
FF 345

Nouvel Hôtel
7 Avenue Boucicaut
Tel: 85 48 07 31
FF 95

Chambêry
Au Prince Eugène de Savoie
Esplanade Curial
Tel: 79 85 06 07
FF 395

Chambord
Hôtel Grand St Michel
Tel: 54 20 31 31
FF 280

Chamonix
Hôtel Albert Ier
119 Impasse du Montenvers
Tel: 50 53 05 09
FF 570

Hôtel International
255 Avenue M. Croz
Tel: 50 53 00 60
FF 353

Hôtel Mont Blanc
Place de l'Eglise
Tel: 50 53 05 64
FF 434

Hôtel Roma
289 Rue Ravanel-le-Rouge
Tel: 50 53 00 62
FF 273

Chantilly
Hôtel Parc
36 Avenue Maréchal Joffre
Tel: 44 58 20 00
FF 380

Chartres
Hôtel Mercure
8 Avenue Jehan de Beauce
Tel: 37 21 78 00
FF 465

Chenonceau
Hôtel Ottoni
Tel: 47 23 90 09
FF 245

Cherbourg
Hôtel Mercure
Gare Maritime
Tel: 33 44 01 11
FF 470

Hôtel Moderna
28 Rue Marine
Tel: 33 43 05 30
FF 160

Clermont-Ferrand
Hôtel Bordeaux
39 Avenue F. Roosevelt
Tel: 73 37 32 32
FF 175

Hôtel Lyon
16 Place Jaude
Tel 73 93 32 55
FF 300

Hôtel Mercure Arverne
Place Delille
Tel: 73 91 92 06
FF 380

Collioure
Hôtel Triton
Rue Jean Bart
Tel: 68 82 06 52
FF 160

Relais des Trois Mas
Route Port Vendres
Tel: 68 82 05 07
FF 545

Colmar
Hôtel Arcade
10 Rue St Eloi
Tel: 89 41 30 14
FF 300

Hôtel St Martin
38 Grand'Rue
Tel: 89 24 11 51
FF 330

Hôtel Terminus Bristol
7 Place Gare
Tel: 89 23 59 59
FF 380

Concarneau
Hôtel Ty Chupen Gwenn
Plage Sables Blancs
Tel: 98 97 01 43
FF 245

Courchevel 1850
Hôtel Airelles
Tel: 79 08 38 38
FF 1200

Hôtel Byblos des Neiges
Tel: 79 08 12 12
FF 1570

Hôtel Le Chamois
Tel: 79 08 01 56
FF 550

Hôtel Les Grandes Alpes
Tel: 79 08 03 35
FF 1040

Hôtel Le Mélézin
Tel: 79 08 01 33
FF 1250

Deauville
Hôtel Marie-Anne
142 Avenue de la République
Tel: 31 88 35 32
FF 370

Hôtel Normandy
38 Rue J Mermoz
Tel: 31 98 66 22
FF 1700

Hôtel Royal
Boulevard E Cornuché
Tel: 31 98 66 33
FF 1700

Dieppe
Hôtel La Présidence
2 Boulevard Verdun
Tel: 35 84 31 31
FF 330

Dijon
Hôtel Altéa
22 Boulevard Marne
Tel: 80 72 31 13
FF 410

Hôtel Pullman la Cloche
14 Place Darcy
Tel: 80 30 12 32
FF 510

Hôtel Victor Hugo
23 Rue Fleurs
Tel: 80 43 63 45
FF 128

Dinard
Grand Hôtel
46 Avenue Georges V
Tel: 99 46 10 28
FF 980

Novotel
Avenue Château Hébert
Tel: 99 82 78 10
FF 580

Fountainebleau
Hôtel Aigle Noir
27 Place Napoléon
Tel: 64 22 32 65
FF 950

Hôtel Ibis
18 Rue Ferrare
Tel: 64 23 45 25
FF 300

Gevrey-Chambertin
Hôtel Les Terroirs
Route de Dijon
Tel: 80 34 30 76
FF 360

Grasse
Hôtel des Parfums
Boulevard E. Charabot
Tel: 93 36 10 10
FF 430

Grenoble
Hôtel Gallia
7 Boulevard Maréchal Joffre
Tel: 76 87 39 21
FF 150

Hôtel Mercure Alpotel
12 Boulevard Maréchal Joffre
Tel: 76 87 88 41
FF 440

Park Hôtel
10 Place Paul Mistral
Tel: 76 87 29 11
FF 625

Le Havre
Hôtel Angleterre
1 Rue Louis-Philippe
Tel: 35 42 48 42
FF 180

Hôtel Mercure
Chaussée d'Angoulême
Tel: 35 21 23 45
FF 550

Honfleur
Hôtel Ferme St Siméon
Rue A. Marais
Tel: 31 89 23 61
FF 990

Hôtel Mercure
Rue Vases
Tel: 31 89 50 50
FF 385

Juan-Les-Pins
Hôtel Belles Rives
Boulevard Baudoin
Tel: 93 61 02 79
FF 1700

Hôtel Juana
La Pinède
Tel: 93 61 08 70
FF 650

Hôtel Pré Catalan
22 Avenue Lauriers
Tel: 93 61 05 11
FF 300

Lille
Hôtel Alliance
Quai du Wault
Tel: 20 30 62 62
FF 580

Hôtel Ibis
Avenue Ch St-Venant
Tel: 20 55 44 44
FF 330

Hôtel Paix
46 Bis Rue de Paris
Tel: 20 54 63 93
FF 280

Lisieux
Gardens Hôtel
Tel: 31 61 17 17
FF 290

Hôtel Régina
14 Rue Gare
Tel: 31 31 15 43
FF 250

Lourdes
Grand Hôtel de la Grotte
66 Rue Grotte
Tel: 62 94 58 87
FF 345

Hôtel Christina
42 Avenue Peyramale
Tel: 62 94 26 11
FF 247

Hôtel Gallia et Londres
26 Avenue B. Soubirous
Tel: 62 94 35 44
FF 800

Lyon
Cour des Loges
6 Rue Boeuf
Tel: 78 42 75 75
FF 1150

Grand Hôtel Concorde
11 Rue Grolé
Tel: 72 40 45 45
FF 540

Holiday Inn Crowne Plaza
29 Rue Bonnel
Tel: 72 61 90 90
FF 810

Hôtel Ibis
68 Avenue Leclerc
Tel: 78 58 30 70
FF 310

Hôtel Mercure Lyon Lumière
71 Cours Albert Thomas
Tel: 78 53 76 76
FF 500

Hôtel Pullman Perrache
12 Cours Verdun
Tel: 78 37 58 11
FF 450

Sofitel
20 Quai Gailleton

Tel: 72 41 20 20
FF 770

Le Mans
Hôtel Concorde
16 Avenue Général Leclerc
Tel: 43 24 12 30
FF 450

Hôtel Élysée
7 Rue Lechesne
Tel: 43 28 83 66
FF 130

Novotel
Boulevard R Schumann
Tel: 43 85 26 80
FF 405

Marseille
Hôtel Hermès
2 Rue Bonneterie
Tel: 91 90 34 51
FF 263

Hôtel Lutétia
38 Allées L Gambetta
Tel: 91 50 81 78
FF 218

Hôtel Mercure Centre
Rue Neuve St Martin
Tel: 91 39 20 00
FF 680

Novotel Marseille Centre
36 Boulevard Ch Livon
Tel: 91 59 22 22
FF 480

Sofitel Vieux Port
36 Boulevard Ch Livon
Tel: 91 52 91 19
FF 660

Megève
Chalet Mt d'Arbois
Route Mont d'Arbois
Tel 50 21 25
FF 1310

Hôtel Coin du Feu
Route Rochebrune
Tel: 50 21 04 94
FF 750

Hôtel Patinoire
Route Mont d'Arbois
Tel: 50 21 11 33
FF 260

Hôtel Week-End
Route Rochebrune
Tel: 50 21 26 49
FF 360

Parc des Loges
100 Rue d'Arly
Tel: 50 93 05 03
FF 750

Menton
Europ Hôtel
35 Avenue Verdun
Tel: 93 35 59 92
FF 410

Hôtel Le Globe
21 Avenue Verdun
Tel: 93 35 73 03
FF 270

Hôtel Londres
15 Avenue Carnot
Tel: 93 35 74 62
FF 230

Hôtel Princess et Richmond
617 Promenade Soleil
Tel: 93 35 80 20
FF 440

Méribel
Hôtel Adrat Télé-Bar
Tel: 79 08 60 26
FF 250

Hôtel Grand Coeur
Tel: 79 08 60 03
FF 600

Hôtel Le Chalet
Tel: 79 00 55 71
FF 1250

Metz
Hôtel Gare
20 Rue Gambetta
Tel: 87 66 74 03
FF 147

Hôtel Ibis
47 Rue Chambière
Tel: 87 31 01 73
FF 280

Hôtel Théâtre
Port St Marcel
Tel: 87 31 10 10
FF 420

Novotel
Place Paraiges
Tel: 87 37 38 39
FF 460

Monaco
Hôtel de Paris
Place du Casino
Tel: 93 50 80 80
FF 2300

Hôtel Hermitage
Square Beaumarchais
Tel: 93 50 67 31
FF 1800

Hôtel Louvre
16 Boulevard Moulins
Tel: 93 50 65 25
FF 900

Le Mont Doré
Hôtel Londres
Rue Meynadier
Tel: 73 65 01 12
FF 180

Hôtel Panorama
Avenue de la Libération
Tel: 73 65 11 12
FF 300

Montpellier
Hôtel Georges V
42 Avenue St Lazare
Tel: 67 72 35 91
FF 350

Hôtel Métropole
3 Rue Clos René
Tel: 67 58 11 22
FF 580

Hôtel Sofitel
Au Triangle
Tel: 67 58 45 45
FF 510

Mulhouse
Hôtel Bâle
19 Passage Central
Tel: 89 46 19 87

Hôtel Bourse
14 Rue Bourse
Tel: 89 56 18 44
FF 320

Hôtel Parc
26 Rue Sinne
Tel: 89 66 12 22
FF 550

Nancy
Central Hôtel
6 Avenue R Poincaré
Tel: 83 32 21 24
FF 190

Grand Hôtel de la Reine
2 Place Stanislas
Tel: 83 35 03 01
FF 590

Hôtel Mercure
5 Rue Carmes
Tel: 83 35 32 10
FF 410

Nantes
Holiday Inn Garden Court
1 Boulevard Martyrs Nantais
Tel: 40 47 77 77
FF 420

Hôtel Astoria
11 Rue Richebourg
Tel: 40 74 39 90
FF 260

Hôtel Paris
2 Rue Boileau
Tel: 40 48 78 79
FF 240

Hôtel Sofitel
Ile Beaulieu

Tel: 40 47 61 03
FF 565

Nice
Hôtel Kent
16 Rue Chauvain
Tel: 93 80 76 11
FF 360

Hôtel Méridien
1 Promenade des Anglais
Tel: 93 82 25 25
FF 1100

Hôtel Négresco
37 Promenade des Anglais
Tel: 93 88 39 51
FF 1550

Hôtel Sofitel
2-4 Parvis de l'Europe
Tel: 92 00 80 00
FF 800

Hôtel West End
31 Promenade des Anglais
Tel: 93 88 79 91
FF 475

Hôtel Windsor
11 Rue Dalpozzo
Tel: 93 88 59 35
FF 390

Star Hôtel
14 Rue Biscarra
Tel: 93 85 19 03
FF 200

Nîmes
Hôtel Majestic
10 Rue Pradier
Tel: 66 29 24 14
FF 200

Hôtel Vatel
140 Rue Vatel
Tel: 66 62 57 57
FF 400

Novotel Atria Nîmes Centre
5 Boulevard Prague
Tel: 66 76 56 56
FF 470

Obernai
Grand Hôtel
Rue Dietrich
Tel : 88 95 51 28
FF 275

Hôtel Parc
169 Rue Général Gouraud
Tel: 88 95 50 08
FF 400

Orange
Hôtel Altéa
Route Caderousse
Tel: 90 34 24 10
FF 410

Hôtel Ibis
Route Caderousse
Tel: 90 34 35 35
FF 280

Orléans
Hôtel Sofitel
44 Quai Barentin
Tel: 38 62 17 39
FF 615

Hôtel Urbis
17 Rue de Paris
Tel: 38 62 40 40
FF 290

Pau
Hôtel Bristol
3 Rue Gambetta
Tel: 59 27 72 98
FF 245

Hôtel Continental
2 Rue Maréchal Foch
Tel: 59 27 69 31
FF 310

Perpignan
Christina Hôtel
50 Cours Lassus
Tel: 68 35 24 61
FF 140

Hôtel Villa Duflot
Avenue V Dalbiez
Tel: 68 56 67 67
FF 490

Hôtel Windsor
8 Boulevard Wilson
Tel: 68 51 18 65
FF 300

Le Puy en Velay
Cris'tel
15 Boulevard A Clair
Tel: 71 02 24 44
FF 240

Hôtel Bristol
7 Avenue Maréchal Foch
Tel: 71 09 13 38
FF 195

Quimper
Hôtel Griffon
131 Route Bénodet
Tel: 98 90 33 33
FF 345

Relais Arcade
21 Bis Avenue de la Gare
Tel: 98 90 31 71
FF 250

Reims
Hôtel Boyer "Les Crayères"
64 Boulevard Vasnier
Tel: 26 82 80 80
FF 990

Hôtel Crystal
86 Place Drouet d'Erlon
Tel: 26 40 52 25
FF 210

Hôtel de la Paix
9 Rue Buirette
Tel: 26 40 04 04
FF 330

Rennes
Hôtel Altéa
1 Rue Cap Maignan
Tel: 99 29 73 73
FF 475

Hôtel Anne de Bretagne
12 Rue Tronjolly
Tel: 99 31 49 49
FF 320

Hôtel Brest
15 Place Gare
Tel: 99 30 35 83
FF 200

Ribeauvillé
Hôtel du Cheval Blanc
122 Grand'Rue
Tel: 89 73 61 38
FF 160

Hôtel Le Ménestrel
27 Avenue Général de Gaulle
Tel: 89 73 80 52
FF 390

Riquewihr
Hôtel Le Riquewihr
Route de Ribeauvillé
Tel: 89 47 83 13
FF 215

Hôtel le Schoenenbourg
Rue Piscine
Tel: 89 49 01 11
FF 325

Rocamadour
Hôtel Beau Site et Notre Dame
Tel: 65 33 63 08
FF 260

Hôtel Ste Marie
Tel: 65 33 69 08
FF 160

La Rochelle
Hôtel France-Angleterre et Champlain
20 Rue Rambaud
Tel: 46 41 34 66
FF 280

Hôtel Le Savary
2 Rue Alsace-Lorraine
Tel: 46 34 83 44
FF 230

Hôtel Urbis
4 Rue L Vieljeux
Tel: 46 50 68 68
FF 330

Novotel
Avenue Porte Neuve
Tel: 46 34 24 24
FF 430

Rouen
Hôtel Altéa Champ de Mars
Avenue A Briand
Tel: 35 52 42 32
FF 450

Hôtel Astrid
Place Gare
Tel: 35 71 75 88
FF 220

Hôtel Colin's
15 Rue Pie
Tel: 35 71 00 88
FF 495

St Jean Cap Ferrat
Hôtel Bel Air Cap Ferrat
Boulevard Général de Gaulle
Tel: 93 76 00 21
FF 910

Hôtel Clair Logis
Avenue Centrale
Tel: 93 76 04 57
FF 260

Hôtel Voile d'Or
Au Port
Tel: 93 01 13 13
FF 910

St Jean de Luz
Hôtel Chantaco
Tel: 59 26 14 76
FF 750

Hôtel Ohartzia
28 Rue Garat
Tel: 59 26 00 06
FF 250

Grand Hôtel
43 Boulevard Thiers
Tel: 59 26 35 36
FF 1040
St Malo
Hôtel Central
6 Grande Rue

Tel: 99 40 87 70
FF 390

Hôtel La Cité
26 Rue Ste Barbe
Tel: 99 40 55 40
FF 340

Hôtel Louvre
2 Rue Marins
Tel: 99 40 86 62
FF 190

St Rémy de Provence
Hostellerie du Vallon de Valrugues
Chemin Canto Cigalo
Tel: 90 92 04 40
FF 740

Hôtel Les Antiques
15 Avenue Pasteur
Tel: 90 92 03 02
FF 330

Hôtel Van Gogh
1 Avenue Jean Moulin
Tel: 90 92 14 02
FF 260

St Tropez
Hôtel Byblos
Avenue P. Signac
Tel: 94 97 00 04
FF 1570

Hôtel La Bastide de St Tropez
Route Carles
Tel: 94 97 58 16
FF 1900

Hôtel Le Yaca
1 Boulevard Aumale
Tel: 94 97 11 79
FF 900

Saintes Maries de la Mer
Hôtel Galoubet
Route Cacharel
Tel: 90 97 82 17
FF 300
Hôtel Mirage
Tel: 90 97 80 43
FF 230

Hôtel Pont des Bannes
Tel: 90 97 81 09
FF 860

Mas du Tadorne
Tel: 90 97 93 11
FF 800

Sarlat-La-Canéda
Hôtel de Selves
21 Avenue de Selves
Tel: 53 31 50 00
FF 320

Hôtel Salamandre
Rue Abbé Surguier
Tel: 53 59 35 98
FF 300

Saumur
Hôtel Central
23 Rue Daillé
Tel: 41 51 05 78

Hôtel Loire
Rue Vieux Port
Tel: 41 67 22 42
FF 375

Hôtel Londres
48 Rue Orléans
Tel: 41 51 23 98
FF 110

Strasbourg
Grand Hôtel
12 Place Gare
Tel: 88 32 46 90
FF 360

Holiday Inn
20 Place Bordeaux
Tel: 88 37 80 00
FF 780

Hôtel Hilton
Avenue Herrenschmidt
Tel: 88 37 10 10
FF 870
Hôtel Dragon
2 Rue Écarlate
Tel: 88 35 79 80
FF 400

Hôtel Rhin
8 Place Gare
Tel: 88 32 35 00
FF 179

Hôtel Sofitel
Place St Pierre le Jeune
Tel: 88 32 99 30
FF 725

Toulouse
Holiday Inn Crowne Plaza
7 Place Capitole
Tel: 61 61 19 19
FF 780

Hôtel Sofitel Centre
84 Allés J. Jaurès
Tel: 61 10 23 10
FF 790

Hôtel Star
17 Rue Baqué
Tel: 61 47 45 15
FF 192

Hôtel Taur
2 Rue Taur
Tel: 61 21 17 54
FF 215

Hôtel Victor Hugo
26 Boulevard Strasbourg
Tel: 61 63 40 41
FF 210

Novotel
Place A. Jourdain
Tel: 61 21 74 74
FF 490

Le Touquet
Grand Hôtel
Boulevard Canche
Tel: 21 06 88 88
FF 800

Hôtel Westminster
Avenue Verger
Tel: 21 05 48 48
FF 675

Novotel
Sur la plage
Tel: 21 09 85 00
FF 390

Tours
Hôtel Cygne
6 Rue Cygne
Tel: 47 66 66 41
FF 120

Hôtel Foch
20 Rue Maréchal Foch
Tel: 47 05 70 59
FF 145

Hôtel Jean Bardet
57 Rue Groison
Tel: 47 41 41 11
FF 650

Hôtel Royal
65 Avenue Grammont
Tel: 47 64 71 78
FF 306

Val d'Isère
Hôtel Blizzard
Tel: 79 06 02 07
FF 500

Hôtel Christiania
Tel: 79 06 08 25
FF 1202

Hôtel La Galise
Tel: 79 06 05 04
FF 720

Sofitel
Tel: 79 06 08 30
FF 770

Vannes
Aquarium Hôtel
Parc du Golfe
Tel: 97 40 44 52
FF 365

Hôtel Bretagne
34 Rue Méné
Tel: 97 47 20 21
FF 145

Verdun
Hostellerie du Coq Hardi
8 Avenue Victoire
Tel: 29 86 36 36
FF 290

Hôtel Montaulbain
4 Rue Vieille Prison
Tel: 29 86 00 47
FF 120

Vézelay
Hôtel Le Pontot
Tel: 86 33 24 40
FF 500

Hôtel Poste et Lion d'Or
Tel: 86 33 21 23

Vichy
Hôtel Louvre
15 Rue Intendance
Tel: 70 98 27 71
FF 185

Hôtel Pavillon Sévigné
50 Boulevard Kennedy
Tel: 70 32 16 22
FF 550

Hôtel Portugal
121 Boulevard des États-Unis
Tel: 70 31 90 66
FF 290

AIRLINES-DOMESTIC (IN PARIS)
Air France
119 Champs Elysées
75384 Paris
Tel: 43 23 81 81

Air Inter
14 Avenue de l'Opéra
75001 Paris
Tel: 42 60 08 52

AIRLINES INTERNATIONAL (IN PARIS)
Aer Lingus
47 Avenue Opéra
75002 Paris

Tel: 47 42 12 50

Aeroflot
33 Avenue Champs Elysées
75008 Paris
Tel: 42 25 31 92

Aerolineas Argentinas
77 Avenue Champs Elysées
75008 Paris
Tel: 43 59 02 96

AeroMexico
12 Rue Auber
75009 Paris
Tel: 47 42 40 50

Air Algerie
28 Avenue de l'Opéra
75002 Paris
Tel: 42 60 31 00

Air Canada
31 Rue Falguière
75015 Paris
Tel: 43 20 12 00

Air China
10 Boulevard Malesherbes
75008 Paris
Tel: 42 66 16 58

Air France
119 Champs Elysées
75384 Paris
Tel: 43 23 81 81

Air Inter
14 Avenue de l'Opéra
75001 Paris
Tel: 42 60 08 52

Air Mauritius
8 Rue Halévy
75009 Paris
Tel: 47 42 75 02

Air Portugal
9 Boulevard de la Madeleine
75001 Paris
Tel: 42 96 15 65

Alitalia
43-45 Avenue de l'Opéra

75002 Paris
Tel: 40 15 01 40

American Airlines
109 Rue du Faubourg St. Honoré
75008 Paris
Tel: 42 89 05 22

Austrian Airlines
9 Boulevard Malesherbes
75008 Paris
Tel: 42 66 34 66

British Airways
12 Rue Castiglione
75001 Paris
Tel: 42 86 08 08

Cathay Pacific Airways
24 Avenue Friedland
75008 Paris
Tel: 42 27 70 05

China Airlines
77 Avenue Champs Elysées
75008 Paris
Tel: 42 25 63 60

Delta Airlines
4 Rue Scribe
75009 Paris
Tel: 47 68 92 92

Egypt Air
1 Bis Rue Auber
75009 Paris
Tel: 48 84 55 46

El Al
24 Boulevard Capucine
75009 Paris
Tel: 47 42 41 29

Garuda Indonesia
75 Avenue Champs Elysées
75008 Paris
Tel: 45 62 45 45

Gulf Air
115 Avenue Champs Elysées
75008 Paris
Tel: 47 23 70 70

Iberia
31 Avenue Montaigne
75008 Paris
Tel: 47 23 01 23

Iran Air
33 Avenue Champs Elysées
75008 Paris
Tel: 43 59 01 20

Iraqi Airways
144 Avenue Champs Elysées
75008 Paris
Tel: 45 62 62 25

Japan Airlines
75 Avenue Champs Elysées
75008 Paris
Tel: 42 25 85 05

KLM
36 Bis Avenue Opéra
75002 Paris
Tel: 47 42 57 29

Korean Airlines
9 Boulevard Madeleine
75001 Paris
Tel: 42 61 58 46

Kuwait Airlines
6 Rue Paix
75002 Paris
Tel: 42 60 30 60

Lufthansa
21 Rue Royale
75008 Paris
Tel: 42 65 19 19

Malaysian Airline System
12 Boulevard Capucines
75002 Paris
Tel: 47 42 26 00

Northwest Airlines
16 Rue Chauveau Lagarde
75008 Paris
Tel: 42 66 90 00

Olympic Airways
3 Rue Auber
75009 Paris
Tel: 47 42 87 99

akistan Airlines
0 Avenue Champs Elysées
'5008 Paris
5 62 92 41

hilippine Airlines
14 Avenue Champs Elysées
'5008 Paris
el: 43 59 20 33

Quantas
' Rue Scribe
'5009 Paris
el: 42 66 53 05

Royal Nepal Airlines
2 Rue St. Victor
'5005 Paris
el: 40 46 95 21

SAS
30 Boulevard des Capucines
'5009 Paris
el: 47 42 06 14

Sabena
9 Rue de la Paix
75002 Paris
el: 47 42 76 00

Saudi Arabian Airlines
55 Avenue George V
75008 Paris
Tel: 48 62 39 54

Singapore Airlines
43 Rue Boissière
75016 Paris
Tel: 45 53 52 44

South African Airways
12 Rue Paix
75002 Paris
Tel: 42 61 57 87

Swissair
Rue Ferrus
75683 Paris
Tel: 40 78 10 00

Thai Airways
123 Avenue Champs Elysées
75008 Paris
Tel: 47 20 86 15

TWA
101 Champs Elysées
75008 Paris
Tel: 47 20 62 11

United Airlines
40 Rue Jean Jaurès
93170 Bagnolet
Tel: 48 97 82 82

UTA
3 Boulevard Malesherbes
75008 Paris
Tel: 47 76 55 55

BANKS
The three largest banking networks in France are **Crédit Lyonnais**, **Société Générale** and **la Banque Nationale de Paris** (BNP). They all have very extensive, countrywide networks. More and more banks have Automatic Teller Machines (ATMs) outside the banks.

CINEMAS
The French are extremely keen cinema-goers, so almost every small town will have at least one cinema, though only in Paris will you be able to see foreign films in *version originale* (original language). Otherwise, they will be dubbed into French. In Paris, cinemas are half-price on Mondays and very crowded over the weekend. The main cinema groups are Gaumont and UGC, both of which have outlets all over the country.

DEPARTMENT STORES
Every town in France will have at least one department store, in the larger cities there will be many stores, and there are several country-wide chains. For food, basic toiletries and household needs, stationery and simple clothing, there are branches of **Monoprix**, **Prisunic** and **Uniprix** all over the country. More upmarket and stocking a far wider range of goods are **Galeries Lafayette** and **Printemps**, both of which have very large stores on Boulevard Haussmann in Paris, as well as branches in most of the large cities. For groceries, there is usually a branch of **Félix Potin** in most towns.

DIPLOMATIC REPRESENTATIONS AND CONSULATES
ALBANIA
Embassy
Rue Skenderberg
Tirana 14
Tel: (355)(42) 34054/34250

ALGERIA
Embassy
6 Rue Larbi Alik
Alger Hydra Alger
Tel: (213)(2) 604488/609844

Consulate
Rue Gouta Sebti
23000 Annaba
Tel: (213)(8) 826391/826936

3 Square Cayla
Oran
Tel: (213)(6) 335803/335300/335575

ANGOLA
Embassy
1 Rua dos Enganos
BP 584
Luanda
Tel: (244)(2) 334841/334335

ARGENTINA
Embassy
Cerrito 1399
Buenos Aires 1010
Tel: (54)(1) 3931071/3931172/3931273

ARMENIA
Embassy
Hotel Hrazdan
Erevan

Tel: (788)(52) 151095/536691

AUSTRALIA
Embassy
6 Perth Avenue
Yarralumla
Canberra
ACT 2600
Tel: (61)(6) 2705111

Consulate
492, St Kilda Road
Melbourn Vic 3004
Tel: (61)(3) 8200921

Consulate
St Martins Tower
31 Market Street
Sydney, NSW 2000
Tel: (61)(2) 2615779

AUSTRIA
Embassy
Technikerstrasse 2
1040 Vienna
Tel: (43)(222) 5054747/
5055100

AZERBAIJAN
Embassy
Hotel Respublika
Bakou
Tel: (789)(22) 927903

BAHRAIN
Embassy
Diplomatic Area 310
Road 1901
PO 11 134
Manama
Tel: (973) 291734

BANGLADESH
Embassy
Road 108 House 18
Gulshan
PO Box 22
Dhaka
Tel: (880)(2) 607083/607084

BELGIUM
Embassy
65 Rue Ducale

1000 Brussells
Tel: (32)(2) 5125171/5125105

Consulate
24 Bosmanslei
2018 Antwerpen
Tel: (32)(3) 2382391/2388591

Consulate
33 Sint-Annaplem
9000 Gent
Tel: (32)(91)259730/259743

Consulate
1 Rue St. Remy
B 4000 Liège
Tel: (32)(41) 236013/234245

Consulate
52C Boulevard Dolez
7000 Mons
Tel: (32)(65) 352304/352142

BENIN
Embassy
Route de l'Aviation
BP 966
Cotonou
Tel: (229) 300225/300226

BOLIVIA
Embassy
Avenida Hernando Siles
No 5390 Obrajes
Casilla 824
La Paz
Tel: (591)(2) 786114/786125

BRAZIL
Embassy
Avenida das Naçoès
lote no 4
70404 Brasilia, DF
CP 07665 70359 Brasilia
Tel: (55)(61) 3129100

Consulate
Edificio San Diego
9th floor
Avenida Dantas Berreto 1200
50020 Recife PE
CP 681
Tel: (55)(81) 2246722/2246980

Consulate
58, Avenida Presidente Antonic
Carlos
20020-010 Rio de Janeiro RJ
Tel: (55)(21) 2101272

Consulate
Avenida Paulista
1073, 17th floor
Conjunto Nacional-Edificio
Horsa I
01395-900 Sao Paulo SP
CP 515309 01495970 Sao Paulo
SP
Tel: (55)(11) 2879522

Chancery
Avenida Presidente Pernambuco
no 269
66000 Belem-Para
Tel: (55)(91) 2246818

BRUNEI
Embassy
Komplex Jalan Sultan
Units 301-306
Jalan Sultan
PO Box 3027
Bandar Seri Begawan 2085
Tel: (673)(2) 220960/220961

BULGARIA
Embassy
29 Rue Oborichté
Sofia
Tel: (359)(2) 441172/441723

BURKINA
Embassy
902 Avenue de l'Indépendance
01 BP 504 Ouagadougou 01
Tel: (226) 306771/306776

BURMA
Embassy
102 Pyidaungsu Yeiktha Road
PO Box 858
Rangoon
Tel: (33)(95) 82122/82418

BURUNDI
Embassy
60 Avenue de l'Uprona
BP 1740

Bujumbara
Tel: (257)(2) 26464/26767

BYLORUSSIA
Embassy
Hotel Belarus
Bureau no 602
Minsk
Tel: (701)(72) 690602

CAMBODIA
Embassy
22 Croisement des rues
242 et 55
Quartier Chaktomuk
Phonm Penh
Tel: (855)(23) 26278/26544

CAMEROON
Embassy
Plateau Atémengué
BP 1631
Yaoundé
Tel: (237) 230463/221462

Consulate
Avenue des Cocotiers
BP 869
Douala
Tel: (237) 425370/426250

Consulate
Route de l'Aviation
BP 127
Garoua
Tel: (237) 271475/271647

CANADA
Embassy
42 Promenade Sussex
Ottawa ONT KIM 2C9
Tel: (1)(613) 2321795

Consulate
300 Highfield Place
10010 106 Street
Edmonton Alberta T51 3L8
Tel: (1)(403) 4280232/4280235

Consulate
250 Lutz Street
CP 1109 Moncton
NB E1C 8P6

Tel: (1)(506) 8574191/8574192

Consulate
2, Elysée, place Bonaventure
Montréal, BP 202
QUE, H5A 1B1
Tel: (1)(514) 878438/8784387

Consulate
1110 Avenue des Laurentides
Quebec
QC G1S 3C3
Tel: (1)(418) 6880430

Consulate
130 Bloor Street West
Suite 400
Toronto - ONT M5S 1N5
Tel: (1)(416) 9258041/925833

Consulate
1201-736 Granville Street
Vancouver BC V6Z 1H9
Tel: (1)(604) 6812301

CAP VERT
Embassy
Quartier Prainha de Praia
(Ile de Santiago)
C.P. 192 Praia
Tel: (238) 615589/615591

CENTRAL AFRICA REPUBLIC
Embassy
Boulevard du Général de Gaulle
BP 784 884 and 914 Bangui
Tel: (236) 613000/610176

CHAD
Embassy
Rue du Lt Franjoux
BP 431
Ndjamena
Tel: (235) 512576/512580

CHILE
Embassy
Avenue Condell
65 Providencia
Santiago
Tel: (56)(2) 2251030

CHINA
Embassy
No 3 Rue 3 Est San Li Tun
Arrondissement Chao Yang
Péking
Tel: (86)(1) 5321331/5321336

Consulate
Hotel White Swan
Ile Schamian
Canton
Tel: (86)(20) 8879101

Consulate
1431 Huai-han Zhong Lu
Shanghai
Tel: (86)(21) 4339437

COLOMBIA
Embassy
Avenida 39 no 7/84
Bogota Apartado aereo 29611
Tel: (57)(1) 6180511/6184066

COMORES
Embassy
Boulevard de Strasbourg
BP 465
Moroni
Tel: (33)(269) 730753

CONGO
Embassy
Rue Alfassa
BP 2089
Brazzaville
Tel: (242) 831423/831425

Consulate
4 Allée Nicolau
BP 720
Pointe-Noir
Tel: (242) 940002/940062

COSTA RICA
Embassy
Carretera Curridabat Del Indoor
Club
AP 10177 San José
Tel: (506) 250733/250933

CROATIA
Embassy
5 Solserove Stube

BP 466
41000 Zagreb
Tel: (38)(41) 272985

CUBA
Embassy
Calle 14 no 312
Miramar Havana
Tel: (53) 332132/332308

CYPRUS
Embassy
6 Ploutarchos Street
Engomi PO Box 1671
Nicosia
Tel: (357)(2) 665258/63687

CZECHOSLAVAKIA
Embassy
Velkoprevorske Namesti 2
16000 Prague 1
Tel: (42)(2) 533042

DENMARK
Embassy
Kongens Nytorv 4
1050 Copenhagen K
Tel: (45)(33) 155122

DJIBOUTI
Embassy
45 Boulevard du Maréchal Foch
BP 2039
Djibouti
Tel: (253) 350325/350963

DOMINICAN REPUBLIC
Embassy
Edificio Heinsen 2 piso
Avenida George Washington
353 AP 780
St Domingue
Tel: (1809) 6892161/6892162

EGYPT
Embassy
29 Avenue de Guizeh
Guizeh BP 1777
Cairo
Tel: (20)(2) 57039/57016

Consulate
2 Place Ahmed Orabi
BP 474

Alexandra
Tel: (20)(3) 4835614/4835615

EQUADOR
Embassy
Avenida General Leonidas Plaza
107 y
Patria no 172101913
Eloy Alfaro
Quito
Tel: (593)(2) 560789/562270

EQUITORIAL GUINEA
Embassy
Carretera del Aeropuerto
Malabo
Tel: (33)(240) 2005/2460

ESTONIA
Embassy
20 Toom Kuninga
Tallin
Tel: (358) 49103275

ETHIOPIA
Embassy
Quartier Kabana
BP 1464
Addis-Ababa
Tel: (251) 550066

FIJI
Embassy
Dominion House
Thomson Street
Private Mail Bag
Suva
Tel: (33)(679) 301894

FINLAND
Embassy
Itainen Puistotie 13
00140 Helsinki
Tel: (358)(0) 171521

GABON
Embassy
Boulevard de l'Indépendence
Pont-Pirah
BP 2125
Libreville
Tel: (241) 762031/761056

Consulate
Avenue Savorgnan de Brazza
BP 511
Port-Gentil
Tel: (241) 752086

GERMANY
Embassy
Kapellenweg 1A
D 5300, Bonn 2
Tel: (49)(228) 362031/362036

Bureau
Unter der Linden 40
1080 Berlin Mitte
Tel: (49)(30) 2315530

Consulate
Cecilienallee 10
4000 Dusseldorf 30
Tel: (49)(211) 499077/499079

Consulate
Ludolfusstrasse 13
6000 Francfort-sur-le-Main
Tel: (49)(69) 7950960

Consulate
Poseldorferweg 32
2000 Hamburg 13
Tel: (49)(40) 4141060

Consulate
6 Springerstrasse
0-7022 Leipzig.
Tel: (49)(341) 51516

Consulate
Kaiserstrasse 39
D-6500 Mainz
Tel: (49)(6131) 674603/674604

Consulate
Mohlstrasse 5
8000 Munich 80
Tel: (49)(89) 475016/475017

Consulate
Johannisstrasse 2
6600 Sarrebrucken
Tel: (49)(681) 30626/30628

Consulate
Richard Wagner Strasse 53

7000 Stuttgart 1
Tel: (49)(711) 235566

GHANA
Embassy
12th Road
Off Liberation Avenue
PO Box 187
Accra
Tel: (233)(21) 774480/774469

GREAT BRITAIN
Embassy
58 Knightsbridge
London SW1
Tel: (44)(71) 2358080

Consulate
11 Randolph Crescent
Edinburgh
Tel: (44)(31) 2257954

Consulate
Philip Le Feuvre House
La Motte Street
Saint-Helier
Jersey
Tel: (44)(534) 26256/26257

GREECE
Embassy
7 Léoforos Vassilissis Sofias
Athens 10671
Tel: (30)(1) 3611663/3638659

GUATEMALA
Embassy
Marbella Building
16th Calle no. 4-53
Zone 10 AP 1252
01014 Guatemala-Ciudad
Tel: (502)(2) 373639/374080

GUINEA
Embassy
'Chavanel' Building
Babadi Hadiri
BP 373 and 570
Conakry Ville
Tel: (33)(224) 441605/441655

GUINEA-BISSAO
67/A Eduardo-Mondlane Street
AP 95 1011 Bissao codex

Tel: (33)(245) 251031/251032

HAITI
Embassy
51, Square of the Independence
Heros
BP 1312
Port-au-Prince
Tel: (509)(1) 220951/220953

HONDURAS
Embassy
Avenida Juan Lindo
Colonia Palmira
AP 3441
Tegucigalpa
Tel: (504) 321800/324432

HONG KONG
Consulate
Admiralty Centre
Tower 2 26th floor
18 Harcourt Road
Hongkong
Tel: (852)(5) 294351/294356

HUNGARY
Embassy
27 Lendvay utca
1062 Budapest VI
Tel: (36)(1) 1324980

ICELAND
Embassy
Tungata no 22
BP 1750
101 Reykjavik
Tel: (354)(1) 17621/17622

INDIA
Embassy
2/50 E Shantipath
Chanakyapuri
New Delhi 110 021
Tel: (91)(11) 604004

Consulate
Datta Prasad 2nd floor
10 N Gamadia Cross Road
Off Pedder Road
Bombay 400 026.
Tel: (91)(22) 4949808/4949917

Chancery
26 Park Mansions
Park Street
PO Box 9034
Calcutta 700 016.
Tel: (91)(33) 213084/240958

Consulate
2 Rue de la Marine
Pondicherry 605 001
Tel: (91)(413) 24058/24174

INDONESIA
Embassy
20 Jalan Huski
Thamrin
Jakarta Pusat
Tel: (62)(21) 332807/332367

IRAN
Embassy
81 Avenue Neauphle-le-
Château
BP 113
Teheran 11365
Tel: (98)(21) 676005/676008

IRELAND
Embassy
36 Ailesbury Road
Ballsbridge
Dublin 4
Tel: (353)(1) 694777

ISRAEL
Embassy
112 Promenade Herbert-Samuel
PO Box 3480
63572 Tel Aviv
Tel: (972)(3) 5245371/5245374

Consulate
37 Hagefen Street
PO Box 9539
35053 Haifa
Tel: (972)(4) 526281

ITALY
Embassy
Piazza Farnese 67
00186 Rome
Tel: (39)(6) 686011

Consulate
Piazza Ognissanti 2
50123 Florence
Tel:(39)(55) 2302556/2302558

Consulate
Corso Venezia 42
20121 Milan
Tel: (39)(2) 794341/784670

Consulate
2 Piazza della Republica
Naples
Tel:(39)(81) 7612275/7612065

Consulate
Via Bogino 8
10123 Turin
Tel: (39)(11) 835252

Consulate
Via Garibaldi 20
16124 Genoa
Tel: (39)(10) 200879

Consulate
Palazzo Clary
Zattere 1397
30123 Venice
Tel: (39)(4) 5224319

IVORY COAST
Embassy
17 Rue Le Coeur
Quartier du Plateau
BP 175/176
Abidjan
Tel: (225) 222033/227305

JAMAICA
Embassy
13 Hillcrest Avenue
PO Box 93
Kingston 6
Tel: (809)(92) 77430/77343

JAPAN
Embassy
11-44 4 Chome
Minami Azabu
Minato-Ku
Tokyo 106
Tel: (81)(3) 54208800

Consulate
Ohbayashi Building
24th floor
4-33 Kitahama-Higashi Chuo-Ku
Osaka 540
Tel: (81)(6) 9466181/9466185

JERUSALEM
Consulate
5 Rue Paul-Emile Botta
PO Box 182
91001 Jerusalem
Tel: (972)(2) 259481/259483

JORDAN
Embassy
Djebel Amman
PO Box 374
Mutanabi Street
Amman
Tel: (962)(6) 641273/641274

KENYA
Embassy
Embassy House
Harambee Avenue
PO Box 41784
Tel: (254)(2) 339783/339784

KOREA
Embassy
30 Hap-dong Sodaemun-ku
Seoul 120-030
Tel: (82)(2) 3123272

KUWAIT
Embassy
Villa 24 Quarter No. 1
13th Street Mansouriah
PO Box 5967 Safat
13060 Safat Kuwait
Tel: (965) 2571061

LAOS
Embassy
Avenue Sethatirath
BP 6
Vientiane
Tel: (33)(856) 2377/2642

LEBANON
Embassy
Mar-Takla
Beirut
Tel: (961)(1) 429629/429590

LETTONIE
Embassy
Hotel Ridzene
1 Endrupa Street
Riga
Tel: (358)(49) 315202

LIBYA
Embassy
Said Loutfi ben Achour Street
PO Box 312
Tripoli
Tel: (218)(21) 607861/607865

LITHUANIA
Embassy
Palais des Artistes
3-8 S Daukanto Aikste
Vilnius
Tel: (701)(22) 358053

LUXEMBOURG
Embassy
9 Boulevard Prince-Henri
BP 359
2013 Luxembourg
Tel: (35)(2) 4755881

MADAGASCAR
Embassy
3 Rue Jean-Jaurès
Ambatomena
BP 204
Tananarive
Tel: (261)(2) 23700

Consulate
Rue Benyowski
BP 220
Diégo-Suarez
Tel: (261)(8) 29354

Consulate
Boulevard La Bourdonnais
BP 155
Tamatave
Tel: (261)(5) 32721/33972

MALAWI
Embassy
BP 30054 & 30055
Lilongwe 3
Tel: (265) 783577/783732

MALAYSIA
Embassy
192-196 Jalan Ampang
PO Box 10700
50722 Kuala Lumpur
Tel: (60)(3) 2484122/2484235

MALI
Embassy
Square Patrice Lumumba
BP 17
Bamako
Tel: (223) 223141/223136

MALTA
Embassy
Villa Séminia
12 Sir Temi Zammit Street
Ta'Xbiex
PO Box 408
Valletta
Tel: (356) 331107/225856

MAURITANIA
Embassy
Rue Ahmed Ould Mohammed
BP 231
Nouakchott
Tel: (222)(2) 5174/51745

MAURITIUS
Embassy
Rue Saint-Georges no14
Port-Louis
Tel: (230)(2) 083755/083756

MEXICO
Consulate
Havre no15
06600 Mexico DF
Tel: (52)(5) 5331360/5331364

MONACO
Monte Carlo Sun Building
74 Boulevard d'Italie BP 365
98006 Monaco Cedex
Tel: (16) 9350 5167

MOROCCO
Embassy
3 Rue Sahnoun Agdal
Rabat
Tel: (212)(7) 777822

Consulate
Boulevard Mohammed Sheik
Saadi
BP 267
Agadir
Tel: (212)(8) 840823/840826

Consulate
Rue du Prince Moulay Abdallah
BA 15810 Casablanca Principal
Tel: (212)(2) 2271418/2265355

Consulate
Avenue Abou Obeida Ibn Jarrah
BP 2227
Fès
Tel: (212)(5) 625547/625549

Consulate
1 Rue Ibn Khaldoun
BP 518
Marrakech
Tel: (212)(4) 441748/441787

Consulate
2 Place de France
BP 401
Tanger
Tel: (212)(9) 932039/932040

MOZAMBIQUE
Embassy
2361 Avenida Julius-Nyerere
2361 Maputo
Tel: (258)(1) 491774/490444

NAMIBIA
Embassy
1 Goethe Street
PO Box 20484
Windhoek
Tel: (264)(61) 229021/229023

NEPAL
Embassy
Lazimpath
BP 452
Kathmandu

Tel: (977) 412332/414734

NETHERLANDS
Embassy
1 Smidsplein
2514-BT The Hague
Tel: (31)(70) 3560606

Consulate
Vijzelgracht 2
Postbus 20018
Amsterdam
Tel: (31)(20) 6248346

NEW ZEALAND
Embassy
1 Willeston Street
PO Box 1695
Wellington
Tel: (64)(4) 4720200

NICARAGUA
Embassy
Avenida de la Iglezia del Carmen
1 Cuadra
1/2 Abajo Managua
Tel: (505)(2) 26210/26615

NIGER
Embassy
Route de Yantala
BP 10660
Niamey
Tel: (227) 722431/722433

NIGERIA
Embassy
1 Queen's Drive
Ikoyi
Lagos
Tel: (234)(1) 603300/603303

NORWAY
Embassy
Drammensveien 69
0271 Oslo
Tel: (47)(2) 441820

OMAN
Embassy
PO Box 50208 MQ
Mascate
Tel: (968) 604222/604233

PAKISTAN
Embassy
Diplomatic Enclave G/5
GPO Box 1068
Islamabad
Tel: (92)(51) 213981/213983

Consulate
12A Mohammed Ali Bogra Road
Bath Island
Karachi 4
Tel: (92)(21) 5691047/5691008

PANAMA
Embassy
Plaza de Francia
AP 869
Panama zona 1
Tel: (507) 287824/287835

PAPUA-NEW GUINEA
Embassy
Pacific View Apartments
9th floor
Unit 2.1/84 Pruth Street
PO Box 1155
Korobosea Port Moresby
Tel: (675) 251323/253740

PARAGUAY
Embassy
Avenida Espana
No 893 CC no 97
Assuncion
Tel: (595)(21) 212439/212449

PERU
Embassy
Avenida Arequipa San Isidro
CC 607
Lima
Tel: (51)(14) 704968

PHILIPPINES
Embassy
Pacific Star Building
Corner Gil Puyat & Makati
Avenue
Metro Manila
Tel: (63)(2) 8101981/8101988

POLAND
Embassy
1 Piekna Street

00-477 Warsaw
Tel: (48)(2) 6288401

Consulate
Ulica Stolarska 15
31-043 Cracow
Tel: (48)(12) 221864/227140

PORTUGAL
Embassy
Rua Santos o Velho No 5
1293 Lisbon Codex
Tel: (351)(1) 608121

Consulate
Rua Eugénio de Castro
352 2nd floor
(Quartier Foco)
4100 Porto
Tel: (351)(2) 694805/694806

QATAR
Embassy
West Bay
PO Box 2669
Doha
Tel: (974) 832283

ROMANIA
Embassy
13-15 Strada Biserica Amzei
BP 143
Bucharest
Tel: (40)(0) 120217/120221

RWANDA
Embassy
40 Avenue du Député
Kamuzinzi
Kigali
Tel: (250) 75225/75263

SAINT LUCIA
Embassy
Clarke Avenue-Vigie
Private Box GPO
Castries Saint Lucia WI
Tel: (1809)(45) 22462/25877

SALVADOR
Embassy
1 ra calle Poniente no 3718
Colonia Escalon
Apartado postal 474

San Salvador
Tel: (503) 794014/794017

SAUDI ARABIA
Embassy
PO Box 94367
Riyadh 11693
Tel: (966)(1) 4881255

Consulate
Adham Commercial Centre
Route de la Médine
BP 145
Jeddah 21411
Tel: (966)(2) 6510082/6511030

SENEGAL
Embassy
1 Rue El Hadj Amadou Assane
Ndoye
BP 4035
Dakar
Tel: (221) 239181

Consulate
Avenue Jean-Mermoz
BP 183
Saint Louis
Tel: (221) 61154

SEYCHELLES
Embassy
'Arpent Vert' Building
Mont Fleuri
PO Box 478
Victoria
Tel: (248) 24523

SIERRA LEONE
Embassy
13 Lamina Sankoh Street
PO Box 510
Freetown
Tel: (33)(232) 22477

SINGAPORE
Embassy
5 Gallop Road
Singapore 1025
Tel: (65) 4664866

SLOVENIA
Embassy
Hotel Union

Ljubljana
Tel: (38)(61) 158221

SOUTH AFRICA
Embassy
1009 Main Tower Cape Town
Centre
Heerengracht 8001 Cape Town
Tel: (27)(21) 212050/212052

Consulate
Carlton Centre 35th floor
Commissioner Street
PO Box 11278
Johannesburg 2000
Tel: (27)(11) 3313460/3313468

SPAIN
Embassy
Calle de Salustiano Olozaga 9
28001 Madrid
Tel: (34)(1) 4355560/4355697

Consulate
8 Calle Arquitecto Morell
03003 Alicante BP 75
Tel: (34)(65) 921836

Consulate
11 Paseo de Gracia
08007 Barcelona
Tel: (34)(3) 3178150/3178208

Consulate
26 Calle Iparraguirre
48011 Bilbao
Tel: (34)(4) 4249000/4249009

Consulate
Calle Carro no 1-1
07013 Palma de Majorque
Tel: (34)(71) 730301/730302

Consulate
Calle Prim no 9-4
20006 St Sébastien
Tel: (34)(43) 423637/423639

Consulate
1 Plaza de Santa Cruz
41004 Séville
Tel: (34)(5) 4222896

Consulate
48 Calle Cirilo Amoros
AP 745 46006 Valence
Tel: (34)(6) 3524125

SRI LANKA
Embassy
Rosmead Place no 89
PO Box 880
Colombo 7
Tel: (94)(1) 599750/599752

SUDAN
Embassy
Junction Street 19 and Street Ali
Dinar
Block 6H East Plot no 2
PO Box 377
Khartoum
Tel: (249) 77619/77620

SURINAM
Embassy
Gravenstraat 5
PO Box 2648
Paramaribo
Tel: (597) 76455

SWEDEN
Embassy
Narvavagen 28
115.23 Stockholm
Tel: (46)(8) 6630270

SWITZERLAND
Embassy
Schosshaldenstrasse 46
BP 3000
3006 Berne
Tel: (41)(31) 432424/432429

Consulate
Elisabethenstrasse 33
BP 255
4010 Bâle
Tel: (41)(61) 2726318

Consulate
11 Rue Imbert-Galloix
BP 1200
Geneva
Tel: (41)(22) 3113441

Chancery
30 Avenue Ruchonnet
1003 Lausanne
Tel: (41)(21) 3114191/3114193

Consulate
Muhlebachstrasse 7
8008 Zurich
Tel: (41)(1) 2518544

SYRIA
Embassy
Rue Ata Ayoubi
BP 769
Damascus
Tel: (963)(11) 247992/247995

Chancery
40 Rue Al Malek Faycal
BP 768
Alep
Tel: (963)(21) 211829/219823

TANZANIA
Embassy
Bagamoyo Kilimani Road
PO Box 2349
Dar es Salaam
Tel: (255)(51) 66021

THAILAND
Embassy
35 Custom House Lane
New Road
Bangkok 10500
Tel: (66)(2) 2340950/2340956

TOGO
Embassy
Avenue du Golfe
BP 337
Lome
Tel: (228) 212571/212573

TRINIDAD & TOBAGO
Embassy
Tatil Building
11 Maraval Road
PO Box 440
Port of Spain
Tel: (1809) 6227446/6227447

TUNISIA
Embassy
2 Place de l'Indépendence
BP 689
1000 Tunis RP
Tel: (216)(1) 347555

Consulate
9 Avenue Habib Bourguiba
3000 Sfax Bab el Bahr
Tel: (216)(4) 20788/20789

TURKEY
Embassy
Paris Caddesi no 70
Kavaklidere
Ankara
Tel: (90)(44) 681154

Consulate
8 Istiklal Caddesi (Taksim)
Istanbul
Tel: (90)(12) 431852/431853

UGANDA
Embassy
9-12 Parliament Avenue
PO Box 7212
Kampala
Tel: (256)(41) 242120/242176

UKRAINE
Embassy
39 Reiterskaya Street
Kiev
Tel: (70)(44) 2287369/2288728

UNITED ARAB EMIRATES
Embassy
Corner of Delma Street and Al
Nahayane Street
PO Box 4014
Abu Dhabi
Tel: (971)(2) 331100

Consulate
PO Box 3314 Deira
Dubai
Tel: (971)(4) 232256/232442

URUGUAY
Embassy
853 Avenida Uruguay
CC 290

11100 Montevideo
Tel: (598)(2) 920077/920078

USA
Embassy
4101 Reservoir Road NW
Washington DC 20007
Tel: (1)(202) 9446195

Consulate
285 Peachtree Centre Avenue
Suite 2800 Marquis Two
Atlanta GA 30303
Tel: (1)(404) 5224226

Consulate
3 Commonwealth Aveenue
Boston MA 02116
Tel: (1)(617) 2669413

Consulate
737 North Michigan Avenue
Olympia Centre Suite 2020
Chicago IL 60611
Tel: (1)(312) 7875359/7875361

Consulate
2 Waterfront Plaza
Suite 300
500 ala Moana Bld
Honolulu
Tel: (1)(808) 5994458/5994459

Consulate
Wortham Tower
Suite 976
2727 Allen Parkway
Houston TX 77019
Tel: (1)(713) 5282181

Consulate
Lykes Centre 300 Poydras
Suite 2105
New Orleans LA 70130
Tel: (1)(504) 5235772

Consulate
10990 Wilshire Boulevard Suite
300
Los Angeles CA 90024
Tel: (1)(310) 4794426

Consulate
1 Biscayne Tower Suite 1710

2 South Biscayne Boulevard
Miami FL 33131
Tel: (1)(305) 3729798

Consulate
934 Fifth Avenue
New York NY 10021
Tel: (1)(212) 6063621

Consulate
540 Bush Street
San Francisco CA 94108
Tel: (1)(415) 3974330

Consulate
Mercantil Plaza suite 720
Ponce de Leon avenue Stop 27
1/2 Hato-rey San Juan
Peurto Rico 00918
Tel: (1)(809) 7531700

USSR
Embassy
43 Oulitsa Dimitrova
Moscow
Tel: (7)(095) 2360003/2379034

Consulate
15 Quai Moika
Saint Petersburg
Tel: (7)(812) 3121130/3141443

UZBEKISTAN
Embassy
Hotel Uzbekistan
Room 928
Tashkent
Tel: (73)(712) 331853/331816

VANUATU
Embassy
Kumul Highway
BP 60
Port-Vila
Tel: (678) 22353/22627

VATICAN
Embassy
Via Pave 23
00187 Rome
Tel : (39) (6) 4883841/4883844

VENEZUELA
Embassy
Edificio Los Frailes
Calle La Guairita-Chuao
AC 60385
Caracas 106
Tel: (58)(2) 910933/910324

VIETNAM
Embassy
57 Pho Tran Hung Dao
Hanoi
Tel: (84)(4) 252719/254367

Consulate
27 Xo Viet Nghé Tinh
Ho Chi Minh Ville
Tel: (84)(2) 97231/97235

YEMEN REPUBLIC
Embassy
Street no 52 off Gamal Abdel
Nasser Street
PO Box 1286
Sanaa
Tel: (967)(1) 275995

YUGOSLAVIA
Embassy
Ulica Pariska no. 11
BP 283
11000 Belgrade
Tel: (38)(11) 636200/635715

ZAIRE
Embassy
97 Avenue du Tchad
BP 3093
Kinshasa
Tel: (243)(12) 22116/24006

ZAMBIA
Embassy
74 Independence Avenue
PO Box 30062
10101 Lusaka
Tel: (260)(1) 228031/228033

ZIMBABWE
Embassy
Ranelagh Road
Off Orange Grove Drive
Highlands
Harare

Tel: (263)(4) 46001/48096

EMBASSIES, CONSULATES AND OTHER DIPLOMATIC REPRESENTATIONS

Embassy of South Africa
59 Quai Orsay
75007 Paris
Tel: 4555 9237

Embassy of Albania
131 Rue Pompe
75016 Paris
Tel: 4553 5132

Embassy of Algeria
50 Rue Lisbonne
75008 Paris
Tel: 4225 7070

Embassy of the Arab Republic of Egypt
56 Avenue Iéna
75016 Paris
Tel: 4720 9770

Embassy of the Arab Republic of Syria
20 Rue Vaneau
75007 Paris
Tel: 4550 2490

Embassy of the Arab Republic of Yemen
21 Avenue Charles Floquet
75007 Paris
Tel: 4306 6622

Embassy of Argentina
Standard 6 Rue Cimarosa
75016 Paris
Tel: 4553 1469

Embassy of Austria
12 Rue Edmond Valentin
75007 Paris
Tel: 4705 2717

Embassy of Australia
4 Rue Jean Rey
75015 Paris
Tel: 4059 3300

Embassy of Bahrain
15 Avenue Raymond Poincaré
75016 Paris
Tel: 4553 4379

Embassy of Bangladesh
5 Sq. Pétrarque
75016 Paris
Tel: 4553 4120

Embassy of Belgium
9 Rue Tilsitt
75017 Paris
Tel: 4380 6100

Embassy of Bolivia
12 Avenue Près Kennedy
75016 Paris
Tel: 4224 9344

Embassy of Brazil
34 Cours Albert Premier
75008 Paris
Tel: 4225 9250

Embassy of Bulgaria
1 Avenue Rapp
75007 Paris
Tel: 4551 8590

Embassy of Burkino Faso
159 Boulevard Haussmann
75008 Paris
Tel: 4359 9063

Embassy of Camaroon
73 Rue Auteuil
75016 Paris
Tel: 4651 8900

Embassy of Canada
35 Avenue Montaigne
75008 Paris
Tel: 4723 0101

Embassy of Chile
2 Avenue La Motte Picquet
75007 Paris
Tel: 4551 4668

Embassy of China
11 Avenue George V
75008 Paris
Tel: 4723 3677

Embassy of Colombia
11 Bis Rue Christophe Colomb
75008 Paris
Tel: 4723 3605

Embassy of Cuba
16 Rue Presles
75015 Paris
Tel: 4567 5535

Embassy of Cyprus
23 Rue Galilée
75008 Paris
Tel: 4720 8628

Embassy of Czechoslovakia
18 Rue Bonaparte
75006 Paris
Tel: 4354 2618

Embassy of Denmark
77 Avenue Marceau
75016 Paris
Tel: 4723 5420

Embassy of Djibouti
26 Rue Emile Menier
75016 Paris
Tel: 4727 4922

Embassy of the Dominican Republic
2 Rue Georges Ville
75016 Paris
Tel: 4501 8881

Embassy of Ecuador
34 Avenue Messine
75008 Paris
Tel: 4256 2259

Embassy of Equatorial Guinea
6 Rue Alfred de Vigny
75008 Paris
Tel: 4766 4433

Embassy of Finland
39 Quai Orsay
75007 Paris
Tel: 4705 3545

Embassy of Germany
13 Avenue Franklin D Roosevelt
75008 Paris
Tel: 4299 7800

Embassy of Ghana
8 Villa Said
75016 Paris
Tel: 4500 0950

Embassy of Great Britain
35 Rue Fbg St Honoré
75008 Paris
Tel: 4266 9142

Embassy of Greece
17 Rue Auguste Vacquerie
75016 Paris
Tel: 4723 7228

Embassy of Guatemala
73 Rue Courcelles
75008 Paris
Tel: 4227 7863

Embassy of Haiti
10 Rue Théodule Ribo
75017 Paris
Tel: 4763 4778

Embassy of Honduras
6 Place Vendôme
75001 Paris
Tel: 4261 3475

Embassy of India
15 Rue Alfred Dehodencq
75016 Paris
Tel: 4520 3930

Embassy of Iraq
53 Rue Faisanderie
75016 Paris
Tel: 4501 5100

Embassy of the Islamic Republic of Iran
16 Rue Fresnel
75016 Paris
Tel: 4720 3087

Embassy of the Islamic Republic of Mauritania
89 Rue Cherche Midi
75006 Paris
Tel: 4548 2388

Embassy of Italy
47 Rue Varenne

75007 Paris
Tel: 4544 3890

Embassy of Ivory Coast
102 Avenue Raymond Poincaré
75016 Paris
Tel: 4501 5310

Embassy of Japan
7 Avenue Hoche
75008 Paris
Tel: 4766 0222

Embassy of Kenya
3 Rue Cimarosa
75016 Paris
Tel: 4553 3500

Embassy of Lebanon
42 Rue Copernic
75016 Paris
Tel: 4500 2225

Embassy of Libya
2 Rue Charles Lamoureux
75016 Paris
Tel: 4553 4070

Embassy of Luxembourg
33 Avenue Rapp
75007 Paris
Tel: 4555 1337

Embassy of Malawi
20 Rue Euler
75008 Paris
Tel: 4070 1846

Embassy of Mauritius
68 Boulevard Courcelles
75017 Paris
Tel: 4227 3019

Embassy of Mexico
9 Rue Longchamp
75016 Paris
Tel: 4553 7643

Embassy of Myanmar
60 Rue Courcelles
75008 Paris
Tel: 4225 5695

Embassy of Nepal
45 Bis rue Acacias
75017 Paris
Tel: 4622 4867

Embassy of the Netherlands
7 Rue Eblé
75007 Paris
Tel: 4306 6188

Embassy of Nicaragua
11 Rue Sontay
75016 Paris
Tel: 4500 3542

Embassy of Nigeria
173 Avenue Victor Hugo
75016 Paris
Tel: 4704 6865

Embassy of Norway
28 Rue Bayard
75008 Paris
Tel: 4723 7278

Embassy of Pakistan
18 Rue Lord Byron
75008 Paris
Tel: 4562 2332

Embassy of Panama
145 Avenue Suffren
75015 Paris
Tel: 4783 2332

Embassy of Peru
50 Avenue Kléber
75016 Paris
Tel: 4704 3453

**Embassy of the People's
Democratic Republic of Laos**
74 Avenue Raymond Poincaré
75016 Paris
Tel: 4553 0298

**Embassy of the People's
Republic of China**
1 Rue Bassano
75016 Paris
Tel: 4723 3821

**Embassy of the People's
Republic of Congo**
37 Bis Rue Paul Valéry
75016 Paris
Tel: 4500 6057

**Embassy of the People's
Republic of Hungary**
92 Rue Bonapart
75006 Paris
Tel: 4326 0644

**Embassy of the People's
Republic of Poland**
1 Rue Talleyrand
75007 Paris
Tel: 4551 6080

Embassy of the Philippines
39 Avenue Georges Mandel
75016 Paris
Tel: 4704 655

Embassy of the Republic of Gabon
26 Bis Avenue Raphael
75016 Paris
Tel: 4224 7960

Embassy of the Republic of Malta
92 Avenue Champs Elysées
75008 Paris
Tel: 4562 5301

Embassy of the Republic of Rwanda
12 Rue Jadin
75017 Paris
Tel: 4227 3631

Embassy of the Republic of Zaire
32 Cours Albert Premier
75008 Paris
Tel: 4225 5750

Royal Embassy of Saudi Arabia
40 Rue Galilée
75016 Paris
Tel: 4720 9045

**Embassy of the Social and
Federal Republic of Yugoslavia**
54 Rue Faisanderie

75016 Paris
Tel: 4504 0505

**Embassy of the Socialist
Republic of Romania**
5 Rue Exposition
75007 Paris
Tel: 4705 8499

Embassy of South Korea
125 Rue Grenelle
75007 Paris
Tel: 4753 0101

Embassy of Spain
13 Avenue George V
75008 Paris
Tel: 4723 6183

Embassy of the State of Kuwait
2 Rue Lubeck
75016 Paris
Tel: 4723 5425

Embassy of Sudan
56 Avenue Montaigne
75008 Paris
Tel: 4225 5573

**Embassy of the Sultanate of
Oman**
50 Avenue léna
75016 Paris
Tel: 4723 0579

Embassy of Sweden
17 Rue Barbet de Jouy
75007 Paris
Tel: 4555 9215

Embassy of Switzerland
142 Rue Grenelle
75007 Paris
Tel: 4550 3446

Embassy of Thailand
8 Rue Greuze
75016 Paris
Tel: 4704 3222

Embassy of Turkey
102 Avenue Champs Elysées
75008 Paris
Tel: 4562 2610

Embassy of Uganda
13 Avenue Raymond Poincaré
75016 Paris
Tel: 4727 4680

Embassy of the United States of America
2 Avenue Gabriel
75008 Paris
Tel: 4296 1202

Embassy of Uruguay
15 Rue Le Sueur
75016 Paris
Tel: 4500 9150

Embassy of USSR
40 Boulevard Lannes
75016 Paris
Tel: 4504 0550

Embassy of Venezuela
42 Avenue Près Wilson
75016 Paris
Tel: 4553 0088

Embassy of Vietnam
62 Rue Boileau
75016 Paris
Tel: 4527 6255

Embassy of Yemen
25 Rue Georges Bizet
75016 Paris
Tel: 4723 6176

Embassy of Zambia
76 Avenue Iéna
75016 Paris
Tel: 4720 2988

Embassy of Zimbabwe
5 Rue Tilsitt
75008 Paris
Tel: 4763 4831

GOVERNMENT MINISTRIES

Ministry of Agriculture & Forestry
(*Ministère de l'Agriculture et de la Forêt*)
78 Rue de Varenne
75700 Paris

Tel: 49 55 49 55

Ministry of the Budget
(*Ministère du Budget*)
139 Rue de Bercy
75572 Paris Cedex 12
Tel: 40 04 04 04

Ministry of the Civil Service & Administrative Reforms
(*Ministère de la Fonction Publique et des Reformes Administratives*)
69 Rue de Varenn
75700 Paris
Tel: 42 75 80 00

Ministry of Commerce & Crafts
(*Ministère du Commerce et du l'Artisanat*)
80 Rue de Lille
75700 Paris
Tel: 45 56 24 24

Ministry of Cooperation & Development
(*Ministère de la Coopération et au Développement*)
20 Rue Monsieur
75700 Paris
Tel: 47 83 10 10

Ministry of Defence
(*Ministère de la Défense*)
14 Rue Saint-Dominique
75700 Paris
Tel: 40 65 30 11

Ministry of Economy & Finance
(*Ministère de l'Economie et des Finances*)
139 Rue de Bercy
75572 Paris Cedex 23
Tel: 40 04 04 04

Ministry of Education & Culture
(*Ministère de l'Education et de la Culture*)
110 Rue de Grenelle
75700 Paris
Tel: 49 55 10 10

Ministry of the Environment
(*Ministère de l'Environnement*)
45 Avenue Georges-Mandel
75016 Paris
Tel: 40 81 21 22

Ministry of Exploration & Outer Space
(*Ministère de la Recherche et de l'Espace*)
1 Rue Descartes
75005 Paris
Tel: 46 34 35 35

Ministry of Foreign Affairs
(*Ministère des Affaires Etrangères*)
37 Quai d'Orsa
75700 Paris
Tel: 47 53 53 53

MInistry of Foreign Trade
(*Ministère du Commerce Extérieur*)
139 Rue de Bercy
75572 Paris Cedex 12
Tel: 40 04 04 04

Ministry of Health & Humantarian Action
(*Ministère de la Santé et de l'Action Humanitaire*)
8 Avenue de Ségur
75700 Paris
Tel: 40 56 60 00

Ministry of Housing
(*Ministère du Logement et du Cadre de Vie*)
Grande-Arche - La Défense
92055 Paris
La Défense Cedex 04
Tel: 40 81 21 22

Ministry of Industry & Foreign Trade
(*Ministère de l'Industrie et du Commerce Extérieur*)
139 Rue de Bercy
75572 Paris Cedex 12
Tel: 40 04 04 04

Ministry of Infrastructure, Housing and Transport
(*Ministère de l'Equipement, du Logement et des Transports*)
Grande-Arche - La Défense
92055 Paris La Défense Cedex 04
Tel: 40 81 21 22

Ministry of the Interior & Public Security
(*Ministère de l'Intérieur et de la Sécurité Publique*)
Place Beauvau
75800 Paris
Tel: 49 27 49 27

Ministry of Justice
(*Ministère de la Justice*)
13 Place Vendôme
75042 Paris
Tel: 44 77 60 60

Ministry of Labour, Government & Vocational Training
(*Ministère du Travail, de l'Emploi et de la Formation Professionnelle*)
127 Rue de Grenelle
75700 Paris
Tel: 40 56 60 00

Ministry of Overseas Departments and Territories
(*Ministère des Départements et Territoires d'Outre-Mer*)
27 Rue Oudinot
75358 Paris 07 SP
Tel: 47 83 01 23

Ministry of Post & Telecommunications
(*Ministère des Postes et Télécommunications*)
20 Avenue de Ségur
75700 Paris
Tel: 45 64 22 22

Ministry of Social Affairs & Integration
(*Ministère des Affaires Sociales et de l'Intégration*)
8 Avenue de Ségur
75700 Paris

Tel: 40 56 60 00

Ministry of Tourism
(*Ministère du Tourisme*)
101 Rue de Grenelle
75700 Paris
Tel: 45 56 20 20

Ministry of Youth & Sports
(*Ministère de la Jeunesse et des Sports*)
78 Rue Olivier de Serres
75015 Paris
Tel: 40 45 90 00

HOSPITALS IN PARIS
American Hospital of Paris
63 Boulevard Victor Hugo
92202 Neuilly
Tel: 46 41 25 25

Hospital of Public Assistance
Hopital Dieu
1 Place du Parvis Notre Dame
75004 Paris
Tel: 42 34 82 34

Institut Pasteur
211 Rue de Vaugirard
75015 Paris
Tel: 45 67 35 09

Hertford British Hospital
3 Rue Barbès
92300 Levallois Perre
Tel: 47 58 13 12

MUSEUMS
Most museums are closed on Tuesdays, but there are always local exceptions, so check first. Standard opening hours may also be changed if the museum is hosting a special exhibition. Some of the major Paris Museums stay open late one night a week – until 10:00 pm.

NIGHTSPOTS
The better known cabarets in Paris are:
Crazy Horse
12 Avenue George V
Tel: 47 23 32 32

Moulin Rouge
82 Boulevard de Clichy
Tel: 46 06 00 19

Le Milliardaire
68 Rue Pierre Charron
Tel: 42 25 25 17

PLACES OF WORSHIP
Catholic churches are the most widely found places of worship but many major cities will also have a synagogue and a mosque, as well as Protestant churches. These are listed in the local telephone directory and service times are available at the tourist office. Many of the major churches discourage visitors from wandering around whilst services are taking place. For Mass in English in Paris, there is a Catholic Church called Saint Joseph's with Irish priests, on Avenue Hoche, very close to the Arc de Triomphe.

POLICE
Other than the riot police who are always heavily armed and in a hurry who look after VIPs or quell riots somewhere, the CRS (state security police) are polite and as helpful as they can be given their lack of spoken English (especially outside Paris). They have a delightful habit of saluting you which makes you feel special.

SHOPPING CENTRES
Other than high street shopping which is available everywhere, if you need, for example, furniture or furnishings, try the large hypermarkets that are usually just outside all main towns.

SECRETARIES OF STATE
Secretary of State for Communication
(*Secrétaire d'Etat à la Communication*)
35 Rue Saint-Dominique

75700 Paris
Tel: 47 53 71 48

Secretary of State for Defence
(*Secrétaire d'Etat à la Défense*)
14 Rue Saint-Dominique
75700 Paris
Tel: 40 65 30 11

Secretary of State for Development
(*Secrétaire d'Etat à l'Amènagement du Territoire*)
40 Rue du Bac
75700 Paris
Tel: 40 81 21 22

Secretary of State for the Family, the Aged and Repatriation
(*Secrétaire d'Etat à la Famille, aux Personnes Agées et aux Repatriés*)
8 Avenue de Ségur
75700 Paris
Tel: 40 56 60 00

Secretary of State for the French Language & Cultural Relation
(*Secrétaire d'Etat à la Francophonie et aux Relations Culturelles*)
37 Quai d'Orsay
75700 Paris
Tel: 47 53 53 53

Secretary of State for the andicapped
(*Secrétaire d'Etat aux Handicapés*)
100 Avenue Raymond-Poincaré
75016 Paris
Tel: 40 67 88 88

Secretary of State for Infrastructure
(*Secrétaire d'Etat aux Grands Travaux*)
23-25 Avenue Franklin-Roosevelt
75008 Paris
Tel: 40 81 21 22

Secretary of State for Integration
(*Secrétaire d'Etat à l'Intégration*)
7 Rue de Talleyrand
75700 Paris
Tel: 45 56 13 13

Secretary of State for Local Councils
(*Secrétaire d'Etat aux Collectivités Locales*)
1 Bis Place des Saussaies
75800 Paris
Tel: 49 27 49 27

Secretary of State for Parliamentary Relations & the Government Spokesman
(*Secrétaire d'Etat aux Relations avec le Parlement, Porte-Parole du Gouvernement*)
72 Rue de Varenne
75700 Paris
Tel: 42 75 80 00

Secretary of State for the Rights of Women & Consumer Goods
(*Secrétaire d'Etat aux Droits des Femmes et à la Consommation*)
58 Rue de Varenne
75700 Paris
Tel: 42 75 80 00

Secretary of State for Road & River Transport
(*Secrétaire d'Etat aux Transports Routiers et Fluviaux*)
Grande-Arche - La Défense
92055 Paris
La Défense Cedex 04
Tel: 40 81 21 22

Secretary of State for the Sea
(*Secrétaire d'Etat à la Mer*)
3 Place de Fontenoy
75700 Paris
Tel: 42 73 55 05

Secretary of State for Technical Education
(*Secrétaire d'Etat à l'Enseignement Technique*)
110 Rue de Grenelle
75700 Paris

Tel: 49 55 10 10

Secretary of State for Urban Affairs
(*Secrétaire d'Etat à la Ville*)
246 Boulevard Saint-Germain
75700 Paris
Tel: 40 81 21 22

Secretary of State for War Veterans and War Victims
(*Secrétaire d'Etat aux Anciens Combattants et Victimes de Guerre*)
37 Rue de Bellechasse
75700 Paris
Tel: 45 56 80 00

TOURIST OFFICES
Information Point of Picardy
(*Point Information Picardie*)
112 Rue Maubeuge
75010 Paris
Tel: 48 78 03 50

Regional Board of Tourism for the Central Pyrénées
(*Comité Regional du Tourisme Midi Pyrénées*)
46 Rue Berger
75001 Paris
Tel: 42 33 73 82

Regional Board of Tourism for the Ille de France
(*Comité Regional du Tourisme d'Ile de France*)
73 Rue Cambronne
75015 Paris
Tel: 45 67 89 41

Tourist Office of the Auvergne
(*Maison de l'Auvergne*)
194 Rue Rivoli
75001 Paris
Tel: 42 61 82 38

Tourist Office of Brittany
(*Maison de la Bretagne*)
17 Rue Arrivée
75015 Paris
Tel: 45 38 73 15

Tourist Office of the Dauphine Alps
(*Maison Alpes Dauphine*)
2 Boulevard André Malraux
75001 Paris
Tel: 42 96 08 43

Tourist Office of Limousin
(*Maison du Limousin*)
18 Boulevard Haussmann
75009 Paris
Tel: 47 70 32 63

Tourist Office of Northern France
(*Maison du Nord Pas de Calais*)
18 Boulevard Haussmann
75009 Paris
Tel: 47 70 59 62

Tourist Office of the Pyrénées
(*Maison des Pyrénées*)
15 Rue St Augustin
75002 Paris
Tel: 42 61 58 18

Tourist Office of the Savoy
(*Maison de Savoie*)
16 Boulevard Haussmann
75009 Paris
Tel: 45 23 26 14

Tourist Office of Southeastern France
(*Maison de la Drome*)
14 Boulevard Haussmann
75009 Paris
Tel: 42 46 66 67

(*Maison des Hautes Alpes*)
4 Avenue de l'Opéra
75001 Paris
Tel: 42 96 05 08

Tourist Office of Southern France
(*Maison de L'Aveyron*)
46 Rue Berger
75001 Paris
Tel: 42 36 84 63

(*Maison du Tarn*)
34 Avenue Villiers
75017 Paris

Tel: 47 55 09 09

Tourist Office of Southwestern France
(*Maison du Lot et Garonne*)
15 Passage Choiseul
75002 Paris
Tel: 42 97 51 43

(*Maison de la Lozere*)
4 Rue Hautefeuille
75006 Paris
Tel: 43 54 26 64

Tourist Office of Western France
(*Maison Poitou-Charentes*)
68 Rue Cherche Midi
75006 Paris
Tel: 42 22 83 74

PHOTO CREDITS

INDEX

A

Abbesses, 164
Abbey of Royaumont, 169
Academie Francaise, 90
Admiralty Office, 151
Adour rivers, 67
aeronautics industry, 279
Aerospace, 55
Africa, 264
African Game Park, 181
Agincourt, 24
agriculture, 1, 5, 64
Agrippa, 311
Aguilar, 283
Aigues Mortes, 310
Airbus Industrie®, 55
aircraft, 57
Aix-en-Provence, 121, 309, 315
Aix-la Chapelle, 13
Ajaccio, 22, 319
Albertville, 287, 297, 298, 324
Albi, 280, 281, 336
Algeria, 40, 41, 42, 112, 113
Algiers, 42
Allée des Cygnes, 165
Allied landing, 38
Aloxe-Corton, 244
Alpes Maritimes, 60, 67
Alpine marmot, 78
Alps, 59, 63, 64, 66, 67, 69, 74, 75, 107, 244, 288
Alsace, 28, 63, 67, 75, 103, 107, 108, 109, 113, 223, 226, 232, 235
Alsace-Lorraine, 37, 111
Alsatian, 236
Amboise, 183, 189, 190
American Civil War, 56
American Museum, 137

American War of Independence, 21
Americans, 39, 98, 123, 173, 329
Andorra, 4, 59, 275, 327
Anet, 181, 189
Angelina, 349
Angers, 183, 194
Angoulême, 197
Animal Cemetery, 165
Anjou plateau, 13, 67
Annam, 39
Annecy, 296, 297
anti-clericalism, 111
Antibes, 305, 307, 315
Antique, 359
Anvers, 164
aprés ski, 291
Aquitaine Basin, 12, 13, 15, 16, 61, 67, 69, 71
Arc de Triomphe, 131, 163, 164, 230, 356
Archaeological Museum, 235
Arch de la Défense, 153
architecture, 4, 158
Ardennes massif, 60, 63, 65, 75
arena, 309
Arles, 12, 121, 122, 124, 246, 309, 310, 315
Armagnacs, 16
Armistice Day, 117
Arples, 352
arrondissement, 144, 360
Arsenal Marina, 156
Art Nouveau, 15, 230, 231
Artois, 66
Ascension Day, 116, 121, 331
Ash Wednesday, 120
Asia Minor, 315

Assemblée Nationale, 145
Assumptionist Order, 110, 111
Astérix the Gaul, 330
ateliers, 56
Atlantic Islands, 60, 198, 275
ATMs, 49
Au Printemps®, 358
Auto-route du Soleil, 248
Autun, 244
Auvergne, 13, 61, 251
Avenue Gabriel, 325
Avenue George V, 352
Avenue Montaigne, 351, 352
Avignon, 121, 312, 313, 314
Avoine-Chinon nuclear power-station, 194
Avril, Jane, 14, 160, 161

B

Babyland, 330
Baccarat, 356
Baden, 63
Baden-Baden, 312
badger, 78
Bagnères de Bigorre, 277
baguette, 5, 343
Bahrain, 55
Ballon de Guebwiller, 63
Balzac, 90, 133
Banque de France, 163
Banque National de Paris, 48
Banyuls, 285
Baptistry of Saint Jean, 196
Barbizon, 179
Barcelona, 13
Bardot, Brigitte, 308
Baron Haussmann, 160, 162
Bartholdi, Frédéric-Auguste, 238

Barzini, Luigi, 335
Bas-Médoc, 266
Basel, 238
Basilica of Notre Dame, 246, 257, 317
Basilica of St Denis, 169
Basilica of St Sernin, 279
Basques, 4, 96, 97, 274, 275, 111, 332, 333
Bastia, 319
Bastide de Domme, 269
Bastille Day, 21, 34, 121, 155, 157, 331
bateaux mouches, 144
Battle for Verdun, 227
Battle of Agincourt, 16
Battle of Austerlitz, 22
Battle of Crécy, 15
Battle of Leipzig, 23
Battle of Trafalgar, 25
Battle of Waterloo, 23, 25
Bay of Biscay, 263
Bayeux, 217, 218
Bayonne, 274
Bazaar de l'Hôtel de Ville, 359
beach, 1, 3, 205, 209, 312
Beaujolais, 123, 247, 353
Beaune, 241, 242, 243
Beauvais, 175
beaver, 78
Belgium, 4, 35, 38, 59, 63, 69, 226
Belle Époque, 135
Benedictine Abbey of St Bénigne, 241
Bergerac, 268
Berlioz, Hector, 134, 161
Bernhardt, Sarah, 14
Berry, 257, 259
Bertholet, 192
Beyle, Henri, 294
Biarritz, 274
Billancourt, 53
Biot, 307
Bishop of Bayeux, 218
Bishop of Beauvais, 174
Bishop of Urgel, 275
Bistros, 345
Bituriges, 259, 260
Black Forest, 67
Blois, 13, 185, 188, 190
Blum, Léon, 34
Boétie de la, Etienne, 270
boeuf à la bourguignon, 238,

340
Bohier, Thomas, 190, 191
Bois de Boulogne, 77
Bonaparte, Napoléon, 22, 23, 25, 28, 97, 104, 105, 106, 107, 163, 170, 172, 178, 181, 221, 249, 256, 307, 319
Bonnard, Pierre, 308
Bordeaux, 69, 75, 251, 256, 257, 263, 264, 265, 266, 268, 343, 344
Bordeaux-Le Verdon, 265
Botero, 138
Boubgre-Sur-Mer, 220
Boucher, François, 131
Boucheron, 352
Boudin, Eugène, 213
bouillabaisse, 340, 341
boulangerie, 343, 354
boules, 331
Boulevard des Pyrénées, 275
Boulevard Haussmann, 162, 358
Boulevard Saint Germain, 353
Boulogne-sur-Mer, 77, 221, 219
bouquinistes, 155, 355, 356
Bourbon monarchy, 17, 23
Bourdeilles, 270
Bourges, 259, 260
bourride, 341
brandade de morue, 341
Brantôme, 270
brasseries, 345, 349
bravade, 119
Brel, Jacques, 134
Brest, 205
Breton, André, 134
Breton cuisine, 208
Bretons, 96, 198
Briçonnet, Catherine, 190
Brides-les-Bains, 299
Brie, 169, 343
Britain, 25, 35, 59, 123
Brittany, 4, 9, 13, 15, 17, 60, 63, 97, 111, 125, 198, 201
Brother Antoine, 295
Brouilly, 247
Brumaire coup, 22
Brussels, 221
bûche de Noel, 117
bull-fighting, 122
Burger King, 98
Burgundians, 12, 16, 24
Burgundy, 12, 13, 15, 16, 24,

66, 75, 223, 236, 238, 243, 244, 266, 340, 343, 353
Butte de Montmartre, 65
buttes, 65
Byzantines, 13

C
Cadouin, 268
Caen, 215, 217
Caesar, Julius, 12, 257, 259, 260
Café-tabac, 345, 346, 347
Calais, 15, 16, 219
calvados, 219
Camargue, 66, 67, 81, 310
Cambodia, 39, 44
Camembert, 219, 343
Camus, Albert, 133
can-can, 135
Canal Saint Martin, 156
Cannes, 23, 118, 119, 301, 302, 303, 317, 346
Cantal Mountains, 61
Cap d'Antibes, 119
Capet, Hugues, 170
Capitole, 279
car industry, 50, 53
Carcassonne, 282, 283, 284
Cardinal de Lorraine, 185
Cardinal Mazarin, 20
Cardinal Richelieu, 17, 90, 163, 311
Carnac, 9, 203
Carolingian, 12, 170
Carousel project, 150
Carpentras, 338
Carsac-Aillac, 269
carte, 85
Carthusians, 295
Cartier, 352
casino, 312
catacombs, 156, 157
Cathedral of Beauvais, 172
Cathedral of Notre Dame, 150, 154, 234, 257
Cathedral of Saint Gatien, 191
Cathedral of Saint Julien, 194
Cathedral of Saint Pierre, 196, 197, 198
Cathedral of St Cécile, 280
Cathedral of St Corentin, 205
Cathedral of St Étienne, 261
Cathedral of St Lazare, 244
Cathédrale St Front, 271

Catherine de Médici, 17, 181, 308
Catholics, 24, 103, 104, 109, 110, 210
Caucasian, 97
causses, 61
Céline, 95
Celtic culture, 9
Celts, 9, 97, 198
Cénac, 269
Centre Georges Pompidou, 158
Cévennes, 61, 66, 78, 81
Cézanne, Paul, 132
chador, 113
Chagall, Marc, 226
Chagall Museum, 305
Chagny, 241
Châine des Puys, 61, 252
Chambéry, 295
Chambord, 183, 184, 188
Chambre Syndicale de la Haute Couture, 94, 354
Chamonix, 78, 292, 293
Champ de Mars, 15, 361
champagne, 66, 74, 75, 223, 224, 225, 226, 337
Champs Elysées, 98, 138, 152, 163, 327
Chanel, Coco®, 94, 351
Channel Tunnel, 54, 60, 219
Chantilly, 170
chapel of Notre Dame de la Gorge, 293
charcuterie, 354
Charlemagne, 13, 260, 270
Charles de Gaulle airport, 330
Charles III, 312
Charles IV, 13, 15
Charles IX, 17
Charles le Téméraire, 239
Charles V, 257, 268
Charles VI, 24
Charles VII, 192, 193, 224, 258, 259, 260
Charles VIII, 189
Charles X, 26
Chartres Cathedral, 102, 169, 175
Chartreuse, 295
Chartreuse de Champmol, 239, 293
Château Comtal, 283
Château de Castelnaud, 269
Château de Chantilly, 169

Chatéau de Dieppe, 209
Château de Fayrac, 269
Château de Lanquais, 268
Château de Montfort, 269
Château de Plaige, 244
Château d'If, 317
Château of Anet, 181
Château of Azay-le-Rideau, 192
Château of Beynac-en-Cazenac, 269
Château of Compiègne, 170
Château of Pierrefonds, 172
Château of Rambouillet, 180
Château of St Germain-en-Laye, 181
Chateau of Thoiry, 181
Château of Ussé, 193
Château of Vaux-le-Vicomte, 179
Chaumet, 352
Chaumont, 189
cheeses, 169, 218, 342, 353
Chénas, 247
Chenonceau, 189, 190, 191, 192
Cherbourg, 209, 215
Cheverny, 187, 188
Chinese cuisine, 335
Chinon, 24, 193
Chios, 259
Chirac, Jacques, 41, 44, 48
Chiroubles, 247
Chopin, Frédéric, 134
choucroute, 340
Christ the King Hotel, 110
Christian Dior®, 351, 354, 355
Christian Lacroix®, 354
Christianity, 13, 260
Christmas Day, 117
Christo, 138
Christofle®, 356
Church of La Madeleine, 352
Church of Les Jacobins, 280
Church of Notre Dame La Grande, 197
Church of Sacré Coeur, 124
Church of Saint Étienne, 217
Church of Saint Eustache, 160
Church of St Étienne-de-la-Cité, 271
Church of St Jean-Baptiste, 274
Church of the Jacobins, 279
Churchill, Winston, 36, 228
cider, 219
Cimiez hill, 305

cinema, 15, 126, 136
Cingle de Montfort, 269
Cingle de Trémolat, 268
Cirolli, Delizia, 110
Cirque de Gavernie, 276
Cisalpine Gaul, 12
Citadel in Verdun, 228, 326
Citroën, André-Gustave, 51
civic holidays, 117
clairet, 264
Clermont-Ferrand, 53, 252, 253, 256
Cliquot, Nicole, 225
Clovis, 12
Cochinchina, 39
Cocteau, 345
Coeur, Jacques, 258, 261
Cognac, 199
coiffer Saint Catherine, 124
Colette, 14, 308
Collioure, 285
Colmar, 238
Colonalism, 39
Colonne de la Grand Armee, 221
Comédie Française, 163, 328, 361
Commedia de l'Arte, 329
Commercial Exchange, 161
Common Market, 41, 343
Communards, 30
Commune, 14, 155
Communists, 38, 39, 41, 43
Compiègne, 36
Compris, 91
Concarneau, 205
Conciergerie, 154
Concordat of 1801, 25, 104, 106
Concorde®, 55, 57
congés payés, 35
Contrexéville, 231
coq au vin, 340
Cordes, 281
Corneille, Pierre, 90, 133, 163
Corot, 179
Corsica, 4, 22, 60, 96, 97, 199, 305, 319
Costa Brava, 66
Côte d'Azur, 60, 67, 118, 119, 121, 273, 301, 309
Côte de Beaune, 242, 243
Côte de Brouilly, 247
Côte de Nuits, 242, 243

Côte d'Or, 242
Côte du Rhône, 247
Côte Sauvage, 198
Coulommiers, 169
Council of Ministers, 233
Count of Foix, 275
Cour du Cheval-Blanc, 178
Cour Napoléon, 153
Courbet, Gustave, 131
Courmayeur, 292, 293, 294
Cours Mirabeau, 315
course à la cocarde, 122
couture, 95
Couvent de la Grande Chartreuse, 295
crèche vivante, 119
Crédit Lyonnais, 48, 49, 327
crise de foie, 85
Croix Rousse, 56, 244
Crozon Peninsula, 205
Crusades, 310
Cubism, 307
cuisine, 3, 337, 339, 340
cuisine minceur, 339
cult of Our Lady of Lourdes, 110
culture, 173
currency, 5
customs, 361
cycling, 322, 323
Czechoslovakia, 35

D

D-Day, 209, 215, 217
D'Estaing, Giscard, President, 158, 252
da Vinci, Leonardo, 150, 184
dance, 135
Danube River, 9
daube à la provençale, 341
Daum®, 231, 356
Daumier, Honoré, 132, 179
dauphin, 16, 24, 176, 258
David, 151
De Fauquembergue, 24
De Gaulle, Charles, 36, 37, 40, 41, 42, 342, 343
de Medici, Catherine, 187, 189, 191
de Poitiers, Diane, 181, 189, 191
de Ronsard, 133
Deauville, 211
Debussy, Claude, 134

Degas, Edgar, 132, 136, 161
Delacroix, Eugène, 131
Deportation Memorial, 155
Descartes, 90
Deutschmark, 34
Diaghilev, Serge, 15
Diderot, 133
Dien Bien Phu, 40, 44
Dieppe, 209
Dijon, 238, 239, 241
Dinard, 204
Dior, Christian, 94
dirigisme, 48
Dordogne caves, 9
Dordogne River, 69, 269
Dordogne Valley, 266, 267, 270
Douaumont Ossuary, 228
dralhons, 78
Dreyfus Affair, 107, 108, 109, 110, 111
Dreyfus, Alfred, 30
Duc de Guise, 17, 185
Duingt, 297
Duke of Anjou, 195
Duke of Guyenne, 15
Dumas, 318
Dumas the Younger, 164
Dunhill®, 354
Dunkerque, 219
Dutch, 315

E

E E C, 42, 74, 75, 226
Early Middle Ages, 12
Easter, 118
École Nationale d'Administration, 91, 233
École Nationale d'équitation, 194
economy, 5, 30
Edict of January, 17
Edict of Nantes, 17, 20, 103
Edward III of England, 15, 264
Église Ste Dévote, 118
Eiffel, Gustave, 164
Eiffel Tower, 3, 15, 150, 164, 173, 323, 361
Elba, 23, 178
Eleanor of Aquitaine, 197, 257, 263
Electricité de France, 54
Émile, Zola, 30
Empress Eugénie, 254, 274
en bandoulière, 92

en famille, 87
Énarques, 91
Enclos Paroissial, 210
English, 54, 59, 66, 68, 303
Environmentalists, 81
Épernay, 223, 224
Epiphany, 119
Ermitage de St Germain, 297
Escoffier, 14
Esplanade des Quinconces, 265
Estates General, 21
Étang de Vaccarès, 81, 124, 310
Étretat, 211, 213
Euro-Disney, 98, 328, 329
European Assembly, 233
European Community, 5, 75, 342
European Parliament, 233
Eurostar train, 54
Eurostat, 83
existentialism, 133

F

faire le pont, 115
farandoles, 124
fashion, 3, 92, 94, 354
Fauchon®, 355
Fauna, 77
Feast of the Assumption, 106, 116, 121, 125
Ferme St-Siméon, 213
Fernand Léger Museum, 307
festival estiraux, 121, 125, 239
Festival of Our Lady of Safe Homecoming, 119
Fifth Republic, 4, 40, 42
films, 355
Fine Arts Museum, 246
First Consul, 25, 104
fishing, 205, 274
Flanders, 13, 15, 66, 111, 221
Flaubert, 133
Fleurie, 247
Fleury, 228
FNAC, 136, 356
foie gras, 117, 280
fondue savoyarde, 340
Fontainebleau, 23, 66, 77, 130, 170, 178, 179
Fontvieille, 312
football, 322, 327
Forest of Chantilly, 169
forest of Chinon, 193
Formula One Grand Prix, 119,

313, 322, 323
Fort de la Bastille, 294
Fort Royal, 303
Forum des Halles Shopping Complex, 159, 356
Fouquet, 179
Fourth Republic, 39, 40, 42
Fourvière Hill, 244, 246
Fra Angelico, 151
Fragonard, Jean-Honoré, 131
France, 35, 57, 235
Franco-German War, 233
François I, 56, 175, 184, 185, 190, 191, 192
Franklin, Benjamin, 152
Franks, 12, 13, 233
Freemasons, 109
French Academy, 131, 137
French Agriculture, 74
French Air Force, 57
French architecture, 130
French Character, 5
French Committee of National Liberation, 42
French Ministry of the Environment, 81
French Polynesia, 44
French Revolution, 22, 56, 91, 98, 103, 104, 155, 157, 264, 270, 315
fromagerie, 355
Fronde civil war, 19
Front Populaire, 34
Futuroscope Park, 196

G

Galerie des Glaces, 176
Galeries Lafayette®, 358
Gallé, Émile, 231
Gallicanism, 105
gardians, 124
garigue, 75
Garnier, Charles, 14, 163, 265, 313
Garonne, 68, 75
Gassin, 307
Gauguin, Paul, 132, 136
Gauls, 12, 203, 225, 257, 260
Gaul, Roman, 9
Gault-Millault, 337
Gavarnie, 276
General Joffre, 33
General Resnier, 197
Geneva, 297

Genoese, 312
Georges Pompidou Centre, 131
Germany, 4, 12, 19, 35, 36, 38, 59, 67, 69, 233, 235
Gevrey-Chambertin, 241
Gide, André, 133
Gironde estuary, 69
Gislebertus, 244
Givenchy®, 95, 354
Giverny, 137
glacia, 64
Gnafron, 329
Gobelins Tapestry Factory, 165
Godard, Jean-Luc, 138
Goethe, 235
Gold Beach, 215
golf, 323, 324
Goncourt, Jules de, 338
Gorges de Verdon, 308
Gorges du Tarn, 61
Gothic cathedrals, 101, 130
Government, 4
Grand Army, 25
grand cru, 344
Grand Prix de Deauville, 211
Grand Théâtre, 265
Grande Arch de la Défense, 164
Grande Chartreuse Monastery, 295
Grandes Écoles, 91
grands magasins, 358
Grasse, 75, 308
Great Depression, 34, 51
Great Louvre Project, 150
Great Schism, 314
Greeks, 315
Grenoble, 294, 295
Grimaldi, Governor Jean, 303, 312
Grotte des Demoiselles, 62
Grünewald, Mathias, 238
Guangzhou, 57
Gucci®, 352
Gueberschwihr, 238
Guerlain®, 352, 355
gueule de bois, 123
guichet, 49
Guignol le Canut, 329
Guignol Puppet Theatre, 329
Guillaumin, 136
Guimard, Hector, 15
Guimiliau, 210
Gulf of Morbihan, 208
Gulf War, 112

Gutenberg, 235
Guyenne, 15

H

Haiphong, 40
Hallyday, Johnny, 134
hang-gliders, 253
Hapsburgs, 17, 19
Haussmann, 164
Haut-Médoc, 266
haute couture, 351, 352
health care, 84, 85
HEC university, 169
Heine, Heinrich, 161
Hemingway, 345
Henri II, 17, 181, 189, 191
Henri III, 185, 195
Henri III of Navarre, 17
Henri IV, 17, 157
Henry II, 263
Henry II of England, 263
Henry V of England, 16, 24
Henry VI of England, 193
Hercynian massifs, 60
Hermès®, 3, 95, 352
Hinault, Bernard, 327
Historical Museum of Lorraine, 230
Historique de Tissus, 56
Hitler, Adolf, 35, 37, 38
Ho Chi Minh, 39, 327
Holarctic Floral Zone, 71
Holland, 69
Honfleur, 211, 213
Hospices de Beaune, 243
Hotel Crillon, 151
Hotel de la Poste aux Chevaux, 302
Hôtel de Ville, 229
Hôtel Dieu, 244
Hôtel du Palais, 274
Hôtel Salé, 158
House of Valois, 15
Hugo, Victor, 90, 133
Huguenots, 17, 18, 20, 103, 190
Hundred Years War, 13, 15, 16, 24, 174, 175, 193, 260, 264, 268, 269, 270
Hyères Islands, 315
hyper-markets, 353

I

Iberian, 97
ibex, 78

INDEX

Ile de France, 13, 65
Ile de la Cité, 67, 143, 154, 155
Ile de Noirmoutier, 198
Ile de Ré, 198
Ile d'Oléron, 199
Ile d'Yeu, 198
Ile Saint Honorat, 303
Ile Saint Louis, 155
Ile Sainte Marguerite, 303, 317
Immigrants, 98
Impressionists, 136, 213, 230
Indianapolis, 322
Indo-China, 39, 40
industry, 64
Ingres, 151
INSEAD, 169
Institute of the Arab World, 165
International Exhibition, 15
International Secretariat of the
  EEC, 233
Island of Ré, 196
Isolde, 201
Issenheim Altar, 238
Italy, 4, 12, 16, 35, 59, 64, 131,
  291, 292, 294, 312

J
J'accuse, 30
Jacquard, Joseph-Marie, 56
Jacques-Louis, David, 131
jambon de Bayonne, 342
Japanese, 51, 123
Jardin des Plantes, 164
jazz festival, 119
Jean de France, 259
Jean sans Peur, 239
Jerusalem, 248
Jeu de Paume, 150, 153
Jews, 38, 102, 103, 107, 108,
  109, 110, 113, 157, 247
Joan of Arc, 16, 24, 25, 185,
  193, 197, 216, 224, 258, 260
joie de vivre, 127
Josserand, Louis, 329
Jour de la Montagne, 66
Jouy-en-Josas, 181
Juan-les-Pins, 119
Juliénas, 247
Juno Beach, 215
Jura, 59, 75, 111, 113
Jura mountains, 64, 67
Jurade de St Emilion, 337

K
Kagyu-Ling, 244
Karl Lagerfeld®, 352
Kelly, Grace, 313
King Arthur, 201
King Harold, 218
Kingdom of Westphalia, 23
Kwangchowan, 39

L
La Baule, 205
La Belle Époque, 30
La Bigorre, 277
La Bouillabaisse, 346
la Butte, 160
La Canebière, 318
La Chanson de Roland, 132, 198
la Cime de Caron, 291
La Cimetière des Innocents, 156,
  157
La Condamine, 312
La Coupole, 345
La Croisette, 119, 302
La galette des rois, 120
La Goulue, 161
La Grande Motte mountain, 289
La Loire, 248
La Madeleine, 145
La Maison Carrée, 310, 311
La Maison de la Boétie, 270
La Maison des Canuts, 56
La Marquise de Pompadour, 176
La Marseillaise, 5, 316, 317
la piperade, 342
La Place de la Concorde, 145,
  150, 352
La Place du Parvis, 155
La Plagne, 299
la pucelle, 24
La Pyramide du Louvre, 153
La Rochefoucauld, 199
La Rochelle, 17, 18, 195, 196,
  199
La Roque-Gageac, 269
La Rotonde, 345
la rouille, 347
La Sainte Chapelle, 154
La Tour d' Argent, 339
La vache qui rit, 343
La Vendée, 111
La Ville Close, 205
LaBelle Epoque, 14
Lacroix, Christian, 94
Lady of Auxerre, 151

Lake Annecy, 296, 297
Lake Geneva, 69
Lalbenque, 338
Lalique®, 356
Lancôme®, 352
Landes, 67, 75
Langeais, 193
Languedoc, 17, 61, 67, 344
Languedoc-Roussillon, 75, 273,
  277
Lanvin®, 352
Laos, 39
Lascaux, 61, 271
Laval, Pierre, 36
Law of Separation, 111
le bon roi René, 315
Le Bourget airport, 169
le Breton, Jean, 191
Le Brun, 179
Le Dôme, 345
Le Figaro, 4
le français, 90
le gardien, 81
le grand monde, 4
le Grand Palais, 150
Le Grand Trianon, 176
Le Havre, 68, 209, 213
Le Mans, 194, 195, 322
le Maréchal d'Estrées, 295
Le Monde, 327
le Moulin de la Galette, 160
Le Musée Condé, 169
Le Nain, 131
Le Nôtre, 179
le Palais Bourbon, 145
Le Pen, Jean-Marie, 43
le Périgord blanc, 270
le Périgord noir, 270
le Périgord pourpre, 268
Le Périgord vert, 270
Le Petit Trianon, 177
le Plomb de Cantal, 254
Le Praz, 291
Le quatorze juillet, 119
Le Remblai, 195
le Rocher Corneille, 248
Le Touquet, 219
le tricolore, 5
Le Vau, 179
Légion d'Honneur, 30
Léopold of Saxe-Cobourg, 172
Leroy, Louis, 136
Les Baux de Provence, 311
Les Bouffes du Nord, 328

Les Corbières, 282
les françaises, 92
les grandes vacances, 331
Les Grands Boulevards, 162
Les Halles, 5, 159, 347
Les Invalides, 23
Les Menuires, 289
les paysans, 74
Les Sables d'Olonne, 195, 198
Les Saintes-Maries-de-la Mer, 124
Liberty Flame, 98
Lido, 135
lieuxdits, 95
Lille, 221
Limeuil, 268
Limoges®, 258, 356
Limousin, 257, 258, 263
Lisieux, 217
Lisle de, Rouget, 235
Little Venice, 238
Livarot, 219
Loire, 13, 63, 67, 75, 130, 183
Lombards, 13
Lord Brougham and Vaux, 302
Lorrain, Claude, 131
Lorraine, 28, 63, 66, 103, 107, 223, 226, 229, 231
Louis IX, 13
Louis V, 170
Louis VII, 263
Louis Vuitton®, 352, 354
Louis XI, 189, 259, 269
Louis XII, 188
Louis XIII, 17, 176, 187
Louis XIV, 19, 20, 170, 176, 179, 184, 194, 274, 311
Louis XV, 170, 176, 184, 194, 230, 256
Louis XVI, 21, 22, 150, 170, 172, 176
Louis XVIII, 26
Louis-Philippe, 26, 172
Louise de Lorraine, 259
Lourdes, 110, 276
Lourdes pilgrimage, 101
Louvre, 131, 145, 150, 153, 159, 161, 326, 360
Louvre des Antiquaires, 163, 360
Louvre museum, 129
Louvre Pyramid, 326
Low Countries, 131
Lozère, 81

Lutèce arena, 12
Lutetia Arena, 165
Luxembourg, 4, 59, 69
Luxor, 151
LVMH®, 354
lynx, 78
Lyon, 56, 244, 247, 248, 328
Lyonnaise cooking, 247

M
Madame de Maintenon, 20, 176
Madame de Montespan, 177
Madame de Sévigné, 254
Madame du Barry, 176, 177
Madame Pelouze, 191
Madelon, 329
Madonna Hotel, 110
Magic Kingdom, 98
Maginot, 35, 38, 228
Main Street USA, 329
Maison Bonaparte, 319
Maison de l'Oeuvre de Notre Dame, 235
Maison Natale de Toulouse-Lautrec, 281
Maison Pfister, 238
Malle, Louis, 138
Malraux, André, 133
Man in the Iron Mask, 303, 317
Manet, Éduard, 132, 136
Mansart, 240
manufacturing, 5
Maquis, 37, 75
Marais district, 353
marathons, 126
Marchais, Georges, 41
Mardi Gras, 120
Maréchal de Saxe, 184
Marguerite de Valois, 17
Marie Antoinette, 21, 74, 154, 172, 176, 177, 181
Marie de Médici, 17
Marie-Louise of Austria, 172
Marie-Thérèse, 274
Marine Museum and Aquarium, 204
Marlenheim, 235
Marne River, 67
Marne-la-Vallée, 329
Marques family, 190
Marquise de Pompadour, 177
Marseillaise, 235
Marseille, 113, 315, 316, 326
Massabielle, 110

Massacre of St. Bartholomew's, 17
Massif Armoricain, 60, 62, 63, 65
Massif Central, 60, 61, 63, 65, 67, 68, 73, 74, 111, 113, 244, 251, 266, 267
Massif de la Chartreuse, 295
Matisse, Henri, 15, 132, 305, 308
Maubec, Brother Jérome, 295
Maupassant, Guy de, 164
Mauriac, François, 133
Maurice of Nassau, Prince, 314
Maurois, André, 271
Maxim's restaurant, 14, 352
McDonalds, 98, 347
Mediterranean, 66, 69, 71, 73, 118, 124, 275, 278, 346
Médoc, 265
Megève, 291
Menton, 312
Mercx, Eddie, 327
Méribel, 289
Mérimée, Prosper, 283
Merlin, 201
Merovingian, 12
Mersault, 243, 244
méthode champenoise, 224
Métro, 15, 49, 92, 145, 360
Metz, 226
Meursault, 241
Meuse River, 63, 69
Michelin, 51, 53, 256, 337
Michelin, André, 256
Michelin, Édouard, 256
Mickey Mouse, 173, 329
Middle Ages, 130
Midi, 95
mignonne, 93
Millet, 179
mimosa festival, 118
Minitel, 48, 49
Mirabeau, 315
Mirage® combat, 57
Mirapolis, 330
Misericord Chapel, 313
Mittelbergheim, 239
Mitterrand, 44
Mitterrand, Danialle, 113
Mitterrand, François, 41
Mitterrand, President, 155, 158, 164
Moët et Chandon®, 354

Moissac, 281
Molière, 90, 133, 163, 184, 361
Mona Lisa, 3, 130, 150, 151, 173
Monaco, 4, 60, 118, 312
Monet, Claude, 132, 136, 137, 153, 215
Mont Aigoual, 66
Mont Blanc, 4, 64, 66, 292, 293, 294
Mont des Avaloirs, 63
Mont Saint Michel, 203, 204
Mont Sainte Odile, 236
Montaigne, 133
Monte-Carlo, 312
Montélimar, 247
Montmartre, 123, 160, 161, 164, 165, 281, 331
Montmorency family, 169
Montparnasse, 156
Montpellier, 17, 258
Montrachet, 243
Montrouge, 156
Monts Dômes, 252, 253
Monts Dore, 61, 252, 253
Monts du Cantal, 252, 253
Montsouris, 156
Monument aux Girondins, 265
Monument des Bourgeois de Calais, 219
Moret-sur-Loing, 178
Morgon, 247
Moroccan cuisine, 335
Morvan, 61
Moscow, 23
Moselle River, 69
motor racing, 15, 323
Moulin de la Galette, 161
Moulin Rouge, 14, 160, 161
Moulin-à-vent, 247
Mount Balaïtous, 277
Mount Canigou, 284, 285
Mount Vignemale, 277
Mourget, Laurent, 329
Mulhouse, 238
Municipal Theatre, 209
Mur des Fédérés, 30
Murat, 23
Musée, 56
Musée Archéologique, 241
Musée Basque, 274
Musée Carnavalet, 158
Musée de la Marine, 319
Musée de la Paix, 326

Musée des Augustins, 279, 280
Musée des Beaux Arts, 239, 249
Musée des Beaux-Arts et de la Dentelle, 220
Musée d'Orsay, 130, 131, 137, 150, 153, 158, 361
Musée Guimet, 361
Musée Historique de Tissus, 246
Musée Stendhal, 295
Museum of Decorative Arts, 235
Museum of Fine Arts, 230, 235
Museum of Gallo-Roman Civilization, 246
Museum of Modern Art, 158
Museum of National Antiquities, 181
Museum of Painting and Sculpture, 294
Museum of Stone relics, 283
Muslim, 98, 112, 113
Mussolini, 35

N

Nancy, 229, 356
Napoléon I, 131
Napoléon III, 28, 172, 256, 274
Napoleonic Wars, 265
National Assembly, 4, 21, 22
National Front party, 43
National Institute of Underwater Archaeology, 296
National Museums, 325
National Necropolis, 238
nationalization, 47, 48
NATO forces, 41
natural gas, 54
Nazis, 39
New Caledonia, 44
Nice, 118, 119, 302, 303, 304, 305, 315
Nicolas®, 354
Nijinsky, 15, 161
Nîmes, 12, 122, 124, 248, 309, 310, 311
Nina Ricci®, 351
Noirmoutier-en-L'Ile, 198
Norman Cuisine, 218
Normandy, 3, 13, 16, 17, 209, 213
North Africa, 112
North-Eastern Plateau, 63
northern zone, 71
Notre Dame, 102, 154, 155, 169, 215, 224, 339

Nouveau Guignol de Lyon, 329
nuclear power, 53
Nuits-St-George, 241

O

Obernai, 236
Oceanographic Museum, 313
Odéon, 248, 328
Odile, 236
OECD, 54
Offenbach, Jacques, 135
Officiel des Spectacles of Pariscope, 328
oil, 47, 54
Oise River, 67
Oléron, 199
Olympics, 287, 298, 299
Omaha Beach, 215
Roman Catholic church, 25
Opéra de la Bastille, 129, 155
Operation Overlord, 215
Orange, 12, 121, 122, 246, 309, 314
Orangerie, 153
Orcofi®, 354
Organic Articles, 105
Orléans, 24, 183, 185
Orly airport, 159, 169
otter, 78
Overseas Dominions and Territories, 44

P

Piaf, Edith, 134
Palace of Fontainebleau, 175
Palace of the Kings of Majorca, 284
Palais de Chaillot, 165
Palais de Justice, 197
Palais de la Berbie, 280
Palais de la Bourse, 319
Palais des Congres, 302
Palais des Papes, 121, 314
Palais d'Europe, 233
Palais Ducal, 230
Palais Rohan, 235
Palais Royal, 159, 163
Palais St Pierre, 246
Palm Beach Casino, 302
Panthéon, 165
Pâques, 116
Parc Astérix, 330
Parc Beaumont, 275
Parc Jouvet, 249

Parc Naturel Régional des Volcans d'Auvergne, 252
Parc Océanique Cousteau, 330
pardons, 125, 208
parfumeries, 352
Paris, 4, 9, 12, 13, 14, 23, 28, 37, 38, 39, 41, 44, 49, 77, 85, 92, 104, 113, 119, 124, 130, 131, 135, 226, 271, 325, 328, 330, 331, 347, 349, 359, 360
Paris Basin, 61, 65, 66, 67, 68, 69, 71
Paris Commune, 28
Paris Dakar race, 323
Paris Mosque, 112, 165, 349
Paris Opera, 14, 163, 265, 313
Paris Parliament, 19, 21
Paris Town Hall, 358
Parish Closes, 210
Parisian architecture, 159
Parisians, 90
Parisii, 143
Parthenon marbles, 151
Pas de Calais, 219
Pascal, Blaise, 253
pâtés, 353
pâtisseries, 340
Patou, Jean, 95, 308
Pau, 275
Payot, 352
Pays Basque, 273
paysans, 3
Pêche-Merle, 61
pelota, 273, 274, 332, 333
Pentecost, 116, 121
Père Lachaise cemetery, 165
perfume, 308
perfume industry, 75
Périgeeux, 271
Pérignon, Dom, 225
Périgord, 251, 263, 266, 338, 340
Périgueux, 270
Péripherique, 145, 165
Perpignan, 284
Perrault, 284
Pétain, 36
Pétain, Maréchal, 198
Pétain, Marshal, 42
Petit Suisse, 342
Petit Trianon, 176
Petite France, 235
Peugeot, Armand, 51
Peyrepertuse, 283

Pfaffenheim, 238
Pfifferdaj, 239
Phare des Baleines, 198
Philip IV the Fair, 13, 15
Philip VI of Valois, 15
Philippe le Bon, 239
Philippe le Hardi, 239
Phoenician, 315
Pic d'Anie, 276
Pic du Midi de Bigorre, 276
Pic du Midi d'Ossau, 276
Picardy, 66
Picasso Museum, 158, 361
Picasso, Pablo, 132, 307
Pigalle, 160, 164
Pilate, Pontius, 248
Pinot Noir, 242
Pissarro, Camille, 132
Pissarro, Pablo, 136
Pithiviers, 169
Place Bellecourt, 246
Place Blanche, 160
Place de la Bastille, 155
Place de la Concorde, 38, 152
Place de la Libération, 240
Place de la Madeleine, 355
Place de la Mairie, 208
Place de la Révolution, 150
Place des Halles, 197
Place des Vosges, 157
Place du Capitole, 279
Place du Palais, 313
Place du President Wilson, 280
Place du Tertre, 161
Place du Théâtre, 221
Place du Vieux Marché, 25, 216
Place Grimaldi, 304
Place Masséna, 304
Place Stanislas, 229
Place Vendôme, 14, 352
Plantaganet, Henri, 15, 193, 263
Plateau de Gergovia, 257
Plateau de Langres, 66
plateaux of Roussillion, 37, 75
Ploumanach, 205
Pointillisme, 136
poisson d'avril, 120
Poitiers, 24, 196, 197
Poitou, 263
Poland, 35
Polidor, Raymond, 327
politicians, 86, 90
Pompidou Centre, 5, 159, 361
Pompidou, Georges, 41

Pompidou, President, 158, 252
Pont de la Concorde, 145
Pont de l'Alma, 165
Pont du Gard, 12, 309, 311
Pont l'Évêque, 219
Pont Neuf, 154
Pope Clement V, 312
Pope Léon X, 174
Pope Pius X, 111
Population, 4
Port Grimaud, 307
Port Vendres, 285
Porte au Vin, 208
Porte d'Arroux, 244
Porte de Clignancourt, 361
Porte St André, 244
Portugal, 22
post-Hiroshima, 39
Post-Impressionists, 132
pot au feu, 340
Poulbot, 161
Poussin, Nicolas, 131
Pralognan-la-Valoise, 299
Procession of the Entombment of Christ, 118
procession of the Sanch, 284
Promenade des Planches, 213
Protestants, 17, 18, 102, 107, 109, 110
Proust, 90, 133
Provence, 12, 13, 75, 119, 122, 303, 309, 310, 341, 344
Provins, 179
Prussians, 28
Puilaurens, 283
Puligny-Montrachet, 241
Puy de Sancy, 61, 253
Puy de-Dômes, 252
Puy Mary, 253, 254
Puy-de-Dôme, 253
Puy-en-Velay, 248
Pyramide du Louvre, 129, 159, 164, 361
Pyrenean brown bear, 79
Pyrénées, 4, 23, 59, 60, 63, 64, 67, 75, 78, 97, 273, 274, 277, 278, 327

Q
quais, 67
Quéribus, 283
Quimper, 205

R

Rabelais, 133
race, 322
Racine, 90, 133, 163
Radet windmill, 161
Rainier III, Prince, 313
Rally for French People, 42
Ramatuelle, 307
Rambouillet, 77, 181
Ramses II, 151
Ravel, Maurice, 134
Raz Point, 205
Reblochon, 343
Régnié, 247
Reign of Terror, 22
Reims, 24, 223, 224
Religion, 4, 16, 17
Renaissance Hôtel Carnavalet, 158
Renault®, 48, 51, 53
Renault Véhicules Industriels, 53
Renaux, Eugène, 253
Rennes, 208
Renoir, 136, 161, 198
Resistance, 37, 38, 39
Revillon®, 352
Revolution, 21, 101, 104, 105, 170, 175, 234, 314
Revolution of July 1830, 26
Reynaud, Paul, 42
Rhine, 35, 63, 67, 69, 226
Rhône, 69, 75, 81, 223, 244, 247
Rhône-Saône, 61, 66, 67
Ribeauvillé, 239
Richard II, 264
Richard the Lionheart, 268
Richelieu, 18, 19, 265, 282
Rio de Janeiro, 55
rioting, 41
Riquewihr, 239
Ritz, César, 14
River, Seine, 183
River Charente, 197, 199
River Cher, 191
River Dordogne, 266, 268
River Garonne, 67, 279, 280
River Gironde, 67
River Indre, 192
River Isère, 294
River Lauch, 238
River Loire, 190, 248
River Maine, 194

River Rhône, 67, 248
River Sâone, 246, 247
River Seine, 38, 68, 143, 215, 355
River Touques, 213
River Vézère, 268
Riviera, 67, 118
Rocamadour, 270
Rocher St Michel, 248
Rodin, 219
Roissy airport, 169
Roman, 122, 151, 254, 305, 309
Roman Catholic, 5, 17, 86, 102, 111, 157
Roman Empire, 12
Roman theatre, 246, 248
Rome, 13, 104, 105, 107
Roquebrune, 312
Roquefort, 343
Rouen, 25, 215
Rousseau, Jean-Jacques, 133, 179, 191
Roussillon, 282, 344
Roussillon coast, 67
Route du Vin, 235, 236, 238
Royat, 254
Rubens, Peter Paul, 230
Rue de Rennes Table Ware, 356
Rue de Rivoli, 360
Rue du Faubourg-St-Honoré, 352
Rue du Paradis, 357
Rue Royale, 359
Rue Saint Sulpice, 353
rugby, 322
Ruggieri, Cosima, 189
Rungis, 159
Rushdie, Salman, 112
Russia, 33, 37
Russian Orthodox Cathedral, 165

S

Saar coal-fields, 231
Saché, 183
Sacré Coeur, 150, 161, 164, 271
Saigon, 39
Saint Bernadette, 110, 276
Saint Catherine of Alexandria, 124
Saint Catherine of Siena, 314
Saint Denis, 169
Saint Laurent, Yves, 94, 352

Saint Louis, 169, 268, 310
Saint Mary Jacob, 124
Saint Mary Salomé, 124
Saint Quentin-en-Yvelines, 167
Saint Sicaire, 270
Saint Suaire, 268, 269
Saint Thégonnec, 210
Saint Theresa of Lisieux, 217
Saint-Nom-la-Bretèche golf course, 325
Sainte Anne d'Auray, 125
Sainte Anne la Palud, 125
Salses Fort, 284
Sambre River, 63
Santiago de Compostela, 279
Sâone, 69, 246, 247
Sarajevo, 33
Sarlat, 270
Sarlat-la-Canéda, 269
Sartre, Jean-Paul, 133
sauce normande, 218
saucisson, 353, 354
Saumur-Champigny, 194
Savoy, 303, 340
Saxons, 13
Scherrer®, 351
Schiaparelli, 352
Second Empire, 28, 39
Sedan, 28
seige of Orléans, 16
Seine, 66, 67, 127, 144, 156, 158, 159, 165
Senate, 4
Senlis, 170
Serbs, 33
Seurat, Georges, 132, 136
shopping, 1, 336, 361
Shrove Tuesday, 118
Signac, 308
Sigolsheim, 239
Silk Industry, 56
Simon de Montfort, 283
Sisley, Alfred, 132, 179
Sisteron, 119
ski resorts, 288
skiing, 1, 288, 289, 291, 322, 323, 324
SNCF, 54
Socialists, 41, 43
Sofitel hotel, 302
Soisson, 65
Somme, 9, 219
Sorbonne, 41
Sorel, Agnès, 258

space technology, 55
Spain, 4, 19, 22, 64, 97, 275
sports, 291
St Amour, 247
St Apollinaire Cathedral, 249
St Bénigne Cathedral, 240
St Bruno, 295
St Émilion, 266, 336
St Étienne, 226
St Germain-en Laye, 181
St Gervais-les-Bains, 293
St Helena, 23, 181
St Jean de Luz, 274
St Martin du Canigou, 285
St Médard's feast day, 78
St Michel de Cuxa, 285
St Nicholas-de-Véroce, 293
St Rémy de Provence, 309
St Sernin Basilica, 279
St Tropez, 119, 307, 308
St-Jean-Cap-Ferrat, 312
St-Malo, 204
St-Martin-de-Ré, 198
St-Pierre-d'Oléron, 199
stamp market, 325
Stanislas, 229
States General, 315
Statue of Liberty, 98, 165
Ste Dévote, 118
Stendhal®, 133, 294
Stock Exchange, 93
storming of the Bastille, 20
Strasbourg, 232, 233, 238, 316
Stravinsky, 15
student riots, 44
summer holiday, 121
Surrealism, 134
Switzerland, 4, 59, 64, 226, 233
Sword Beach, 215

T
tartine, 347
Tati, Jacques, 138
Tea Drinkers' Club, 336
technology, 7, 48
Technopole, 231
telecommunications, 57
téléphérique, 254
Temple of Augustus and Livia, 248
Temple of Luxor, 151
tennis, 313, 322, 323, 327
Termes, 283
terrorism, 44, 97, 319

textiles, 231
TGV train, 173, 233
The Big Bang Schtroumpf, 330
The Citadel, 131
The Louvre, 130
The Mahabharat, 328
The Second Republic, 26
The Three Valleys, 289
Theatre, 326
Théâtre guignol, 328
Theme Parks, 328
théophiles, 349
Thierry Mugler®, 351
Third Republic, 30, 36, 42
Thirty Years War, 19, 179
Thoiry, 181
Three Valleys, 291
Tignes, 288, 289
Tonkin, 39
Toulouse, 13, 55, 269, 279, 280, 281, 340
Toulouse-Lautrec, 14, 132, 160, 161, 280, 281
Tour de France, 273, 322, 327
Touraine hills, 67
tourism, 1
Tours, 38
Toussaint, 117
Tower of Constance, 310
Train à Grande Vitesse, 54
traiteurs, 94
Transhumance, 78
Treaty of Calais, 15, 257
Treaty of Rome, 75
Treaty of the Pyrénées, 284
Treaty of Troyes, 24
Treaty of Versailles, 34
Treaty of Westphalia, 19
Trégastel-Plage, 205
Trémolat, 268
Très Riches Heures du duc de Berry, 259
Tristan, 201
Trophée Lancôme, 325
Trouville, 211, 213
Troyes, 223
Truffaut, François, 138
truffles, 269, 270
Tuileries, 38
Tuileries gardens, 150, 152, 158, 159
Tunisia, 113
Tunisian cuisine, 335
Tunnel du Mont Blanc, 292

Turgot, 21
Turquet Etienne, 56
Twingo, 53

U
Ungaro, 351
Universal Exhibition, 158
Unterlinden Museum, 238
Utrillo, 161

V
Vaison-la-Romaine, 12, 309
Val d'Aoste, 292
Val d'Isère, 288
Val-Thorens, 289
Valence, 248
Valentia, 249
Valéry, Paul, 15
Valéry, Valéry Giscard, 41
Vallée de la Dordogne, 268
Vallée de la Vézère, 268
Valois, 65
Value Added Tax, 359
Van Cleef, 352
Van Dyck, 151
Van Gogh, Vincent, 136, 161, 309
Vannes, 208
Vatican, 110, 111
Vaucluse, 338
vendanges, 123
Vendée, 67, 195
Venus de Milo, 151
Vercingetorix, 12, 257, 260
Verdun, 34, 131, 226, 228
Versailles, 19, 20, 21, 130, 170, 176, 177, 179, 240, 311
version originale, 90, 137
Vézère Valley, 271
Vicennes Forest, 77
Vichy, 39, 61, 254, 256
Vichy France, 38, 42
Vichy government, 37
Victory in Europe Day, 117
Vieille Bourse, 221
Vienne, 248
Vietnam, 39, 41, 42, 44, 335
Vieux Port, 318
Village Suisse, 360
Villandry, 183, 191
Villefranche-sur-Saône, 247
vin de pays, 344
vineyards, 74, 75, 241
Viollet-le-Duc, 172, 283

Virgin Mary, 124
Viscount Trencavel, 283
Visigoths, 12
Vittel, 231
Voiron, 295
Voltaire, 90, 133
Volvic, 254
von Choltitz, General Dietrich, 38
Vosges, 59, 60, 63, 65, 74, 75, 111
vulture, 81

W

waiters' race, 126
Walpole, 176
War of Spanish Succession, 20
Wars of Religion, 17, 264, 270, 311
Watteau, Antoine, 131, 151
William the Conqueror, 218
William the Silent, 314
wind-surfing, 126
wine, 3, 115, 123, 194, 223, 225, 230, 247, 265, 278, 285, 341, 343, 344, 347, 353
Winter Olympics, 294, 324
Winter sports, 287, 324
World Cup, 322
WWI, 14, 15, 33, 35, 51, 112, 117, 131, 172, 221, 224, 227, 233, 338
WWII, 30, 35, 42, 47, 52, 75, 113, 119, 155, 172, 194, 198, 205, 208, 209, 215, 217, 218, 221, 256

Y

Yonne River, 67

Z

Zola, Émile, 14, 90, 133
Zouave, 165
Zygofolis in Nice, 330

NOTES

NOTES

NOTES